JUMI BA'S

MONKEY MEAT

MONKEY MEAT
MULTINATIONAL
JUMI
BA

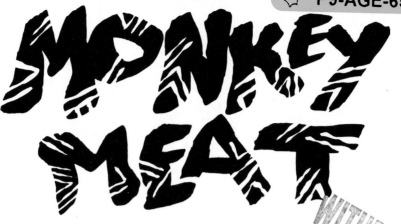

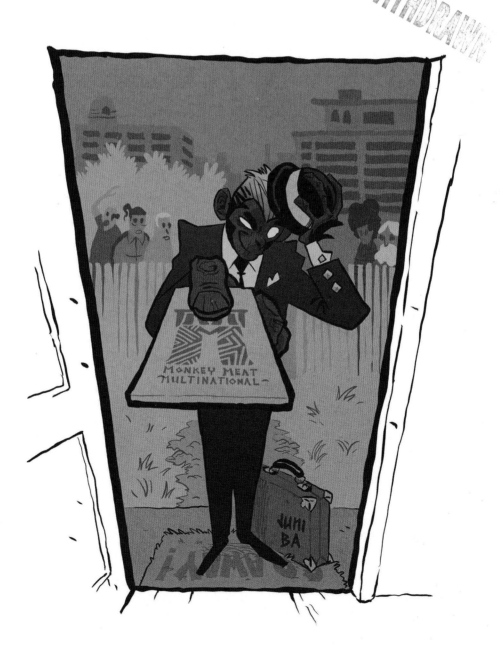

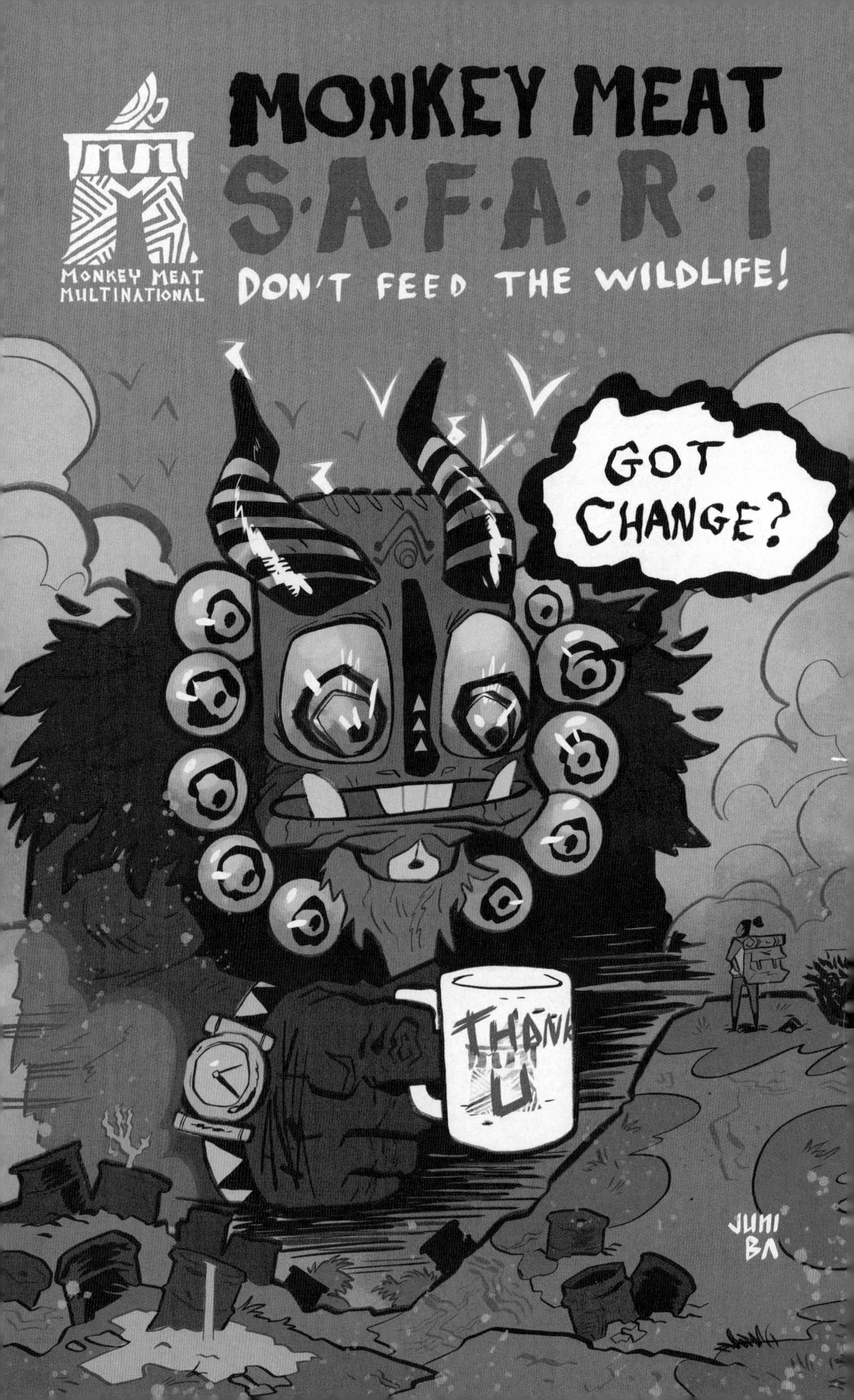
MONKEY MEAT
S·A·F·A·R·I
DON'T FEED THE WILDLIFE!
MONKEY MEAT MULTINATIONAL
GOT CHANGE?
THANK U
JUNI BA

MONKEY·MEAT

A COMIC CREATED BY JUNI BA

With special authorization from the Monkey Meat Company

IMAGE COMICS, INC.
Robert Kirkman: Chief Operating Officer • **Erik Larsen**: Chief Financial Officer • **Todd McFarlane**: President • **Marc Silvestri**: Chief Executive Officer • **Jim Valentino**: Vice President • **Eric Stephenson**: Publisher / Chief Creative Officer • **Nicole Lapalme**: Controller • **Leanna Caunter**: Accounting Analyst • **Sue Korpela**: Accounting & HR Manager • **Matt Parkinson**: Vice President of Sales & Publishing Planning • **Lorelei Bunjes**: Vice President of Digital Strategy • **Dirk Wood**: Vice President of International Sales & Licensing • **Ryan Brewer**: International Sales & Licensing Manager • **Alex Cox**: Director of Direct Market Sales • **Chloe Ramos**: Book Market & Library Sales Manager • **Emilio Bautista**: Digital Sales Coordinator • **Jon Schlaffman**: Specialty Sales Coordinator • **Kat Salazar**: Vice President of PR & Marketing • **Deanna Phelps**: Marketing Design Manager • **Drew Fitzgerald**: Marketing Content Associate • **Heather Doornink**: Vice President of Production • **Drew Gill**: Art Director • **Hilary DiLoreto**: Print Manager • **Tricia Ramos**: Traffic Manager • **Melissa Gifford**: Content Manager • **Erika Schnatz**: Senior Production Artist • **Wesley Griffith**: Production Artist • **IMAGECOMICS.COM**

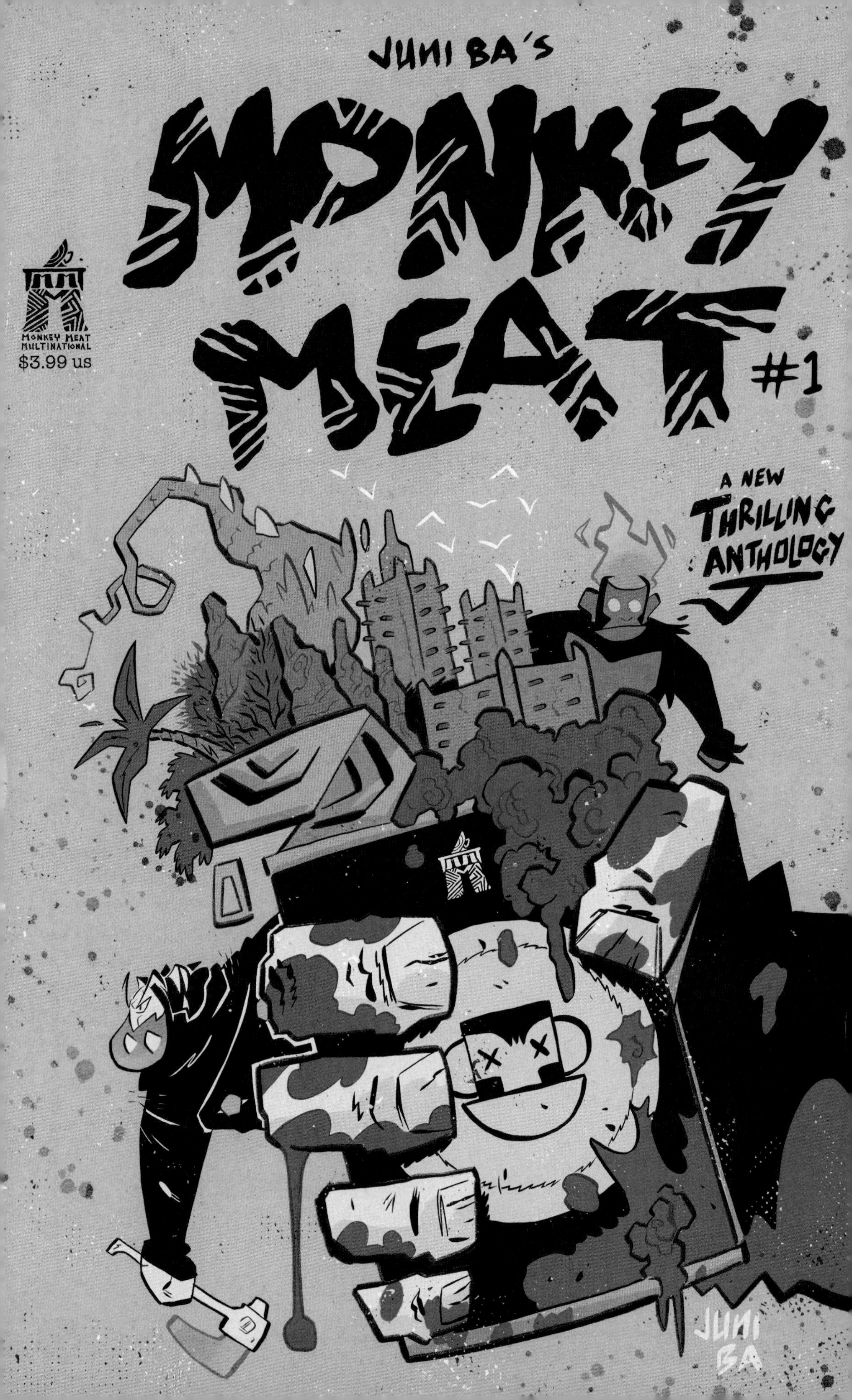
JUNI BA'S
MONKEY MEAT
#1
MONKEY MEAT MULTINATIONAL
$3.99 US
A NEW THRILLING ANTHOLOGY
JUNI BA

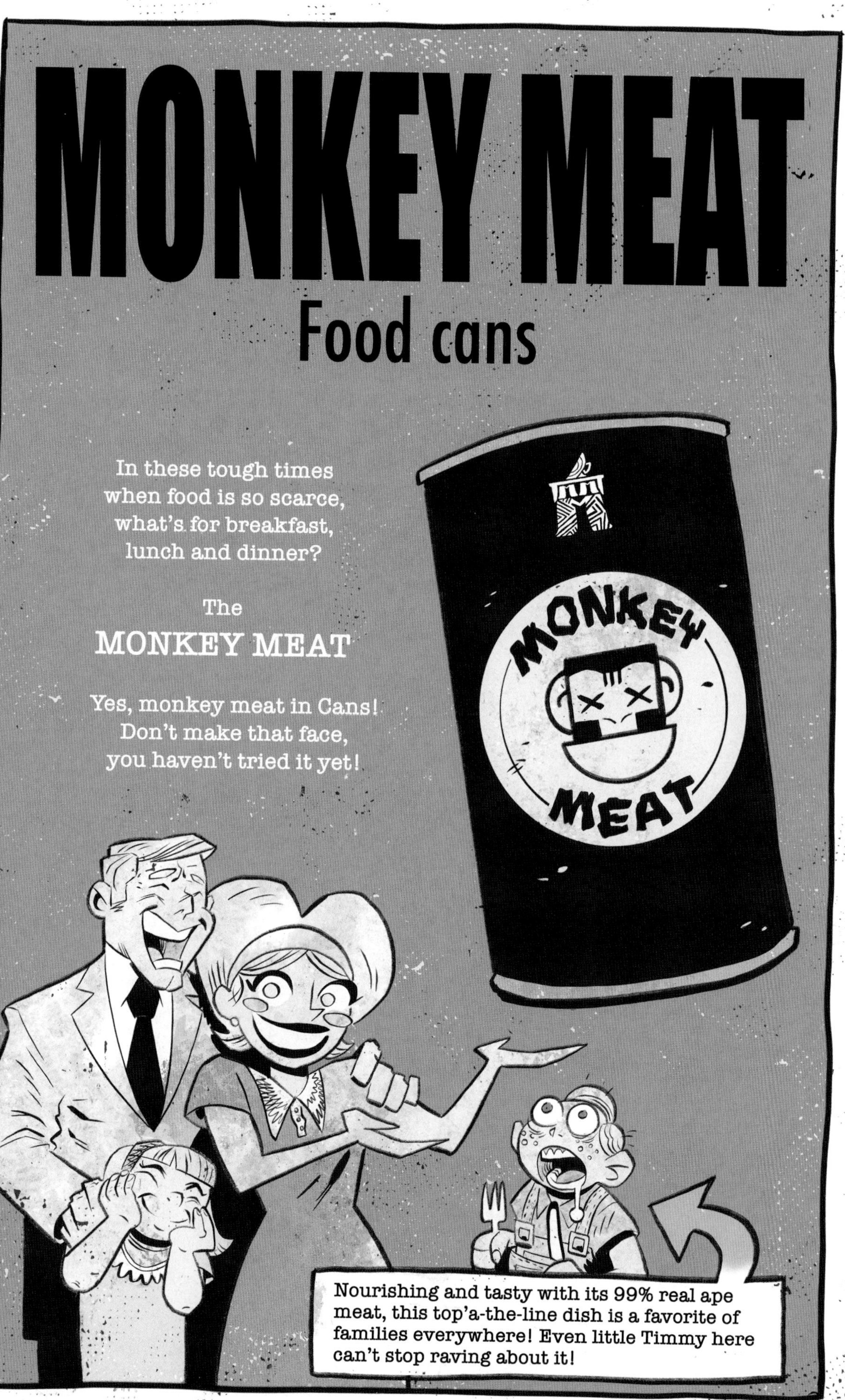

MONKEY MEAT
Food cans
In these tough times when food is so scarce, what's for breakfast, lunch and dinner?
The MONKEY MEAT
Yes, monkey meat in Cans! Don't make that face, you haven't tried it yet!
MONKEY MEAT
Nourishing and tasty with its 99% real ape meat, this top'a-the-line dish is a favorite of families everywhere! Even little Timmy here can't stop raving about it!

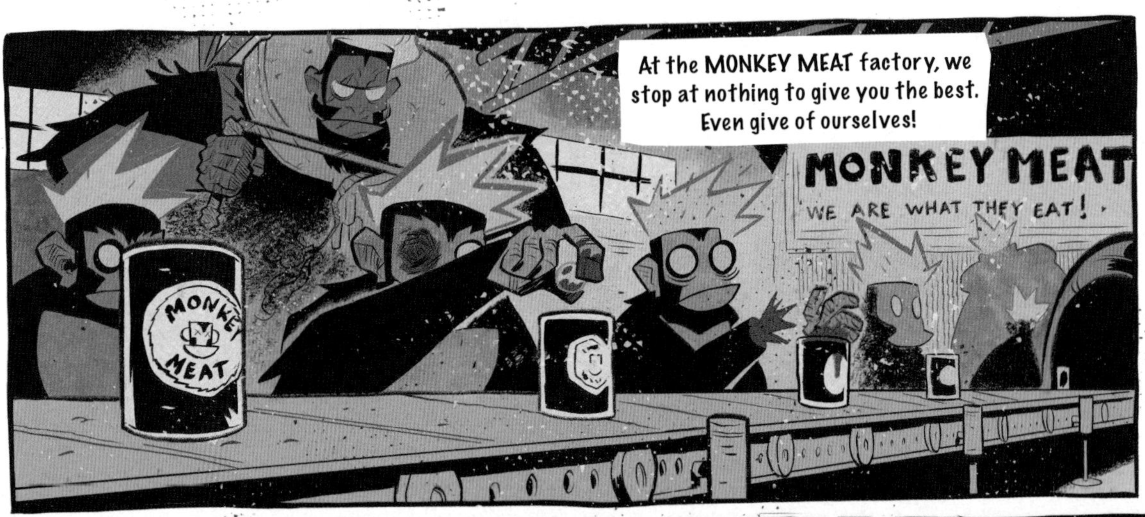
At the MONKEY MEAT factory, we stop at nothing to give you the best. Even give of ourselves!
MONKEY MEAT
WE ARE WHAT THEY EAT!
MONKEY MEAT

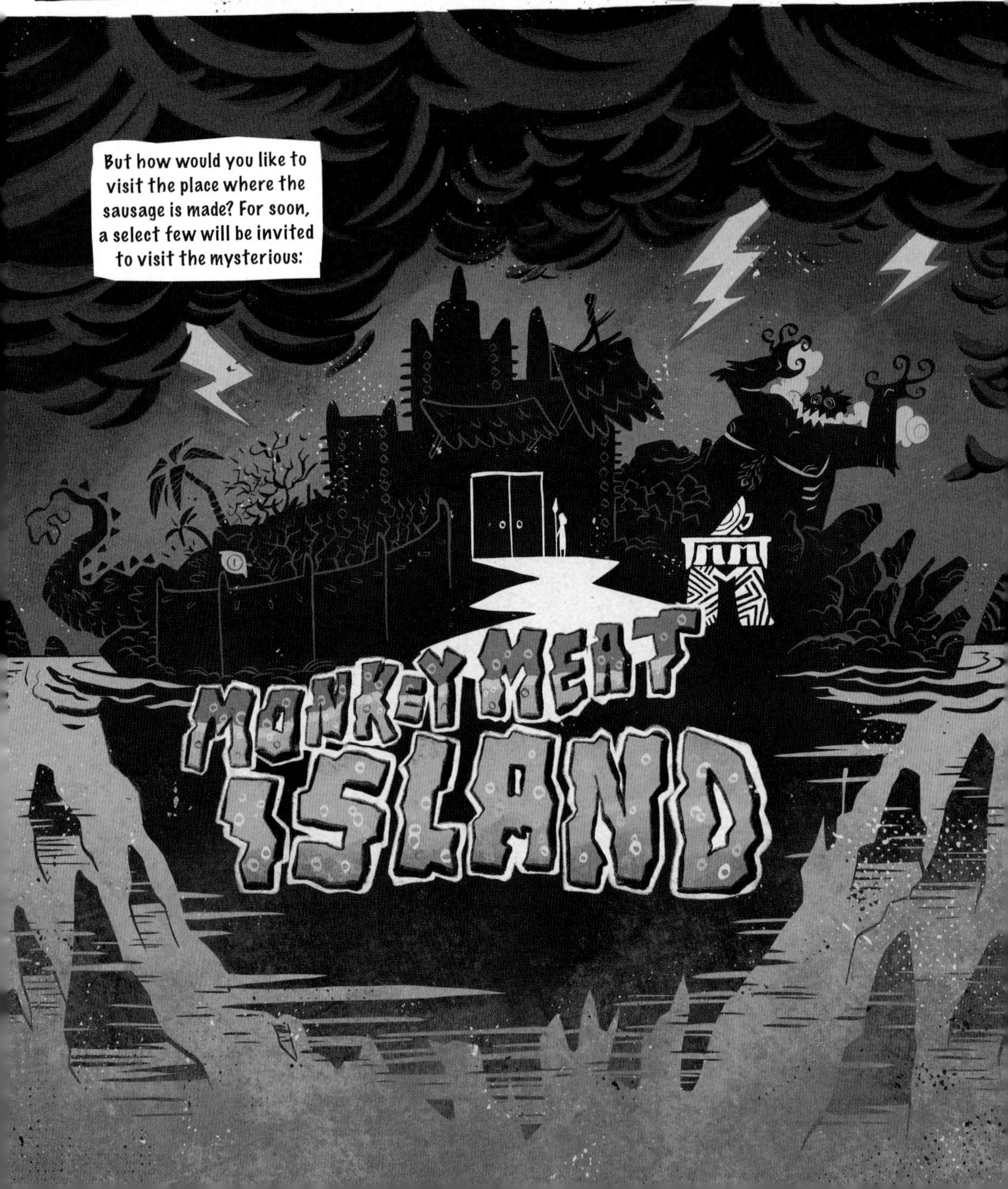
But how would you like to visit the place where the sausage is made? For soon, a select few will be invited to visit the mysterious:
MONKEY MEAT ISLAND

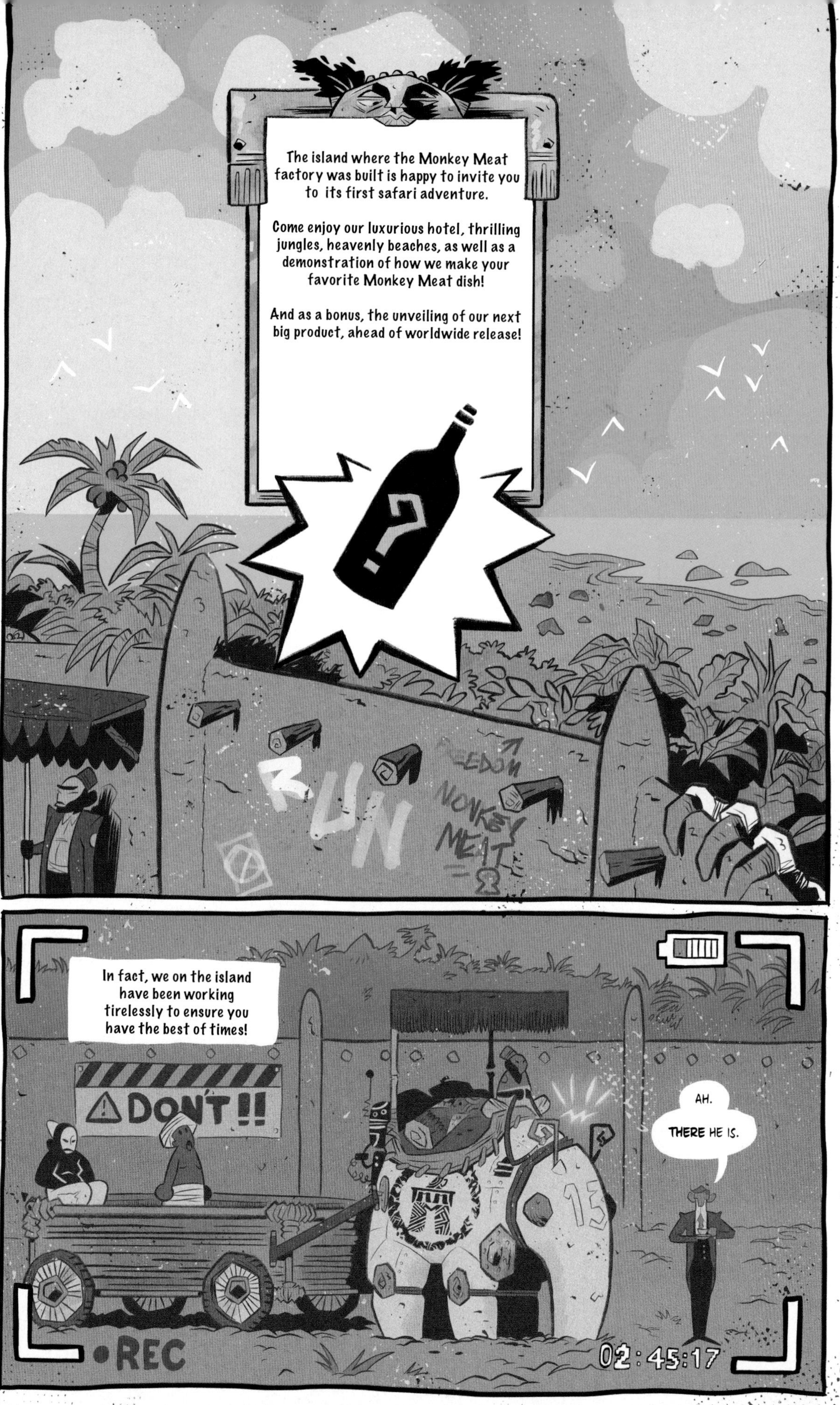

The island where the Monkey Meat factory was built is happy to invite you to its first safari adventure.
Come enjoy our luxurious hotel, thrilling jungles, heavenly beaches, as well as a demonstration of how we make your favorite Monkey Meat dish!
And as a bonus, the unveiling of our next big product, ahead of worldwide release!
RUN
MONKEY MEAT
In fact, we on the island have been working tirelessly to ensure you have the best of times!
DON'T!!
AH.
THERE HE IS.
13
•REC
02:45:17

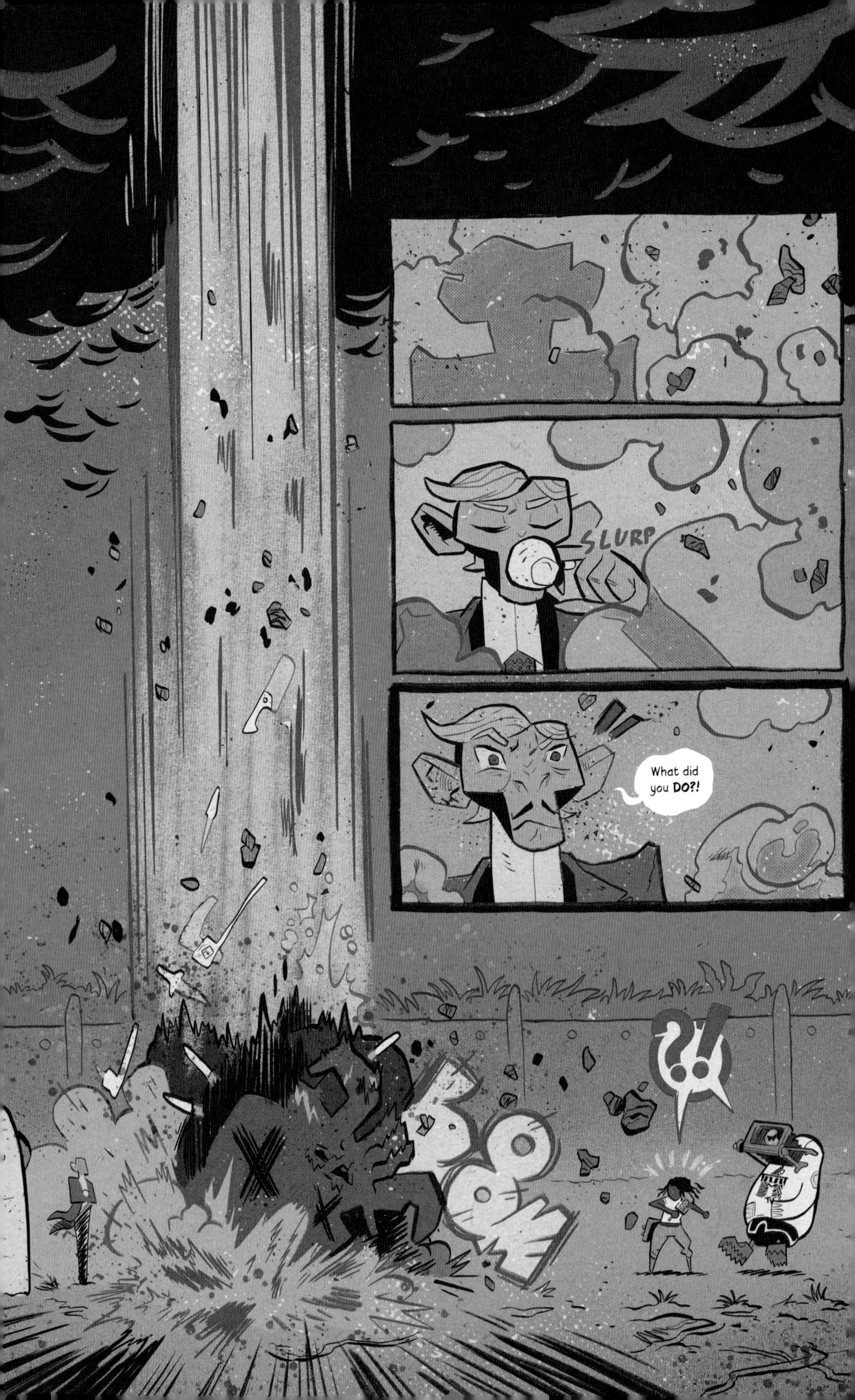
SLURP
What did you DO?!
BOOM

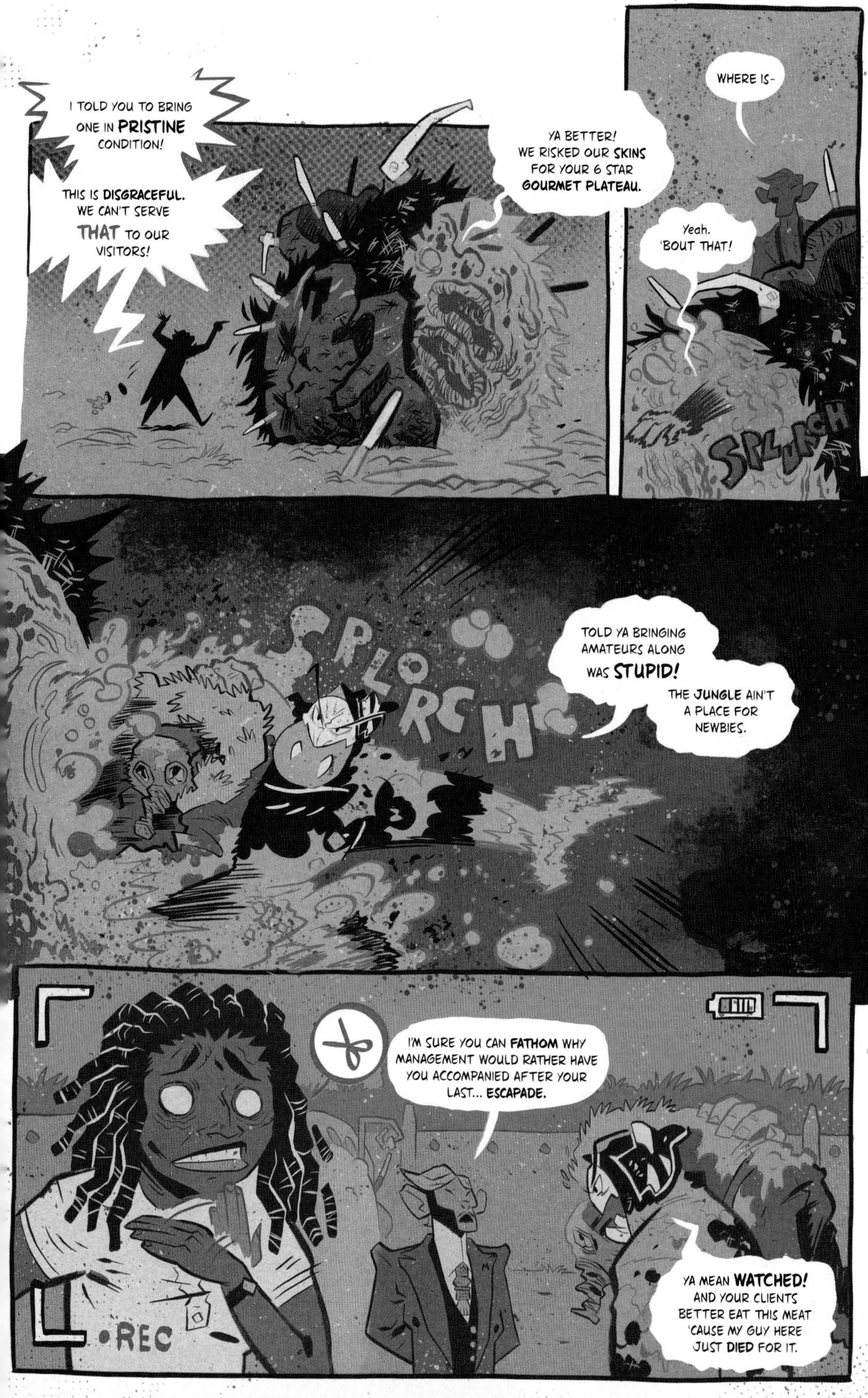
I TOLD YOU TO BRING ONE IN PRISTINE CONDITION!
THIS IS DISGRACEFUL. WE CAN'T SERVE THAT TO OUR VISITORS!
YA BETTER! WE RISKED OUR SKINS FOR YOUR 6 STAR GOURMET PLATEAU.
WHERE IS-
Yeah. 'BOUT THAT!
SPLURCH
SPLORCH
TOLD YA BRINGING AMATEURS ALONG WAS STUPID!
THE JUNGLE AIN'T A PLACE FOR NEWBIES.
I'M SURE YOU CAN FATHOM WHY MANAGEMENT WOULD RATHER HAVE YOU ACCOMPANIED AFTER YOUR LAST... ESCAPADE.
YA MEAN WATCHED! AND YOUR CLIENTS BETTER EAT THIS MEAT 'CAUSE MY GUY HERE JUST DIED FOR IT.
•REC

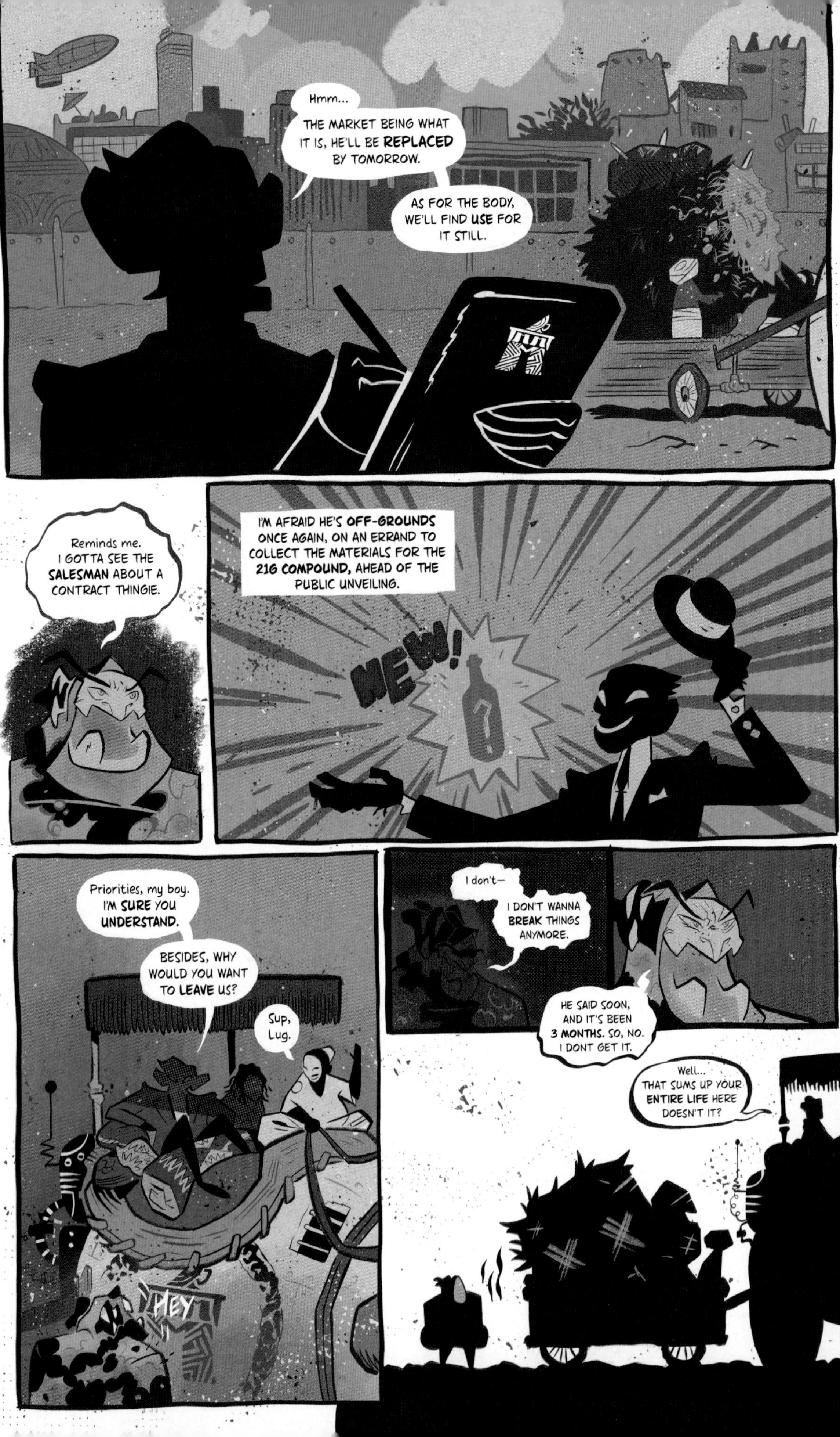
Hmm...
THE MARKET BEING WHAT IT IS, HE'LL BE **REPLACED** BY TOMORROW.
AS FOR THE BODY, WE'LL FIND **USE** FOR IT STILL.
Reminds me. I GOTTA SEE THE **SALESMAN** ABOUT A CONTRACT THINGIE.
I'M AFRAID HE'S **OFF-GROUNDS** ONCE AGAIN, ON AN ERRAND TO COLLECT THE MATERIALS FOR THE **216 COMPOUND,** AHEAD OF THE PUBLIC UNVEILING.
NEW!
Priorities, my boy. I'M **SURE** YOU **UNDERSTAND.**
BESIDES, WHY WOULD YOU WANT TO **LEAVE** US?
Sup, Lug.
HEY
I don't—
I DON'T WANNA **BREAK** THINGS ANYMORE.
HE SAID SOON, AND IT'S BEEN **3 MONTHS.** SO, NO. I DONT GET IT.
Well... THAT SUMS UP YOUR **ENTIRE LIFE** HERE DOESN'T IT?

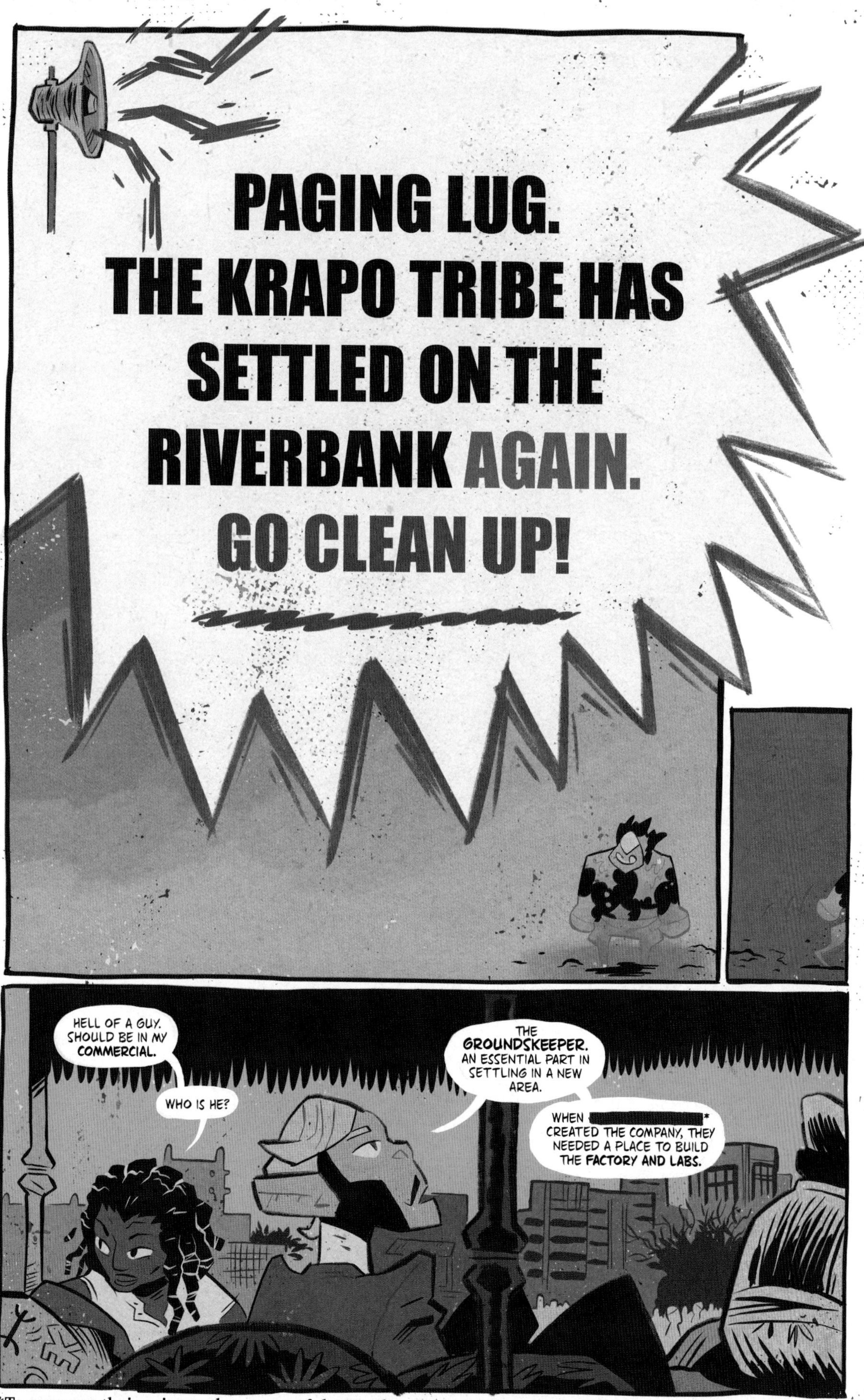
PAGING LUG.
THE KRAPO TRIBE HAS SETTLED ON THE RIVERBANK AGAIN.
GO CLEAN UP!
HELL OF A GUY. SHOULD BE IN MY COMMERCIAL.
WHO IS HE?
THE GROUNDSKEEPER. AN ESSENTIAL PART IN SETTLING IN A NEW AREA.
WHEN [redacted]* CREATED THE COMPANY, THEY NEEDED A PLACE TO BUILD THE FACTORY AND LABS.

*To preserve their privacy, the owner of the Monkey Meat company copyrighted and forbade the use of their own name. Because they can.

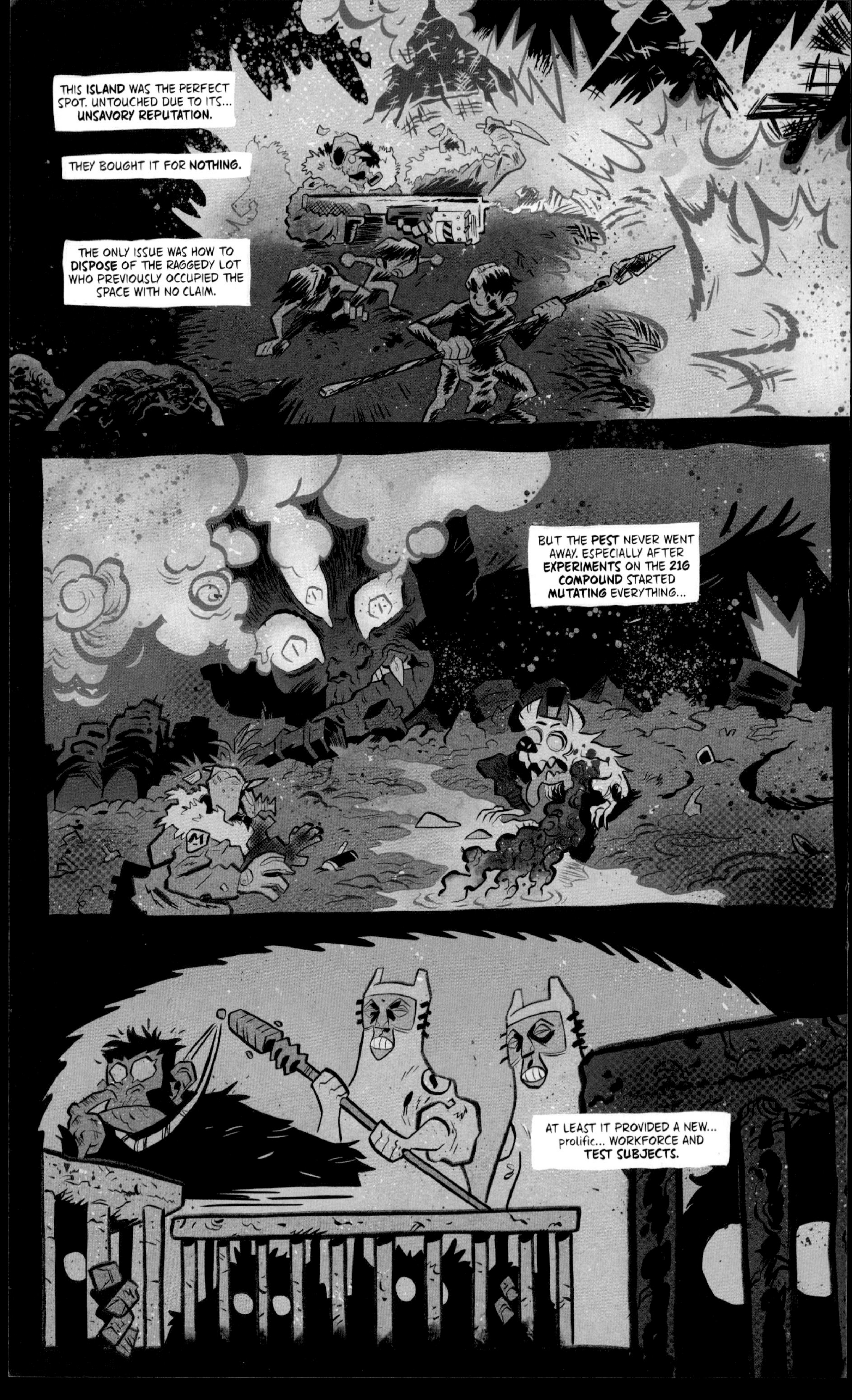
THIS ISLAND WAS THE PERFECT SPOT. UNTOUCHED DUE TO ITS... UNSAVORY REPUTATION.
THEY BOUGHT IT FOR NOTHING.
THE ONLY ISSUE WAS HOW TO DISPOSE OF THE RAGGEDY LOT WHO PREVIOUSLY OCCUPIED THE SPACE WITH NO CLAIM.
BUT THE PEST NEVER WENT AWAY. ESPECIALLY AFTER EXPERIMENTS ON THE 216 COMPOUND STARTED MUTATING EVERYTHING...
AT LEAST IT PROVIDED A NEW... prolific... WORKFORCE AND TEST SUBJECTS.

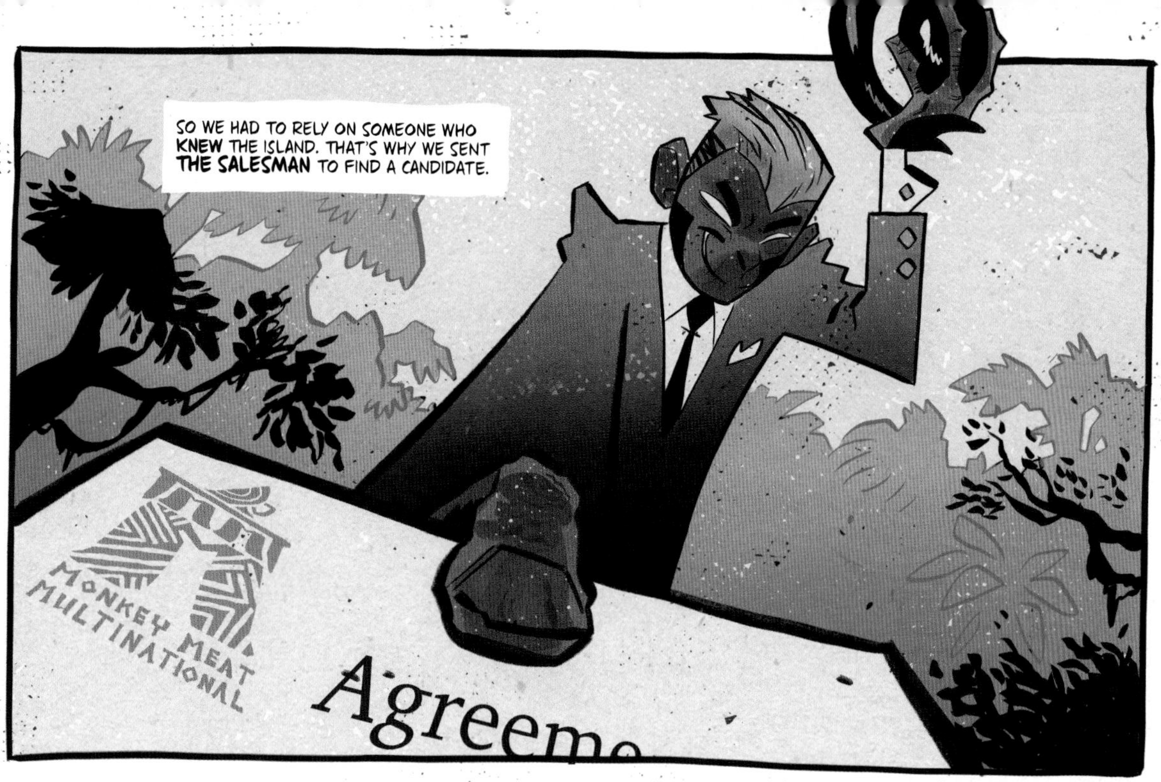
SO WE HAD TO RELY ON SOMEONE WHO KNEW THE ISLAND. THAT'S WHY WE SENT THE SALESMAN TO FIND A CANDIDATE.
MONKEY MEAT MULTINATIONAL
Agreeme

AND HE FOUND **THADDEUS LUG**. A WOODLAND CREATURE WHO HAD BEEN LIVING ON THE ISLAND RENT-FREE FOR YEARS, SO HE WAS ALL BUT **STUCK**.

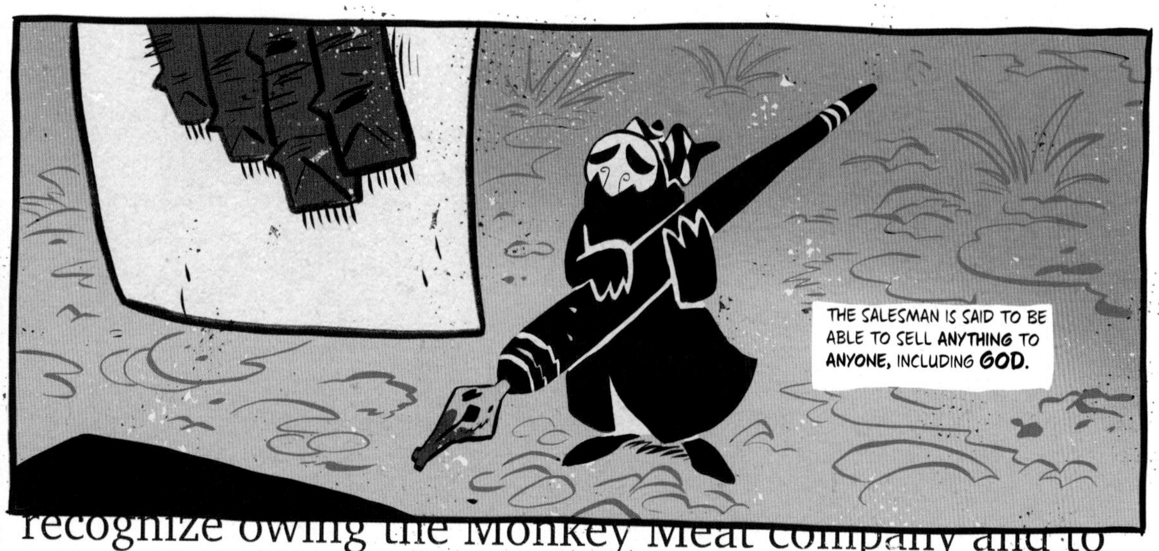
THE SALESMAN IS SAID TO BE ABLE TO SELL ANYTHING TO ANYONE, INCLUDING GOD.

recognize owing the Monkey Meat company and to
assure service until my debt is paid as they see fit.

Signed:.....X..........

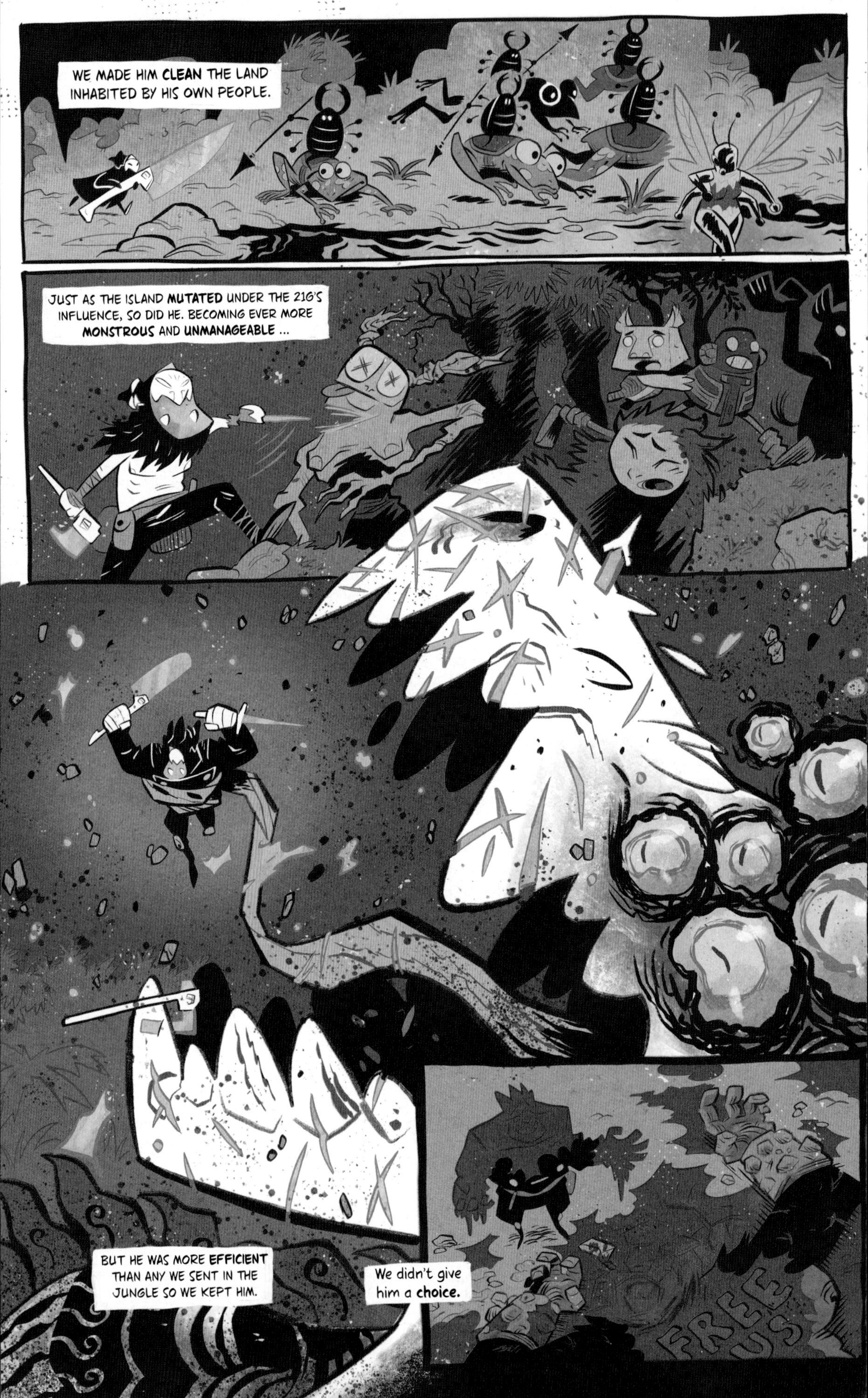

WE MADE HIM **CLEAN** THE LAND INHABITED BY HIS OWN PEOPLE.
JUST AS THE ISLAND **MUTATED** UNDER THE 216'S INFLUENCE, SO DID HE. BECOMING EVER MORE **MONSTROUS** AND **UNMANAGEABLE** ...
BUT HE WAS MORE **EFFICIENT** THAN ANY WE SENT IN THE JUNGLE SO WE KEPT HIM.
We didn't give him a **choice.**
FREE US

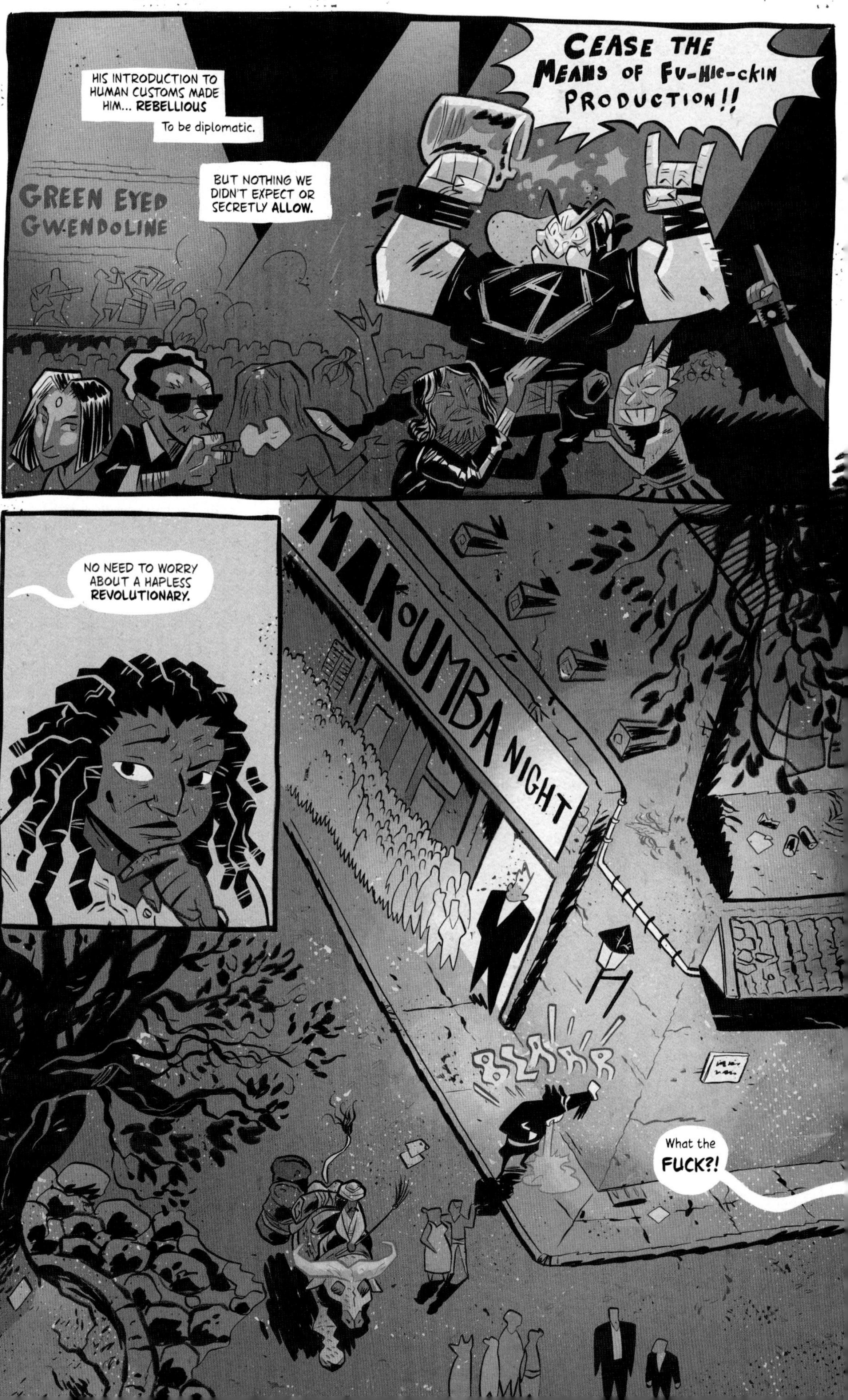
HIS INTRODUCTION TO HUMAN CUSTOMS MADE HIM... REBELLIOUS
To be diplomatic.
GREEN EYED GWENDOLINE
BUT NOTHING WE DIDN'T EXPECT OR SECRETLY ALLOW.
CEASE THE MEANS OF FU-HIC-CKIN PRODUCTION!!
NO NEED TO WORRY ABOUT A HAPLESS REVOLUTIONARY.
MAKOUMBA NIGHT
BLARR
What the FUCK?!

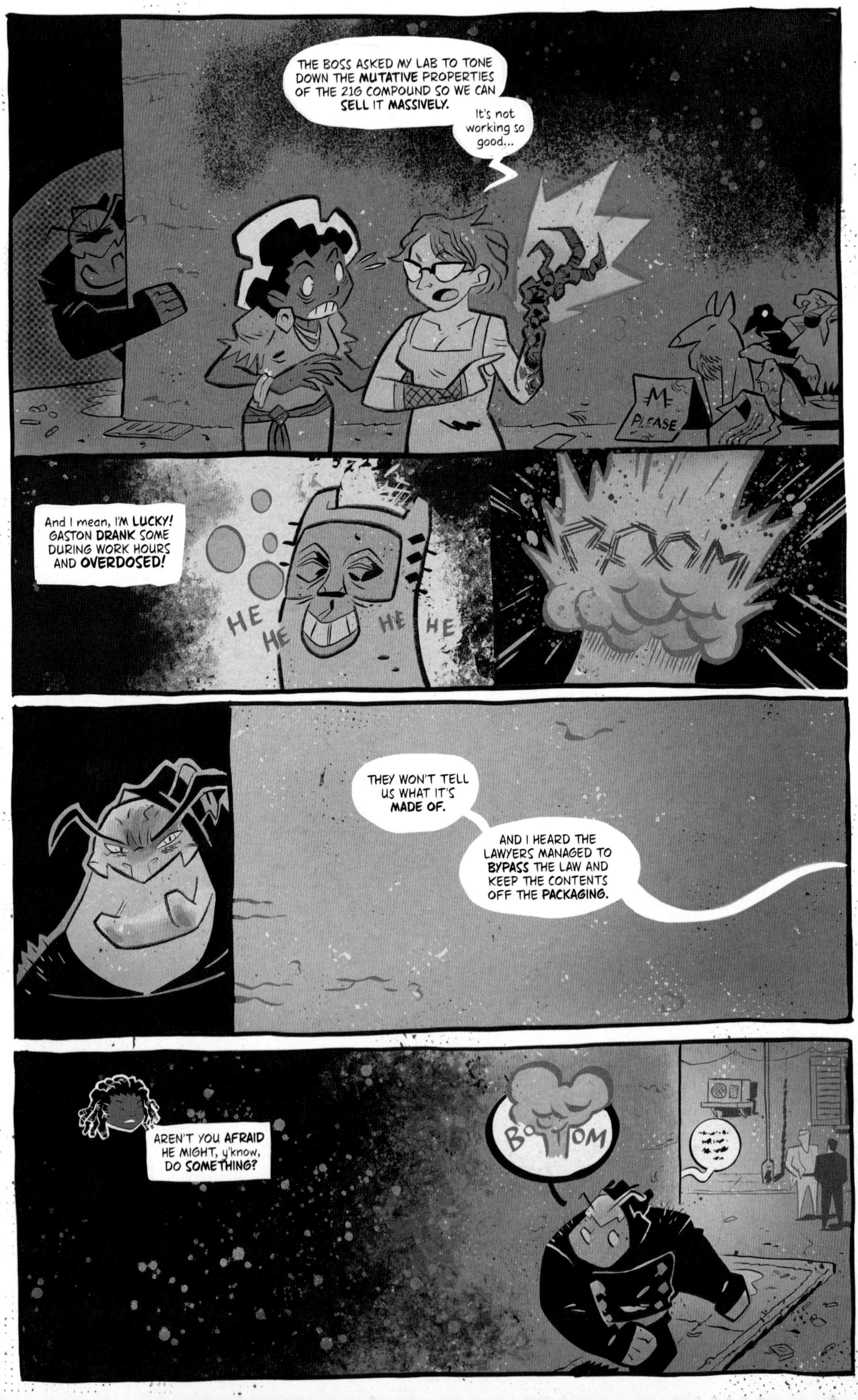

THE BOSS ASKED MY LAB TO TONE DOWN THE MUTATIVE PROPERTIES OF THE 21G COMPOUND SO WE CAN SELL IT MASSIVELY.
It's not working so good...
M PLEASE
And I mean, I'M LUCKY! GASTON DRANK SOME DURING WORK HOURS AND OVERDOSED!
HE HE HE HE
PFOOM
THEY WON'T TELL US WHAT IT'S MADE OF.
AND I HEARD THE LAWYERS MANAGED TO BYPASS THE LAW AND KEEP THE CONTENTS OFF THE PACKAGING.
AREN'T YOU AFRAID HE MIGHT, y'know, DO SOMETHING?
BOTTOM

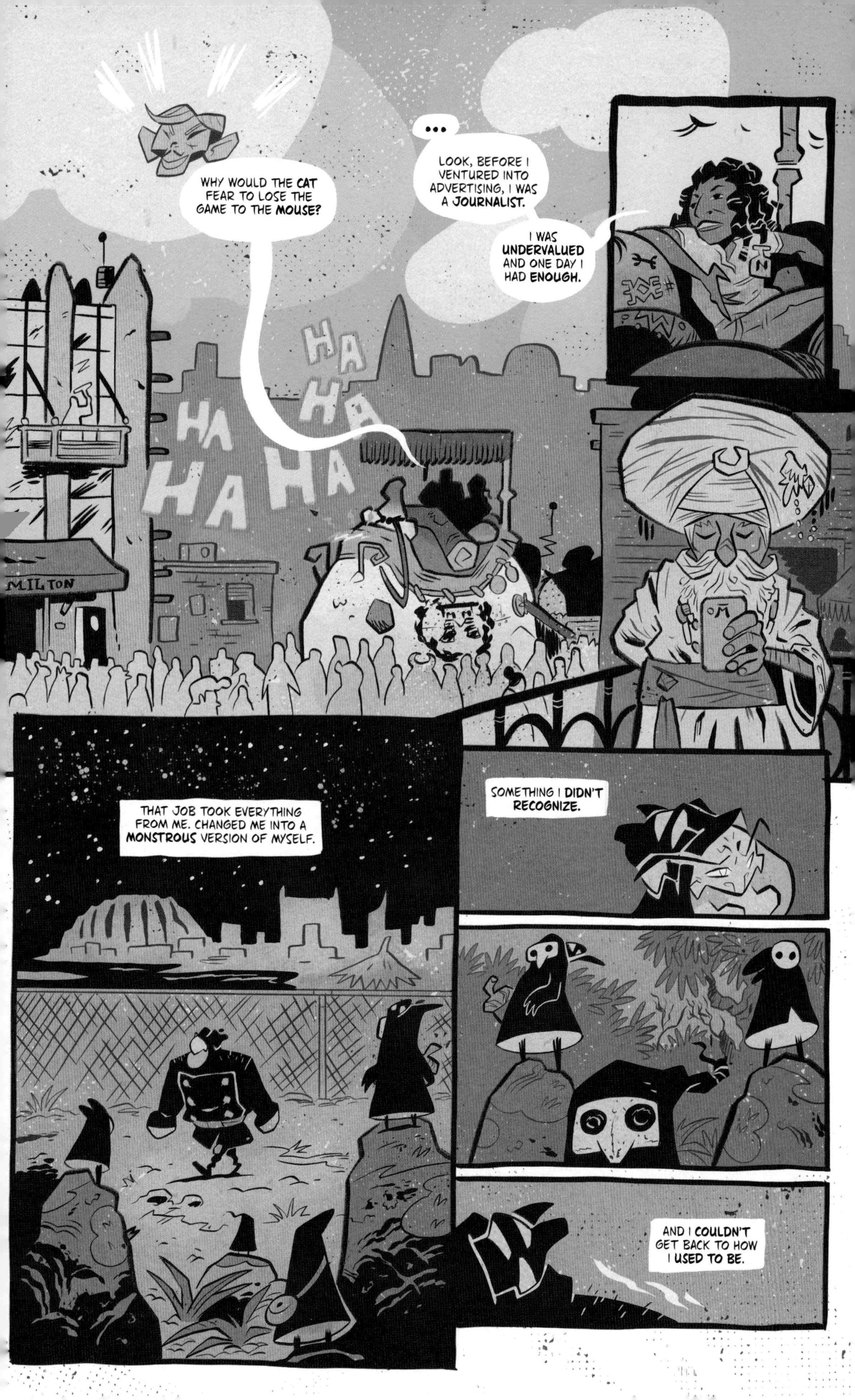
WHY WOULD THE CAT FEAR TO LOSE THE GAME TO THE MOUSE?
HA HA HA HA HA HA
...
LOOK, BEFORE I VENTURED INTO ADVERTISING, I WAS A JOURNALIST.
I WAS UNDERVALUED AND ONE DAY I HAD ENOUGH.
MILTON
THAT JOB TOOK EVERYTHING FROM ME. CHANGED ME INTO A MONSTROUS VERSION OF MYSELF.
SOMETHING I DIDN'T RECOGNIZE.
AND I COULDN'T GET BACK TO HOW I USED TO BE.

SO I HAD TO RECLAIM A SENSE OF SELF. TO BE **HEARD**.

LAB 21

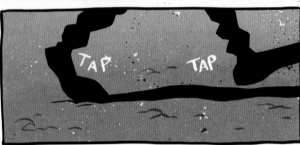

TAP   TAP

TAP

TAP   TAP   TAP

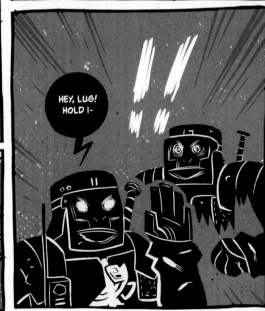

HEY, LUG! HOLD I—

SHTACK

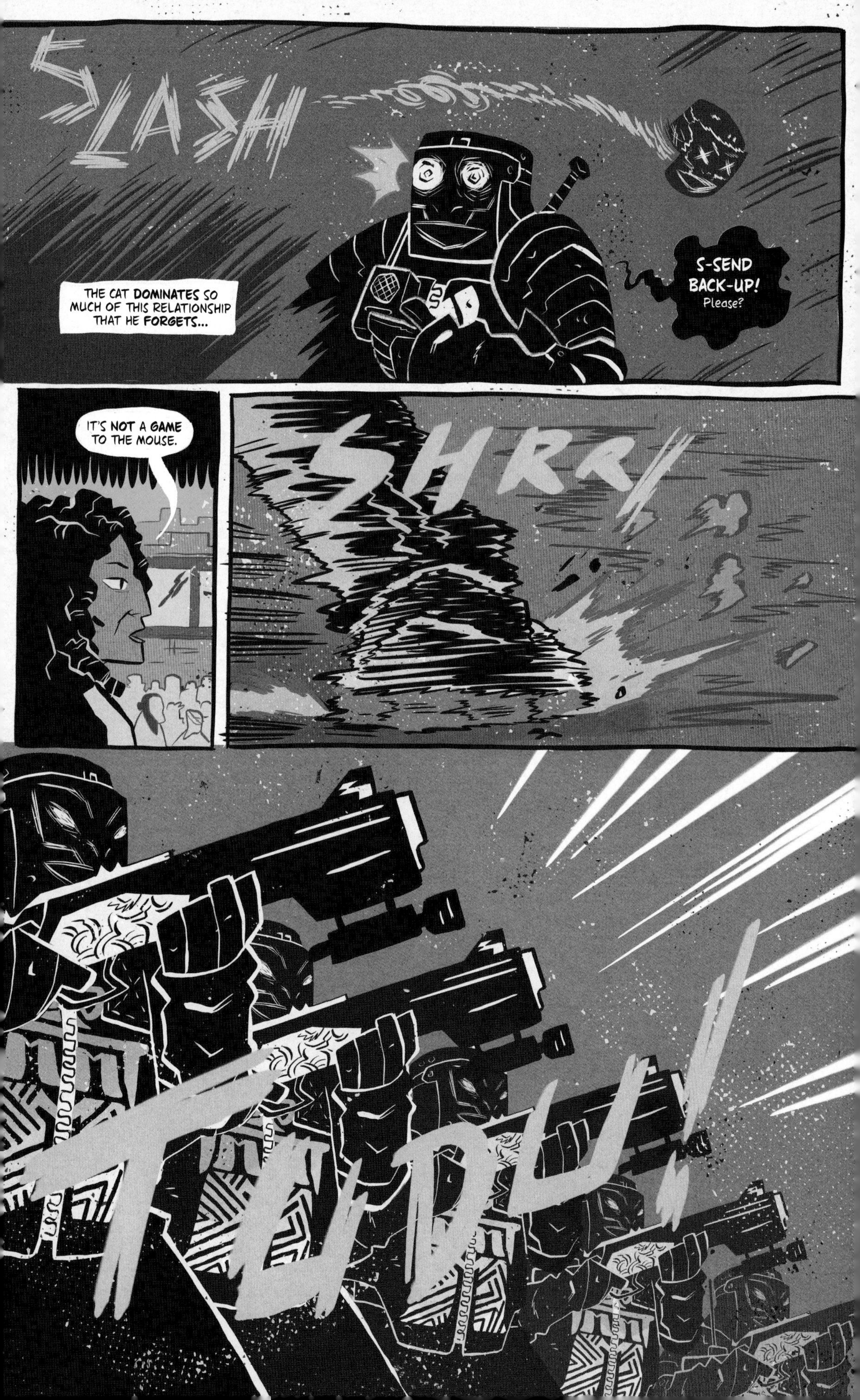
SLASH
THE CAT DOMINATES SO MUCH OF THIS RELATIONSHIP THAT HE FORGETS...
S-SEND BACK-UP! Please?
IT'S NOT A GAME TO THE MOUSE.
SHRR!
TOOM!!

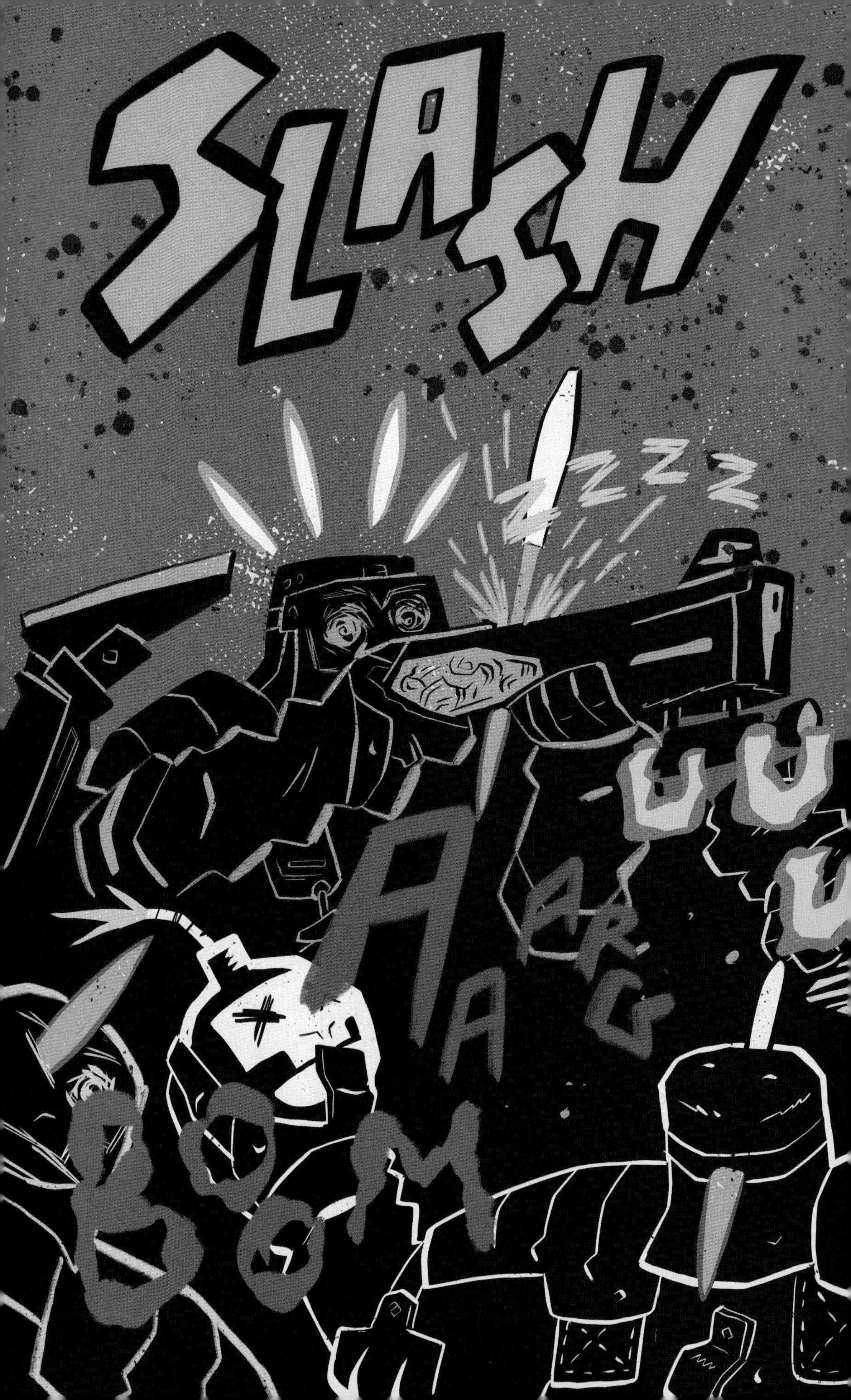
SLASH
ZZZZZ
UUU
AARG
AA
BOOM

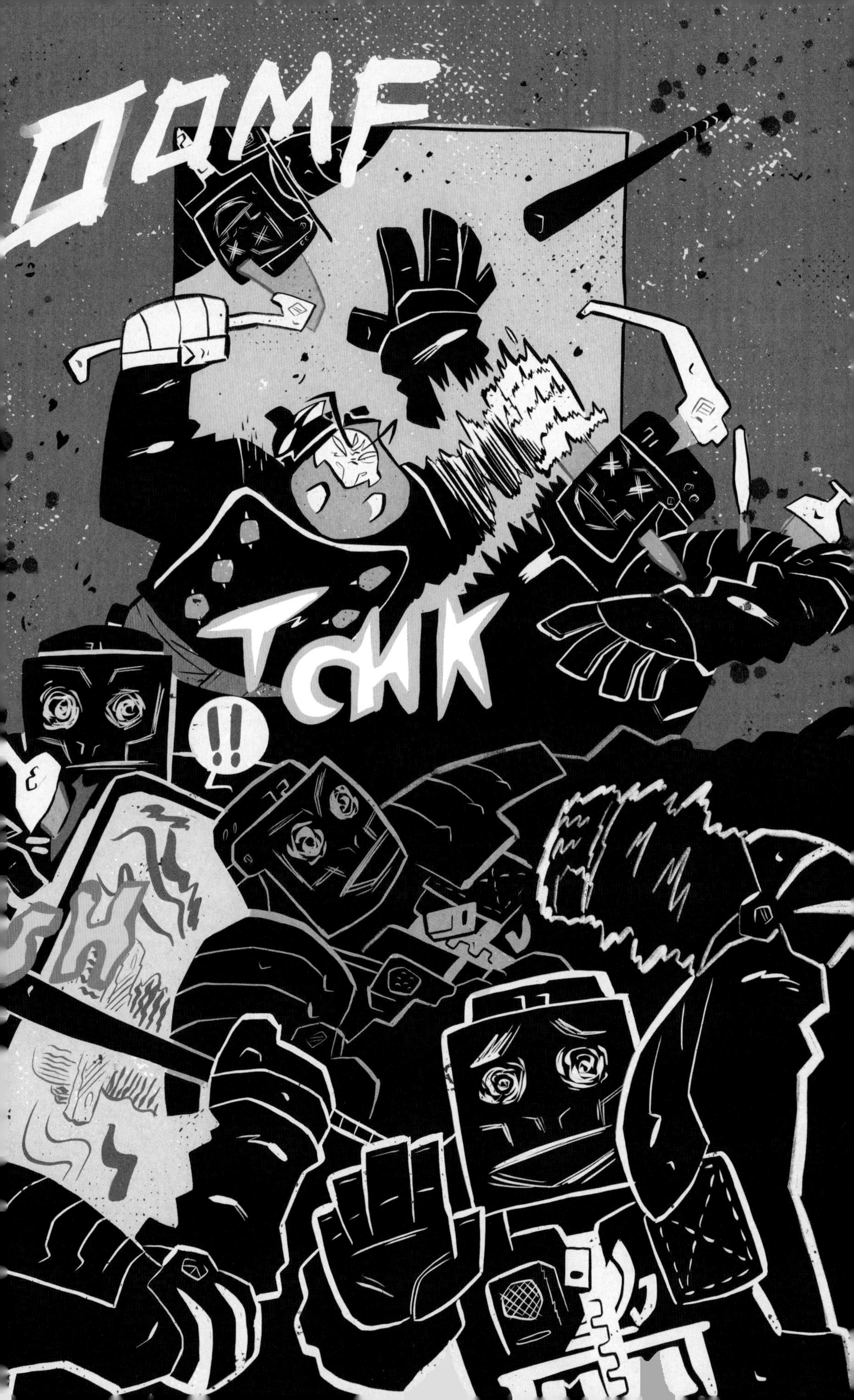
DOMF
TCHK
!!

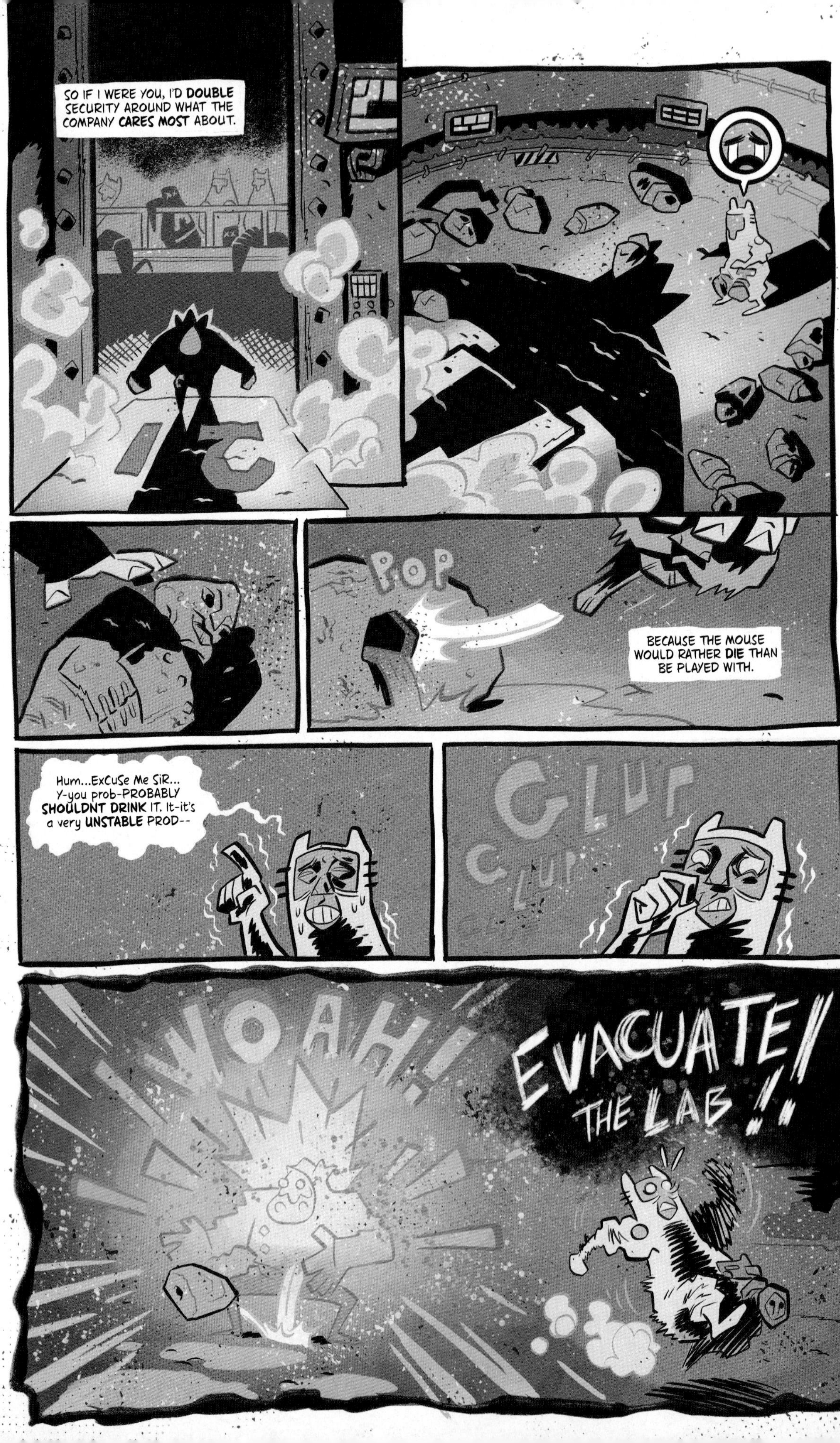
SO IF I WERE YOU, I'D DOUBLE SECURITY AROUND WHAT THE COMPANY CARES MOST ABOUT.
POP
BECAUSE THE MOUSE WOULD RATHER DIE THAN BE PLAYED WITH.
Hum...ExCuSe Me SiR... Y-you prob-PROBABLY SHOULDNT DRINK IT. It-it's a very UNSTABLE PROD--
GLUP
GLUP
WOAH!
EVACUATE THE LAB!!

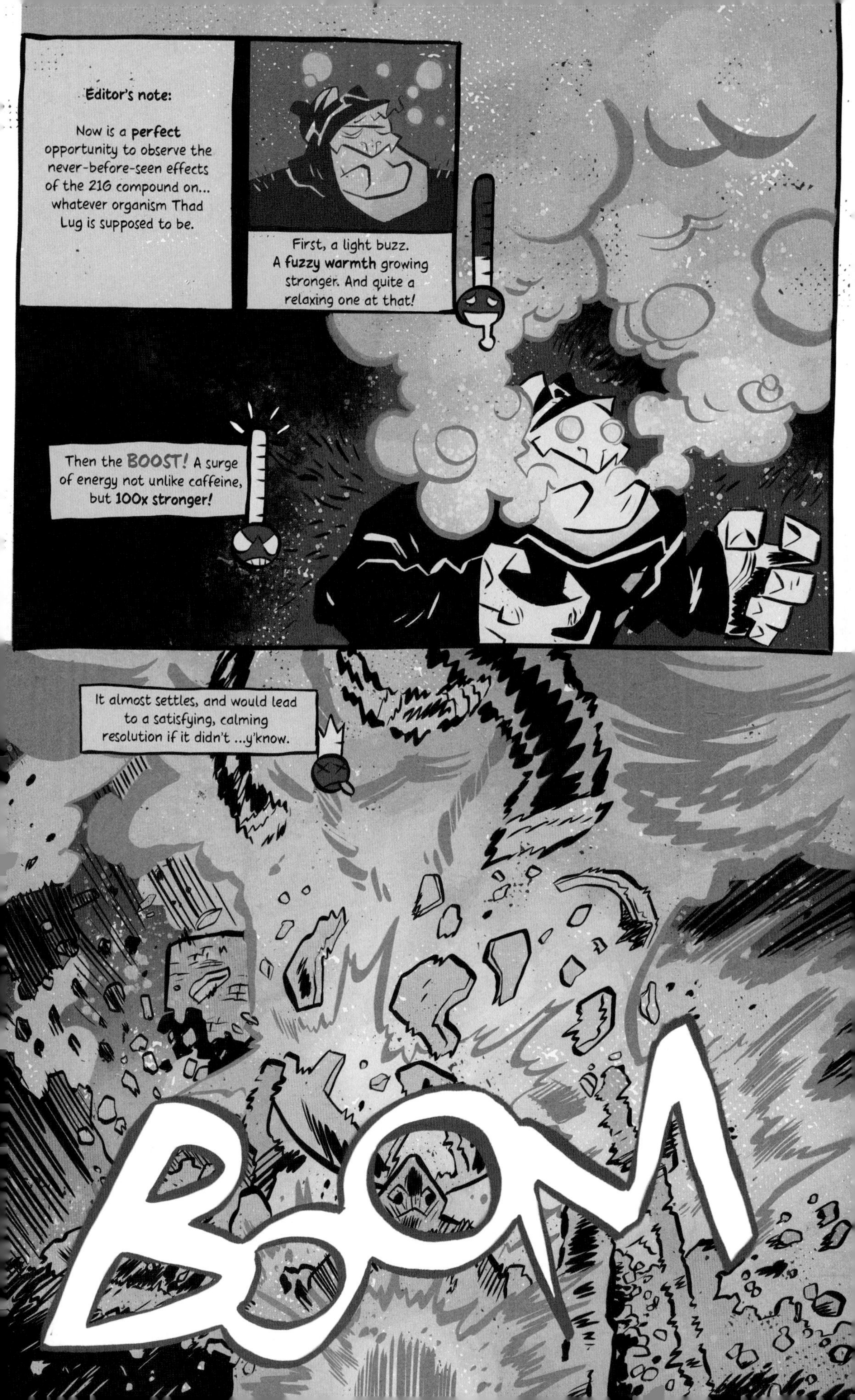
Editor's note:
Now is a **perfect** opportunity to observe the never-before-seen effects of the 216 compound on... whatever organism Thad Lug is supposed to be.
First, a light buzz. A **fuzzy warmth** growing stronger. And quite a relaxing one at that!
Then the **BOOST!** A surge of energy not unlike caffeine, but **100x stronger!**
It almost settles, and would lead to a satisfying, calming resolution if it didn't ...y'know.
BOOM

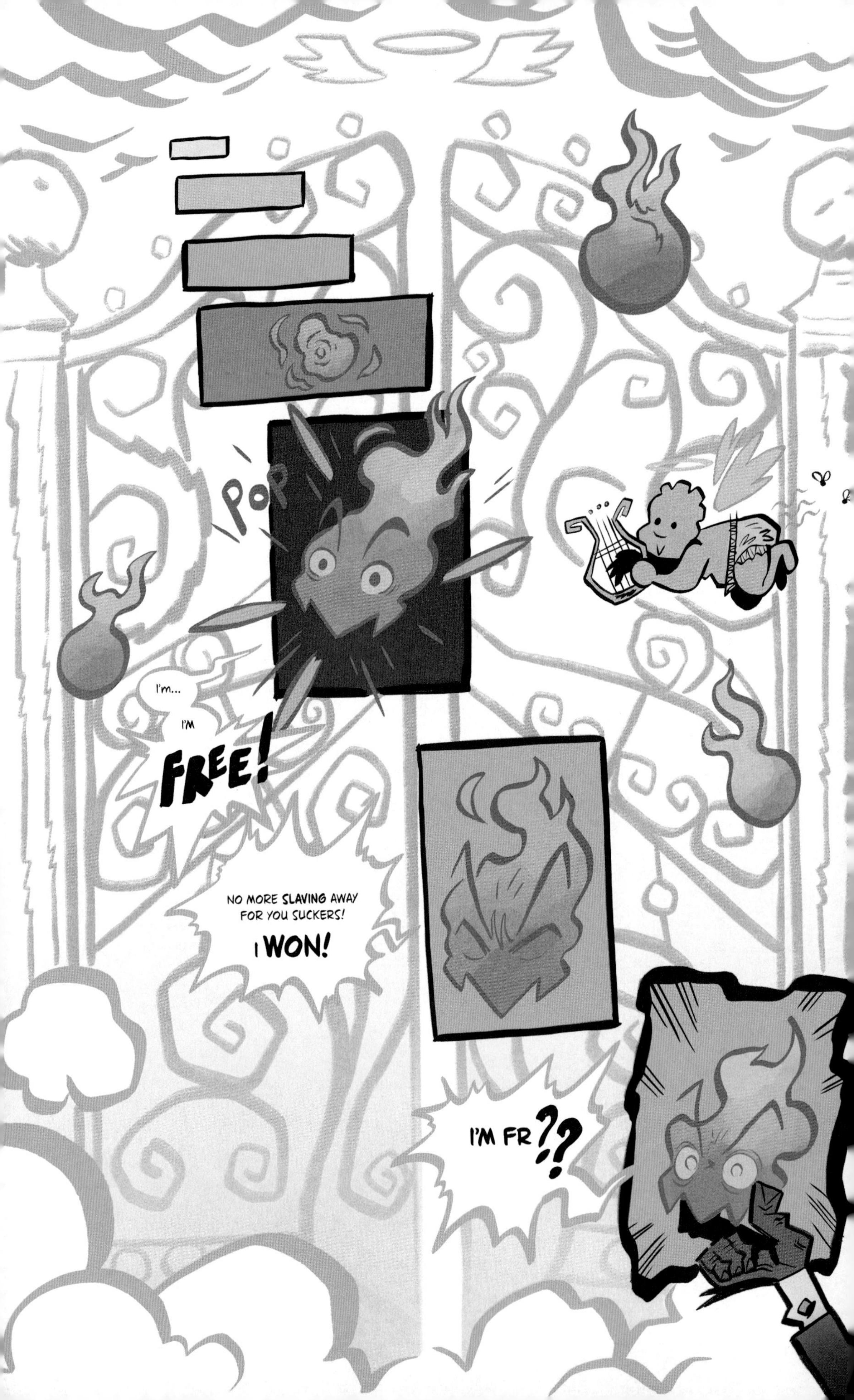
POP
I'm...
I'M
FREE!
NO MORE SLAVING AWAY
FOR YOU SUCKERS!
I WON!
I'M FR??

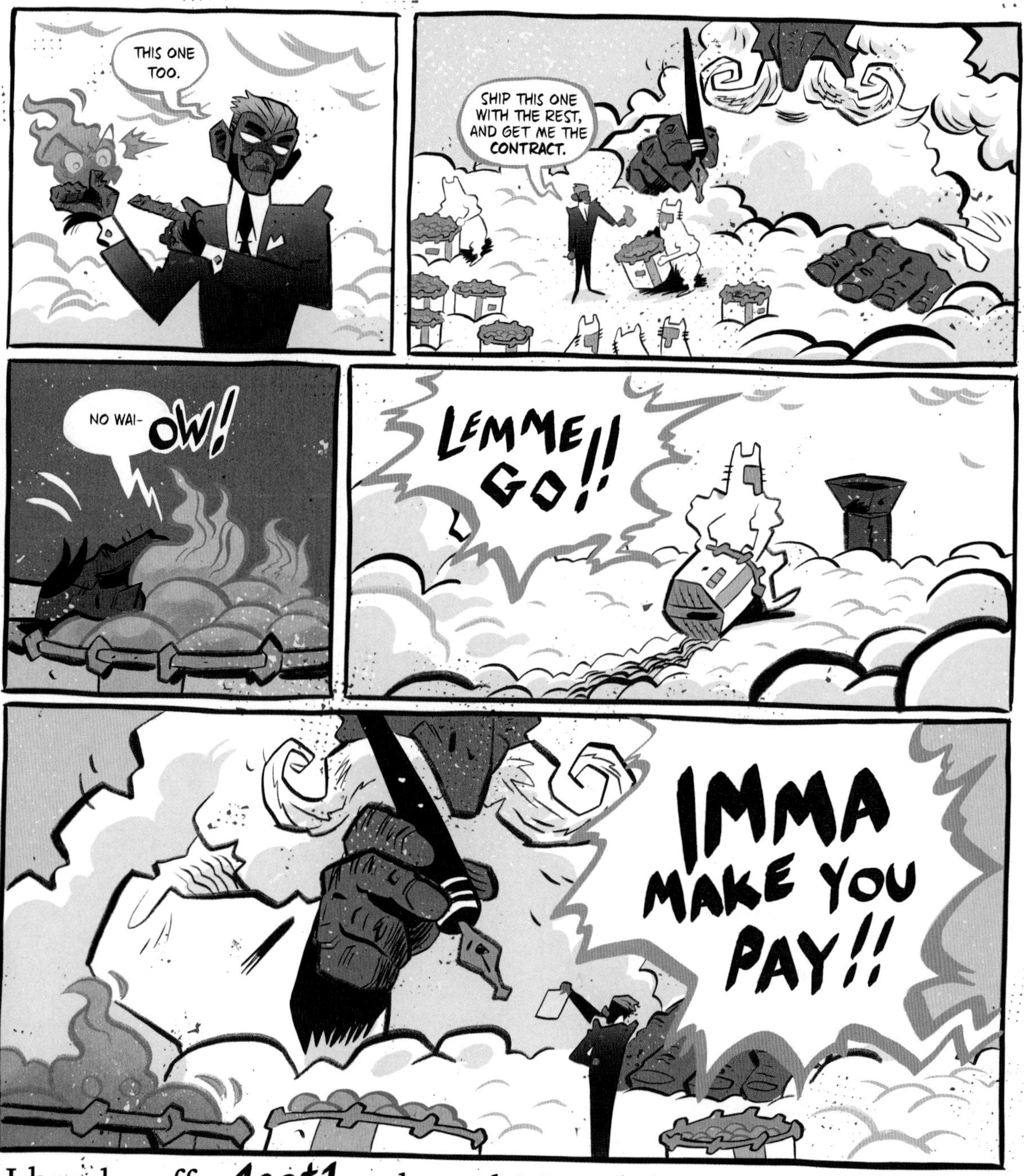

THIS ONE TOO.
SHIP THIS ONE WITH THE REST, AND GET ME THE **CONTRACT.**
NO WAI- OW!
LEMME GO!!
IMMA MAKE YOU PAY!!

I hereby offer...100+1... souls to the Monkey Meat Corporation, to use as raw material for the 21G experimental compound.

Signed:...GOD...

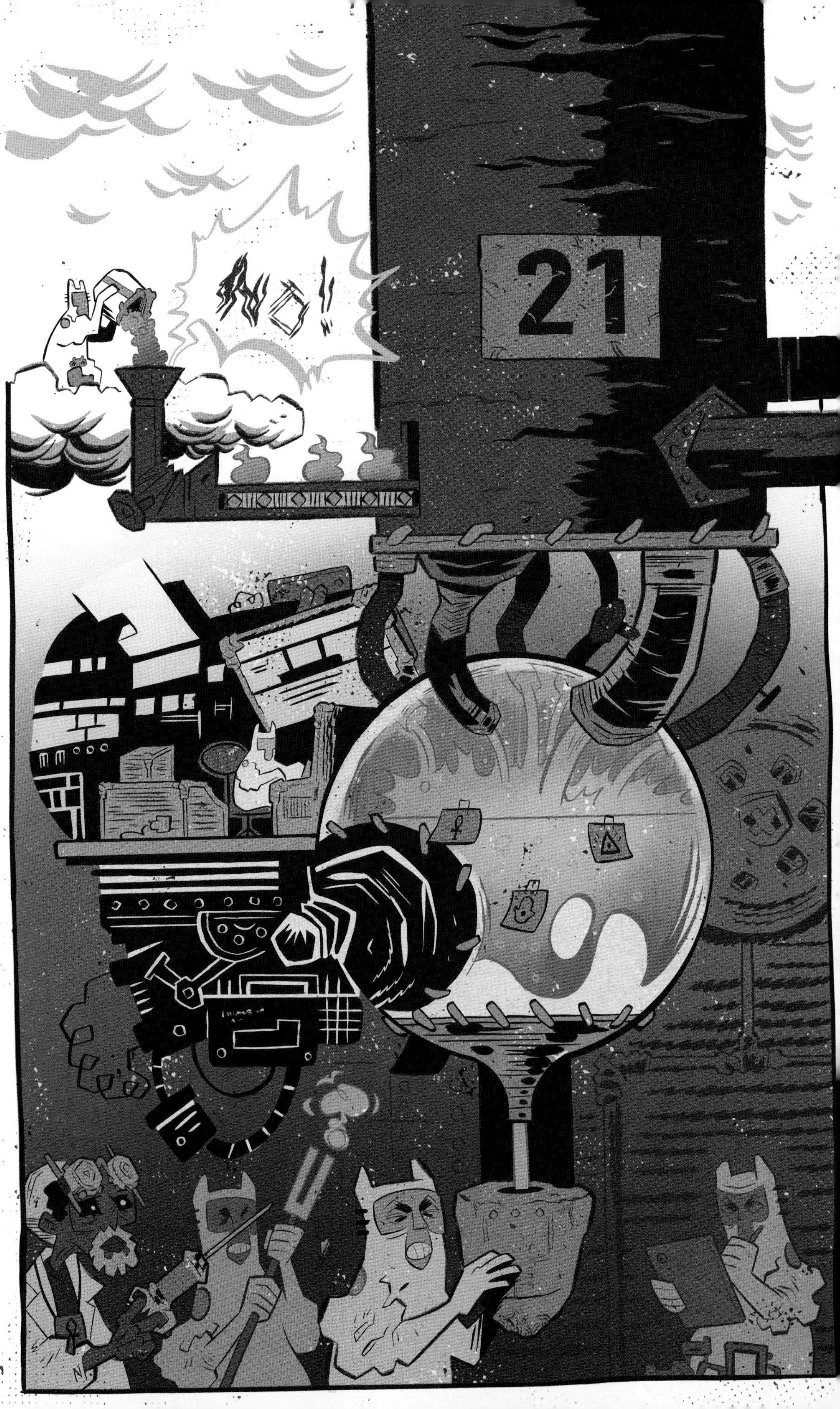
NO!!
21

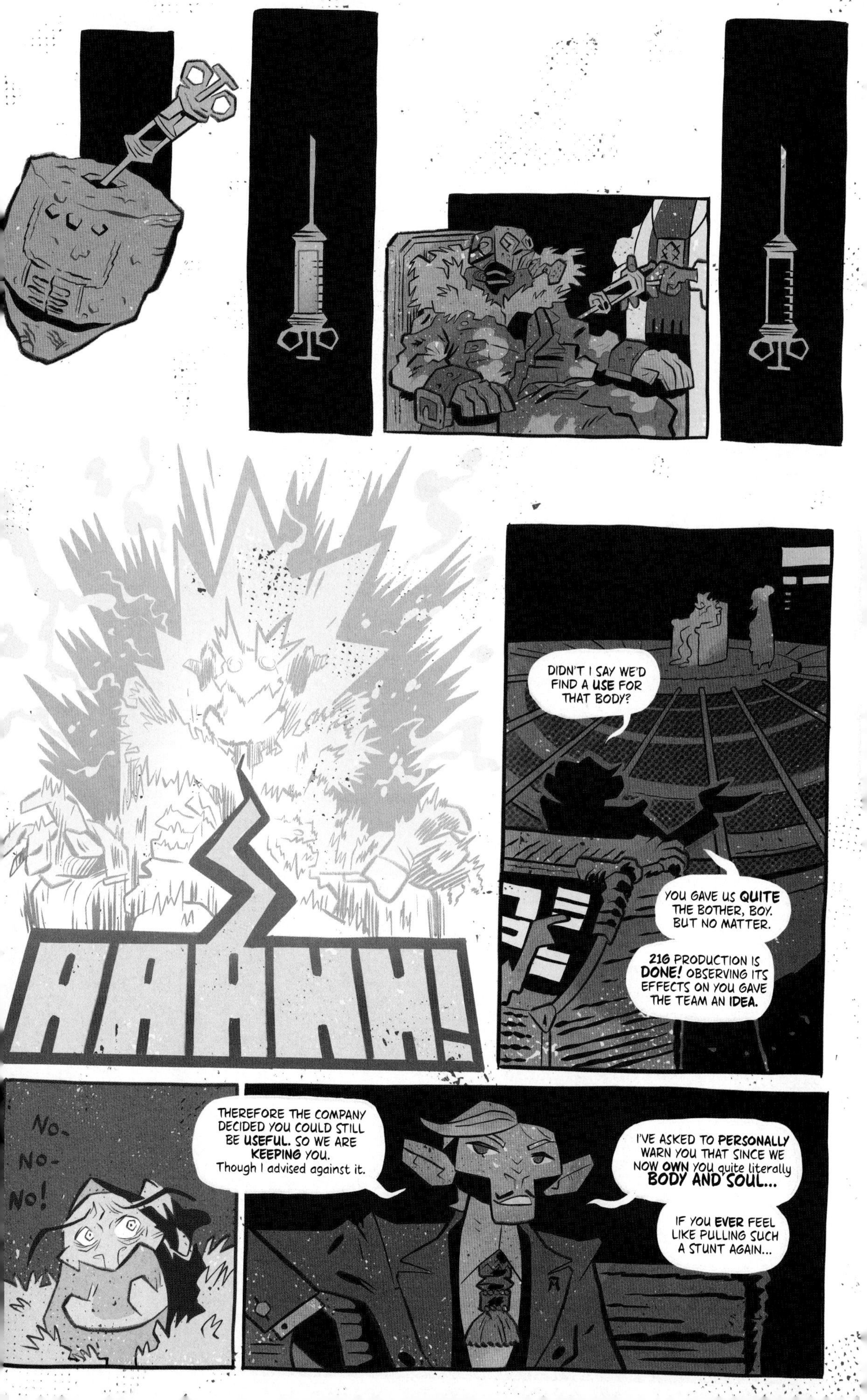
AAAHH!
DIDN'T I SAY WE'D FIND A USE FOR THAT BODY?
YOU GAVE US QUITE THE BOTHER, BOY. BUT NO MATTER.
216 PRODUCTION IS DONE! OBSERVING ITS EFFECTS ON YOU GAVE THE TEAM AN IDEA.
No- No- No!
THEREFORE THE COMPANY DECIDED YOU COULD STILL BE USEFUL. SO WE ARE KEEPING YOU. Though I advised against it.
I'VE ASKED TO PERSONALLY WARN YOU THAT SINCE WE NOW OWN YOU quite literally BODY AND SOUL...
IF YOU EVER FEEL LIKE PULLING SUCH A STUNT AGAIN...

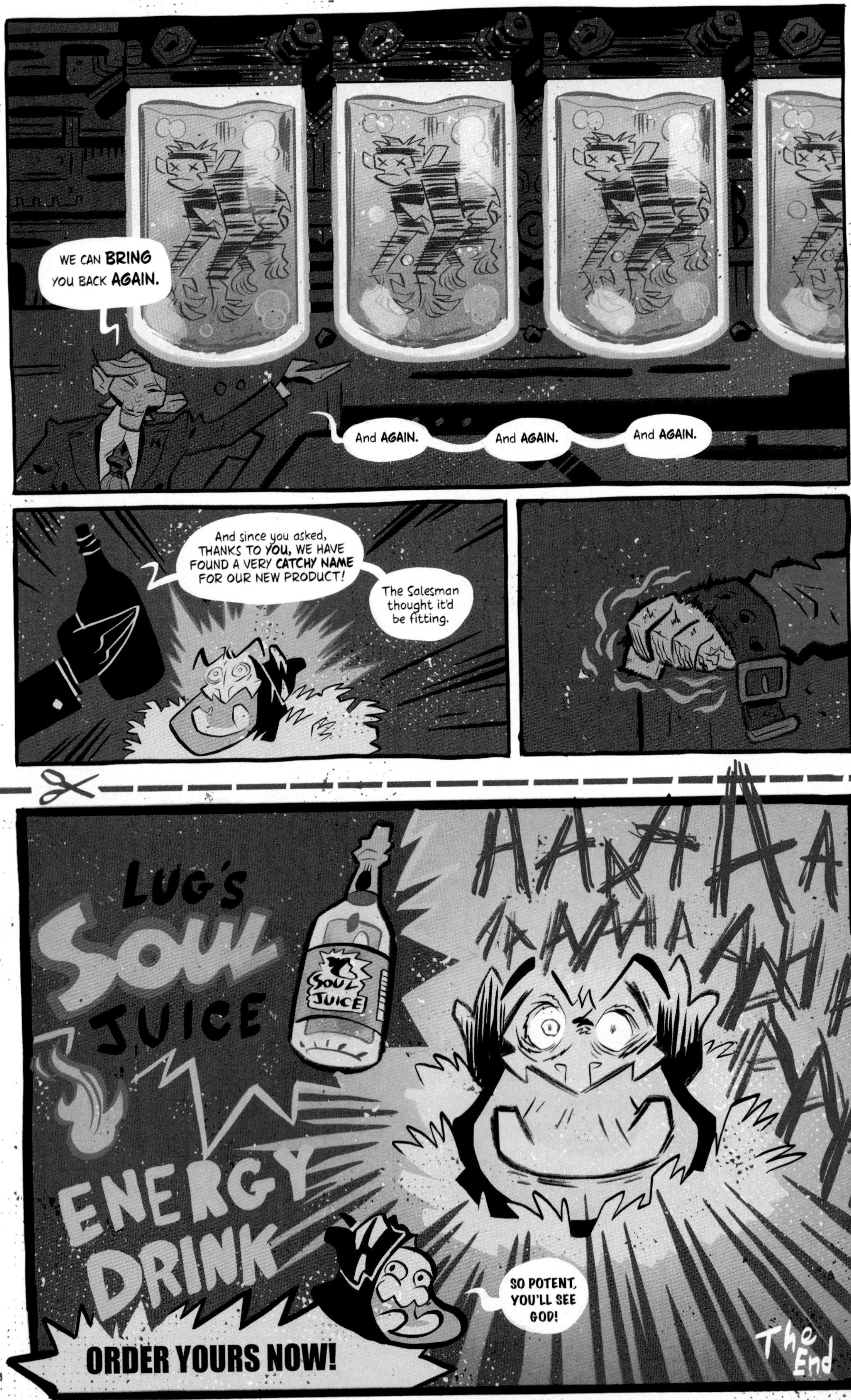
WE CAN BRING YOU BACK AGAIN.
And AGAIN.
And AGAIN.
And AGAIN.
And since you asked, THANKS TO YOU, WE HAVE FOUND A VERY CATCHY NAME FOR OUR NEW PRODUCT!
The Salesman thought it'd be fitting.
LUG'S SOUL JUICE
SOUL JUICE
ENERGY DRINK
AAAAA AAAAAA AAAAAAA
SO POTENT, YOU'LL SEE GOD!
ORDER YOURS NOW!
The End

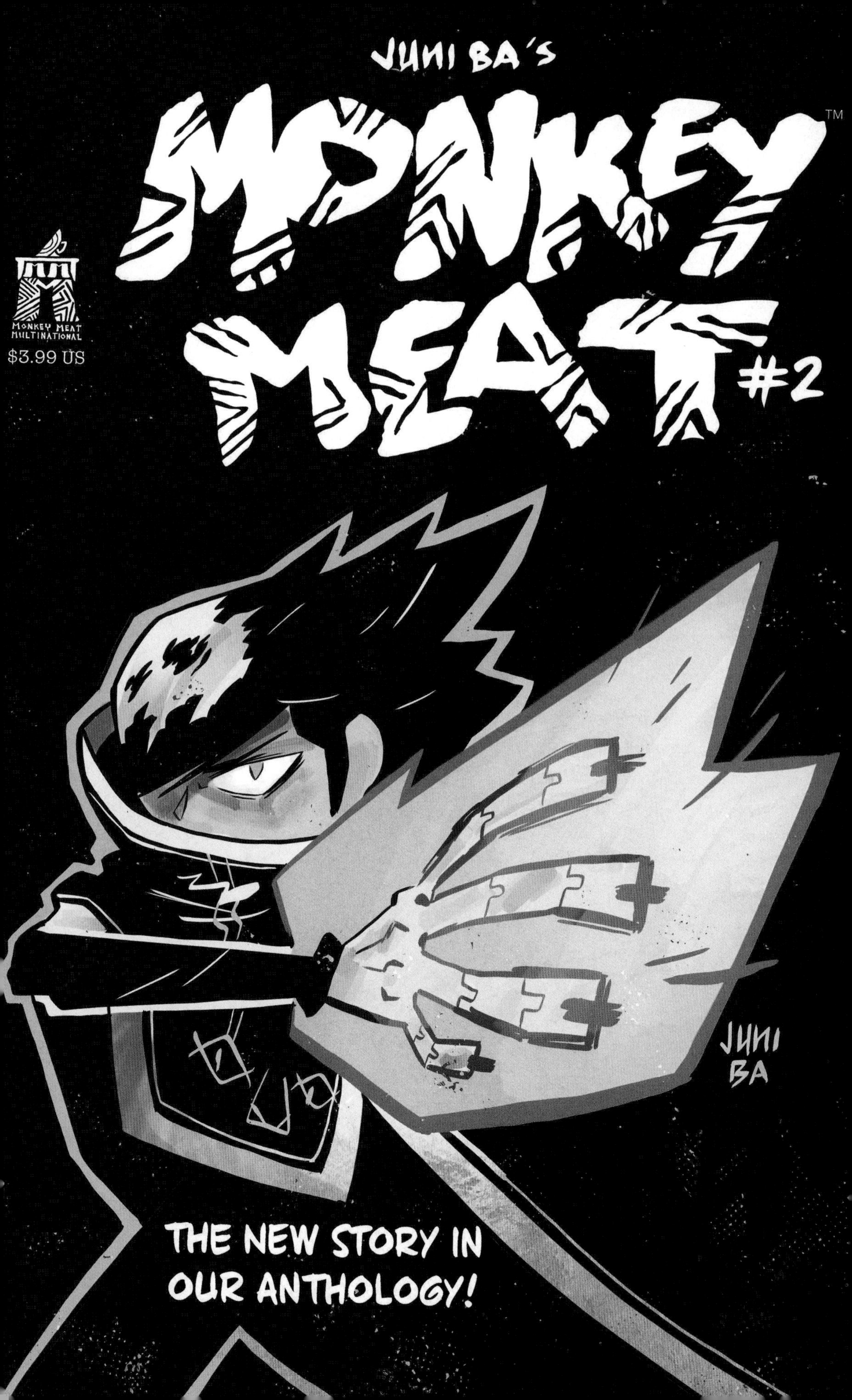
JUNI BA'S
MONKEY MEAT™
#2
MONKEY MEAT MULTINATIONAL
$3.99 US
JUNI BA
THE NEW STORY IN OUR ANTHOLOGY!

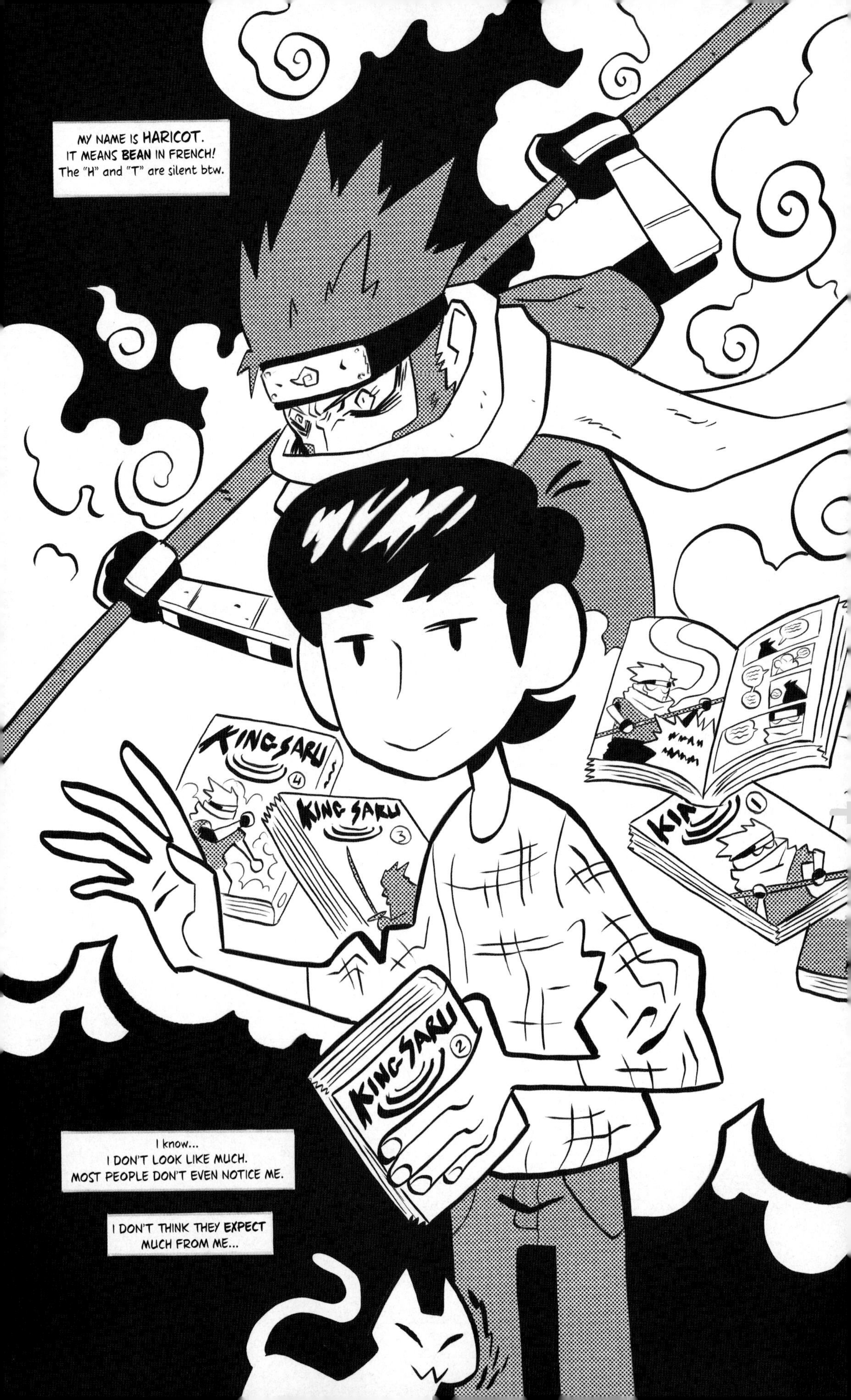
MY NAME IS HARICOT.
IT MEANS BEAN IN FRENCH!
The "H" and "T" are silent btw.
KING SARU 4
KING SARU 3
KING SARU 2
I know...
I DON'T LOOK LIKE MUCH.
MOST PEOPLE DON'T EVEN NOTICE ME.
I DON'T THINK THEY EXPECT
MUCH FROM ME...

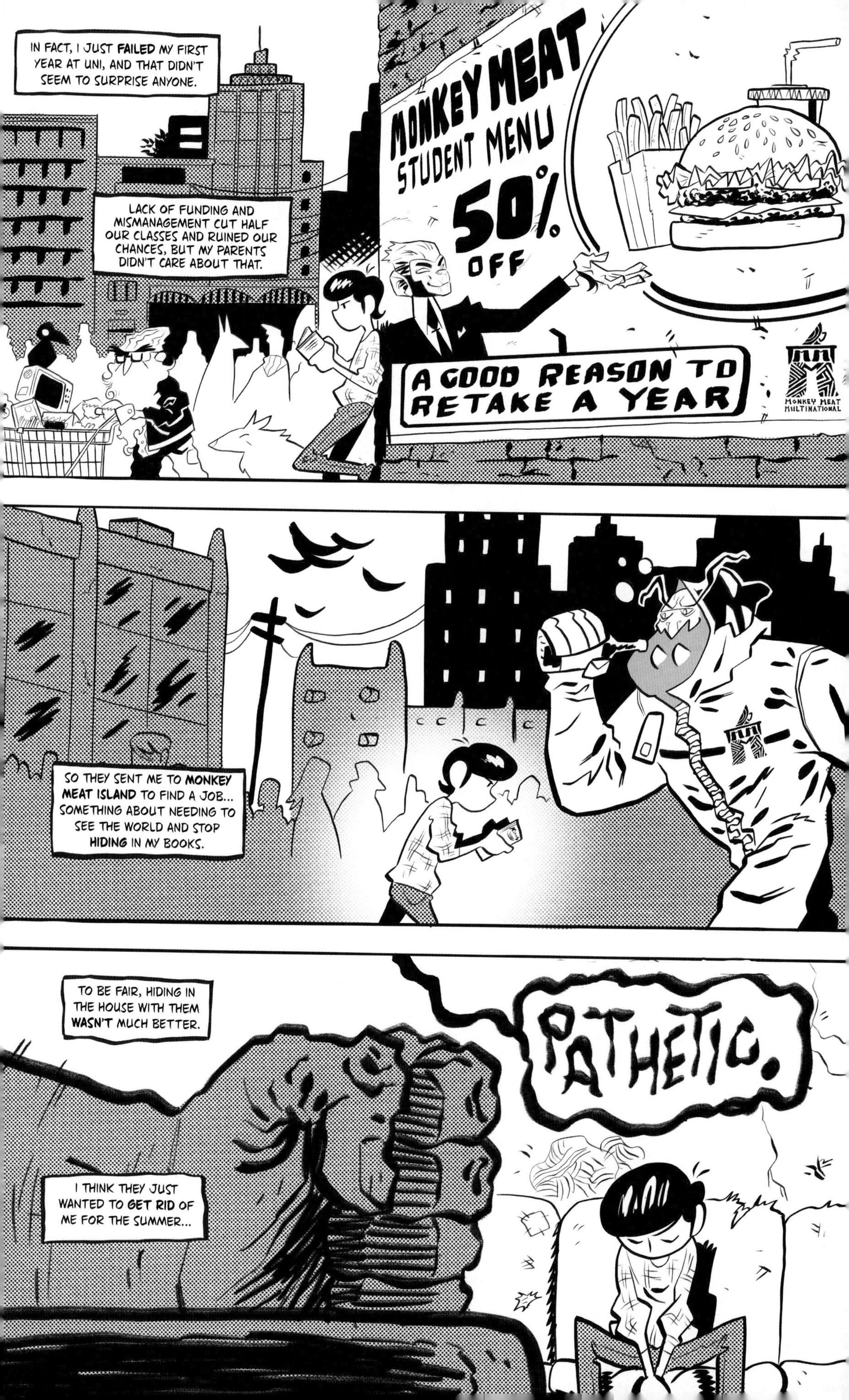
IN FACT, I JUST FAILED MY FIRST YEAR AT UNI, AND THAT DIDN'T SEEM TO SURPRISE ANYONE.
MONKEY MEAT
STUDENT MENU
50% OFF
LACK OF FUNDING AND MISMANAGEMENT CUT HALF OUR CLASSES AND RUINED OUR CHANCES, BUT MY PARENTS DIDN'T CARE ABOUT THAT.
A GOOD REASON TO RETAKE A YEAR
MONKEY MEAT MULTINATIONAL
SO THEY SENT ME TO MONKEY MEAT ISLAND TO FIND A JOB... SOMETHING ABOUT NEEDING TO SEE THE WORLD AND STOP HIDING IN MY BOOKS.
TO BE FAIR, HIDING IN THE HOUSE WITH THEM WASN'T MUCH BETTER.
PATHETIC.
I THINK THEY JUST WANTED TO GET RID OF ME FOR THE SUMMER...

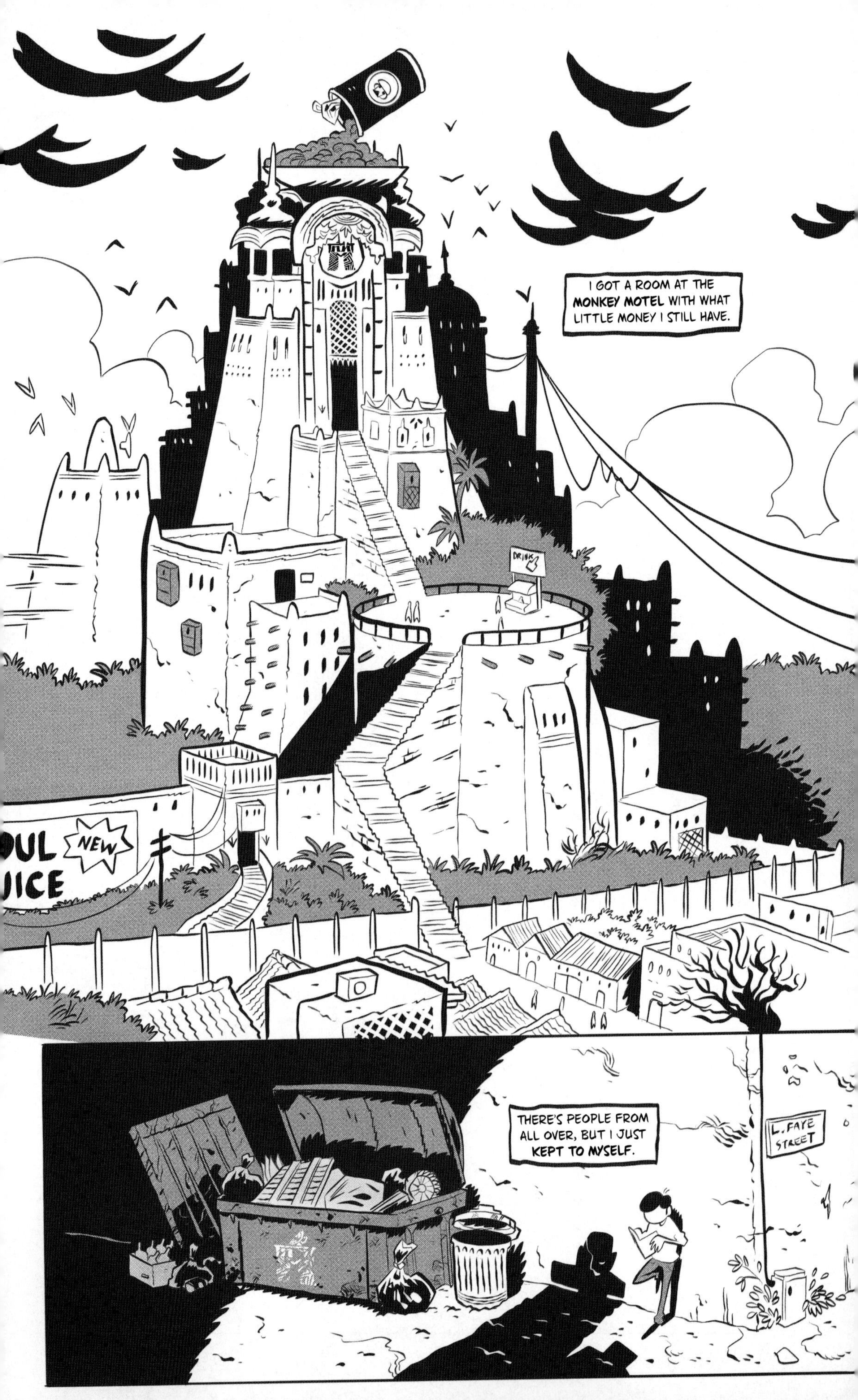
I GOT A ROOM AT THE **MONKEY MOTEL** WITH WHAT LITTLE MONEY I STILL HAVE.
DRINKS
NEW
THERE'S PEOPLE FROM ALL OVER, BUT I JUST **KEPT TO MYSELF.**
L. FAYE STREET

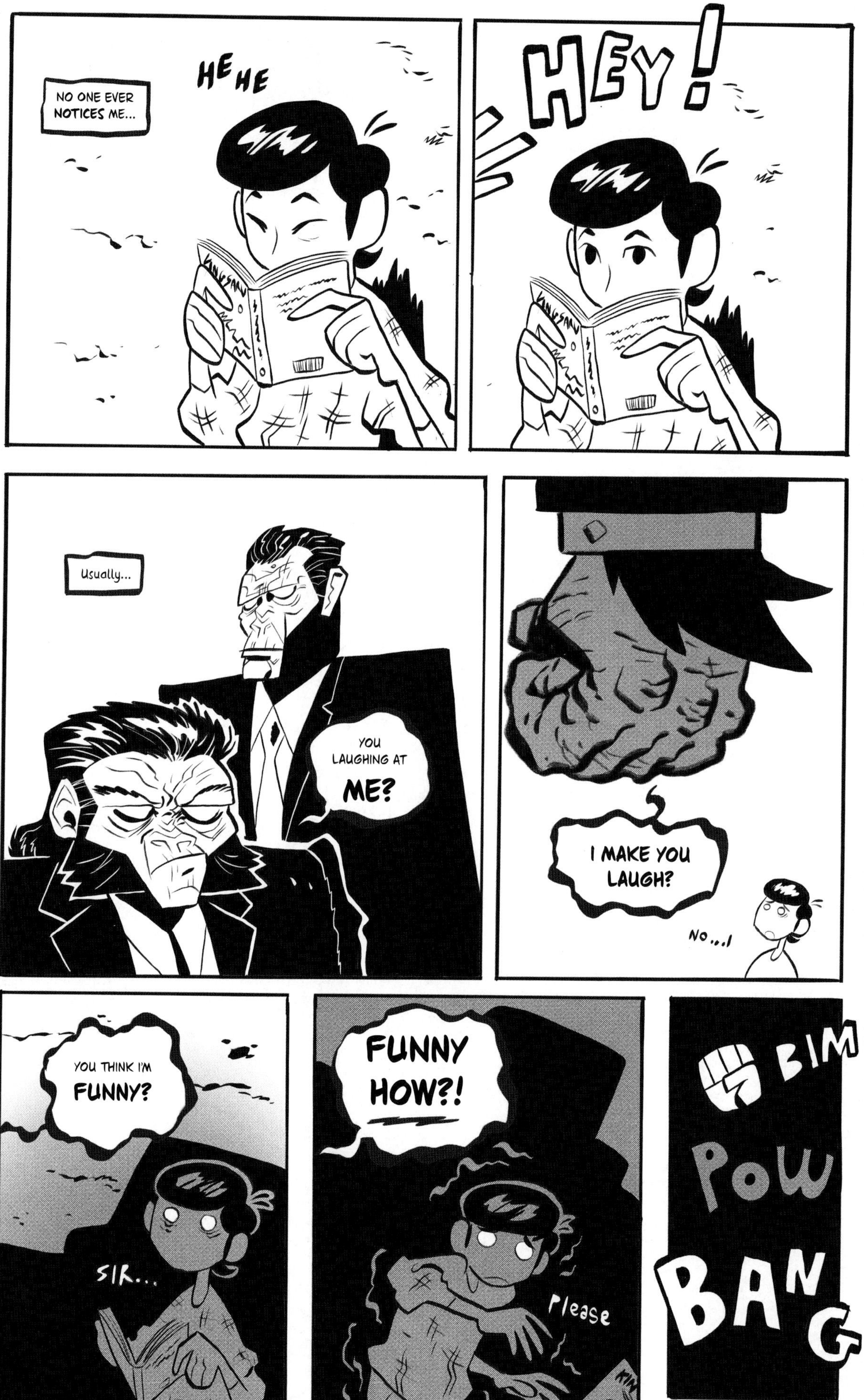
NO ONE EVER NOTICES ME...
HE HE
HEY!
Usually...
YOU LAUGHING AT ME?
I MAKE YOU LAUGH?
NO...!
YOU THINK I'M FUNNY?
SIR...
FUNNY HOW?!
Please
BIM
POW
BANG

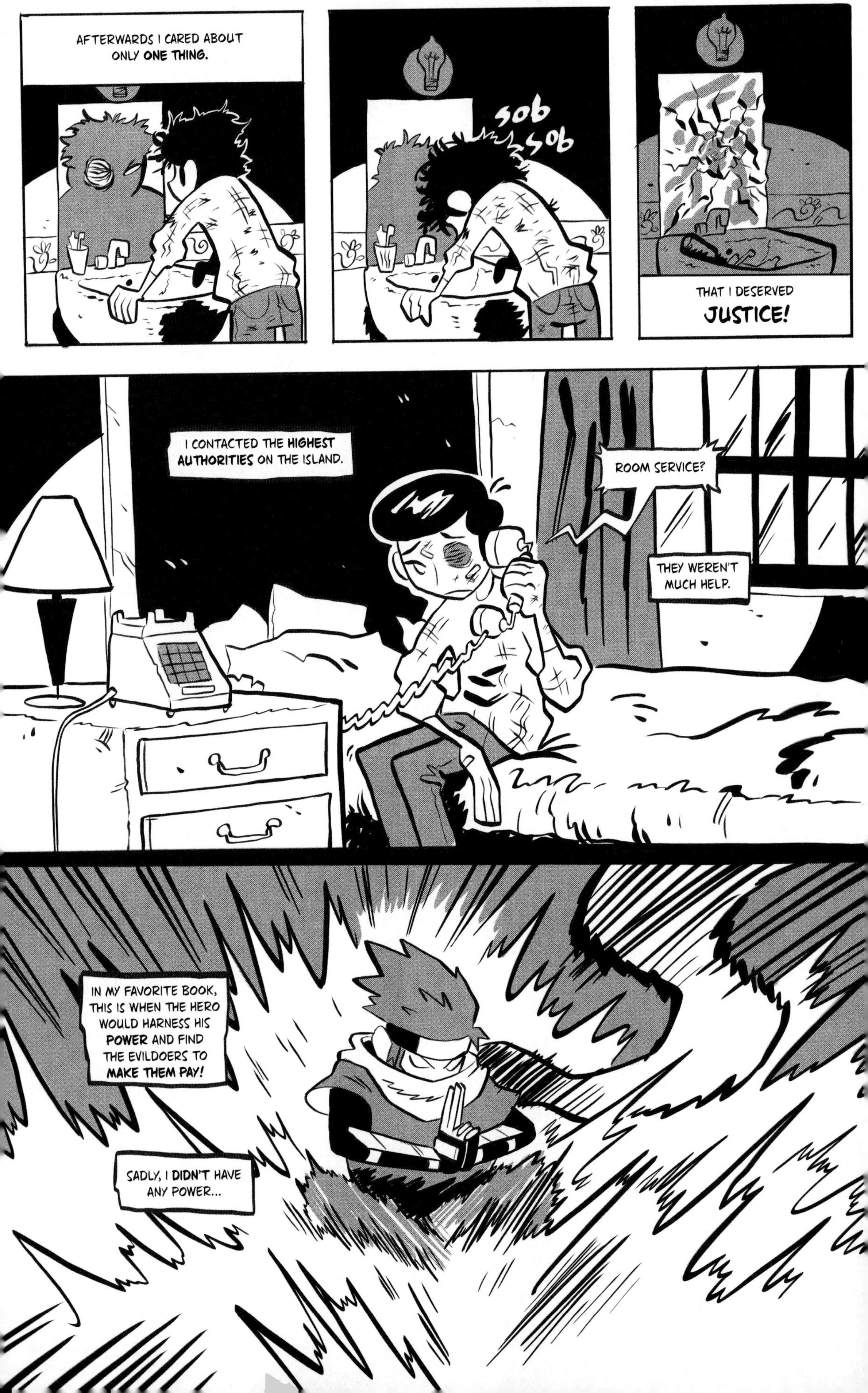
AFTERWARDS I CARED ABOUT ONLY **ONE THING.**
sob sob
THAT I DESERVED **JUSTICE!**
I CONTACTED THE **HIGHEST AUTHORITIES** ON THE ISLAND.
ROOM SERVICE?
THEY WEREN'T MUCH HELP.
IN MY FAVORITE BOOK, THIS IS WHEN THE HERO WOULD HARNESS HIS **POWER** AND FIND THE EVILDOERS TO **MAKE THEM PAY!**
SADLY, I **DIDN'T** HAVE ANY POWER...

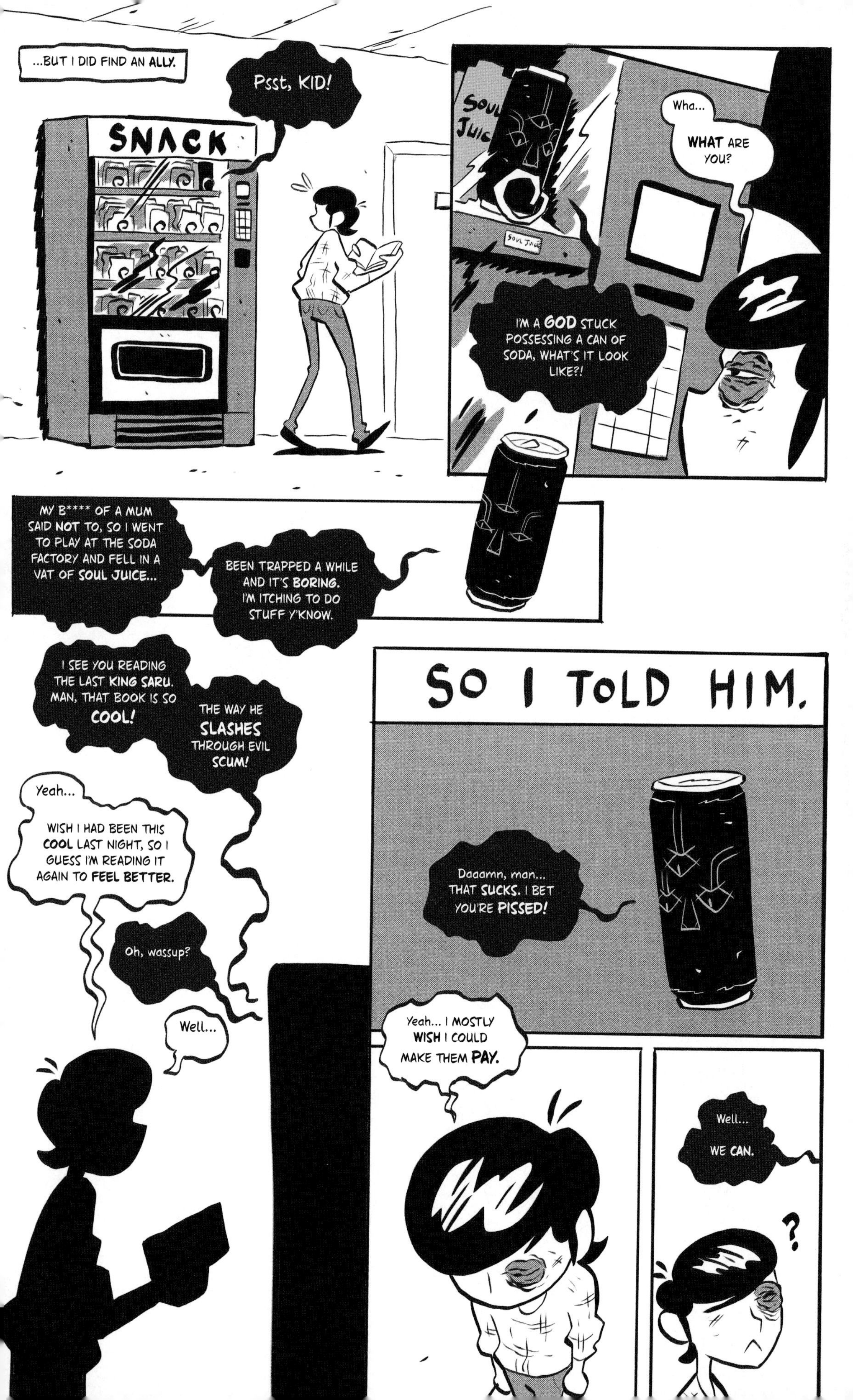
...BUT I DID FIND AN ALLY.
Psst, KID!
SNACK
SOUL JUICE
Wha...
WHAT ARE YOU?
I'M A GOD STUCK POSSESSING A CAN OF SODA, WHAT'S IT LOOK LIKE?!
MY B**** OF A MUM SAID NOT TO, SO I WENT TO PLAY AT THE SODA FACTORY AND FELL IN A VAT OF SOUL JUICE...
BEEN TRAPPED A WHILE AND IT'S BORING. I'M ITCHING TO DO STUFF Y'KNOW.
I SEE YOU READING THE LAST KING SARU. MAN, THAT BOOK IS SO COOL!
THE WAY HE SLASHES THROUGH EVIL SCUM!
Yeah...
WISH I HAD BEEN THIS COOL LAST NIGHT, SO I GUESS I'M READING IT AGAIN TO FEEL BETTER.
Oh, wassup?
Well...
SO I TOLD HIM.
Daaamn, man... THAT SUCKS. I BET YOU'RE PISSED!
Yeah... I MOSTLY WISH I COULD MAKE THEM PAY.
Well...
WE CAN.
?

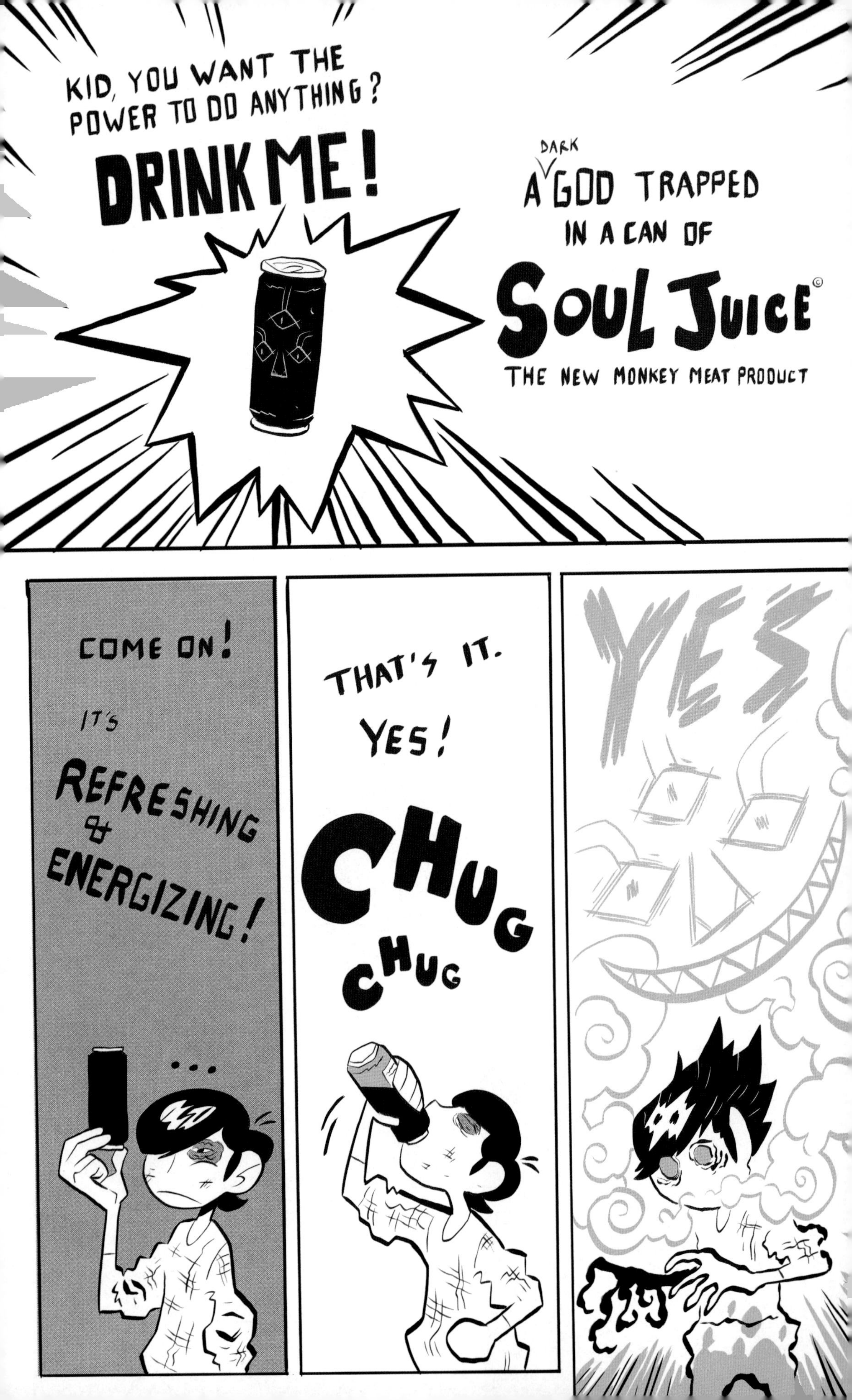
KID, YOU WANT THE POWER TO DO ANYTHING?
DRINK ME!
A DARK GOD TRAPPED IN A CAN OF
SOUL JUICE©
THE NEW MONKEY MEAT PRODUCT
COME ON!
IT'S REFRESHING & ENERGIZING!
...
THAT'S IT.
YES!
CHUG CHUG
YES

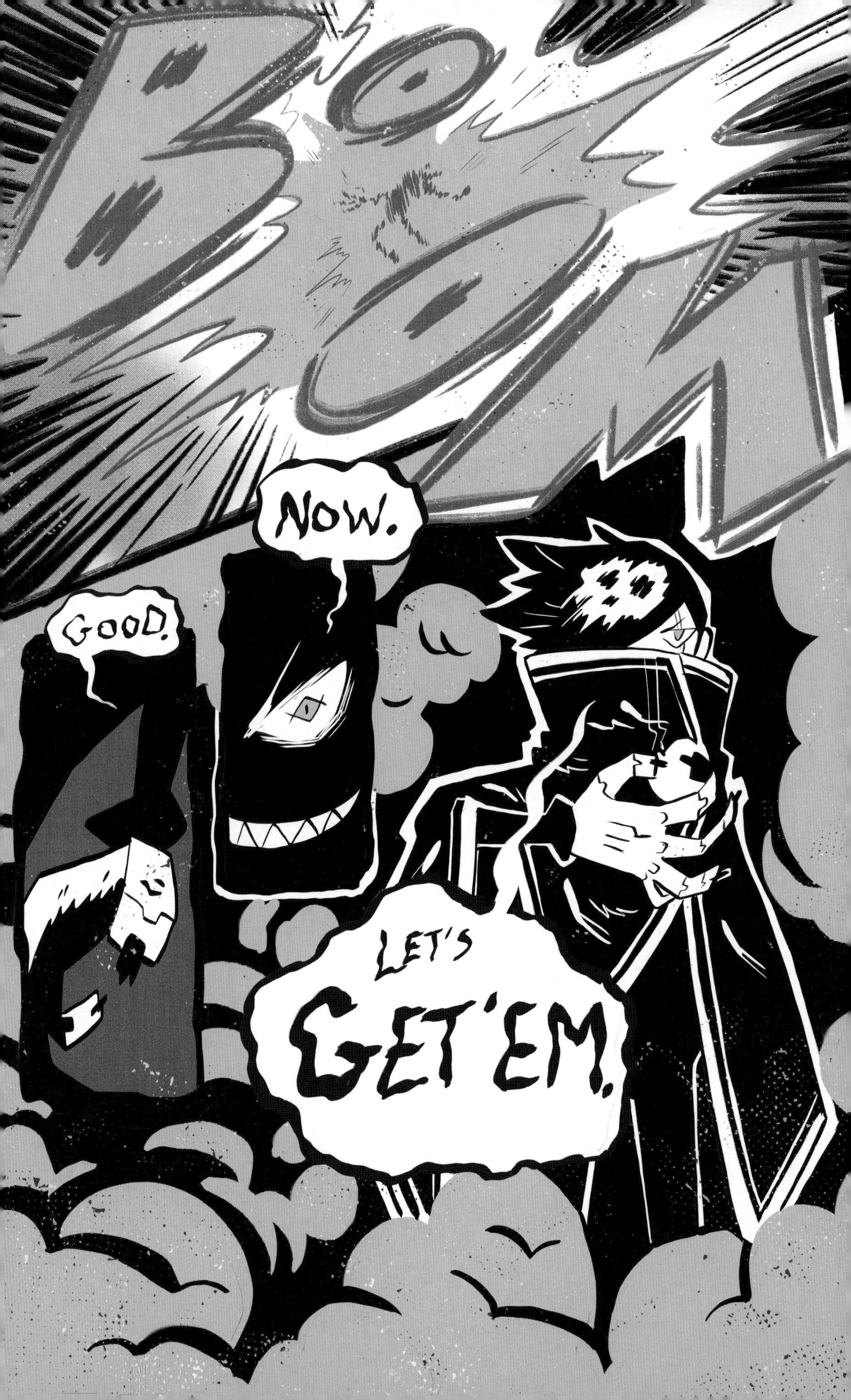
BOOOM
NOW.
GOOD.
LET'S GET'EM.

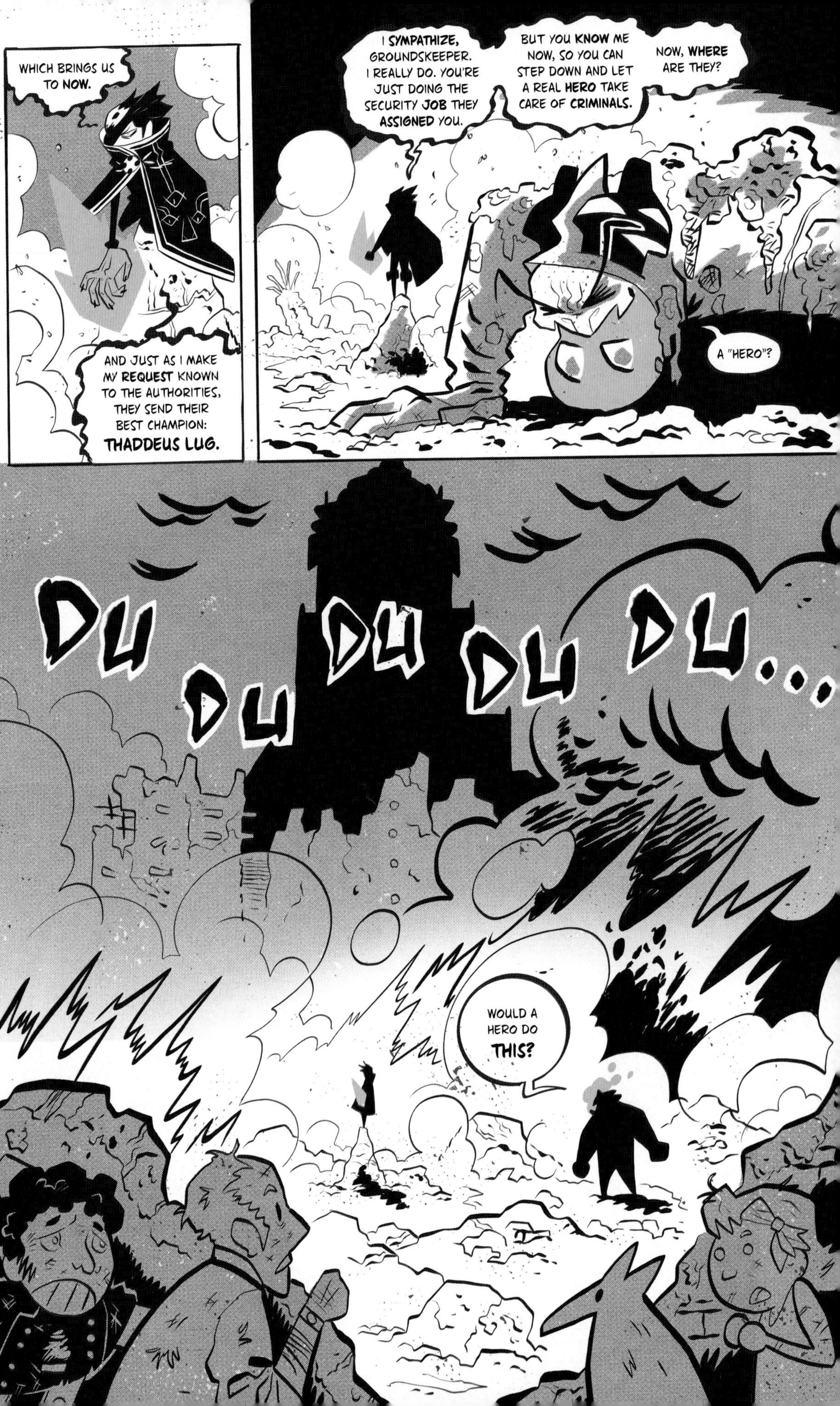
WHICH BRINGS US TO NOW.
AND JUST AS I MAKE MY REQUEST KNOWN TO THE AUTHORITIES, THEY SEND THEIR BEST CHAMPION: THADDEUS LUG.
I SYMPATHIZE, GROUNDSKEEPER. I REALLY DO. YOU'RE JUST DOING THE SECURITY JOB THEY ASSIGNED YOU.
BUT YOU KNOW ME NOW, SO YOU CAN STEP DOWN AND LET A REAL HERO TAKE CARE OF CRIMINALS.
NOW, WHERE ARE THEY?
A "HERO"?
DU DU DU DU DU...
WOULD A HERO DO THIS?

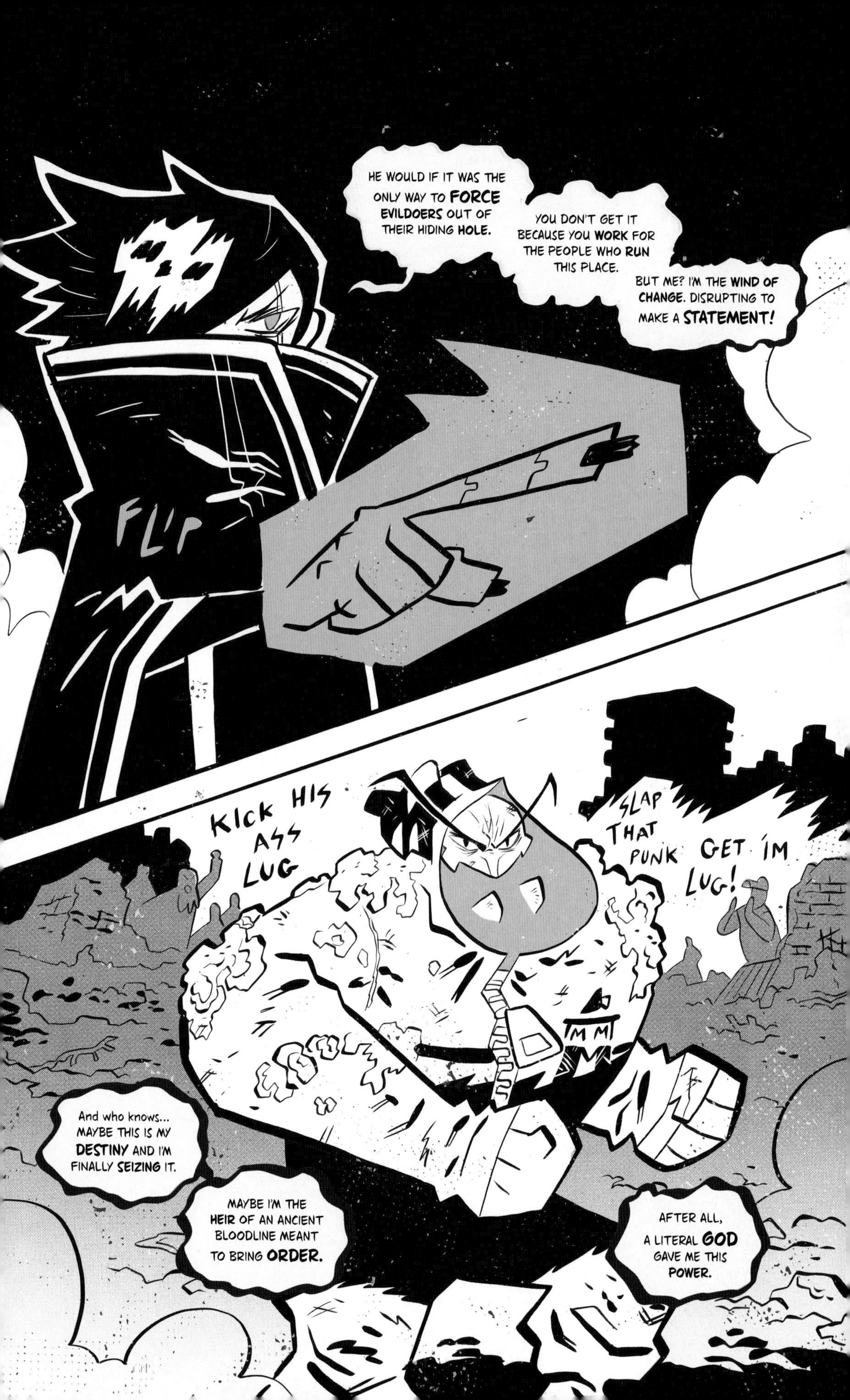
HE WOULD IF IT WAS THE ONLY WAY TO FORCE EVILDOERS OUT OF THEIR HIDING HOLE.
YOU DON'T GET IT BECAUSE YOU WORK FOR THE PEOPLE WHO RUN THIS PLACE.
BUT ME? I'M THE WIND OF CHANGE. DISRUPTING TO MAKE A STATEMENT!
FLIP
KICK HIS ASS LUG
SLAP THAT PUNK
GET 'IM LUG!
MMM
And who knows... MAYBE THIS IS MY DESTINY AND I'M FINALLY SEIZING IT.
MAYBE I'M THE HEIR OF AN ANCIENT BLOODLINE MEANT TO BRING ORDER.
AFTER ALL, A LITERAL GOD GAVE ME THIS POWER.

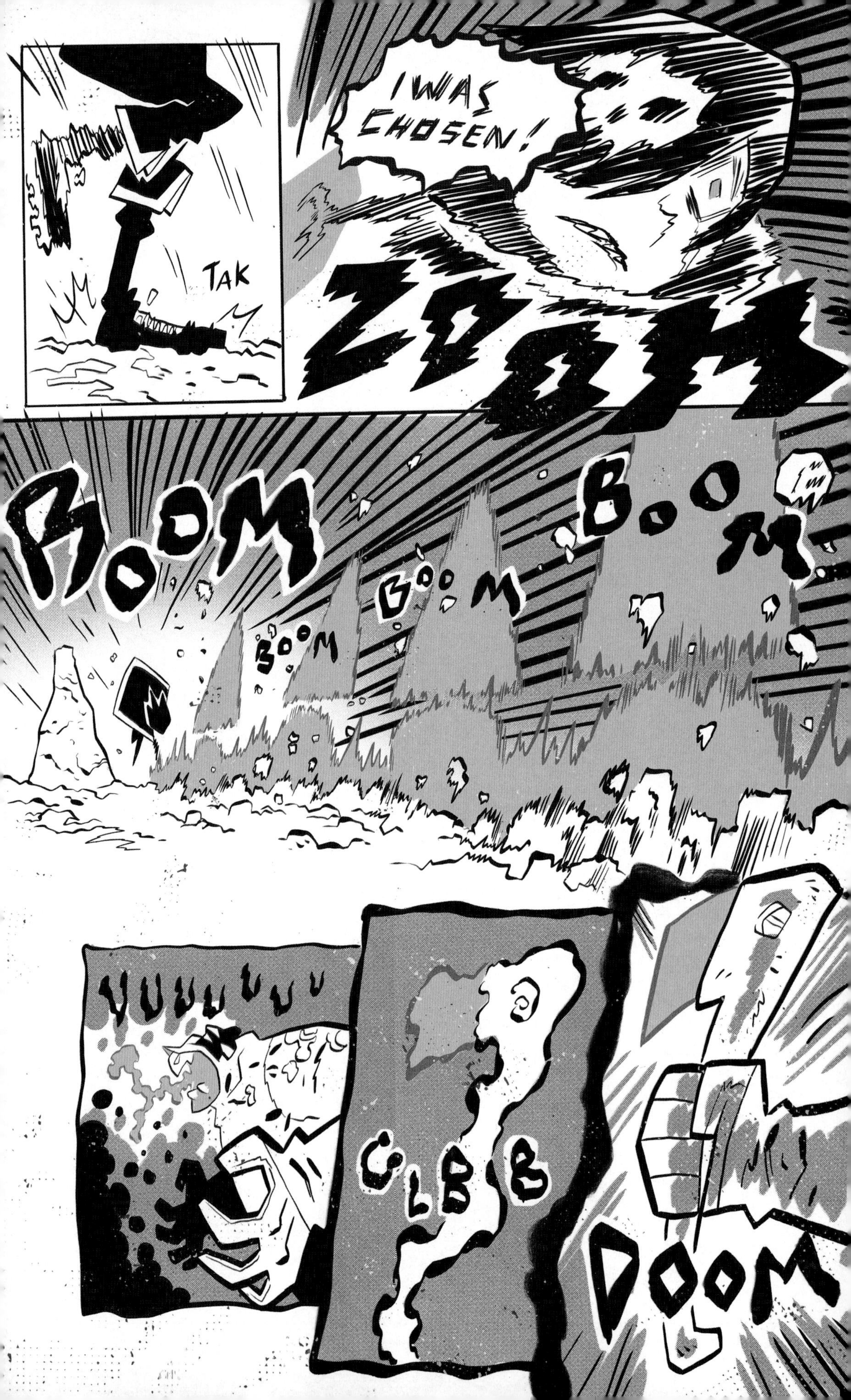
TAK
I WAS CHOSEN!
ZOOM
BOOM
BOOM
BOOM
BOOM
VUUUUUU
GLBB
DOOM

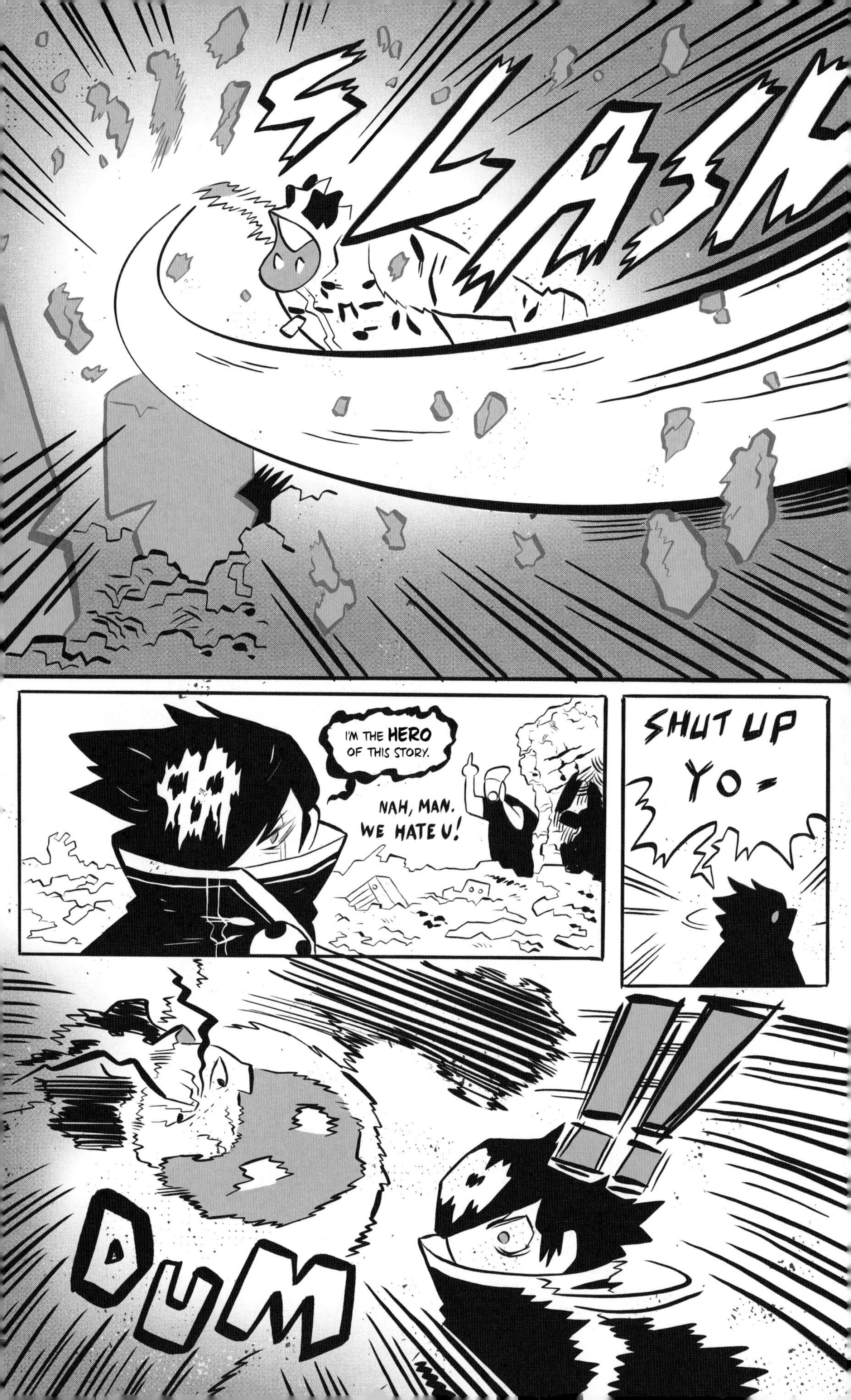
SLASH
I'M THE HERO OF THIS STORY.
NAH, MAN. WE HATE U!
SHUT UP YO-
DUM
!!

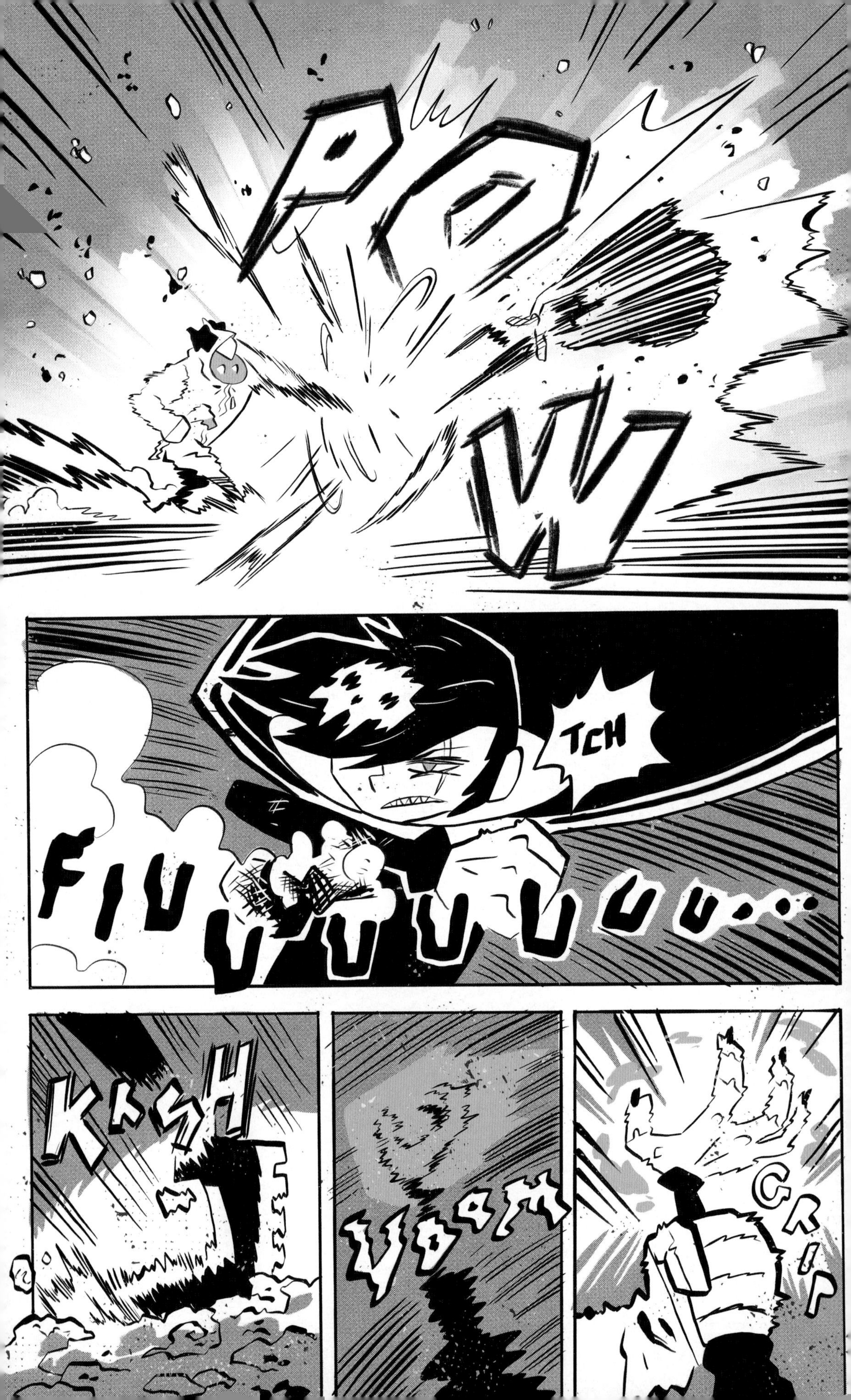
POW
TCH
FIVUUUUUU...
KASH
VOOM
GRIP

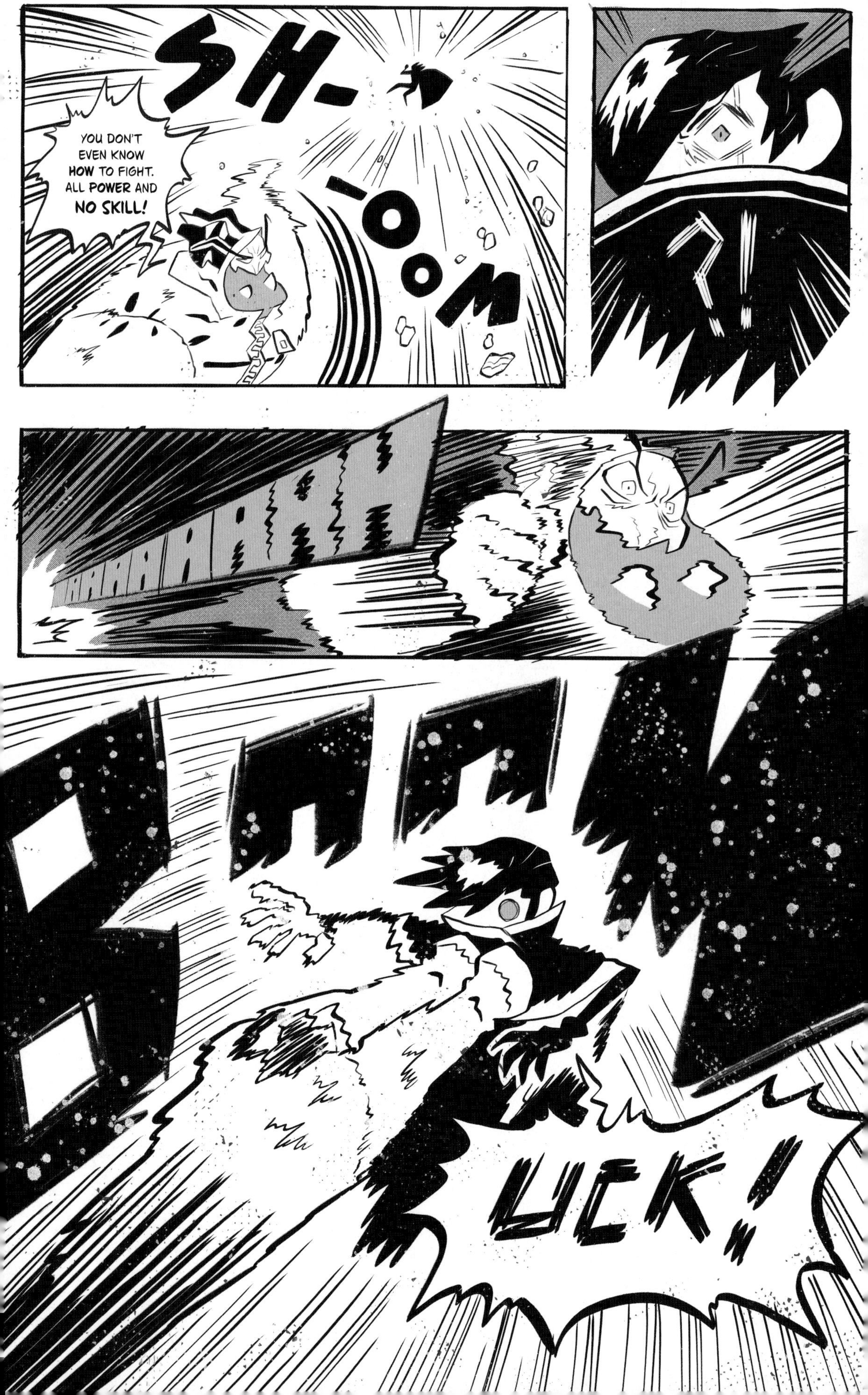
SH-
-OOM
YOU DON'T EVEN KNOW HOW TO FIGHT. ALL POWER AND NO SKILL!
?!
AAAAAAAAAH
UCK!

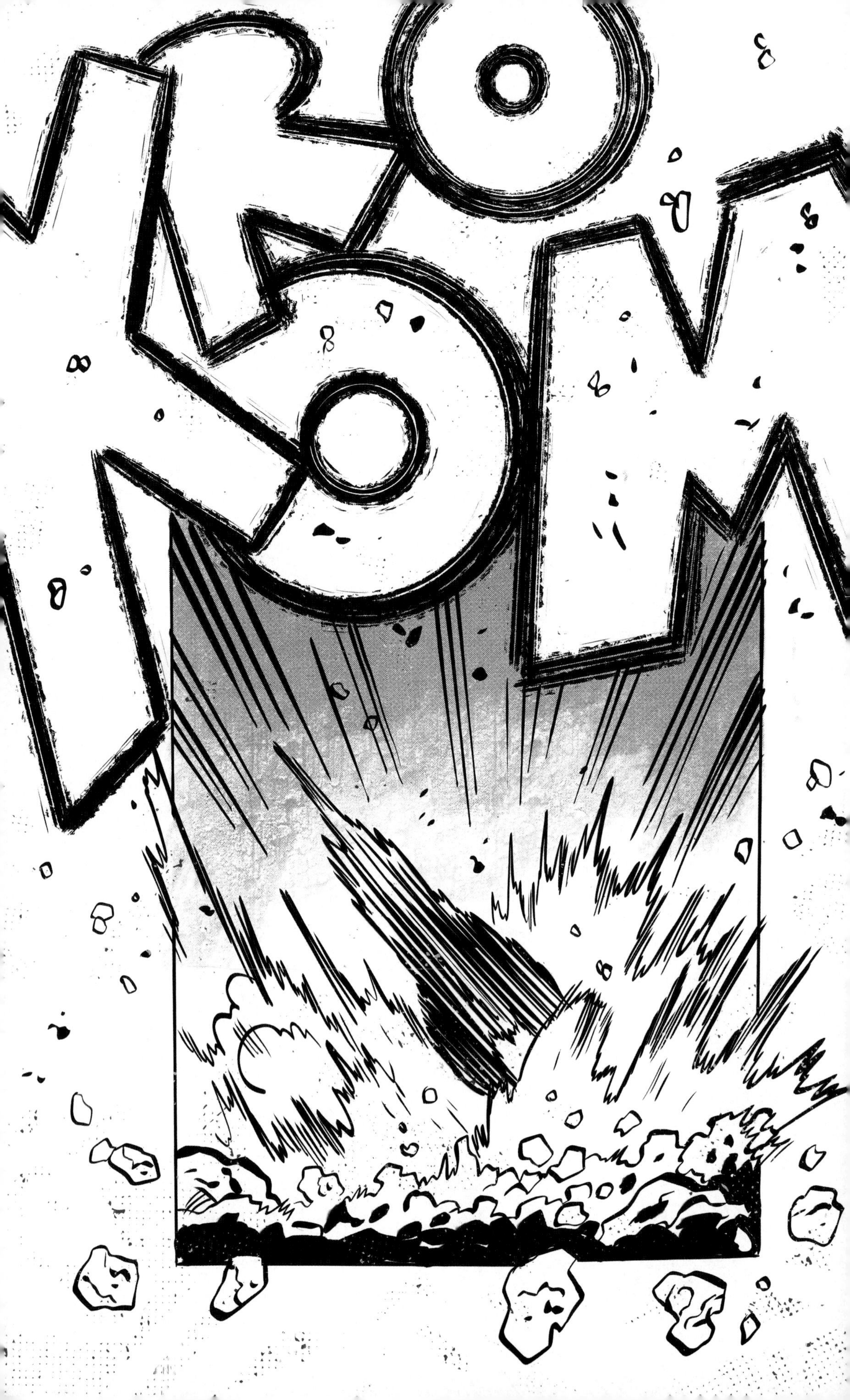
KROOM

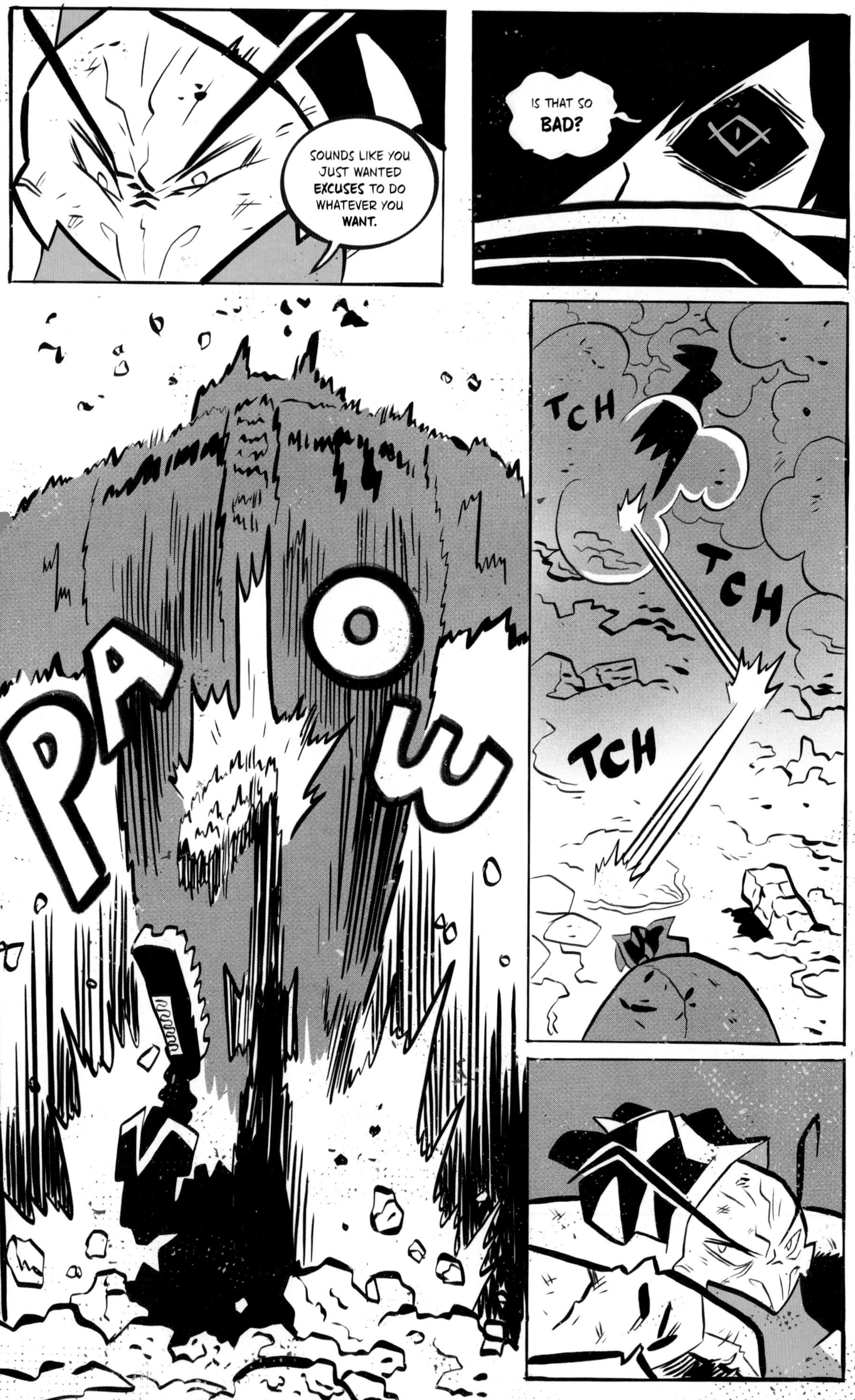
SOUNDS LIKE YOU JUST WANTED EXCUSES TO DO WHATEVER YOU WANT.
IS THAT SO BAD?
PAOW
TCH
TCH
TCH

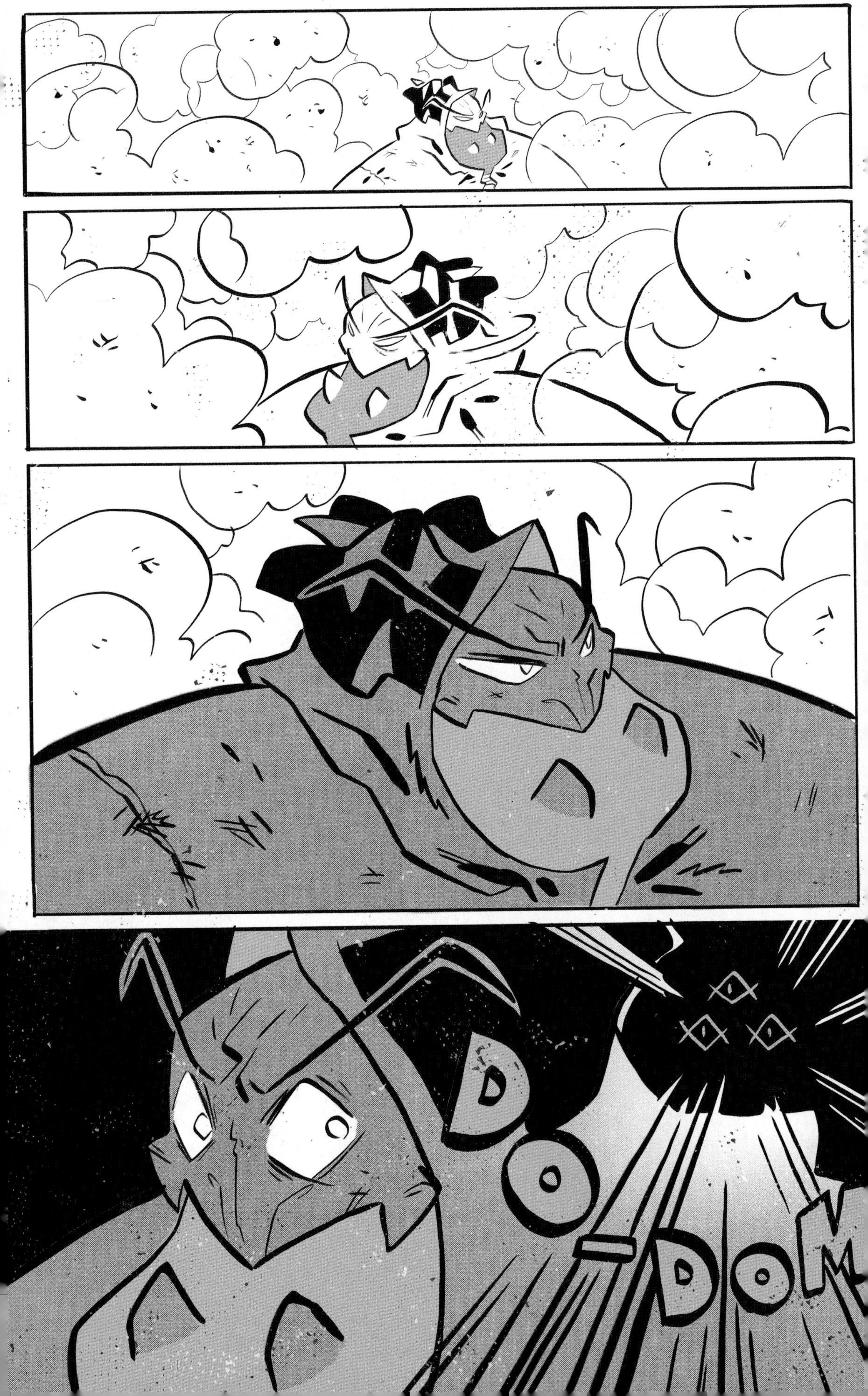
DOO-DOOM

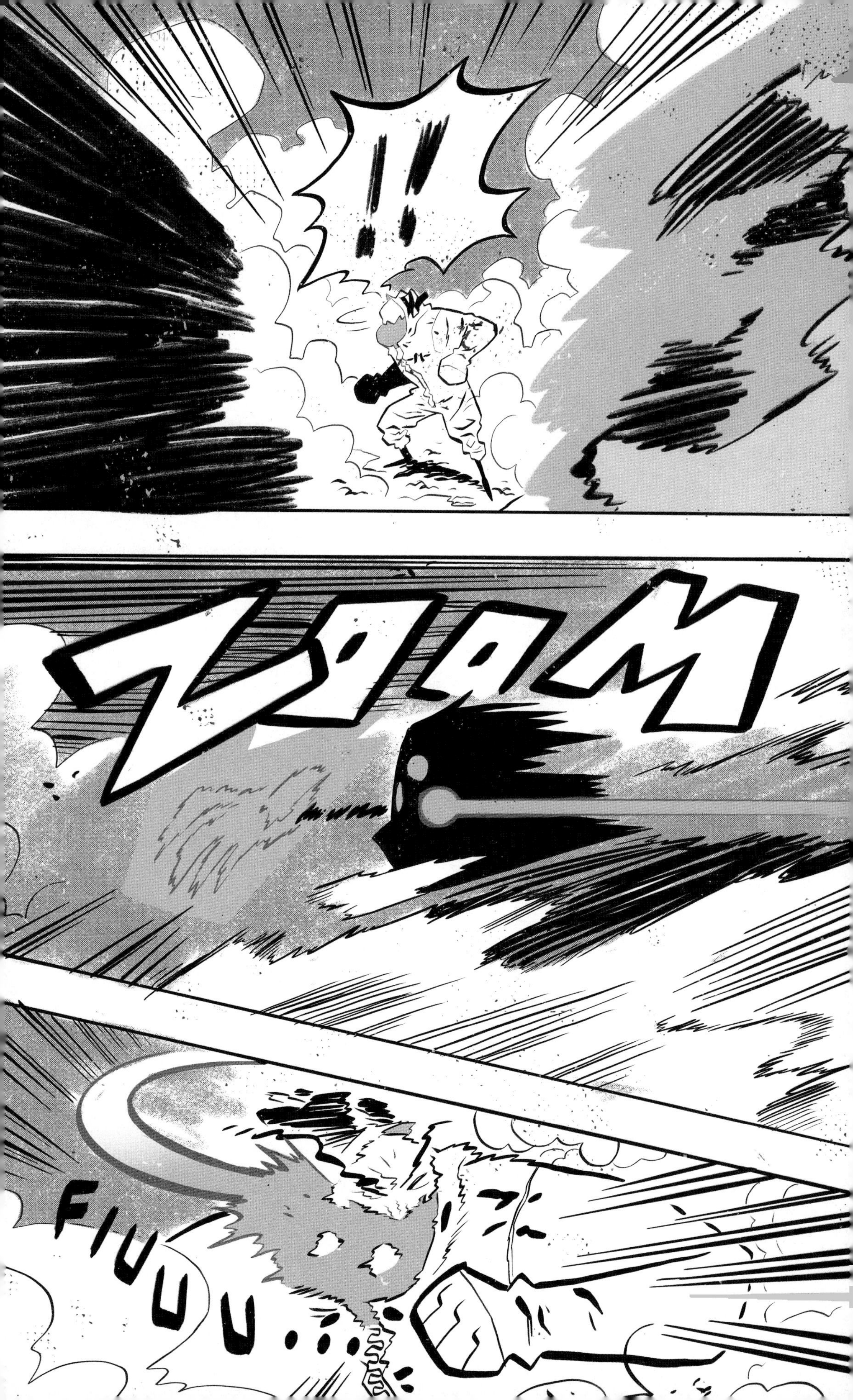
!!
ZOOM
FIUUU...

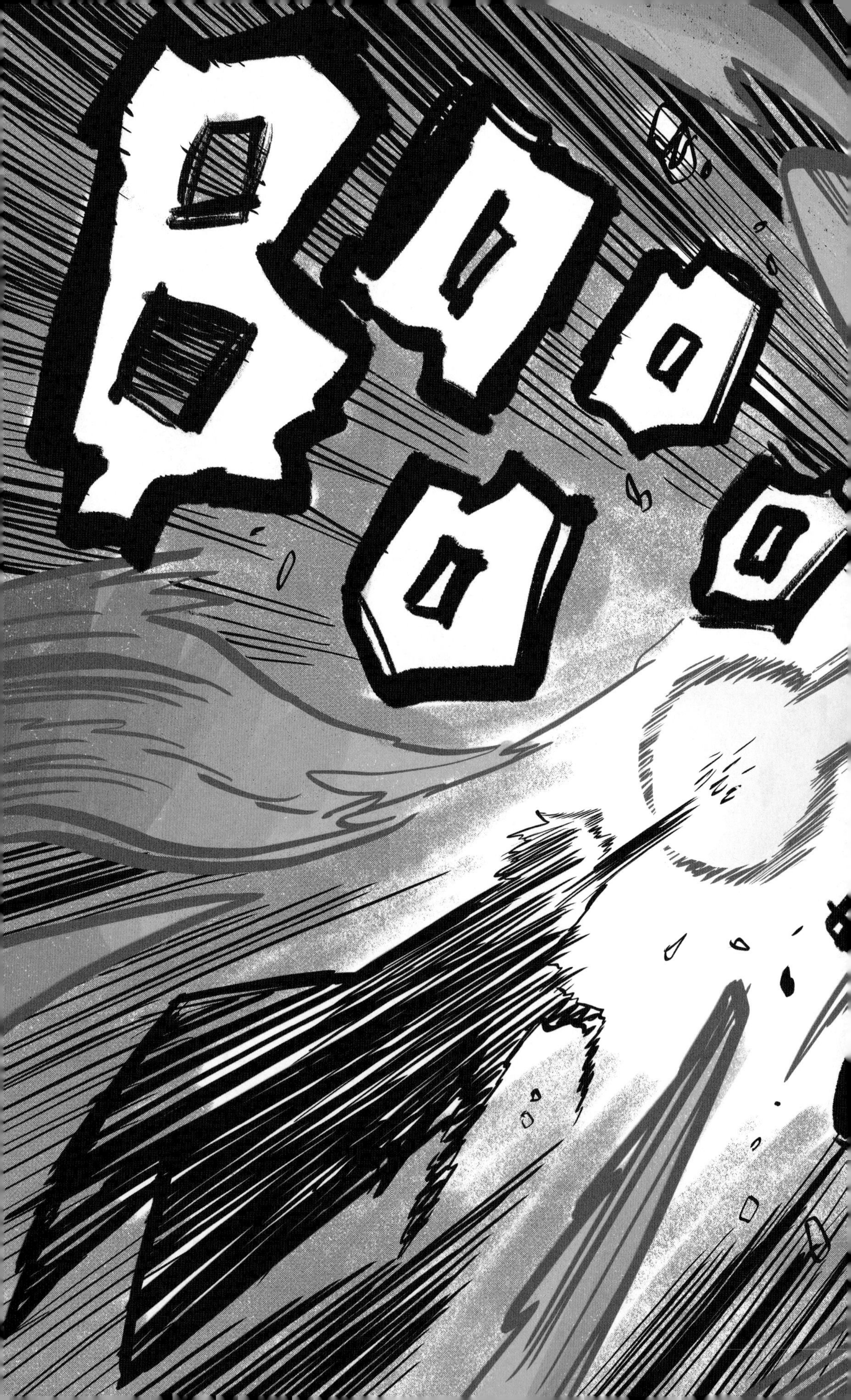

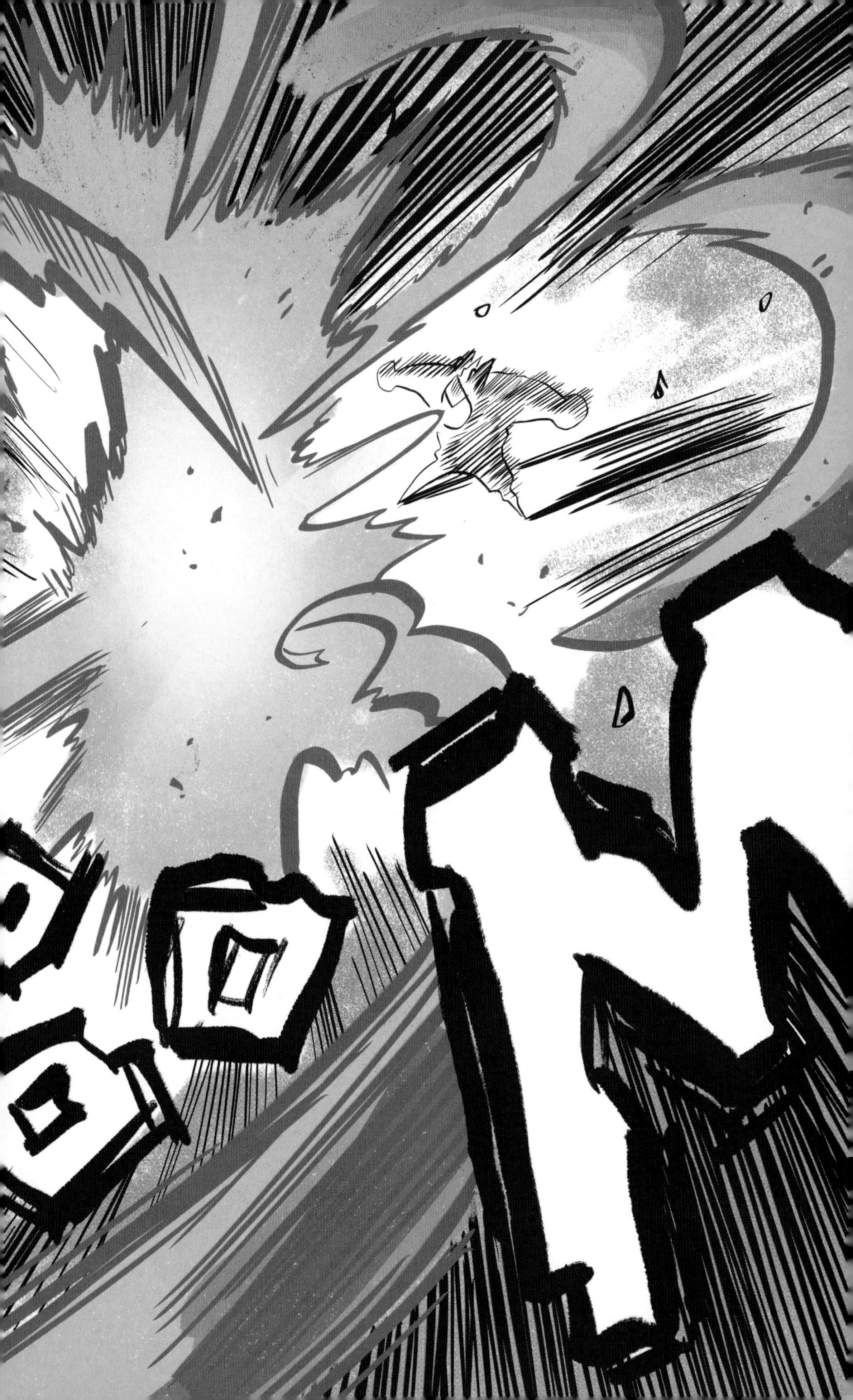

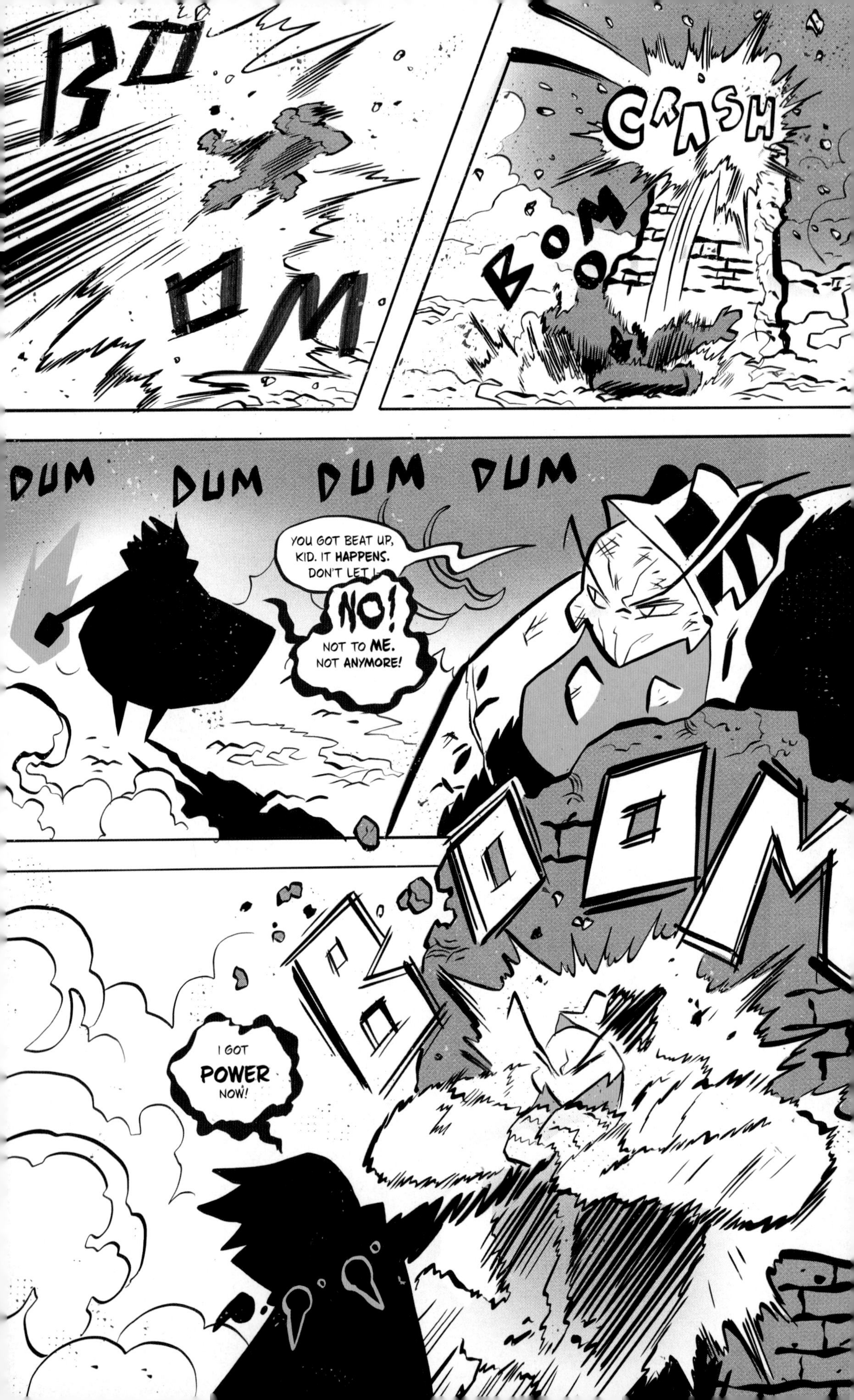
BOOM
CRASH
BOOM
DUM DUM DUM DUM
YOU GOT BEAT UP, KID. IT HAPPENS. DON'T LET I
NO! NOT TO ME. NOT ANYMORE!
BOOM
I GOT POWER NOW!

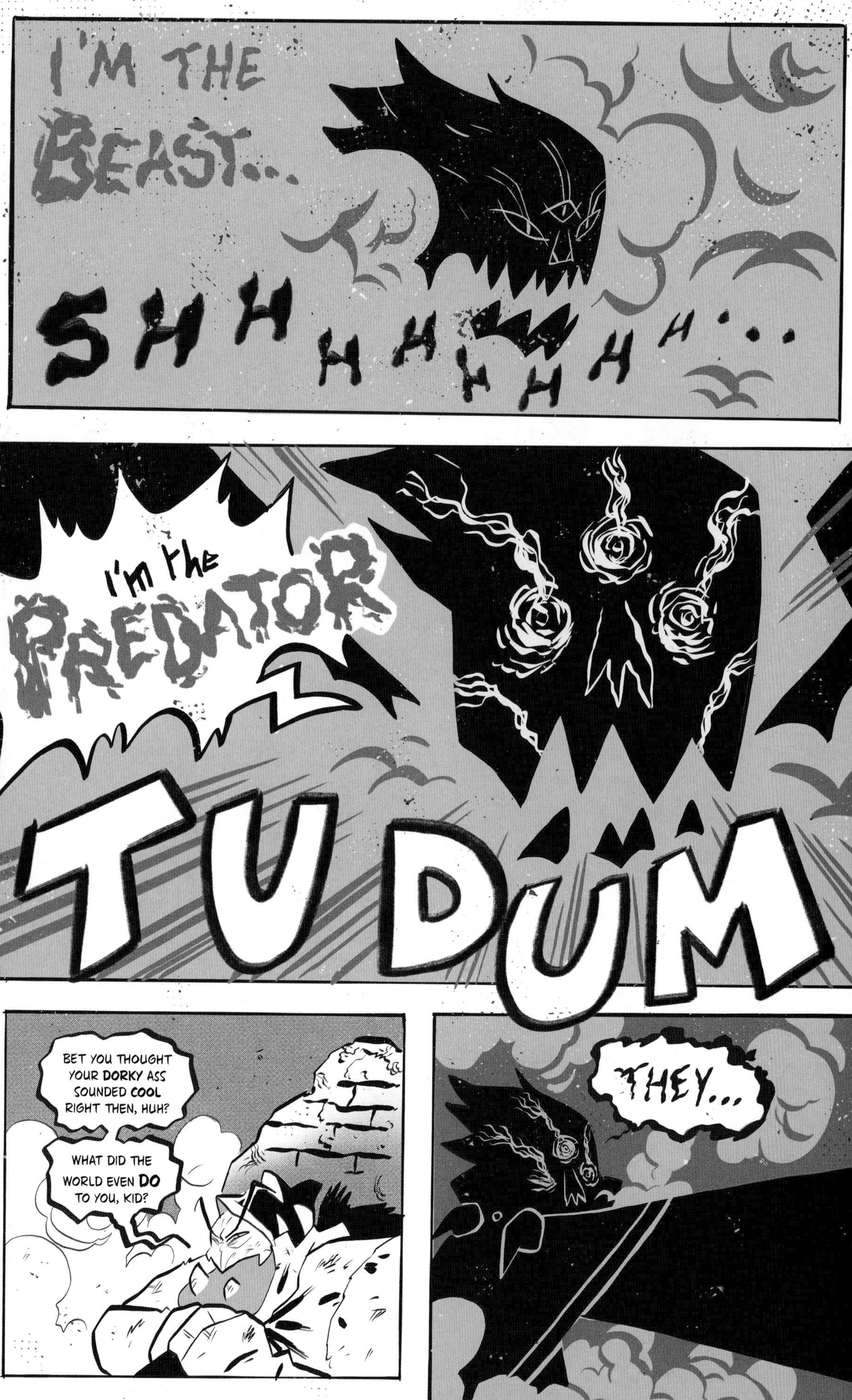

I'M THE BEAST...
SHHHHHHHHHHHH...
I'm the PREDATOR
TU DUM
BET YOU THOUGHT YOUR DORKY ASS SOUNDED COOL RIGHT THEN, HUH?
WHAT DID THE WORLD EVEN DO TO YOU, KID?
THEY...

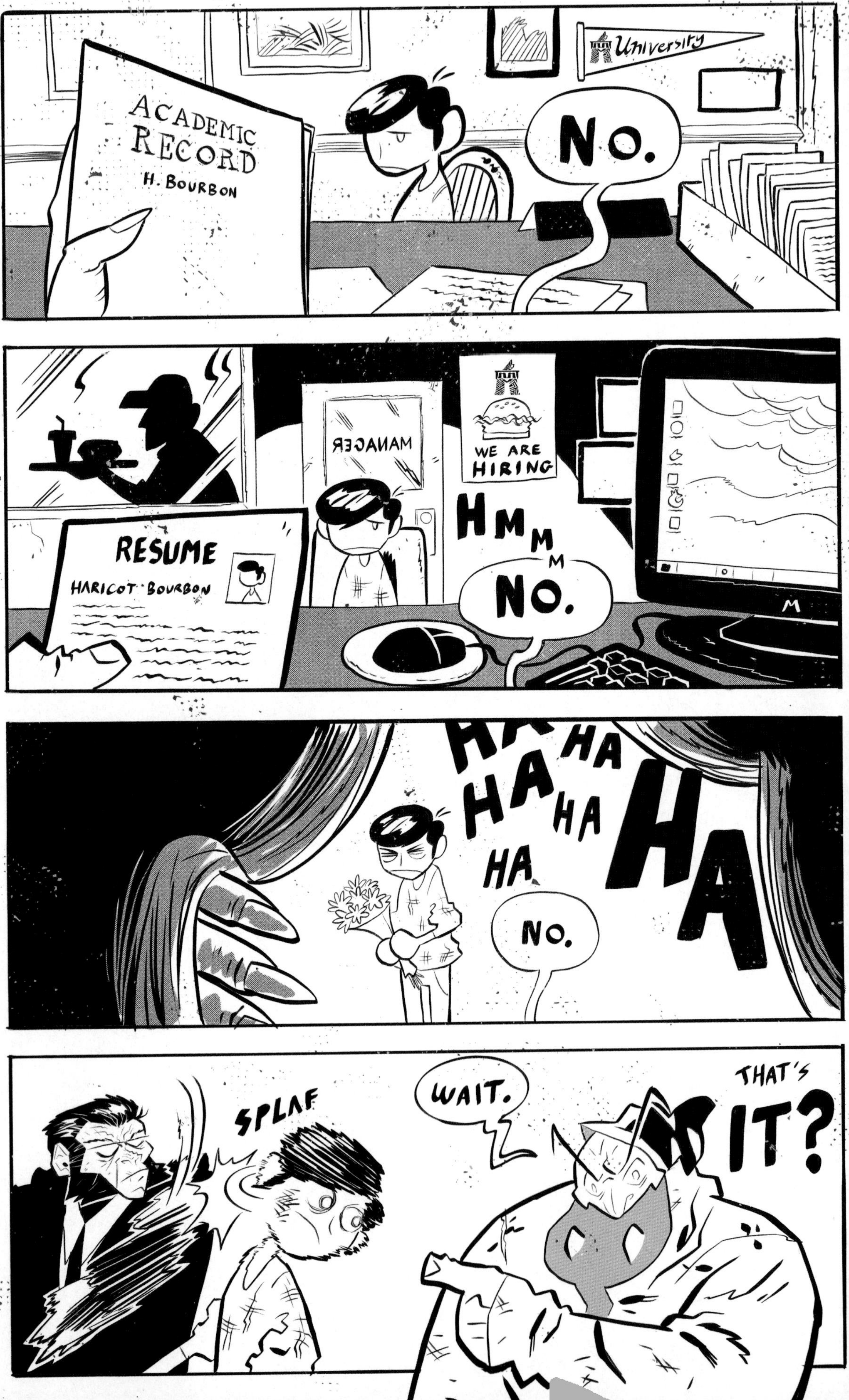

ACADEMIC RECORD
H. BOURBON
University
NO.
MANAGER
WE ARE HIRING
RESUME
HARICOT BOURBON
HMMM
NO.
HA HA HA HA HA HA HA
NO.
SPLAF
WAIT.
THAT'S IT?

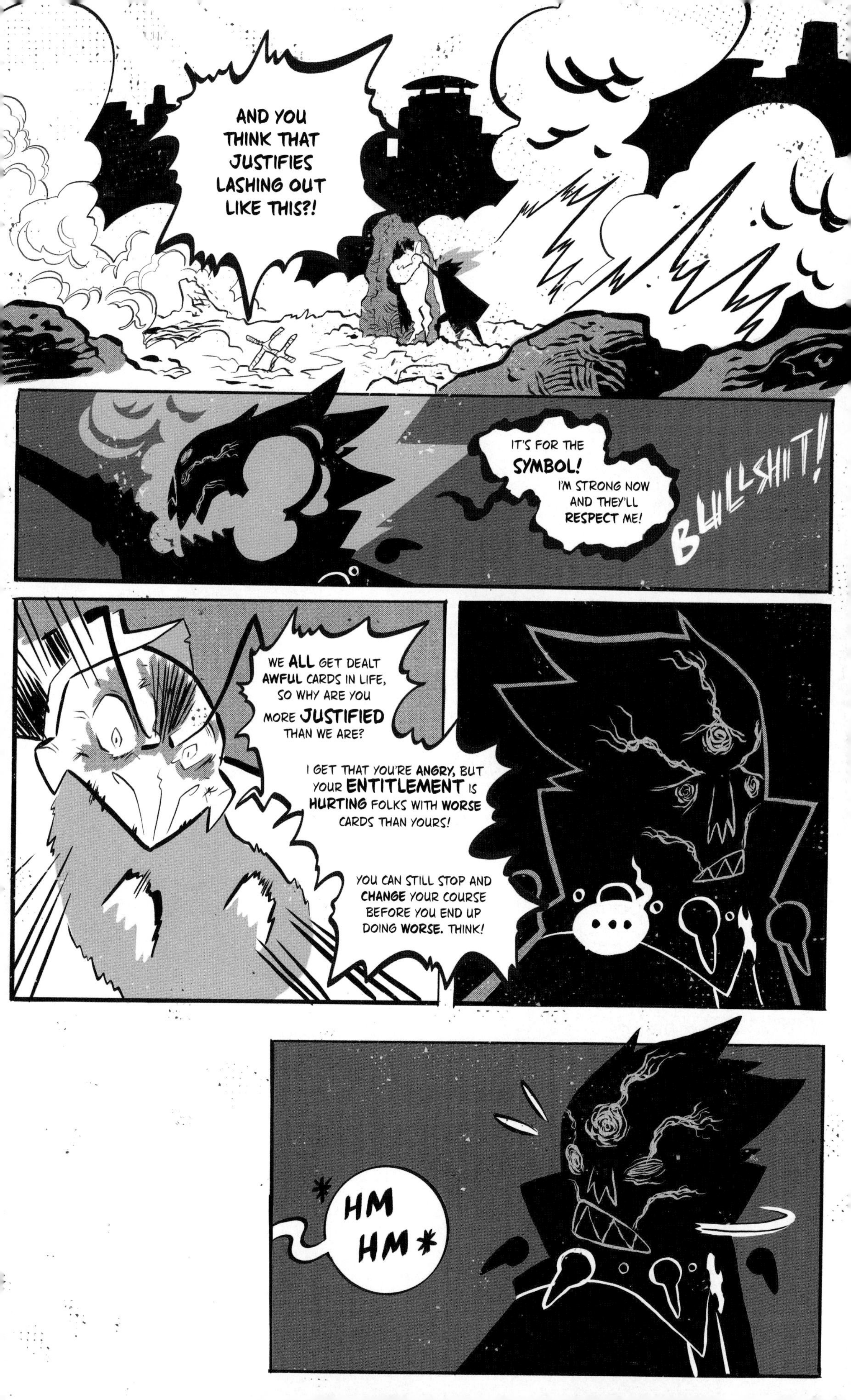
AND YOU THINK THAT JUSTIFIES LASHING OUT LIKE THIS?!
IT'S FOR THE SYMBOL! I'M STRONG NOW AND THEY'LL RESPECT ME!
BULLSHIT!
WE ALL GET DEALT AWFUL CARDS IN LIFE, SO WHY ARE YOU MORE JUSTIFIED THAN WE ARE?
I GET THAT YOU'RE ANGRY, BUT YOUR ENTITLEMENT IS HURTING FOLKS WITH WORSE CARDS THAN YOURS!
YOU CAN STILL STOP AND CHANGE YOUR COURSE BEFORE YOU END UP DOING WORSE. THINK!
...
HM HM

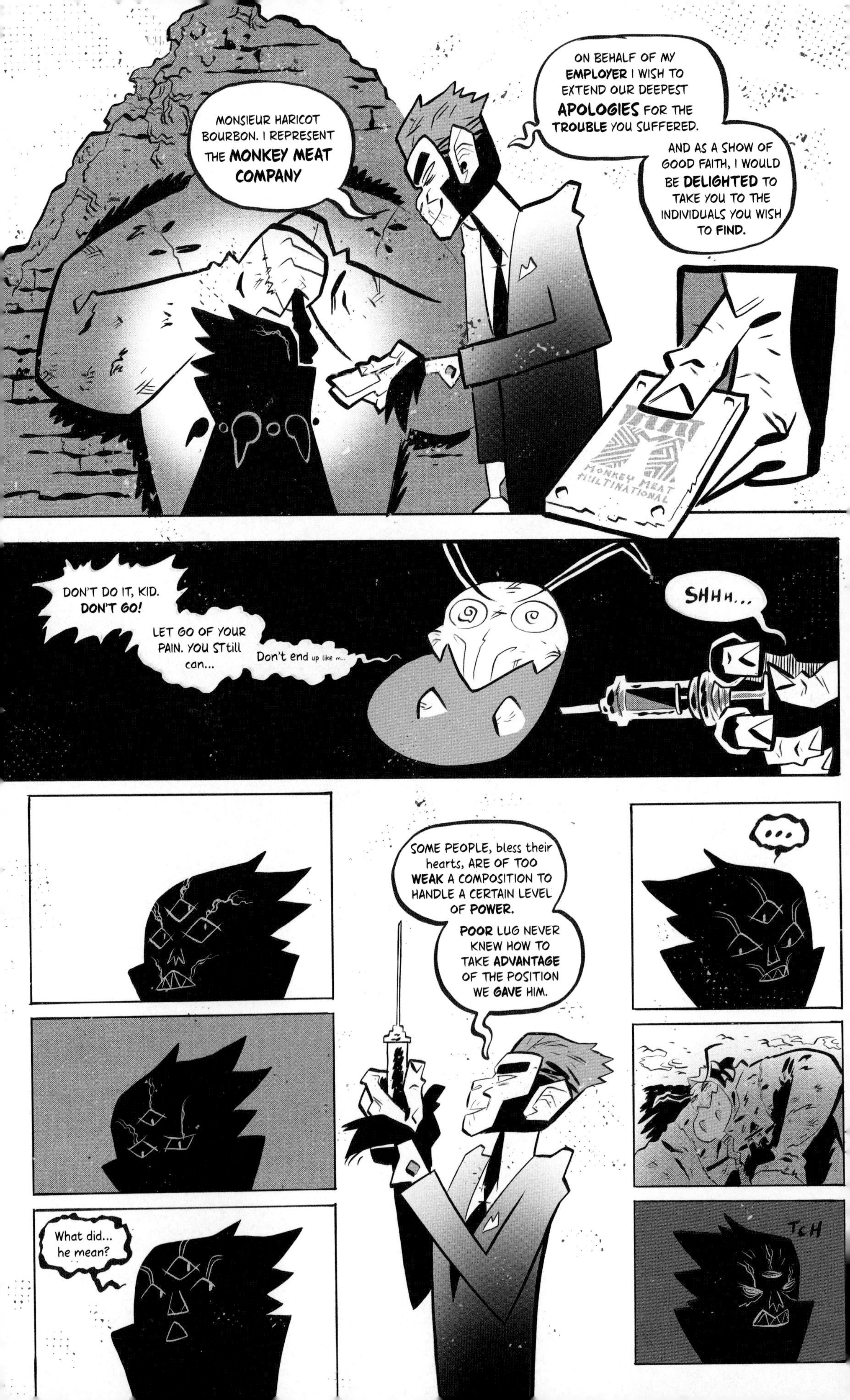

MONSIEUR HARICOT BOURBON. I REPRESENT THE MONKEY MEAT COMPANY
ON BEHALF OF MY EMPLOYER I WISH TO EXTEND OUR DEEPEST APOLOGIES FOR THE TROUBLE YOU SUFFERED.
AND AS A SHOW OF GOOD FAITH, I WOULD BE DELIGHTED TO TAKE YOU TO THE INDIVIDUALS YOU WISH TO FIND.
MONKEY MEAT MULTINATIONAL
DON'T DO IT, KID. DON'T GO!
LET GO OF YOUR PAIN. YOU STill can...
Don't end up like m...
SHHH...
SOME PEOPLE, bless their hearts, ARE OF TOO WEAK A COMPOSITION TO HANDLE A CERTAIN LEVEL OF POWER.
POOR LUG NEVER KNEW HOW TO TAKE ADVANTAGE OF THE POSITION WE GAVE HIM.
...
What did... he mean?
TCH

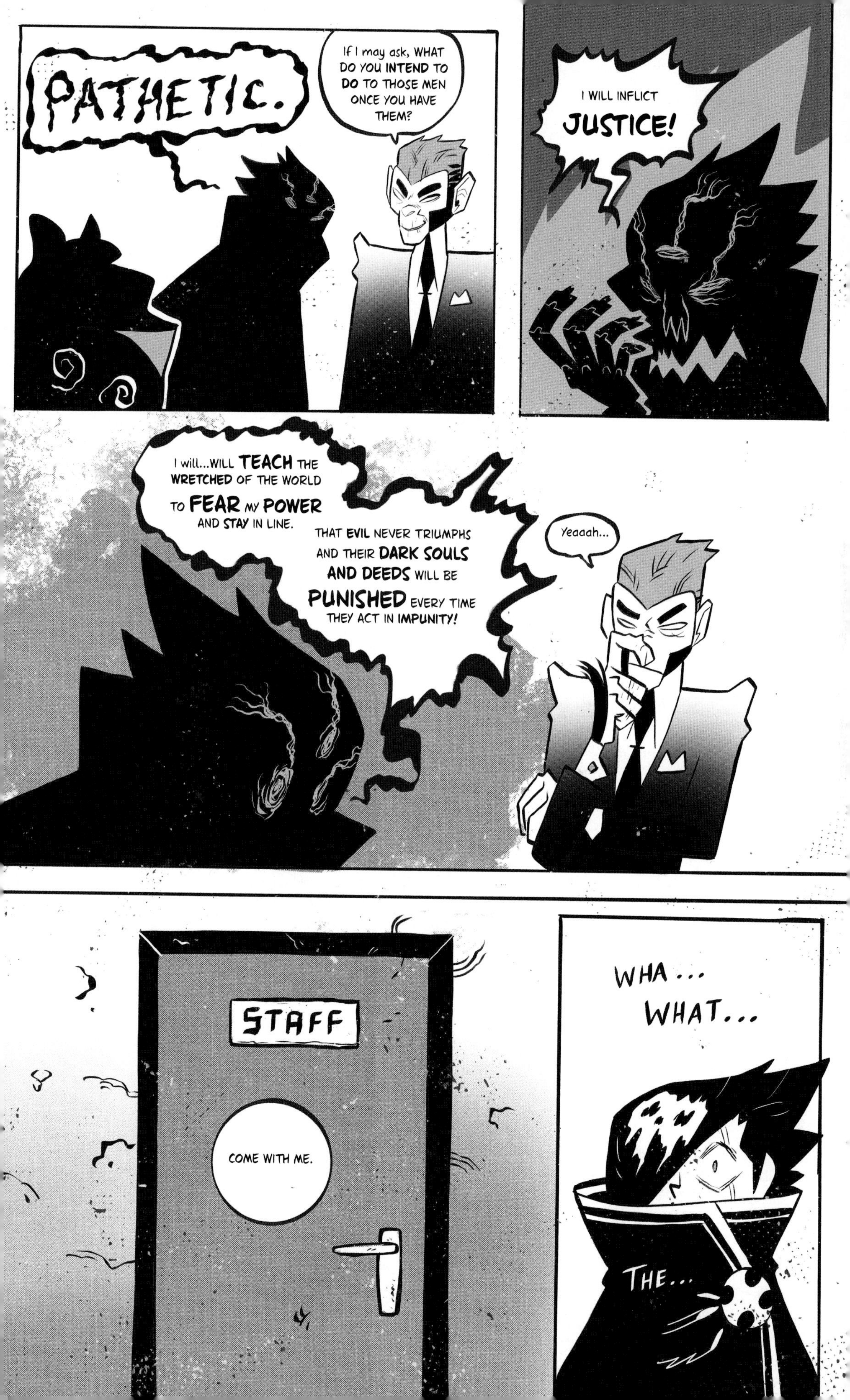
PATHETIC.
If I may ask, WHAT DO YOU INTEND TO DO TO THOSE MEN ONCE YOU HAVE THEM?
I WILL INFLICT JUSTICE!
I will...WILL TEACH THE WRETCHED OF THE WORLD TO FEAR MY POWER AND STAY IN LINE.
THAT EVIL NEVER TRIUMPHS AND THEIR DARK SOULS AND DEEDS WILL BE PUNISHED EVERY TIME THEY ACT IN IMPUNITY!
Yeaaah...
STAFF
COME WITH ME.
WHA...
WHAT...
THE...

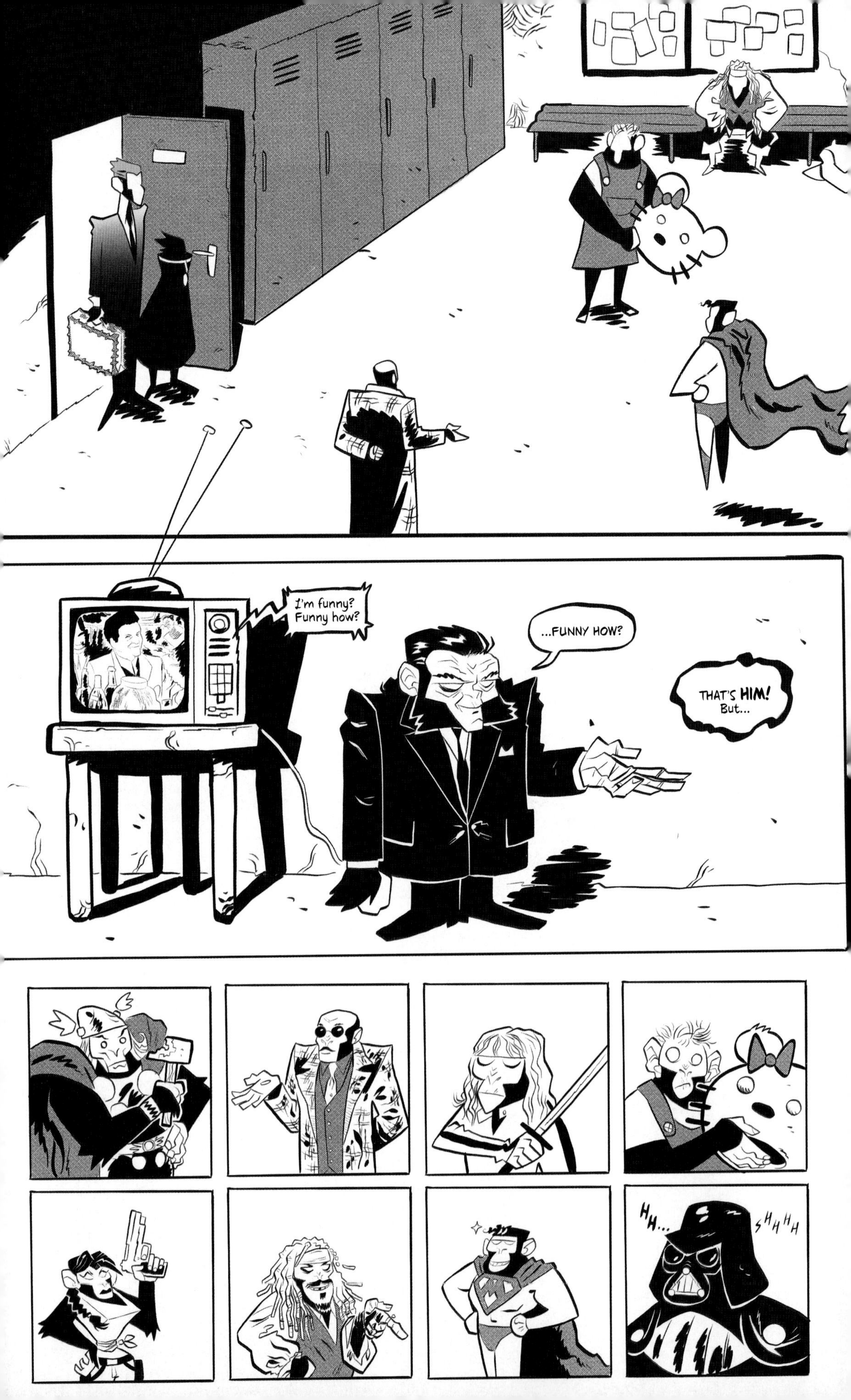
I'm funny? Funny how?
...FUNNY HOW?
THAT'S HIM! But...
HH...
SHHHH

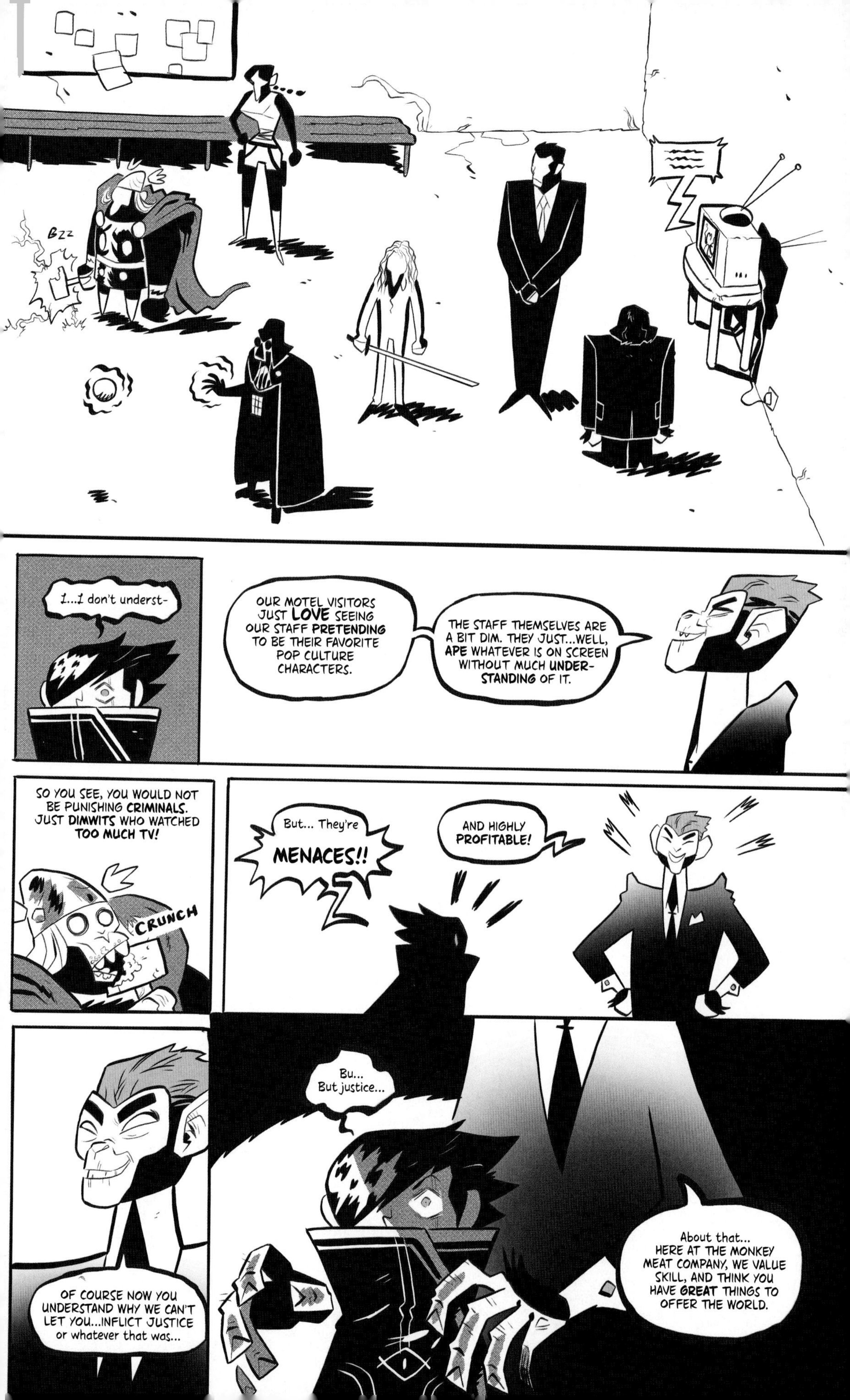
BZZ
I...I don't underst-
OUR MOTEL VISITORS JUST LOVE SEEING OUR STAFF PRETENDING TO BE THEIR FAVORITE POP CULTURE CHARACTERS.
THE STAFF THEMSELVES ARE A BIT DIM. THEY JUST...WELL, APE WHATEVER IS ON SCREEN WITHOUT MUCH UNDER-STANDING OF IT.
SO YOU SEE, YOU WOULD NOT BE PUNISHING CRIMINALS. JUST DIMWITS WHO WATCHED TOO MUCH TV!
CRUNCH
But... They're MENACES!!
AND HIGHLY PROFITABLE!
OF COURSE NOW YOU UNDERSTAND WHY WE CAN'T LET YOU...INFLICT JUSTICE or whatever that was...
Bu... But justice...
About that... HERE AT THE MONKEY MEAT COMPANY, WE VALUE SKILL, AND THINK YOU HAVE GREAT THINGS TO OFFER THE WORLD.

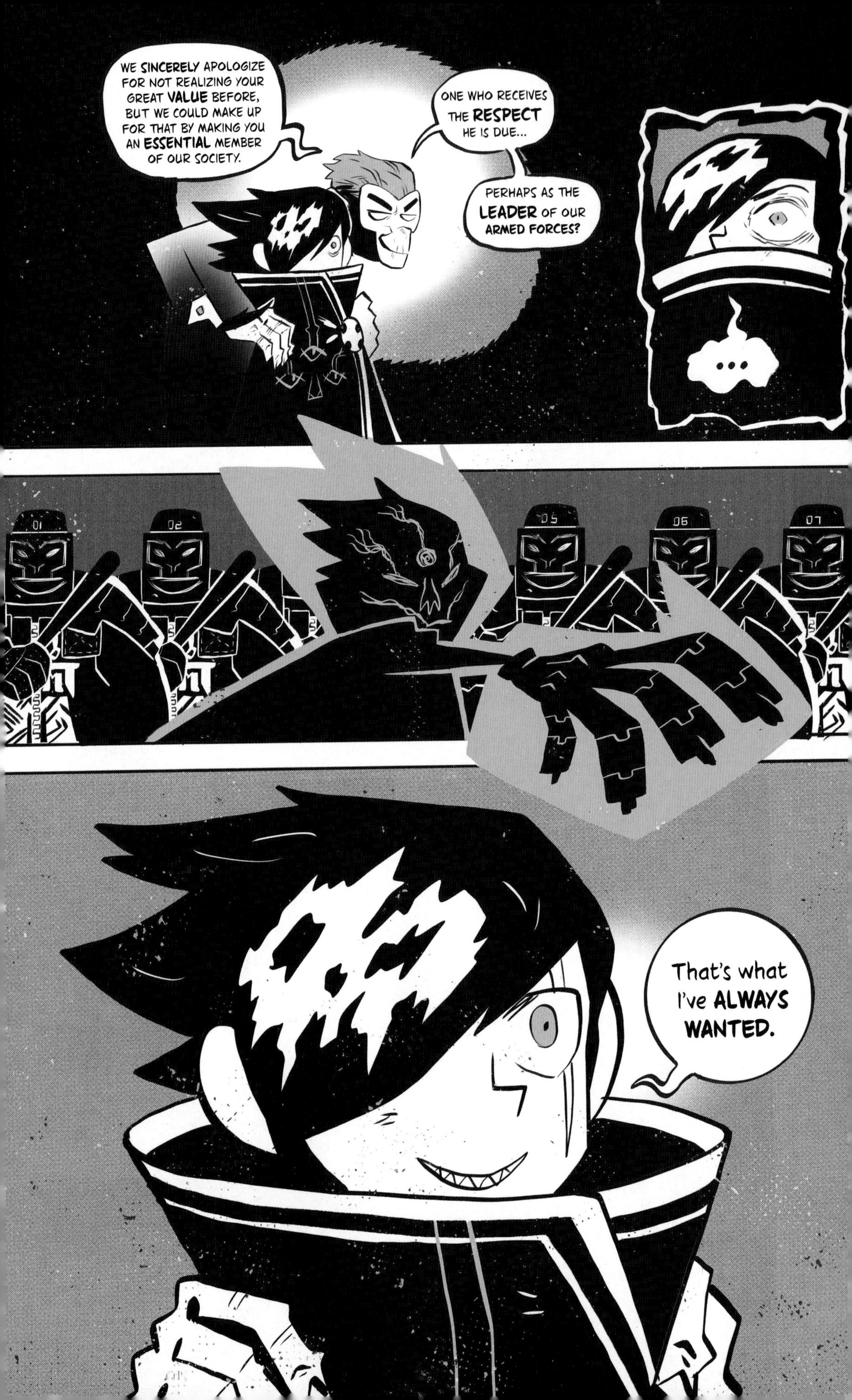
WE SINCERELY APOLOGIZE FOR NOT REALIZING YOUR GREAT VALUE BEFORE, BUT WE COULD MAKE UP FOR THAT BY MAKING YOU AN ESSENTIAL MEMBER OF OUR SOCIETY.
ONE WHO RECEIVES THE RESPECT HE IS DUE...
PERHAPS AS THE LEADER OF OUR ARMED FORCES?
...
01
02
05
06
07
That's what I've ALWAYS WANTED.

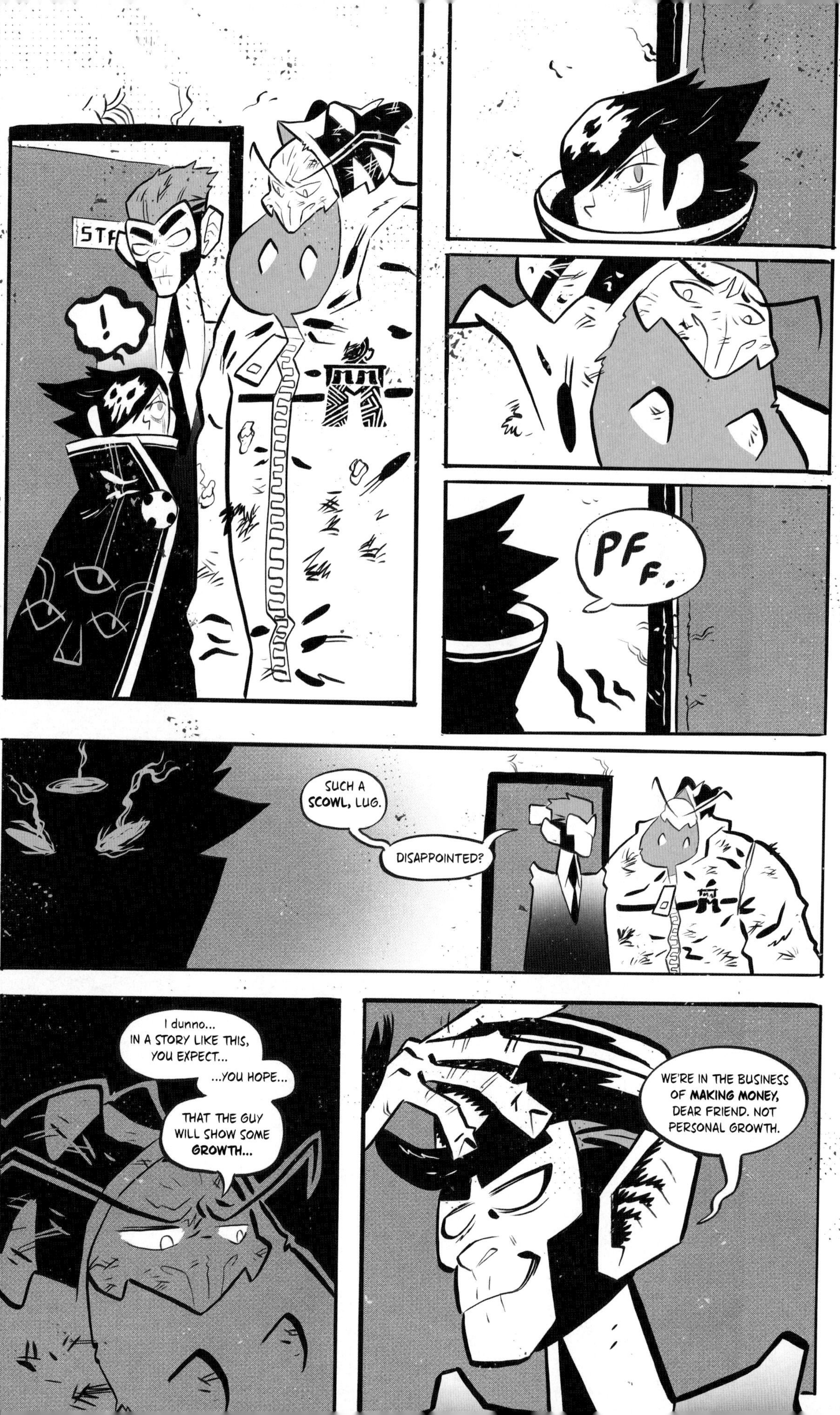
STF
!
PFF.
SUCH A SCOWL, LUG.
DISAPPOINTED?
I dunno... IN A STORY LIKE THIS, YOU EXPECT...
...YOU HOPE...
THAT THE GUY WILL SHOW SOME GROWTH...
WE'RE IN THE BUSINESS OF MAKING MONEY, DEAR FRIEND. NOT PERSONAL GROWTH.

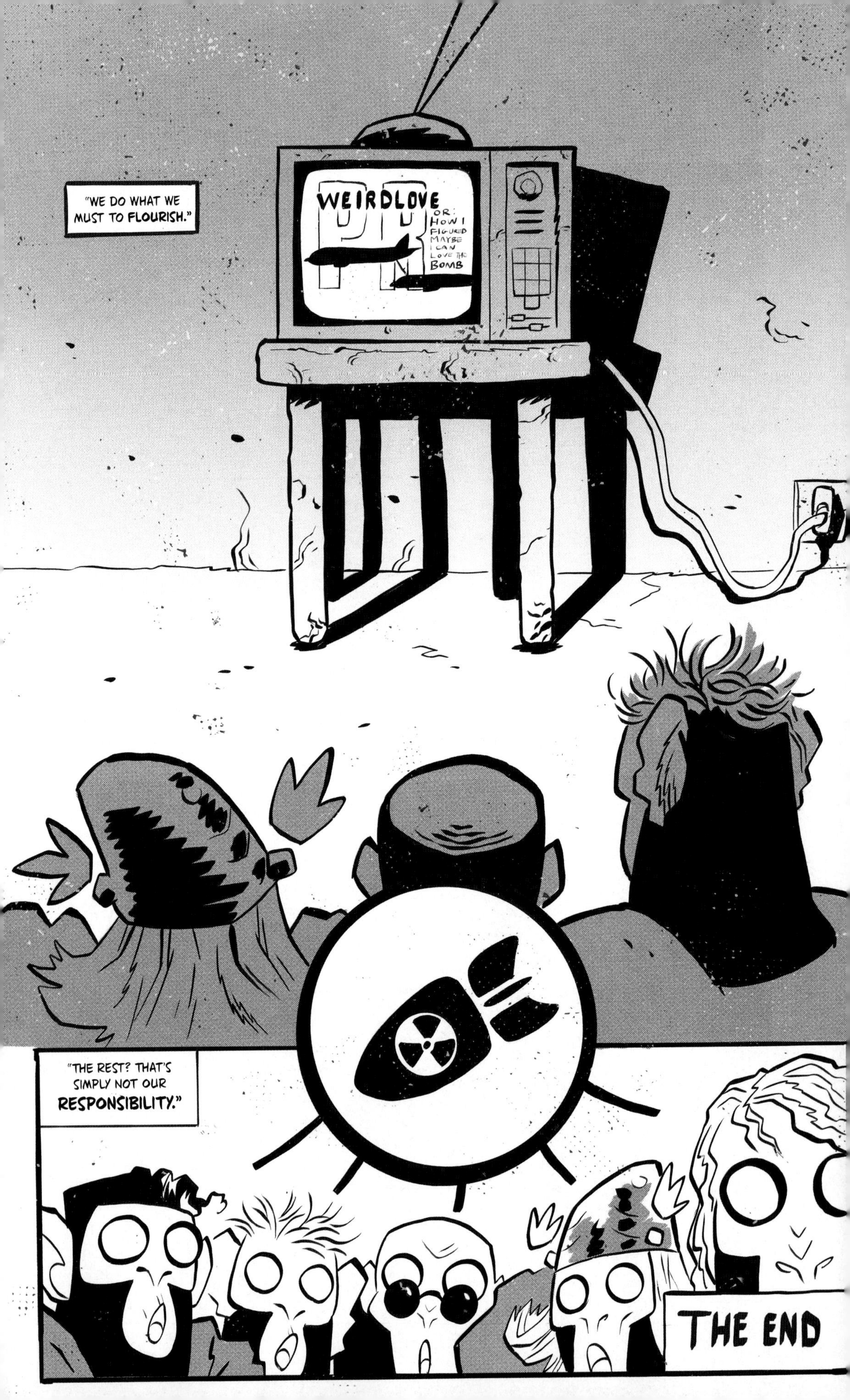
"WE DO WHAT WE MUST TO FLOURISH."
WEIRDLOVE
OR: HOW I FIGURED MAYBE I CAN LOVE THE BOMB
"THE REST? THAT'S SIMPLY NOT OUR RESPONSIBILITY."
THE END

ROOM SERVICE MENU

DISHES 🍴🍽️

- Golo skull roasted on a plate of prime local man-eating vegetables.

- Yam fries and Sahroo tails

- Spider legs spaghetti

- Jollof rice and rohf

SPECIAL

Simian metacarpal barbecue

SPICY

DRINKS 🍹

FRESH COCKTAILS

- Golden Fish Eye
- Soul Juice
- Aloe Vera and bat spit
- Red Matter (Brain juice)

A product of our best brains!

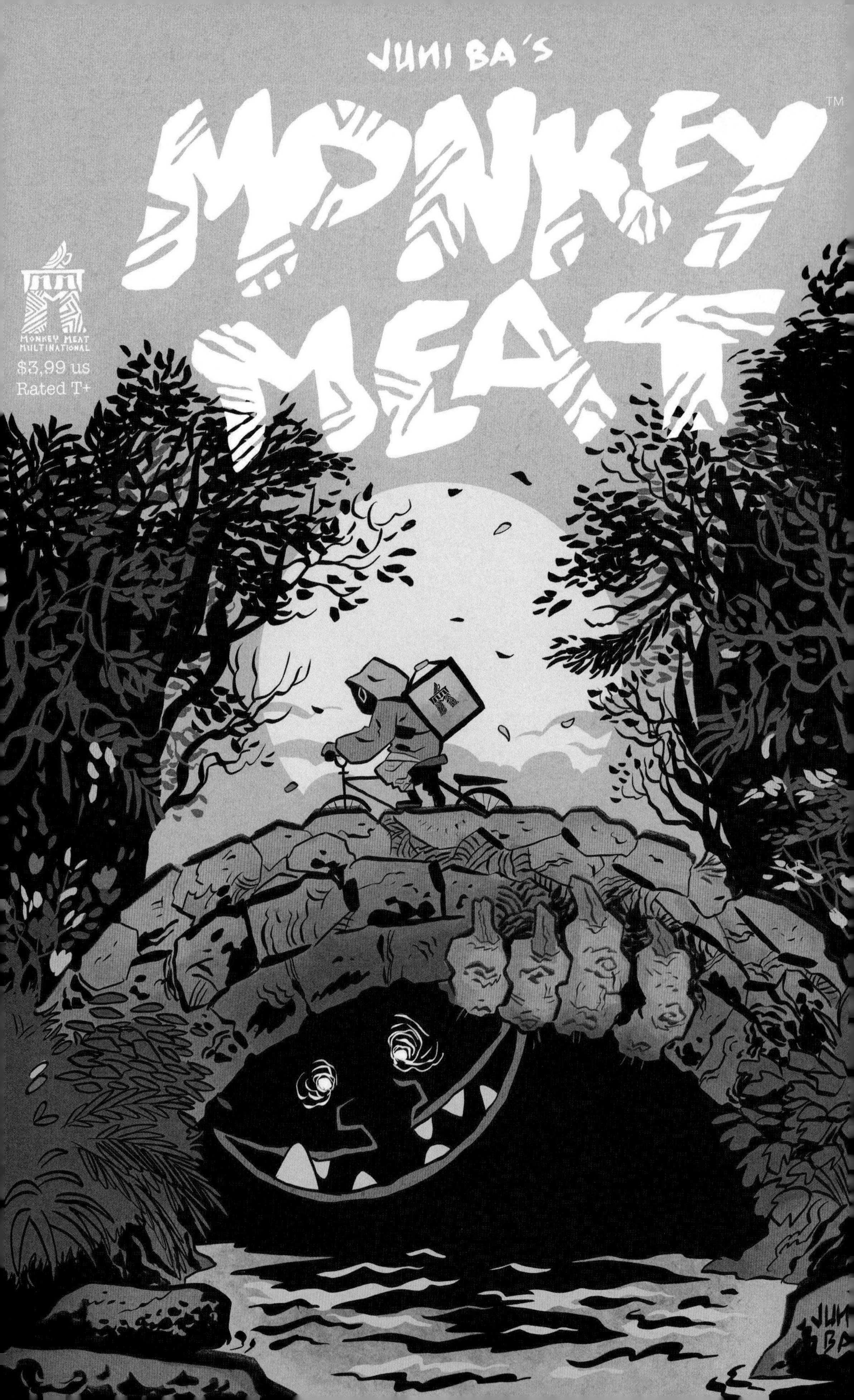
JUNI BA'S
MONKEY MEAT™
MONKEY MEAT MULTINATIONAL
$3,99 us
Rated T+
JUNI BA

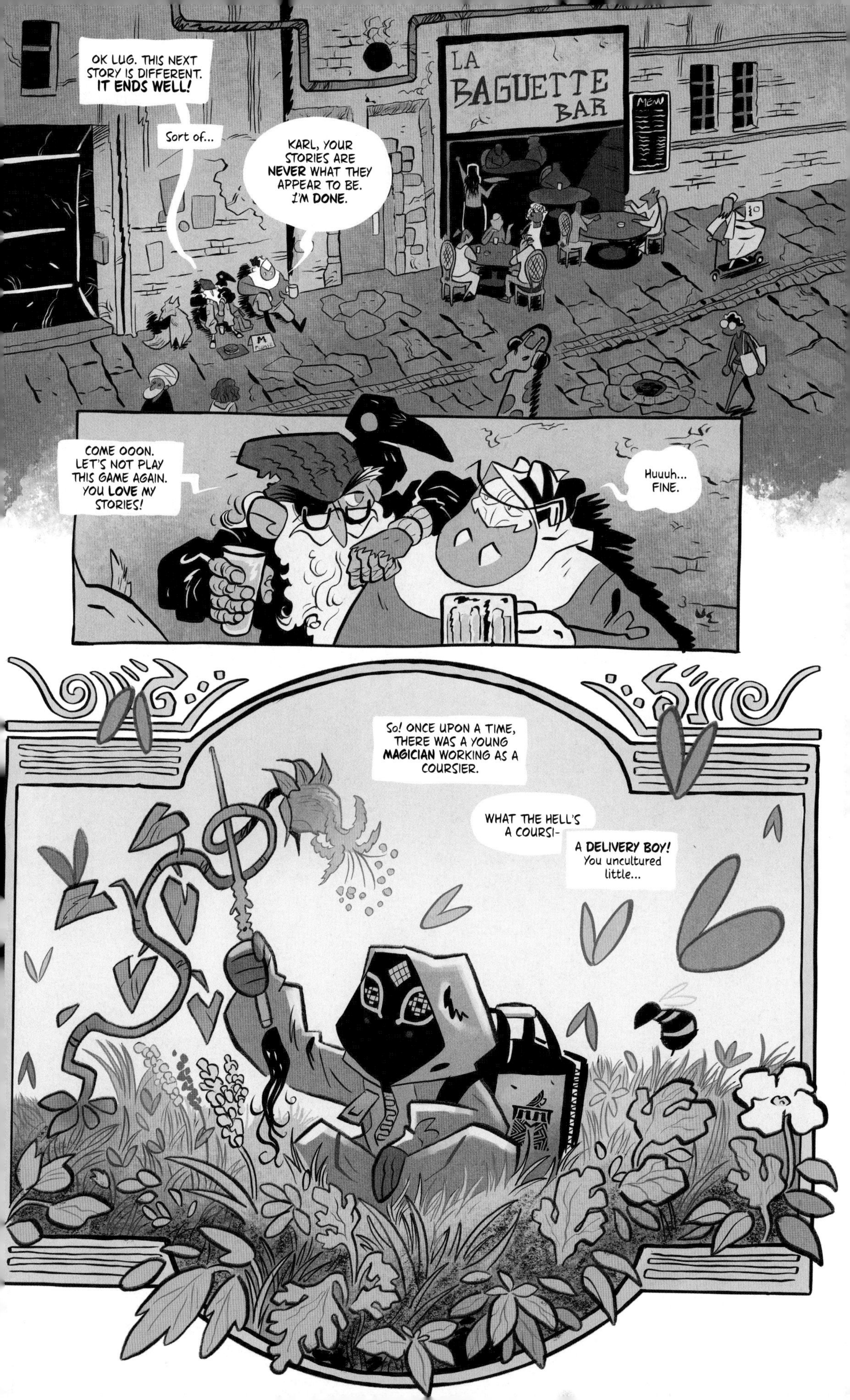

OK LUG. THIS NEXT STORY IS DIFFERENT. IT ENDS WELL!
Sort of...
KARL, YOUR STORIES ARE NEVER WHAT THEY APPEAR TO BE. I'M DONE.
LA BAGUETTE BAR
MENU
COME OOON. LET'S NOT PLAY THIS GAME AGAIN. YOU LOVE MY STORIES!
Huuuh... FINE.
So! ONCE UPON A TIME, THERE WAS A YOUNG MAGICIAN WORKING AS A COURSIER.
WHAT THE HELL'S A COURSI-
A DELIVERY BOY! You uncultured little...

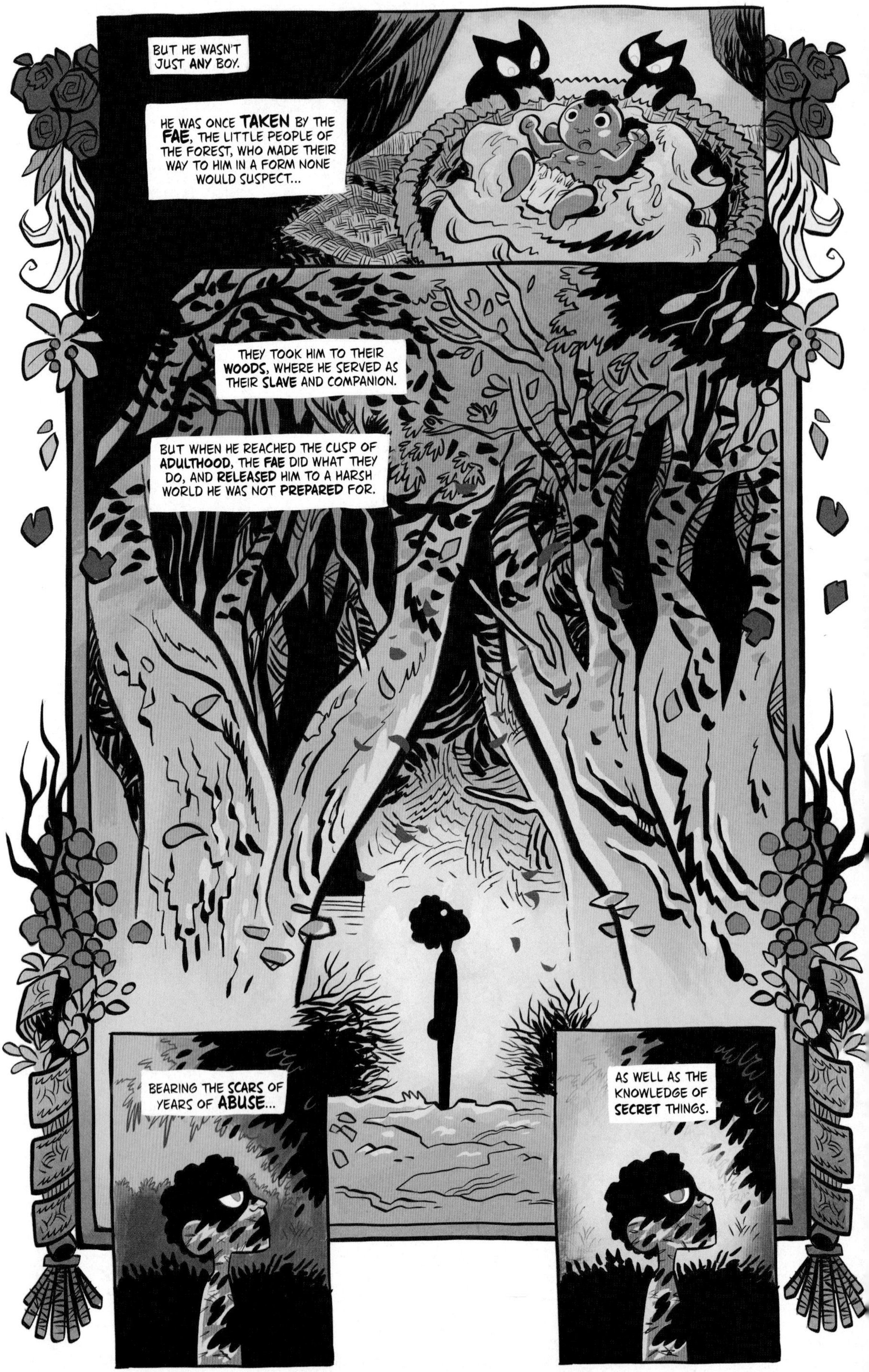

BUT HE WASN'T JUST ANY BOY.
HE WAS ONCE TAKEN BY THE FAE, THE LITTLE PEOPLE OF THE FOREST, WHO MADE THEIR WAY TO HIM IN A FORM NONE WOULD SUSPECT...
THEY TOOK HIM TO THEIR WOODS, WHERE HE SERVED AS THEIR SLAVE AND COMPANION.
BUT WHEN HE REACHED THE CUSP OF ADULTHOOD, THE FAE DID WHAT THEY DO, AND RELEASED HIM TO A HARSH WORLD HE WAS NOT PREPARED FOR.
BEARING THE SCARS OF YEARS OF ABUSE...
AS WELL AS THE KNOWLEDGE OF SECRET THINGS.

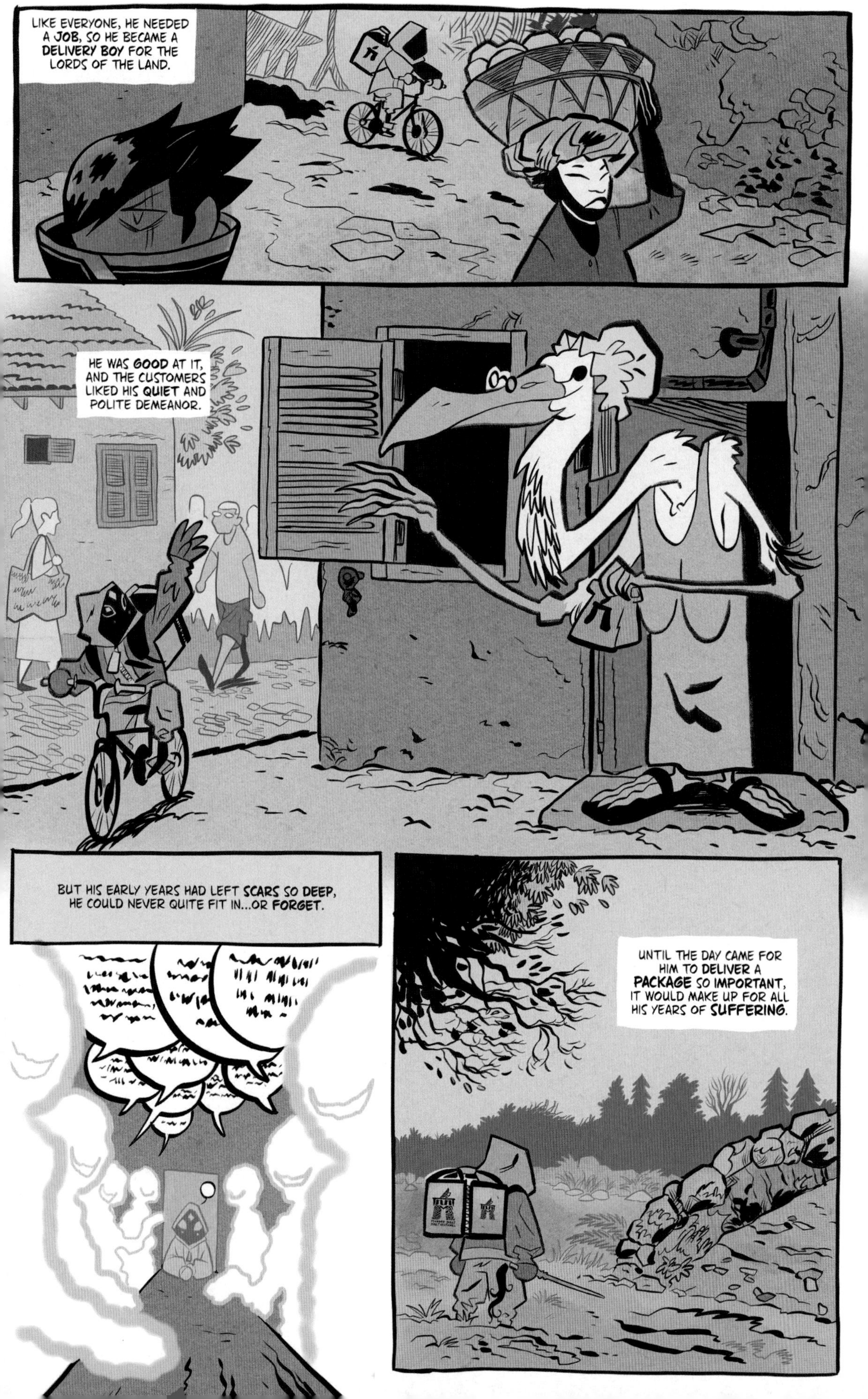

LIKE EVERYONE, HE NEEDED A JOB, SO HE BECAME A DELIVERY BOY FOR THE LORDS OF THE LAND.
HE WAS GOOD AT IT, AND THE CUSTOMERS LIKED HIS QUIET AND POLITE DEMEANOR.
BUT HIS EARLY YEARS HAD LEFT SCARS SO DEEP, HE COULD NEVER QUITE FIT IN...OR FORGET.
UNTIL THE DAY CAME FOR HIM TO DELIVER A PACKAGE SO IMPORTANT, IT WOULD MAKE UP FOR ALL HIS YEARS OF SUFFERING.

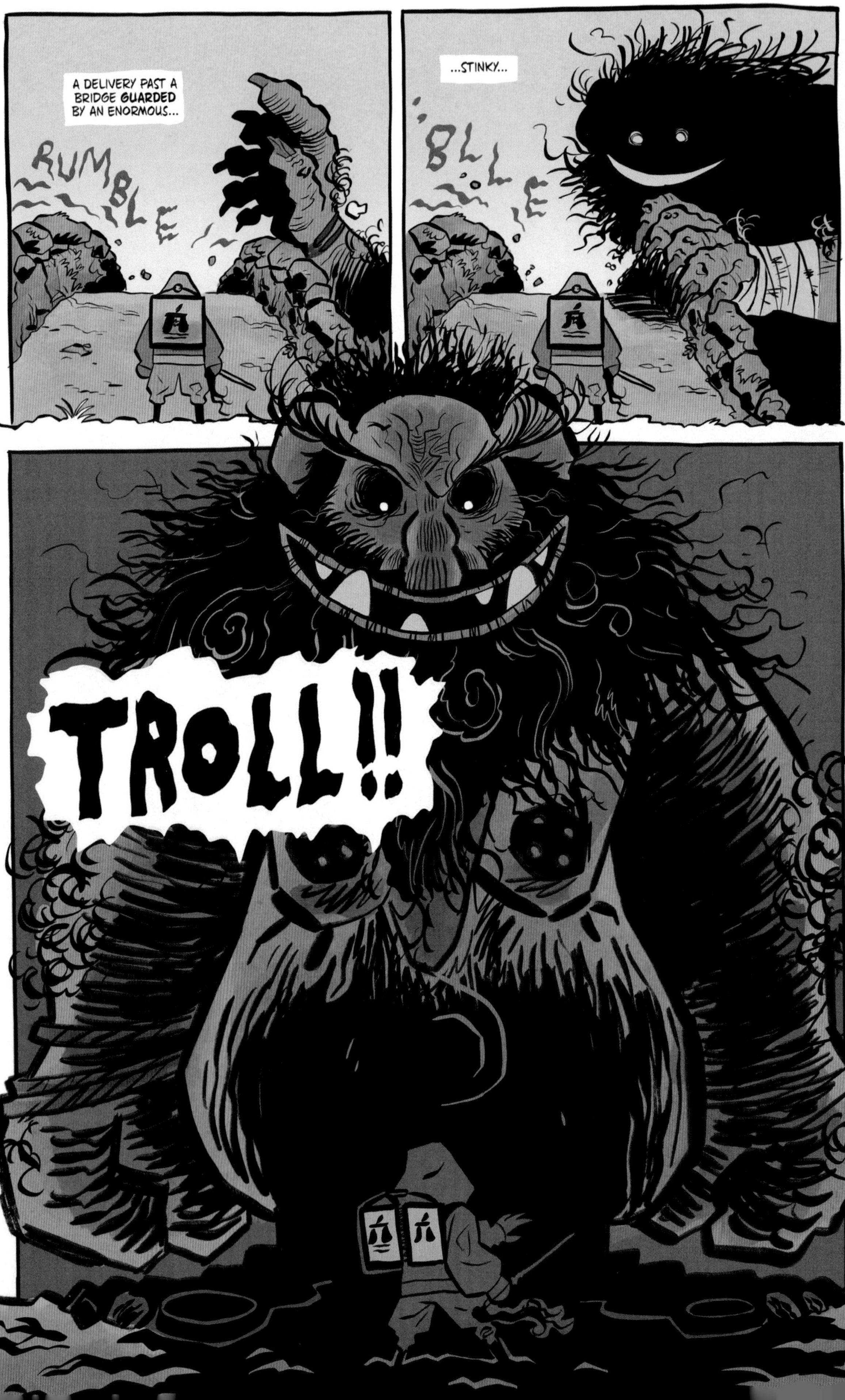
A DELIVERY PAST A BRIDGE GUARDED BY AN ENORMOUS...
RUMBLE
...STINKY...
TROLL!!

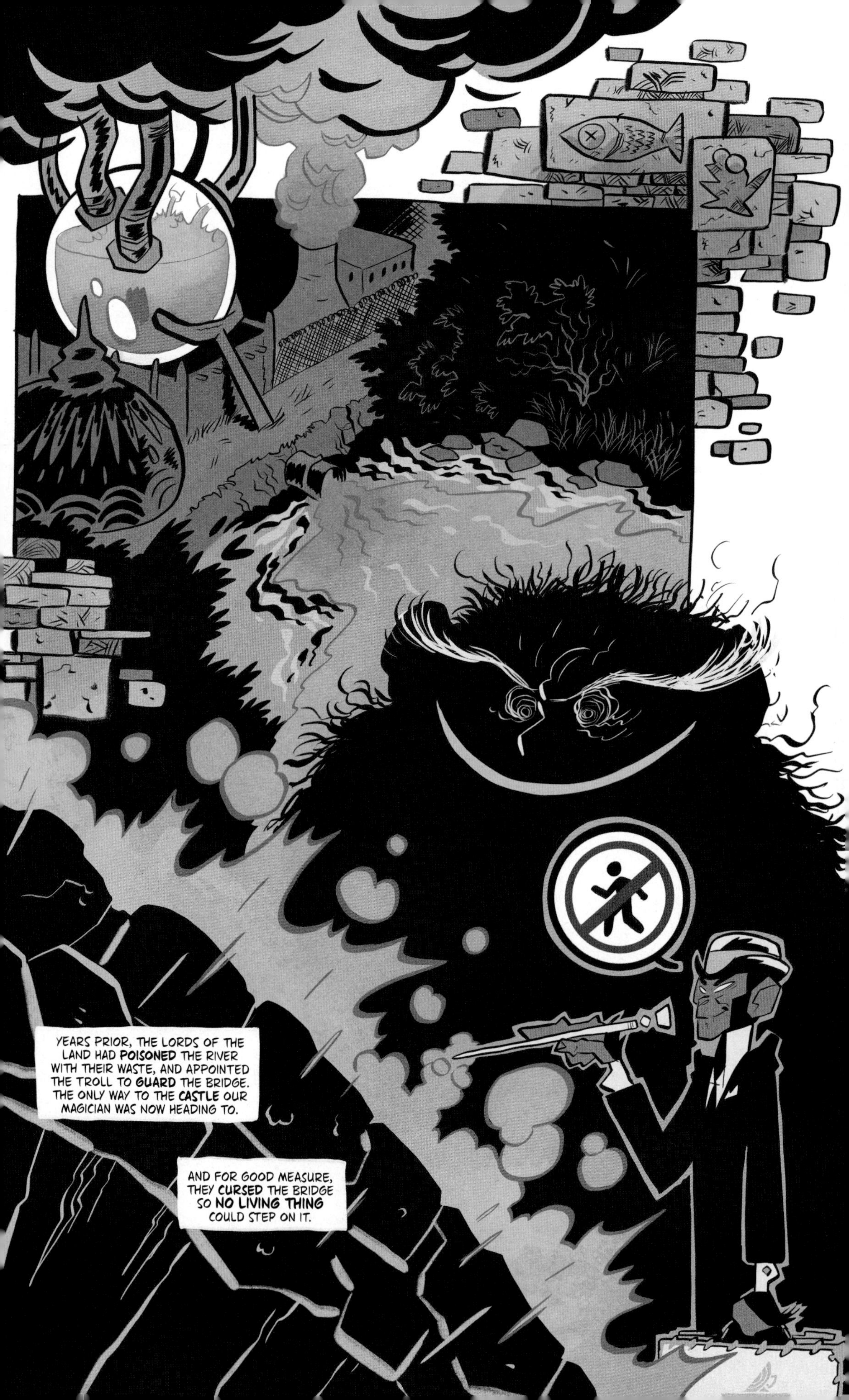
YEARS PRIOR, THE LORDS OF THE LAND HAD **POISONED** THE RIVER WITH THEIR WASTE, AND APPOINTED THE TROLL TO **GUARD** THE BRIDGE. THE ONLY WAY TO THE **CASTLE** OUR MAGICIAN WAS NOW HEADING TO.
AND FOR GOOD MEASURE, THEY **CURSED** THE BRIDGE SO **NO LIVING THING** COULD STEP ON IT.

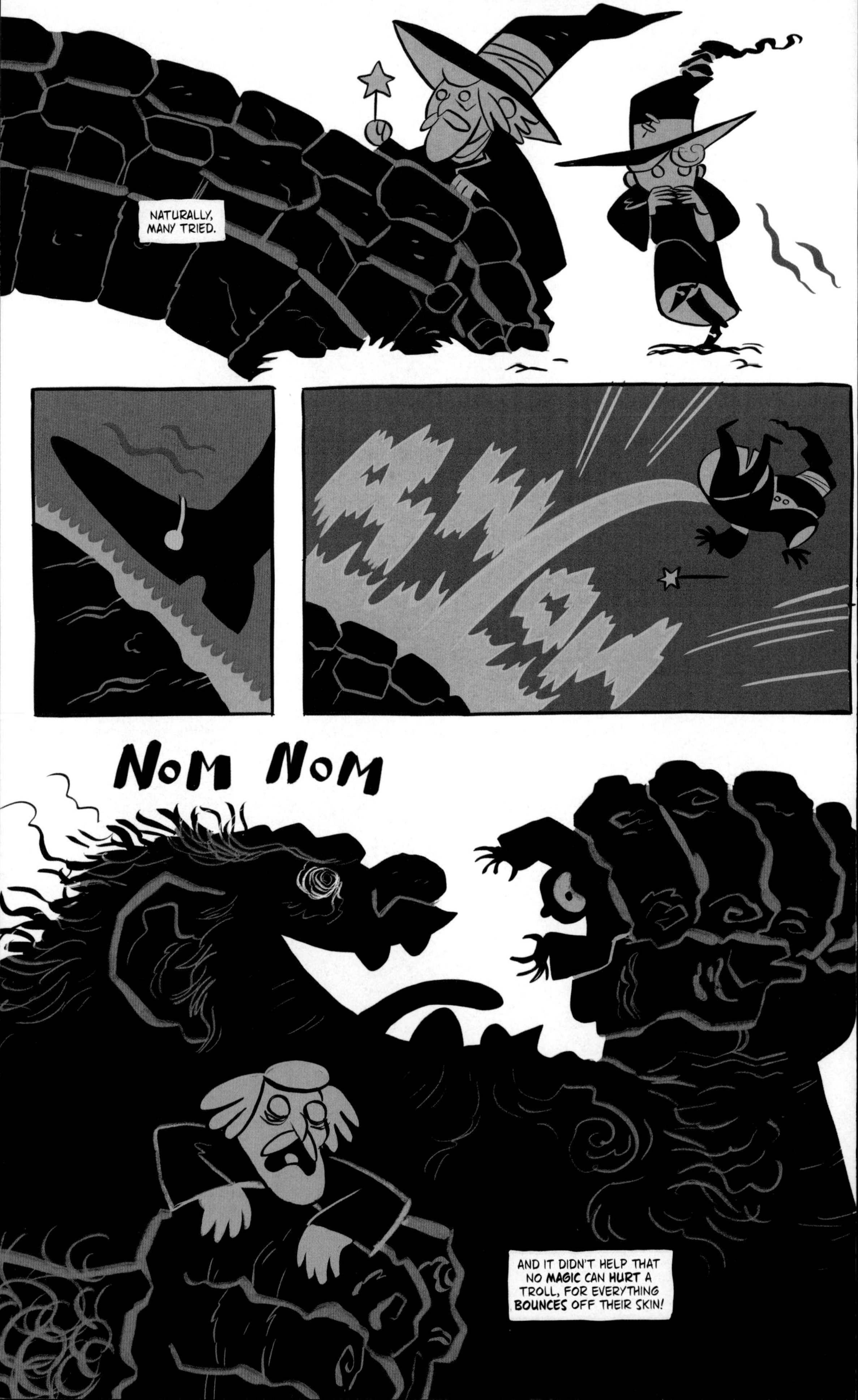
NATURALLY, MANY TRIED.
NOM NOM
AND IT DIDN'T HELP THAT NO MAGIC CAN HURT A TROLL, FOR EVERYTHING BOUNCES OFF THEIR SKIN!

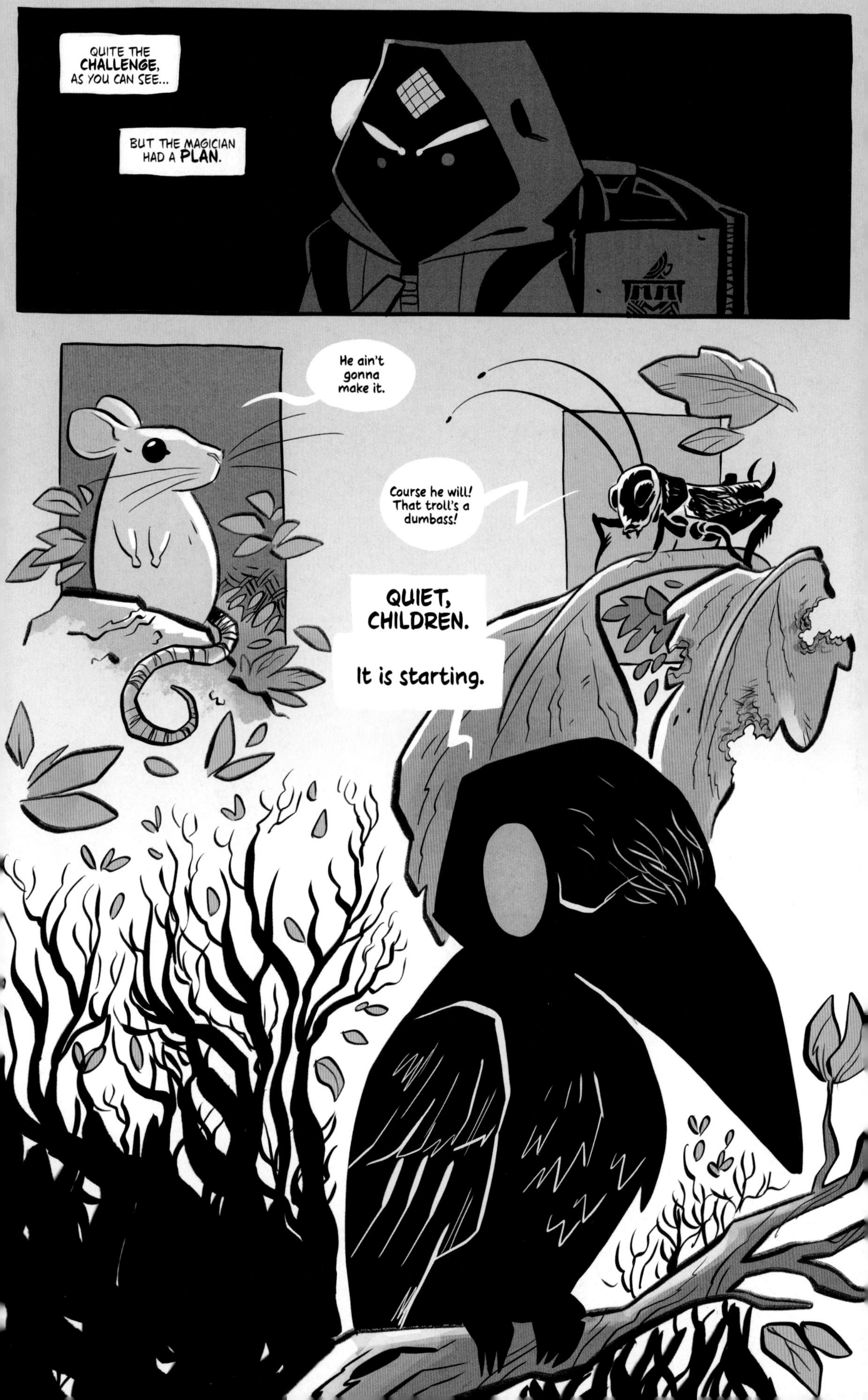
QUITE THE CHALLENGE, AS YOU CAN SEE...
BUT THE MAGICIAN HAD A PLAN.
He ain't gonna make it.
Course he will! That troll's a dumbass!
QUIET, CHILDREN.
It is starting.

FIRST, TO **PROTECT** HIS PRECIOUS CARGO.

BONK

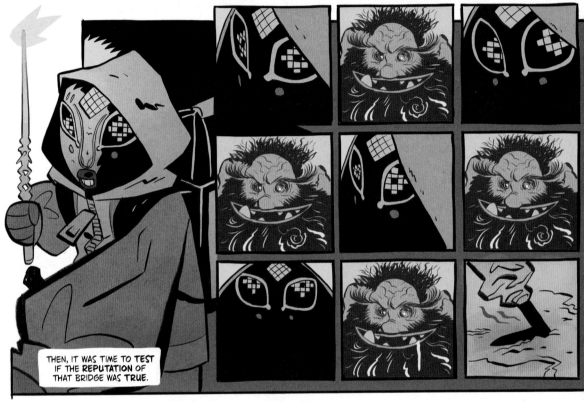

THEN, IT WAS TIME TO **TEST** IF THE **REPUTATION** OF THAT BRIDGE WAS **TRUE.**

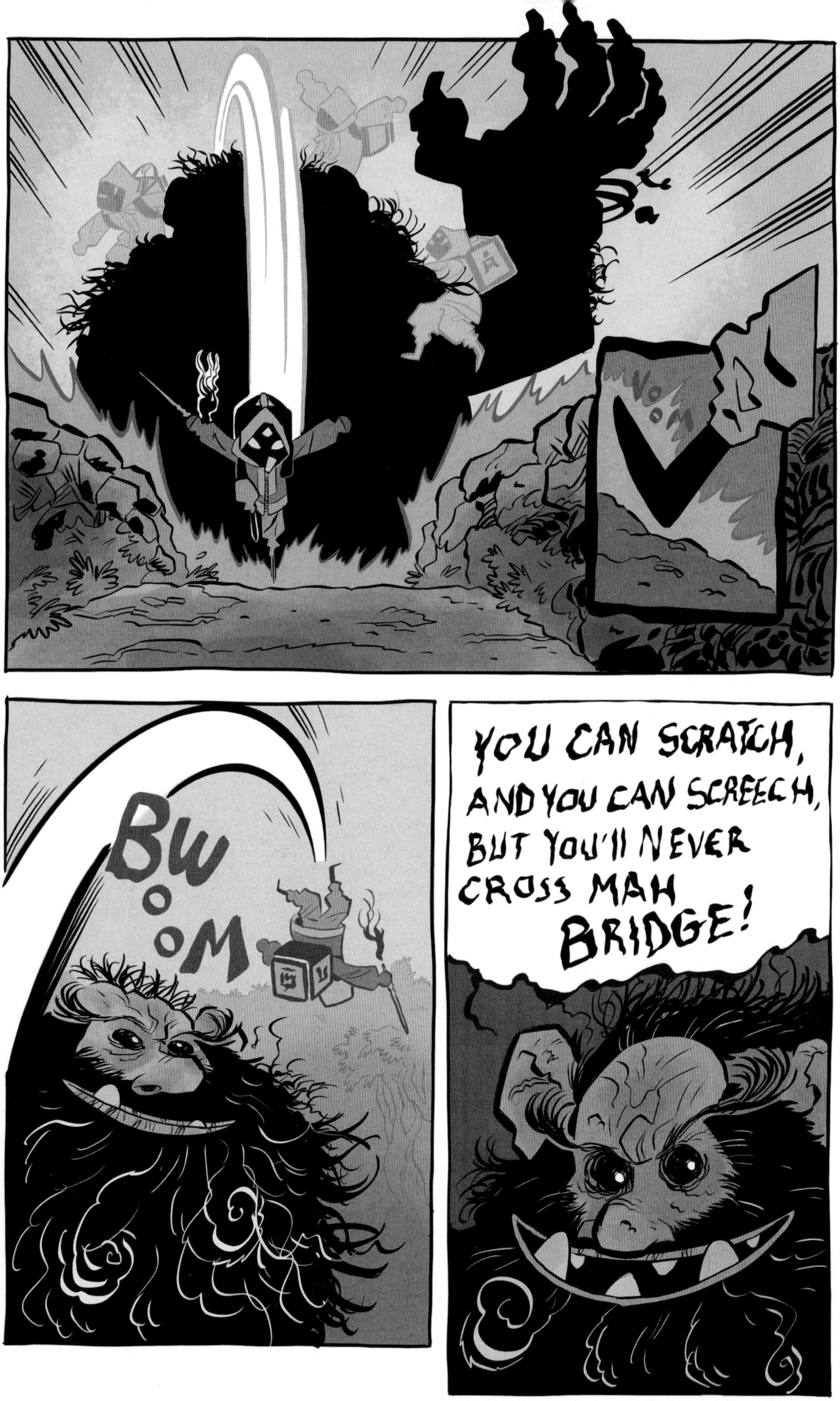
VooM
BWooM
YOU CAN SCRATCH, AND YOU CAN SCREECH, BUT YOU'll NEVER CROSS MAH BRIDGE!

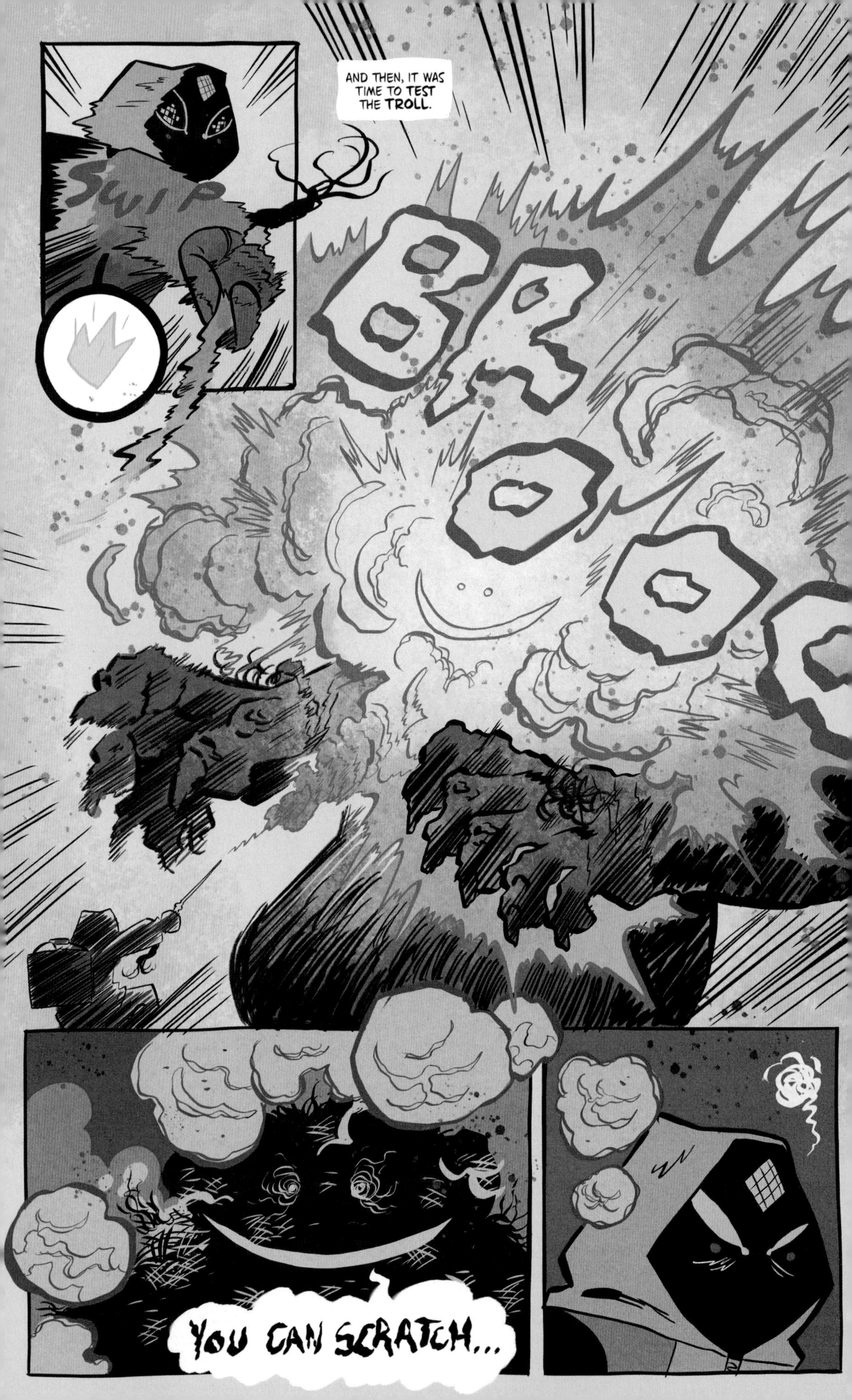
SWIP
AND THEN, IT WAS TIME TO TEST THE TROLL.
BROOOO
YOU CAN SCRATCH...

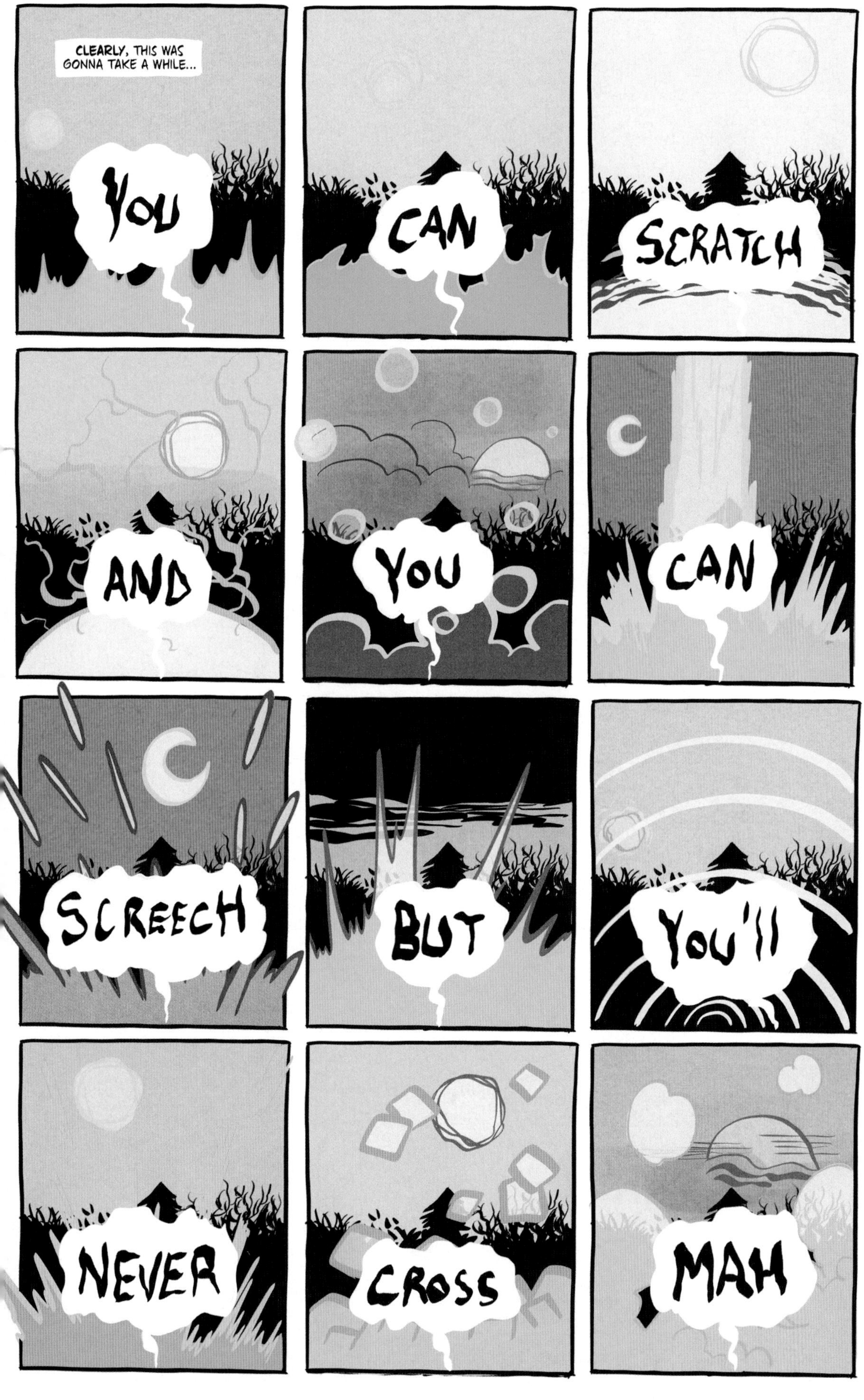
CLEARLY, THIS WAS GONNA TAKE A WHILE...
YOU
CAN
SCRATCH
AND
YOU
CAN
SCREECH
BUT
YOU'LL
NEVER
CROSS
MAH

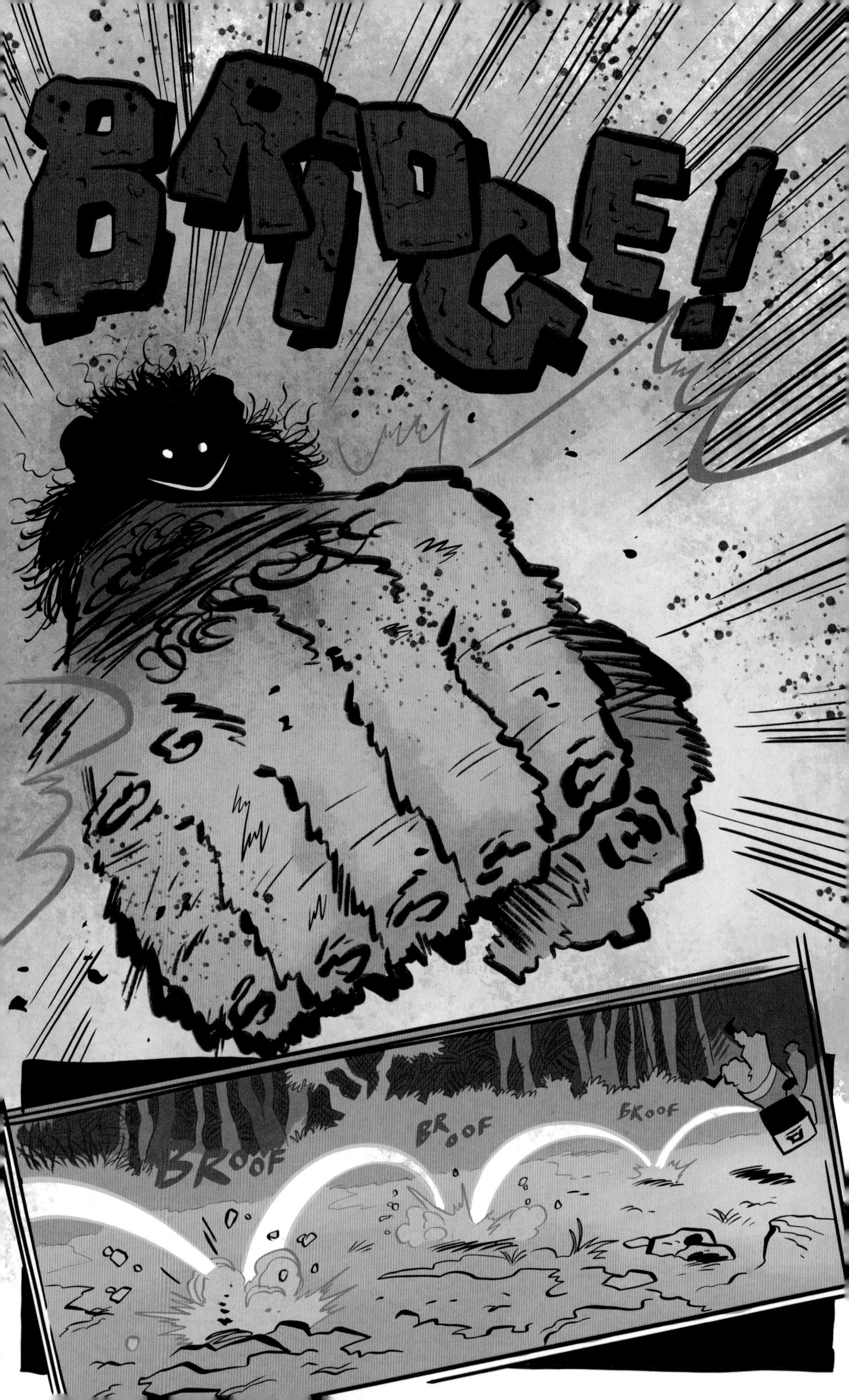
BRIDGE!
BROOF
BROOF
BROOF

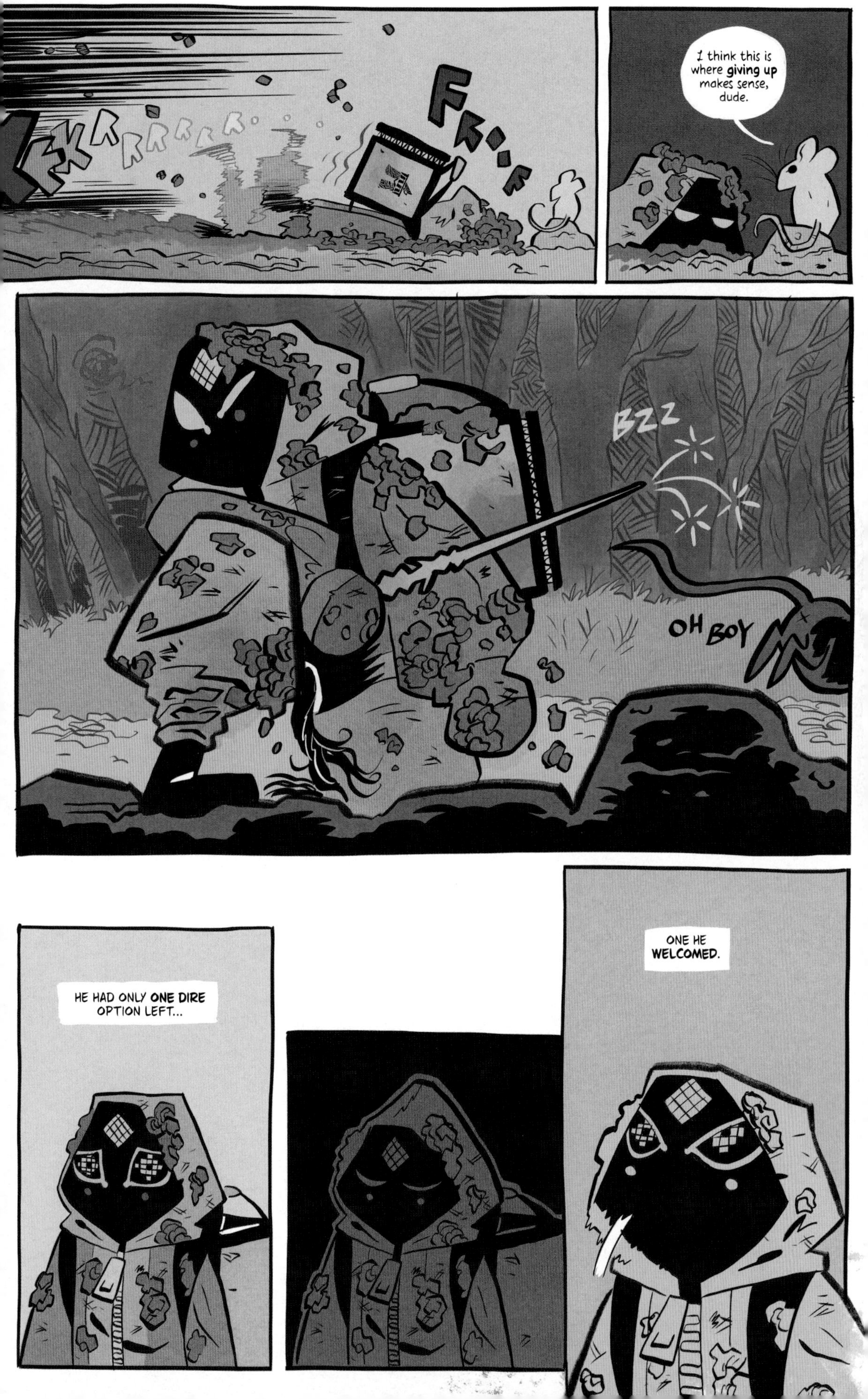
KKRRRRRRK
FROOF
I think this is where **giving up** makes sense, dude.
BZZ
OH BOY
HE HAD ONLY **ONE DIRE** OPTION LEFT...
ONE HE **WELCOMED.**

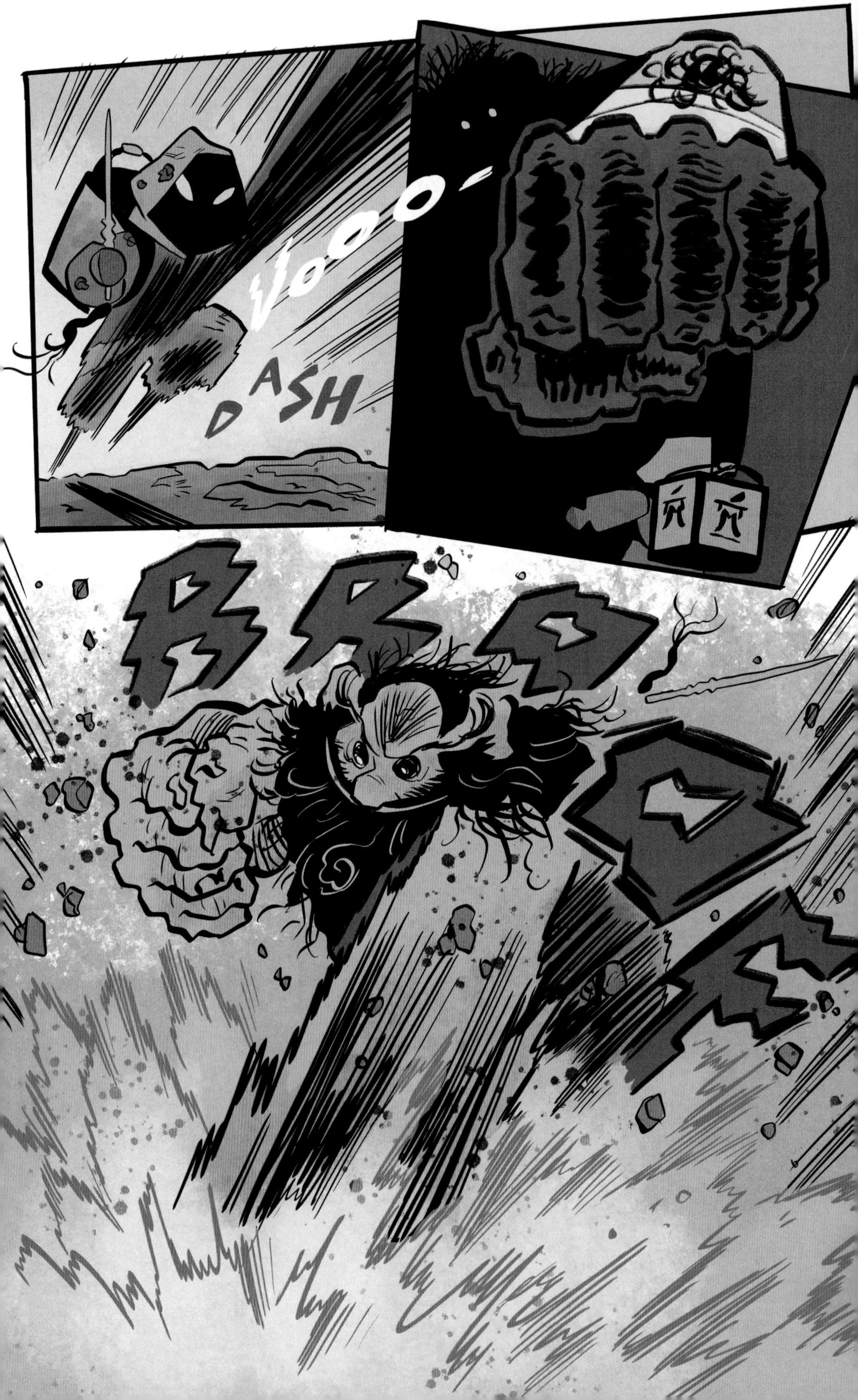
VOOOO-
DASH

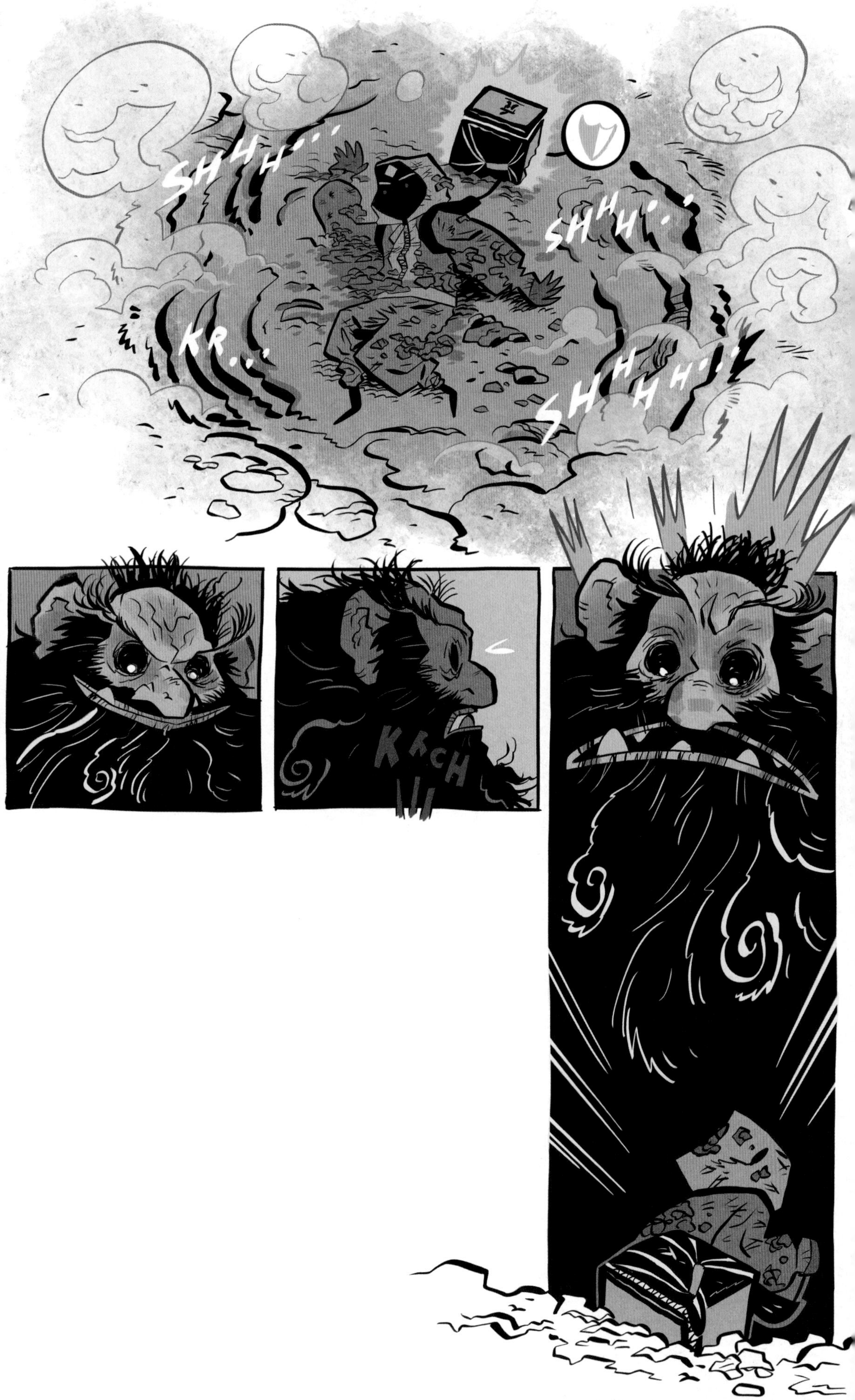
SHHH...
SHHH...
KR...
SHHHH...
KRCH

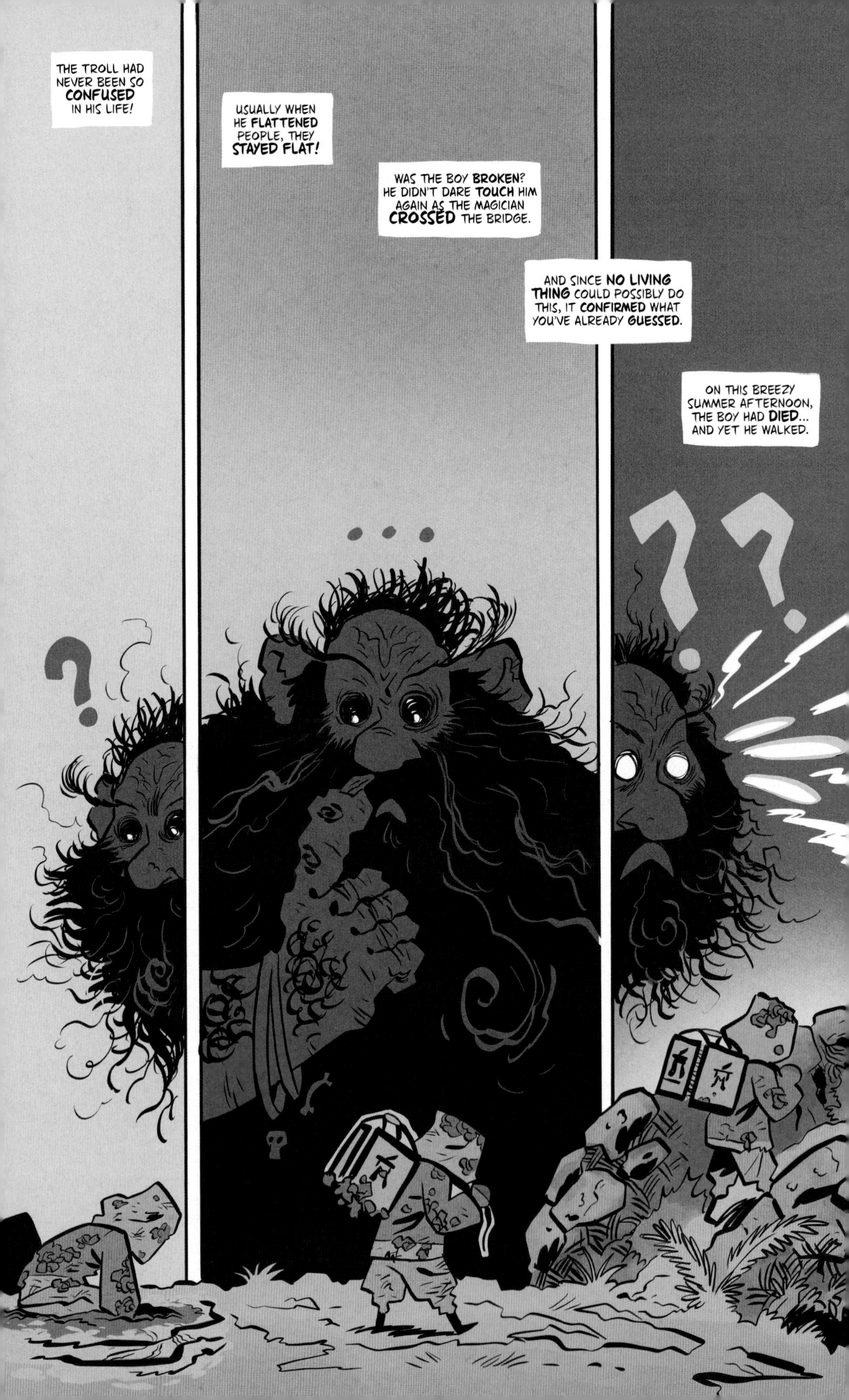
THE TROLL HAD NEVER BEEN SO CONFUSED IN HIS LIFE!
USUALLY WHEN HE FLATTENED PEOPLE, THEY STAYED FLAT!
WAS THE BOY BROKEN? HE DIDN'T DARE TOUCH HIM AGAIN AS THE MAGICIAN CROSSED THE BRIDGE.
AND SINCE NO LIVING THING COULD POSSIBLY DO THIS, IT CONFIRMED WHAT YOU'VE ALREADY GUESSED.
ON THIS BREEZY SUMMER AFTERNOON, THE BOY HAD DIED... AND YET HE WALKED.

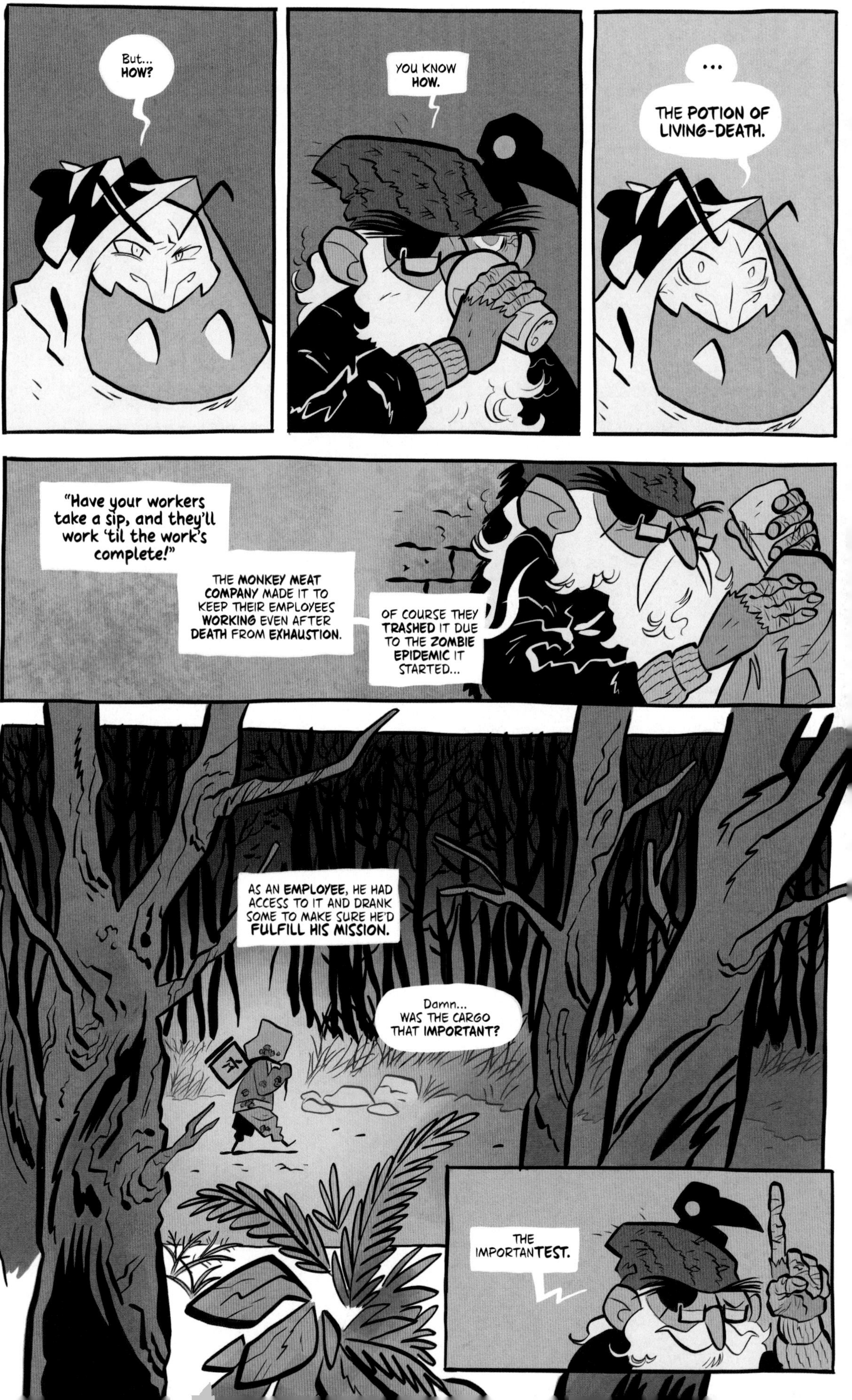
But...
HOW?
YOU KNOW
HOW.
...
THE POTION OF
LIVING-DEATH.
"Have your workers take a sip, and they'll work 'til the work's complete!"
THE MONKEY MEAT COMPANY MADE IT TO KEEP THEIR EMPLOYEES WORKING EVEN AFTER DEATH FROM EXHAUSTION.
OF COURSE THEY TRASHED IT DUE TO THE ZOMBIE EPIDEMIC IT STARTED...
AS AN EMPLOYEE, HE HAD ACCESS TO IT AND DRANK SOME TO MAKE SURE HE'D FULFILL HIS MISSION.
Damn... WAS THE CARGO THAT IMPORTANT?
THE IMPORTANTEST.

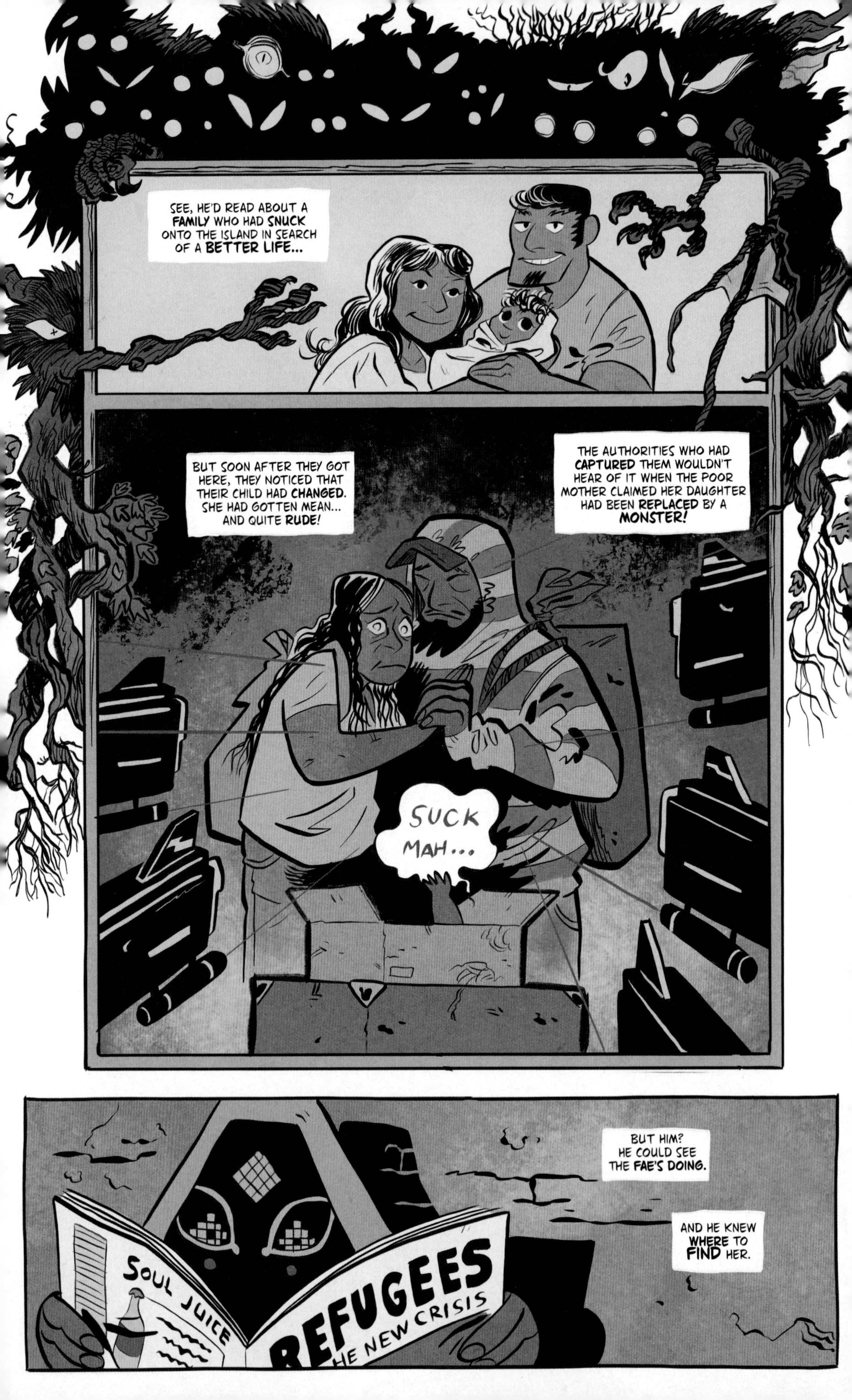
SEE, HE'D READ ABOUT A FAMILY WHO HAD SNUCK ONTO THE ISLAND IN SEARCH OF A BETTER LIFE...
BUT SOON AFTER THEY GOT HERE, THEY NOTICED THAT THEIR CHILD HAD CHANGED. SHE HAD GOTTEN MEAN... AND QUITE RUDE!
THE AUTHORITIES WHO HAD CAPTURED THEM WOULDN'T HEAR OF IT WHEN THE POOR MOTHER CLAIMED HER DAUGHTER HAD BEEN REPLACED BY A MONSTER!
SUCK MAH...
SOUL JUICE
REFUGEES
THE NEW CRISIS
BUT HIM? HE COULD SEE THE FAE'S DOING.
AND HE KNEW WHERE TO FIND HER.

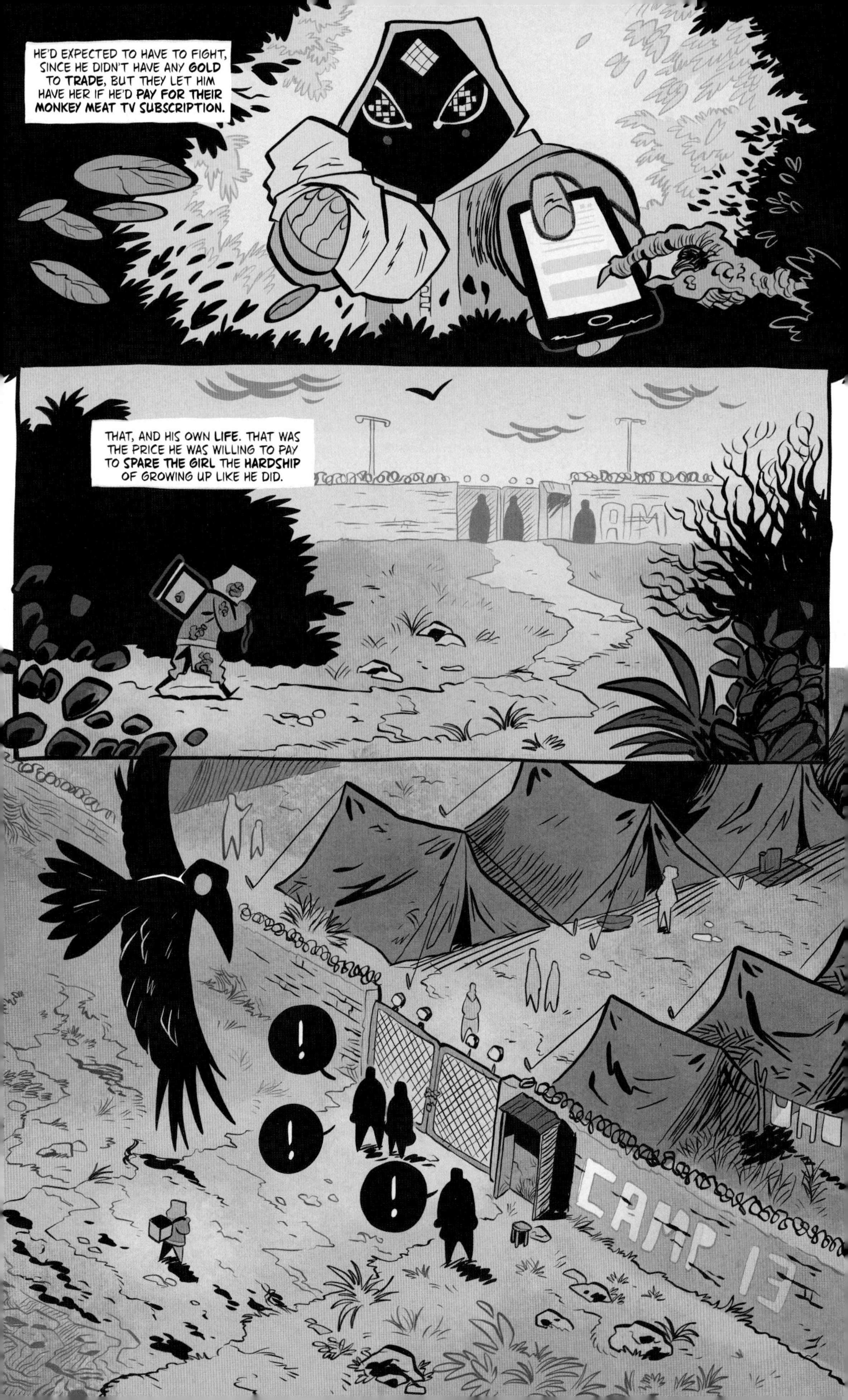
HE'D EXPECTED TO HAVE TO FIGHT, SINCE HE DIDN'T HAVE ANY GOLD TO TRADE, BUT THEY LET HIM HAVE HER IF HE'D PAY FOR THEIR MONKEY MEAT TV SUBSCRIPTION.
THAT, AND HIS OWN LIFE. THAT WAS THE PRICE HE WAS WILLING TO PAY TO SPARE THE GIRL THE HARDSHIP OF GROWING UP LIKE HE DID.
!
!
!
CAMP 13

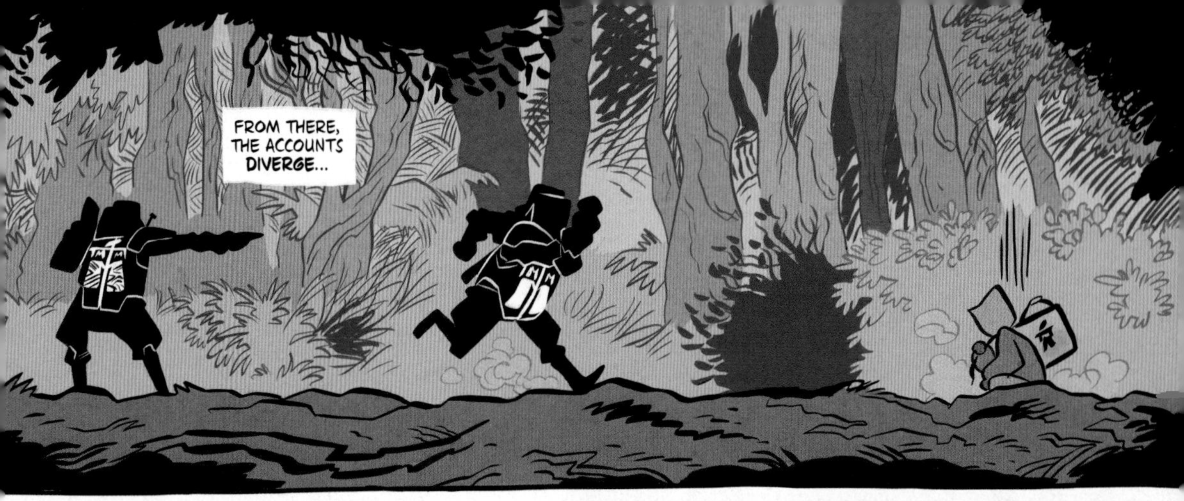
FROM THERE, THE ACCOUNTS DIVERGE...

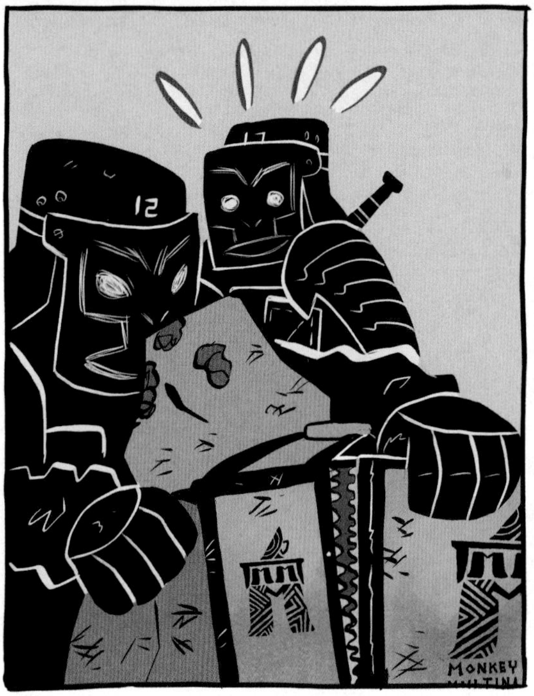
12
MONKEY

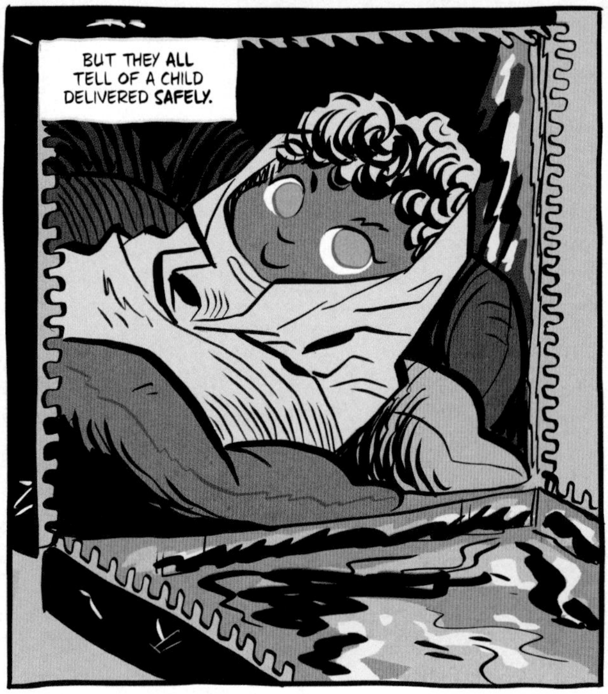
BUT THEY ALL TELL OF A CHILD DELIVERED SAFELY.

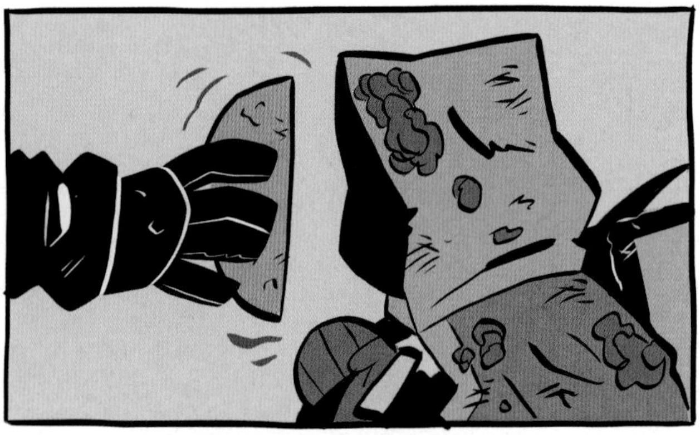

AND OF A BOY WHO **THOUGHT** HIMSELF **EMPTY** FOREVER, BUT WHEN HIS FACE WAS **REVEALED** TO THE WORLD...

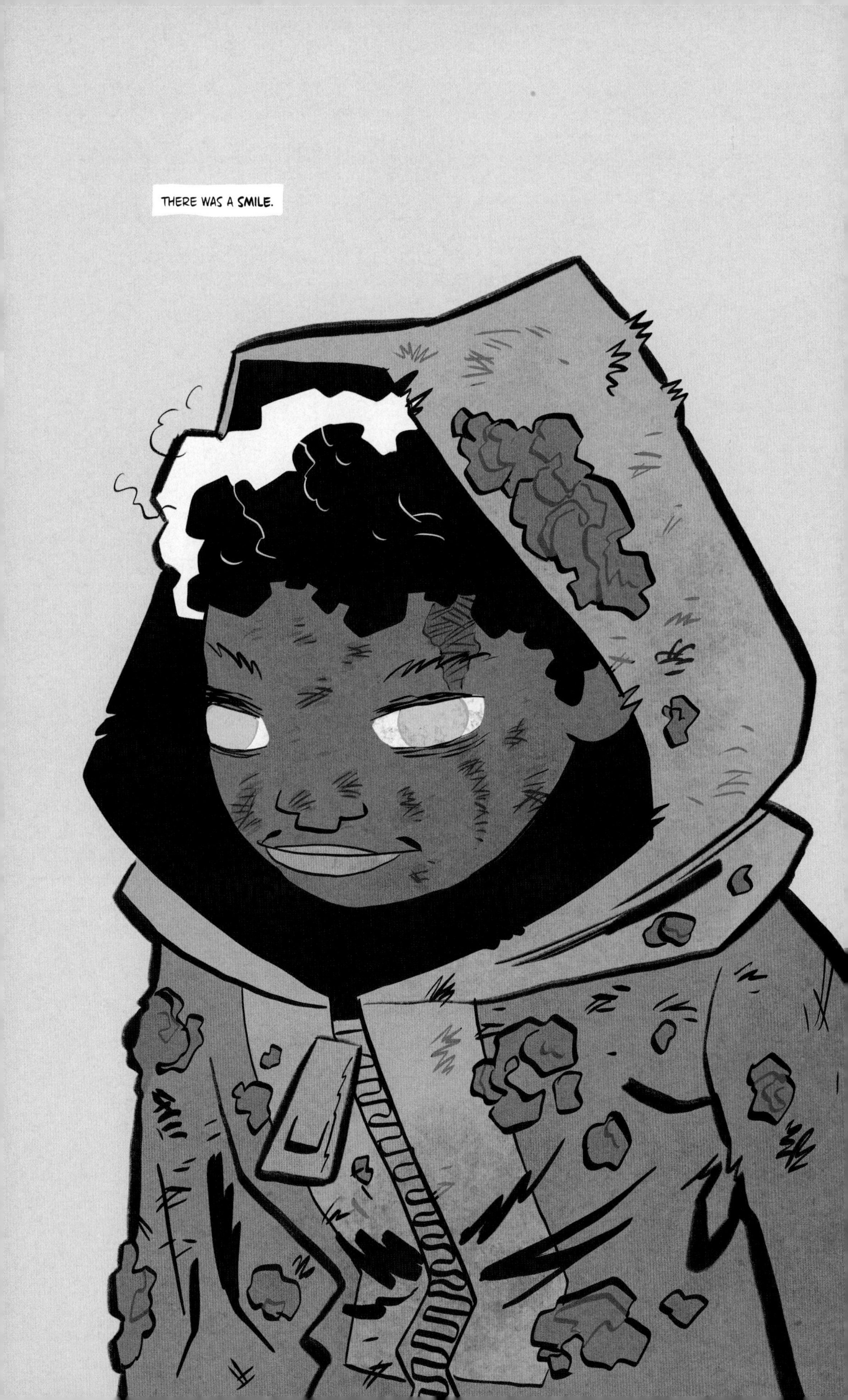
THERE WAS A SMILE.

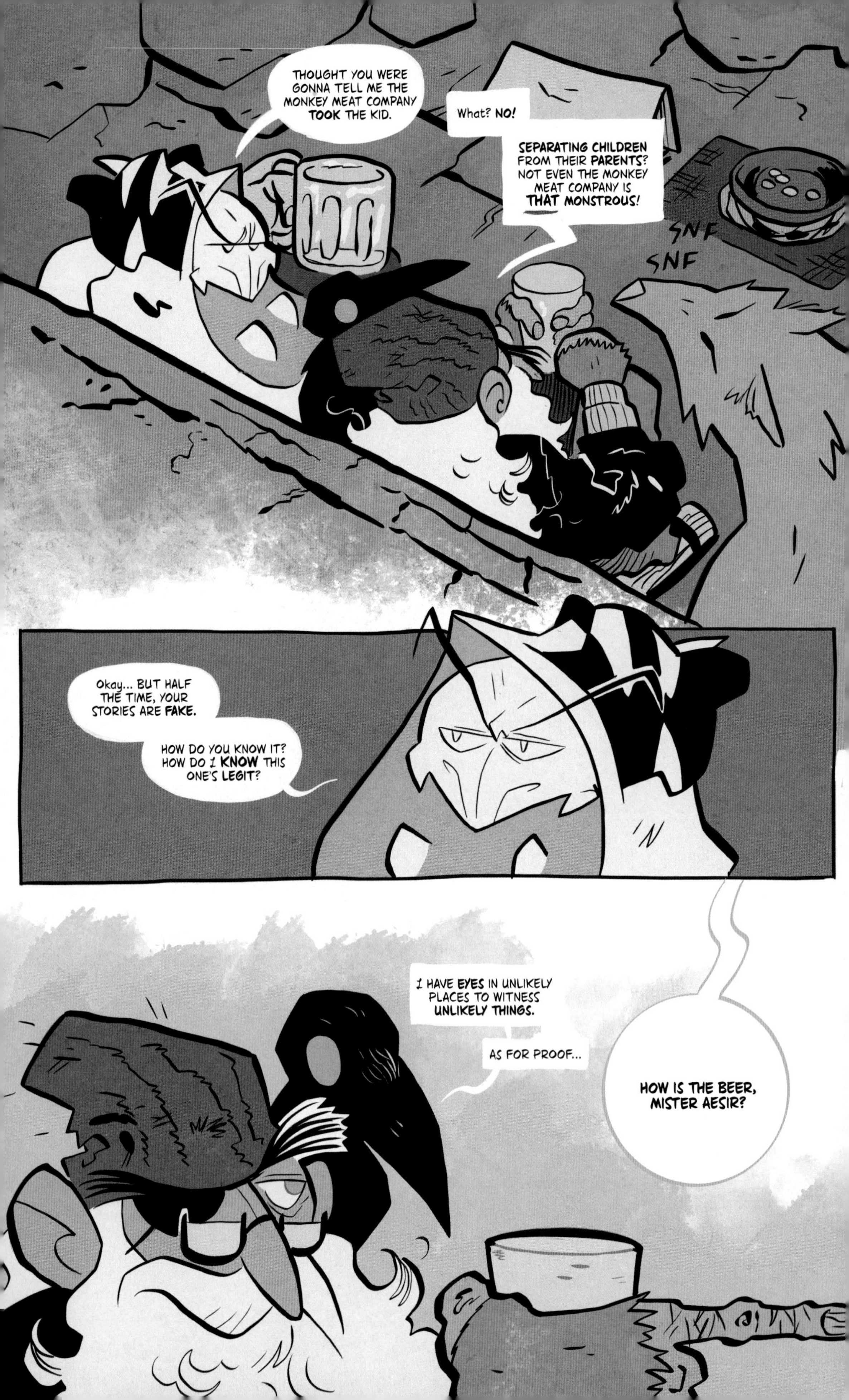
THOUGHT YOU WERE GONNA TELL ME THE MONKEY MEAT COMPANY TOOK THE KID.
What? NO!
SEPARATING CHILDREN FROM THEIR PARENTS? NOT EVEN THE MONKEY MEAT COMPANY IS THAT MONSTROUS!
SNF
SNF
Okay... BUT HALF THE TIME, YOUR STORIES ARE FAKE.
HOW DO YOU KNOW IT? HOW DO I KNOW THIS ONE'S LEGIT?
I HAVE EYES IN UNLIKELY PLACES TO WITNESS UNLIKELY THINGS.
AS FOR PROOF...
HOW IS THE BEER, MISTER AESIR?

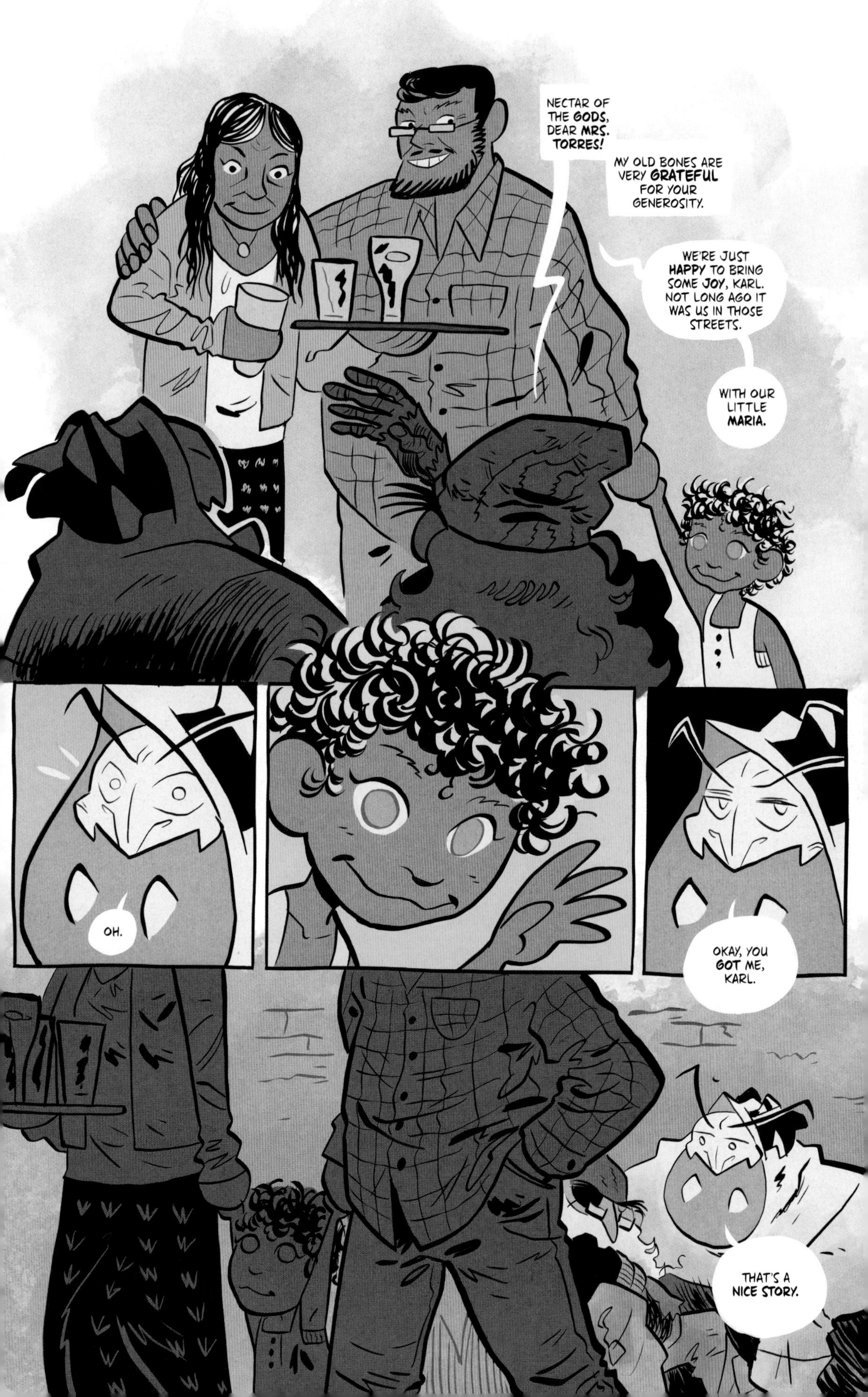
NECTAR OF THE GODS, DEAR MRS. TORRES!
MY OLD BONES ARE VERY GRATEFUL FOR YOUR GENEROSITY.
WE'RE JUST HAPPY TO BRING SOME JOY, KARL. NOT LONG AGO IT WAS US IN THOSE STREETS.
WITH OUR LITTLE MARIA.
OH.
OKAY, YOU GOT ME, KARL.
THAT'S A NICE STORY.

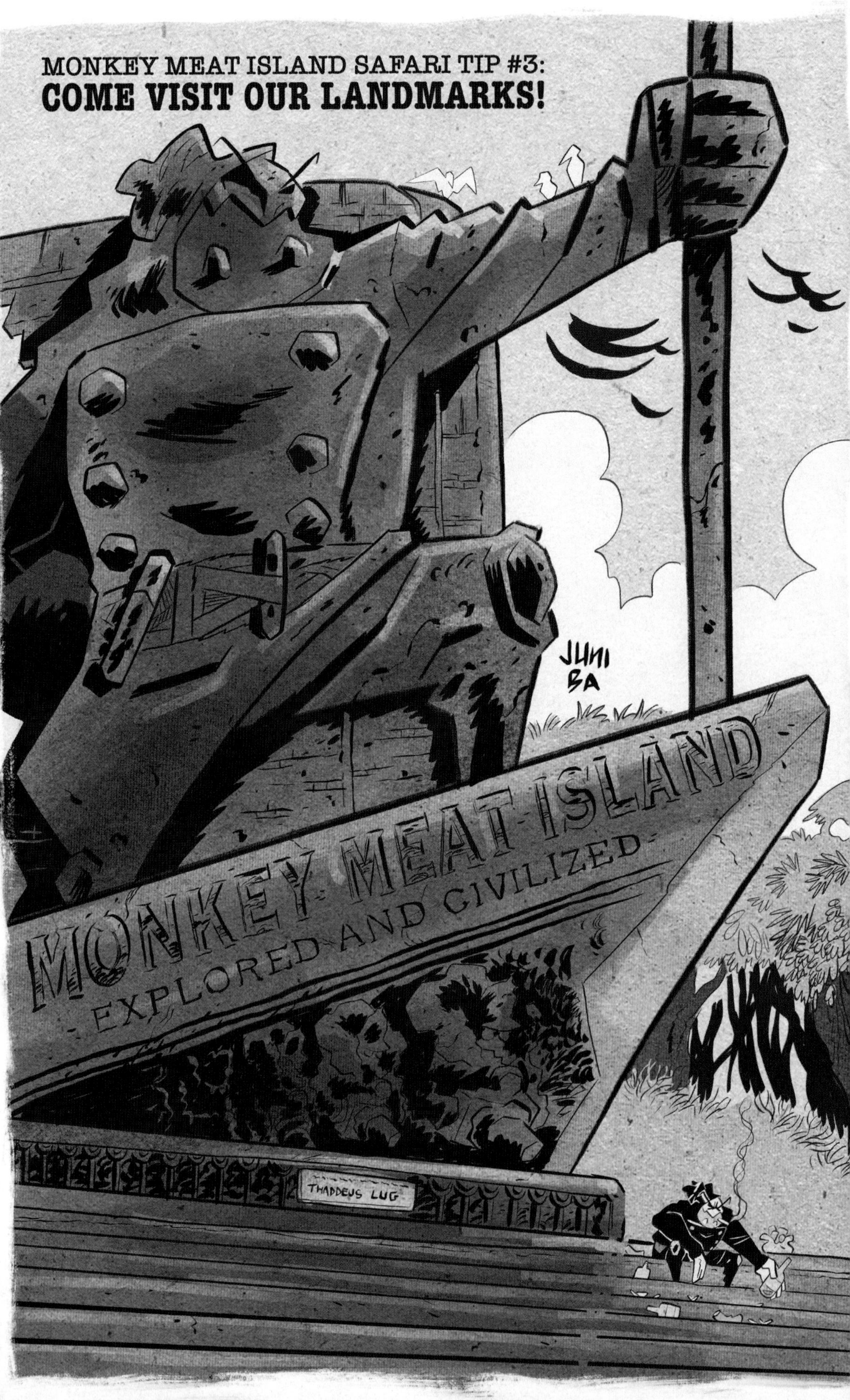
MONKEY MEAT ISLAND SAFARI TIP #3:
COME VISIT OUR LANDMARKS!
JUNI BA
MONKEY MEAT ISLAND
EXPLORED AND CIVILIZED
THADDEUS LUG

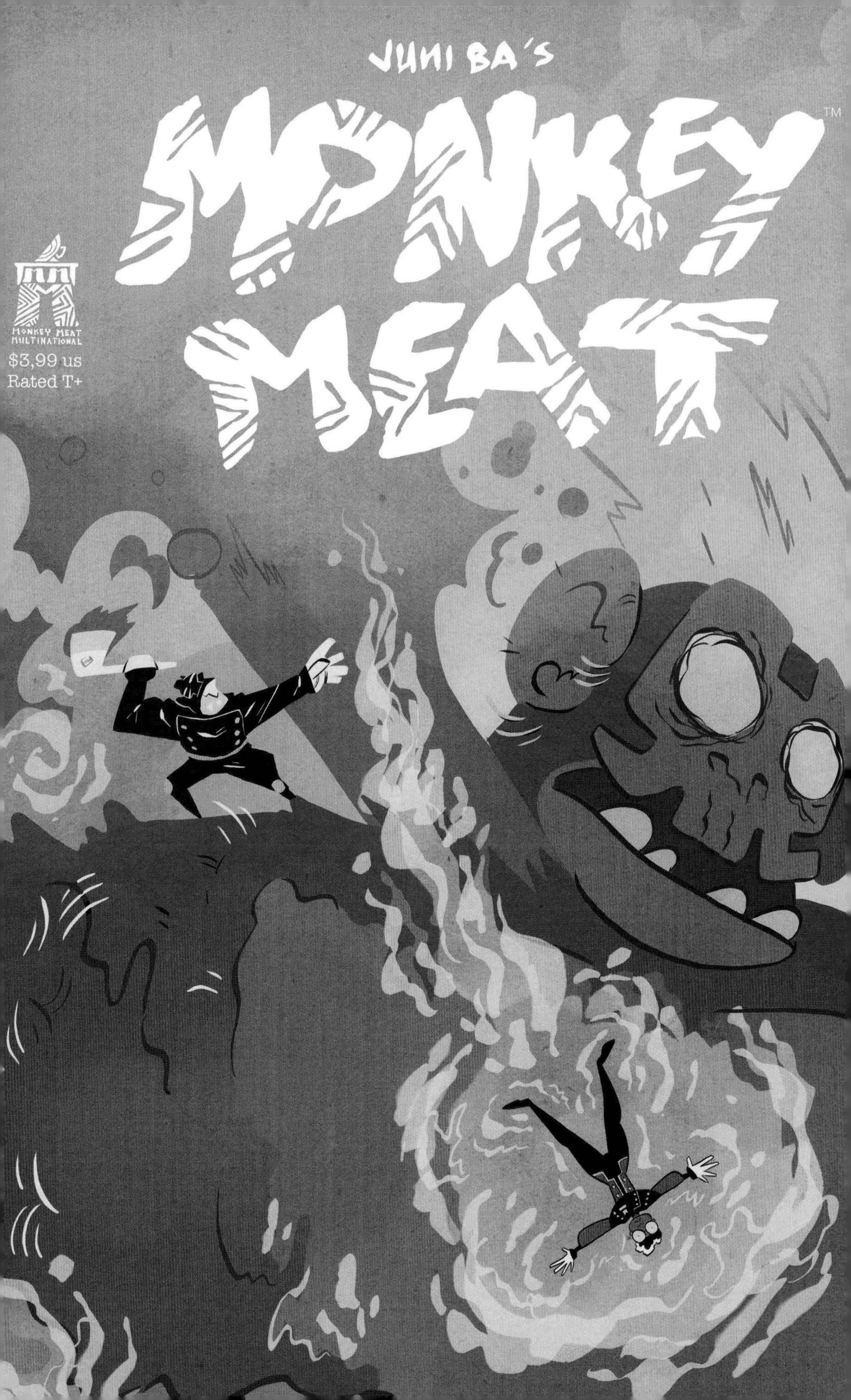
JUNI BA'S
MONKEY MEAT™
MONKEY MEAT MULTINATIONAL
$3,99 us
Rated T+

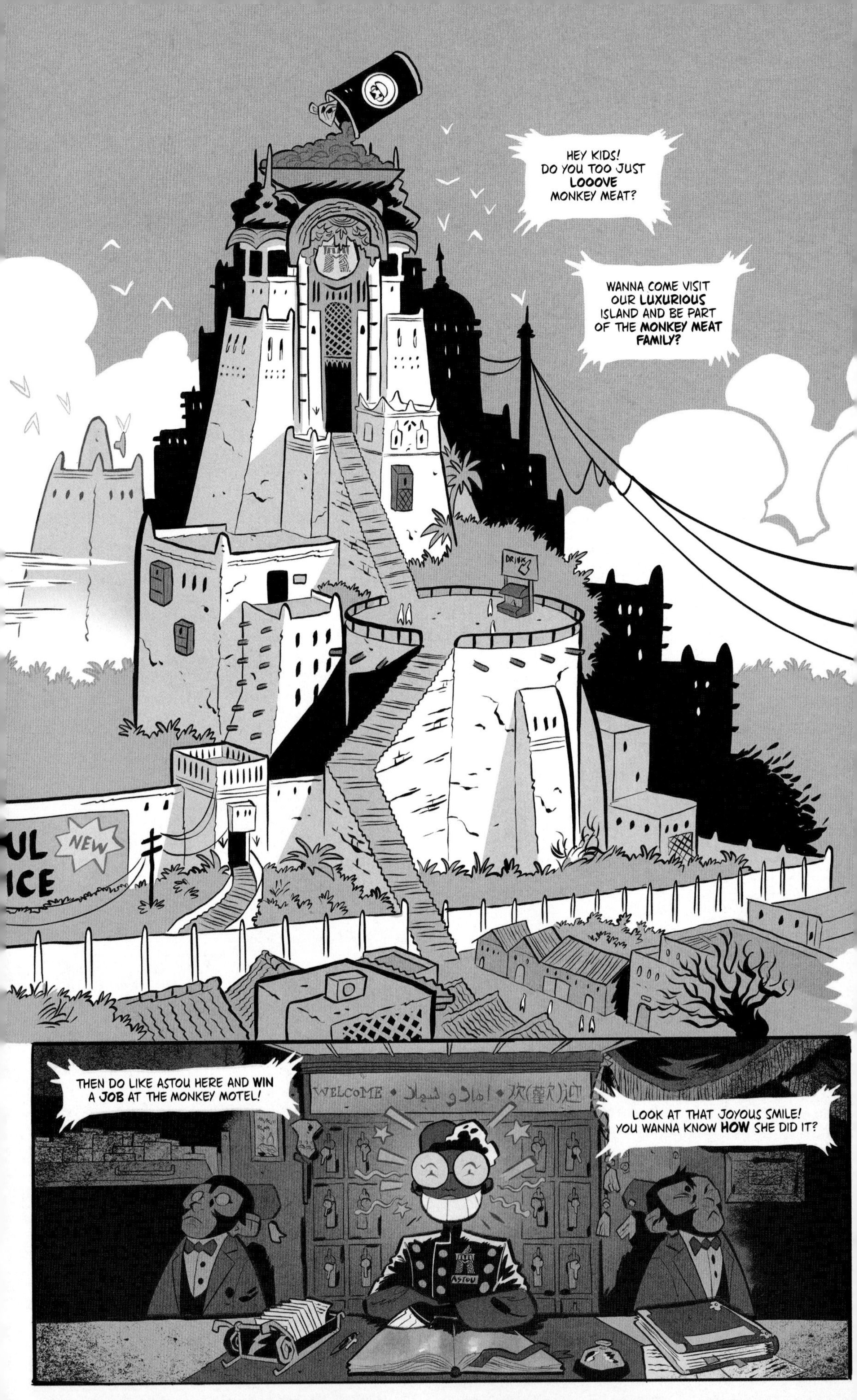
HEY KIDS! DO YOU TOO JUST LOOOVE MONKEY MEAT?
WANNA COME VISIT OUR LUXURIOUS ISLAND AND BE PART OF THE MONKEY MEAT FAMILY?
NEW
WELCOME
THEN DO LIKE ASTOU HERE AND WIN A JOB AT THE MONKEY MOTEL!
LOOK AT THAT JOYOUS SMILE! YOU WANNA KNOW HOW SHE DID IT?

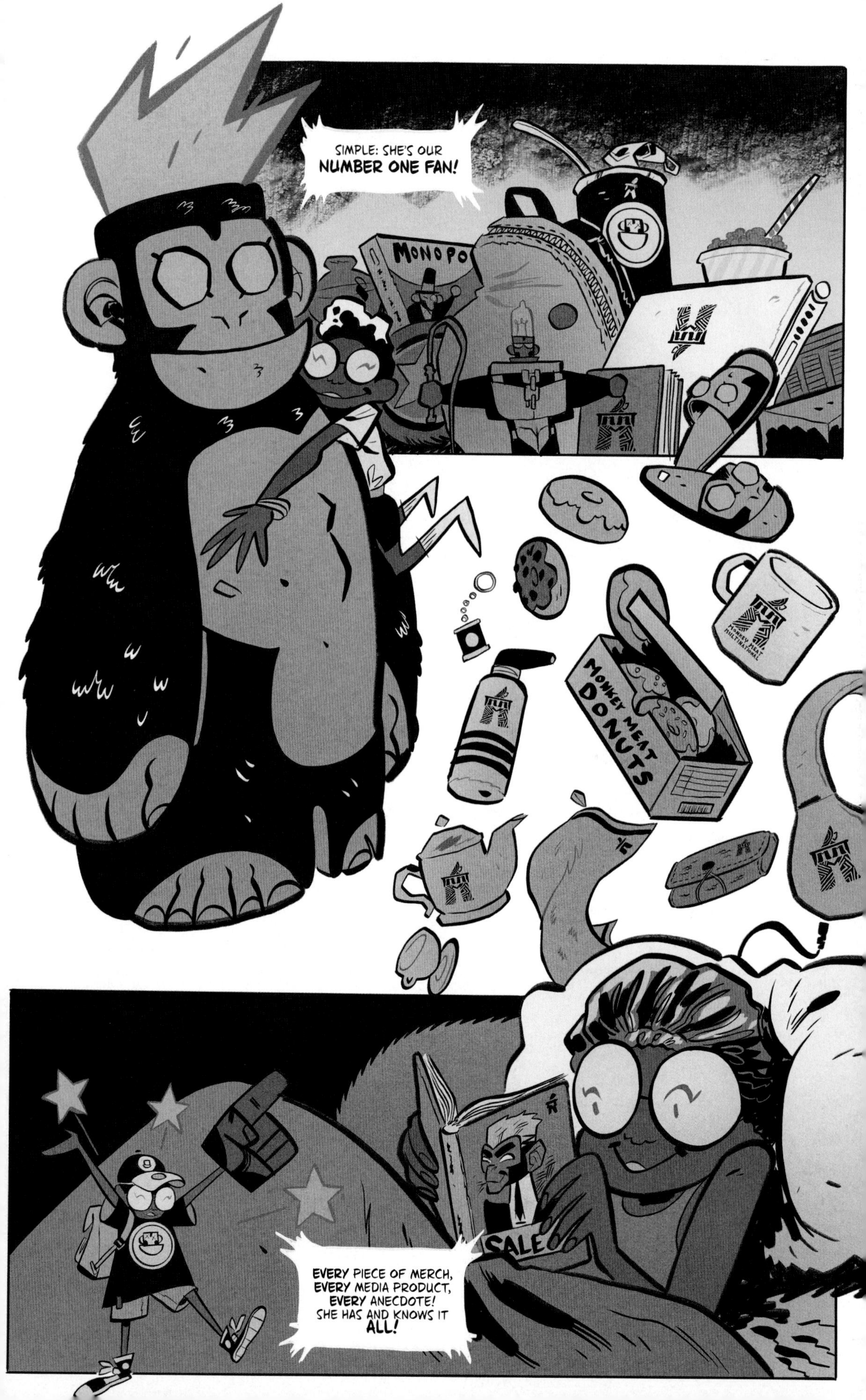
SIMPLE: SHE'S OUR NUMBER ONE FAN!
MONOPO
MONKEY MEAT DONUTS
SALE
EVERY PIECE OF MERCH, EVERY MEDIA PRODUCT, EVERY ANECDOTE! SHE HAS AND KNOWS IT ALL!

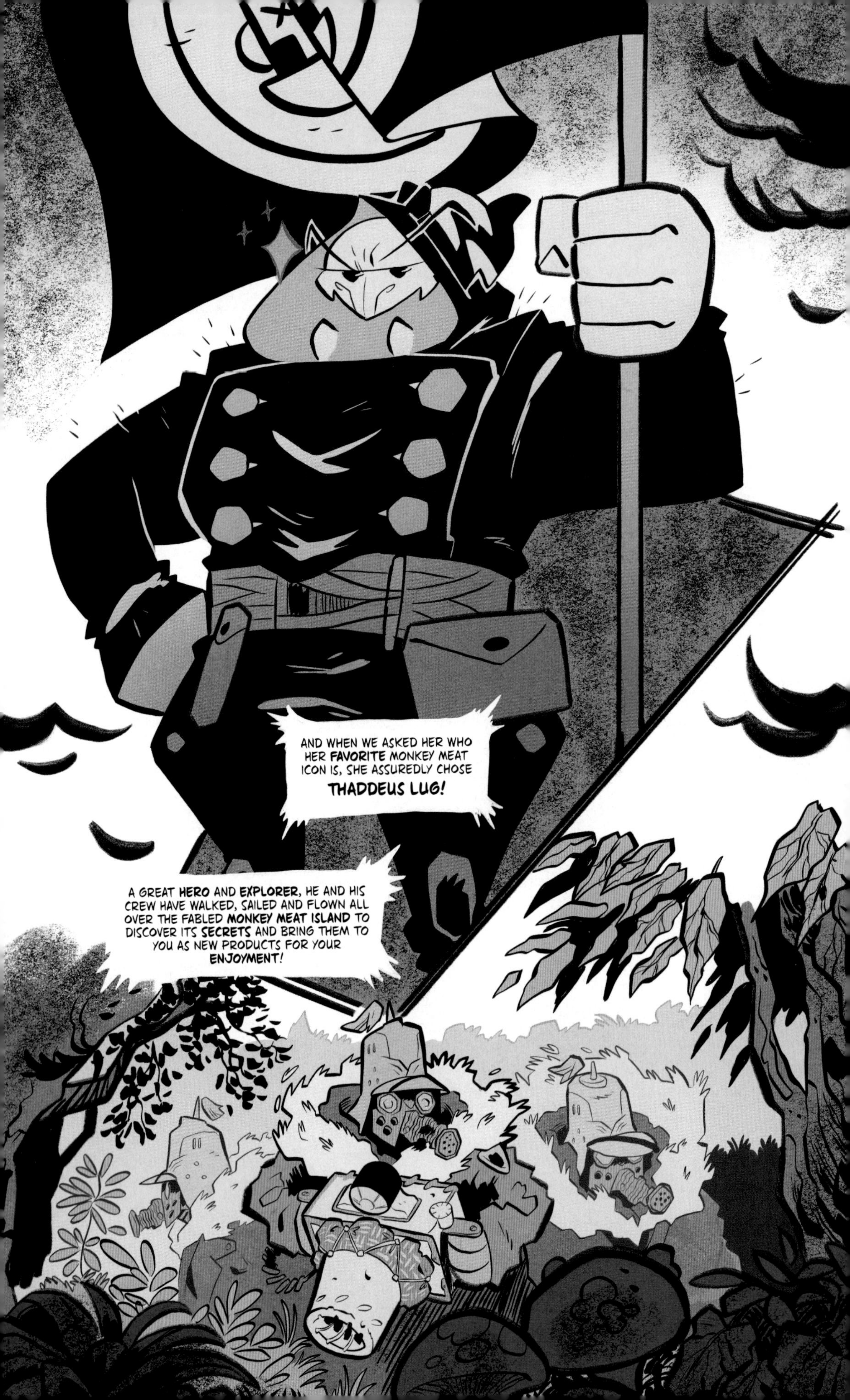
AND WHEN WE ASKED HER WHO HER FAVORITE MONKEY MEAT ICON IS, SHE ASSUREDLY CHOSE THADDEUS LUG!
A GREAT HERO AND EXPLORER, HE AND HIS CREW HAVE WALKED, SAILED AND FLOWN ALL OVER THE FABLED MONKEY MEAT ISLAND TO DISCOVER ITS SECRETS AND BRING THEM TO YOU AS NEW PRODUCTS FOR YOUR ENJOYMENT!

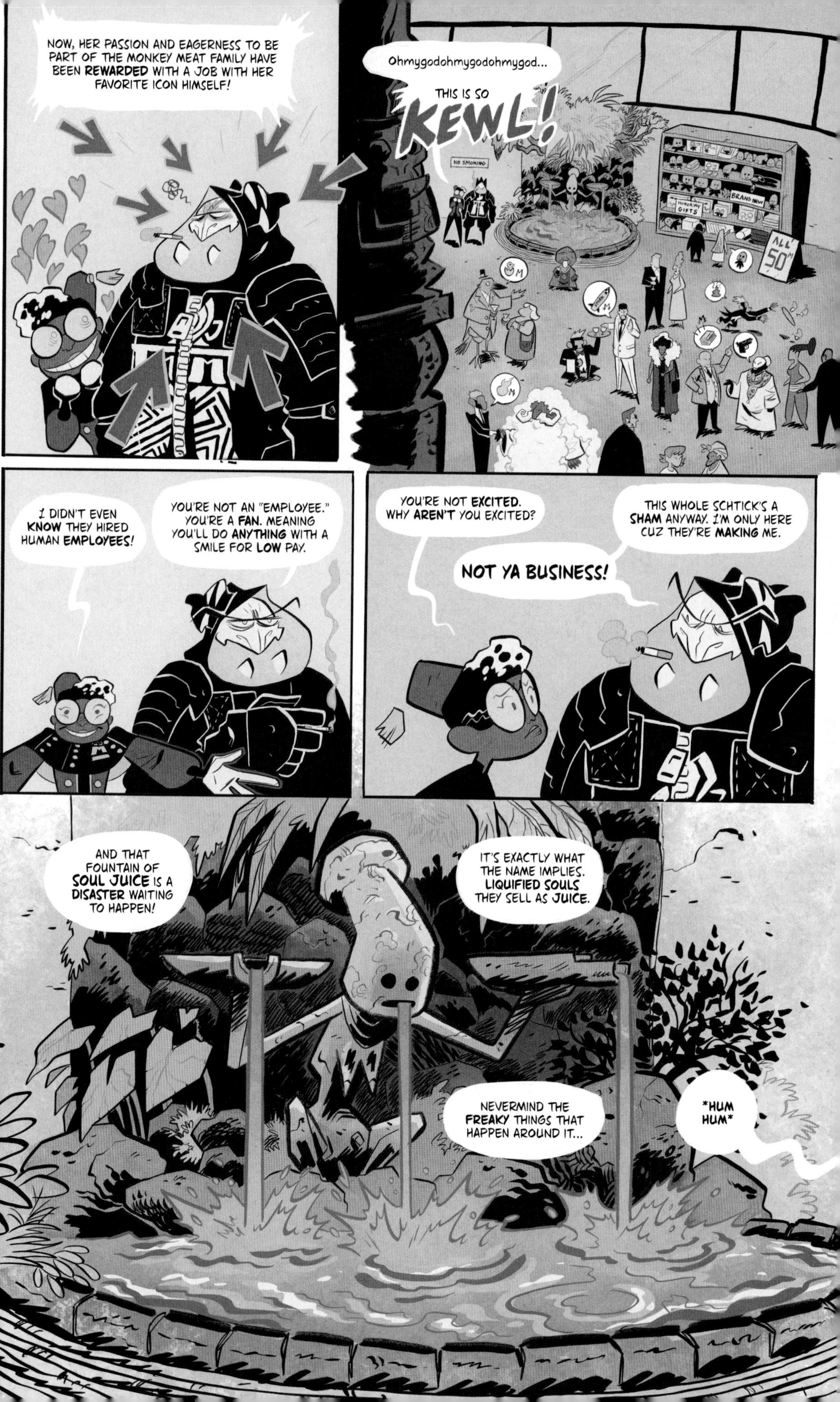
NOW, HER PASSION AND EAGERNESS TO BE PART OF THE MONKEY MEAT FAMILY HAVE BEEN REWARDED WITH A JOB WITH HER FAVORITE ICON HIMSELF!
Ohmygodohmygodohmygod...
THIS IS SO
KEWL!
NO SMOKING
HONORARY GIFTS
BRAND NEW
ALL 50
I DIDN'T EVEN KNOW THEY HIRED HUMAN EMPLOYEES!
YOU'RE NOT AN "EMPLOYEE." YOU'RE A FAN. MEANING YOU'LL DO ANYTHING WITH A SMILE FOR LOW PAY.
YOU'RE NOT EXCITED. WHY AREN'T YOU EXCITED?
THIS WHOLE SCHTICK'S A SHAM ANYWAY. I'M ONLY HERE CUZ THEY'RE MAKING ME.
NOT YA BUSINESS!
AND THAT FOUNTAIN OF SOUL JUICE IS A DISASTER WAITING TO HAPPEN!
IT'S EXACTLY WHAT THE NAME IMPLIES. LIQUIFIED SOULS THEY SELL AS JUICE.
NEVERMIND THE FREAKY THINGS THAT HAPPEN AROUND IT...
HUM HUM

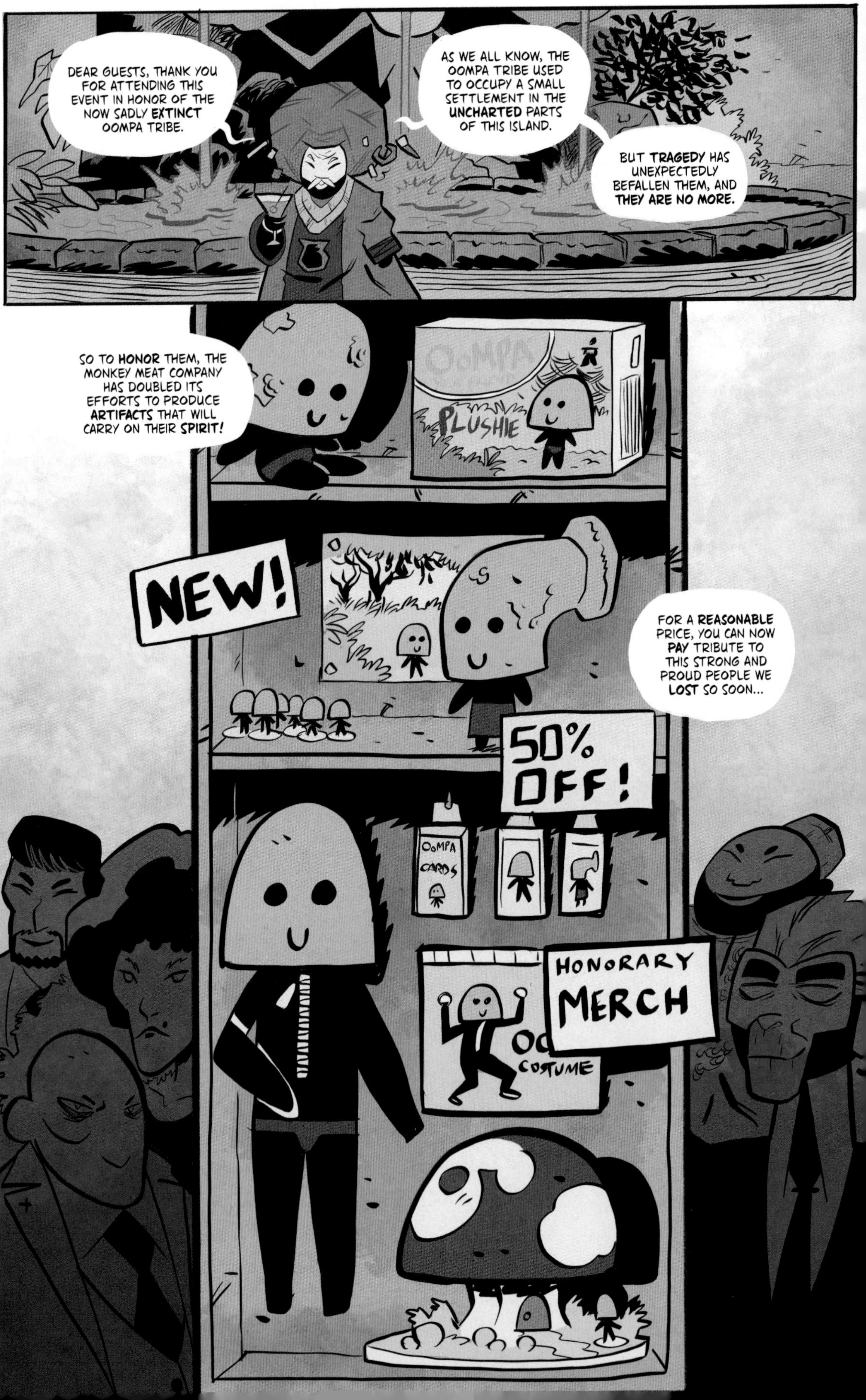
DEAR GUESTS, THANK YOU FOR ATTENDING THIS EVENT IN HONOR OF THE NOW SADLY **EXTINCT** OOMPA TRIBE.
AS WE ALL KNOW, THE OOMPA TRIBE USED TO OCCUPY A SMALL SETTLEMENT IN THE **UNCHARTED** PARTS OF THIS ISLAND.
BUT **TRAGEDY** HAS UNEXPECTEDLY BEFALLEN THEM, AND **THEY ARE NO MORE.**
SO TO **HONOR** THEM, THE MONKEY MEAT COMPANY HAS DOUBLED ITS EFFORTS TO PRODUCE **ARTIFACTS** THAT WILL CARRY ON THEIR **SPIRIT!**
OOMPA
PLUSHIE
NEW!
FOR A **REASONABLE** PRICE, YOU CAN NOW **PAY** TRIBUTE TO THIS STRONG AND PROUD PEOPLE WE **LOST** SO SOON...
50% OFF!
OOMPA CARDS
HONORARY MERCH
COSTUME

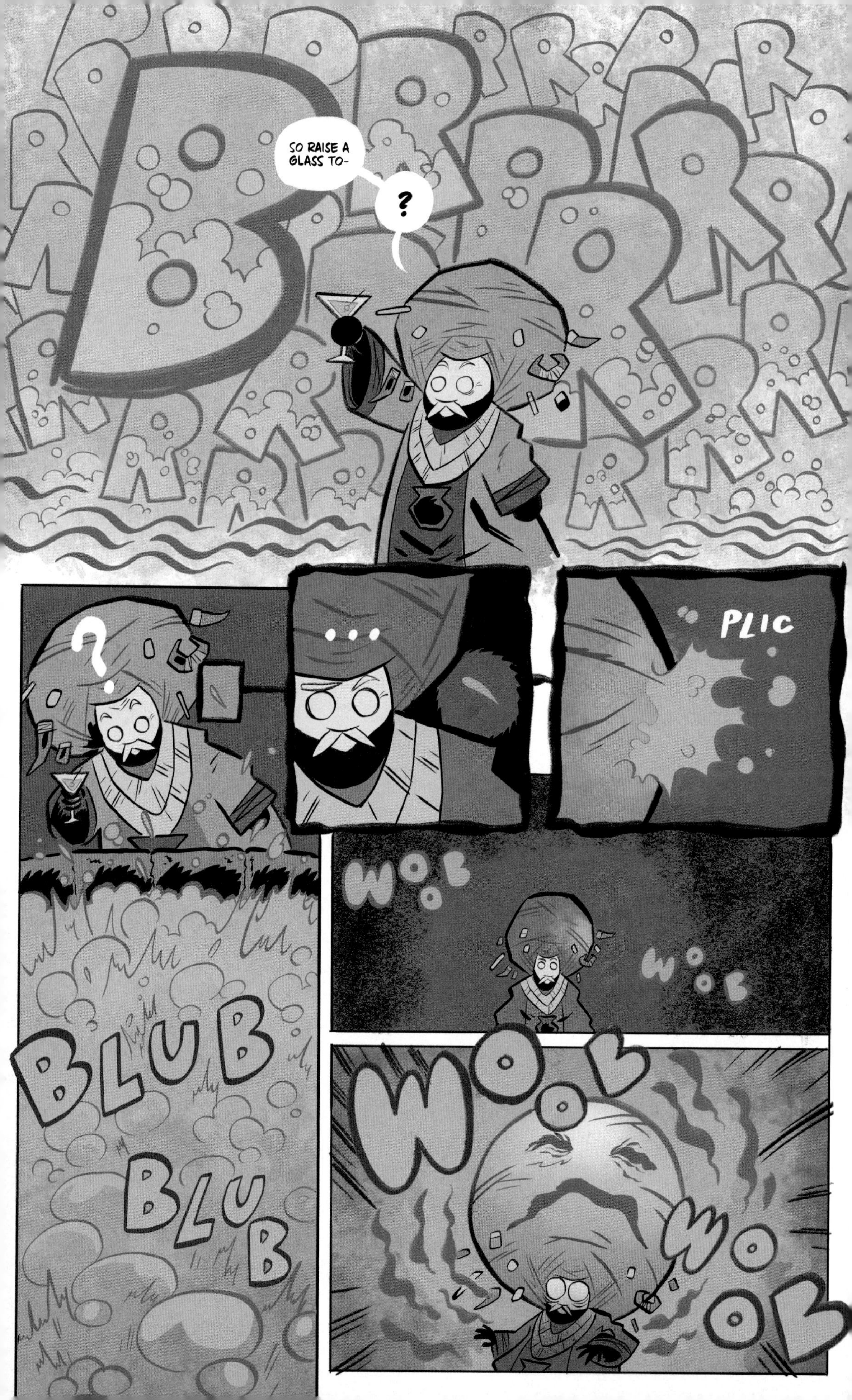
SO RAISE A GLASS TO-
?
?
...
PLIC
BLUB
BLUB
WOOB
WOOB
WOOB
WOOB

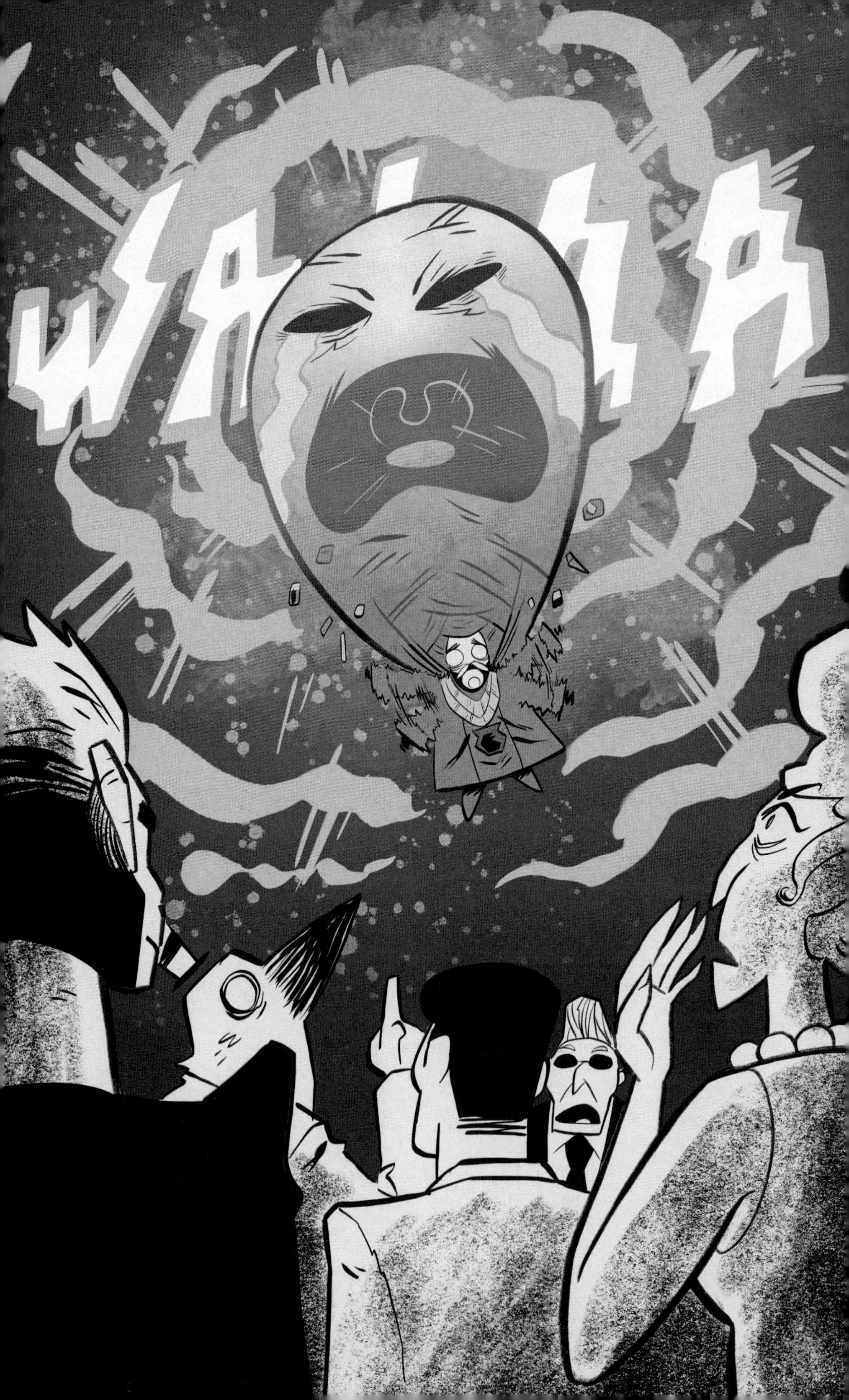

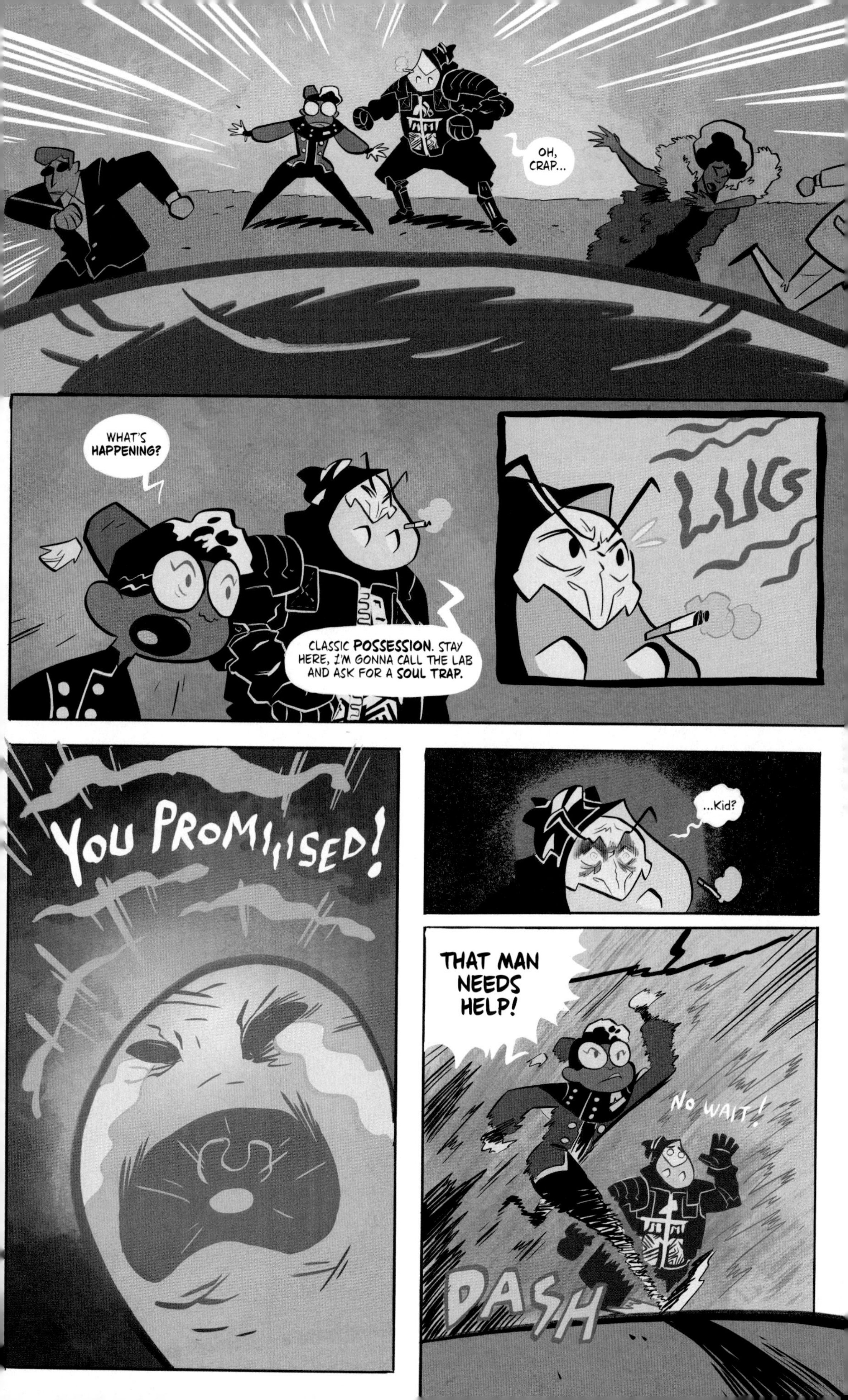
OH, CRAP...
WHAT'S HAPPENING?
CLASSIC POSSESSION. STAY HERE, I'M GONNA CALL THE LAB AND ASK FOR A SOUL TRAP.
LUG
YOU PROMIIISED!
...Kid?
THAT MAN NEEDS HELP!
NO WAIT!
DASH

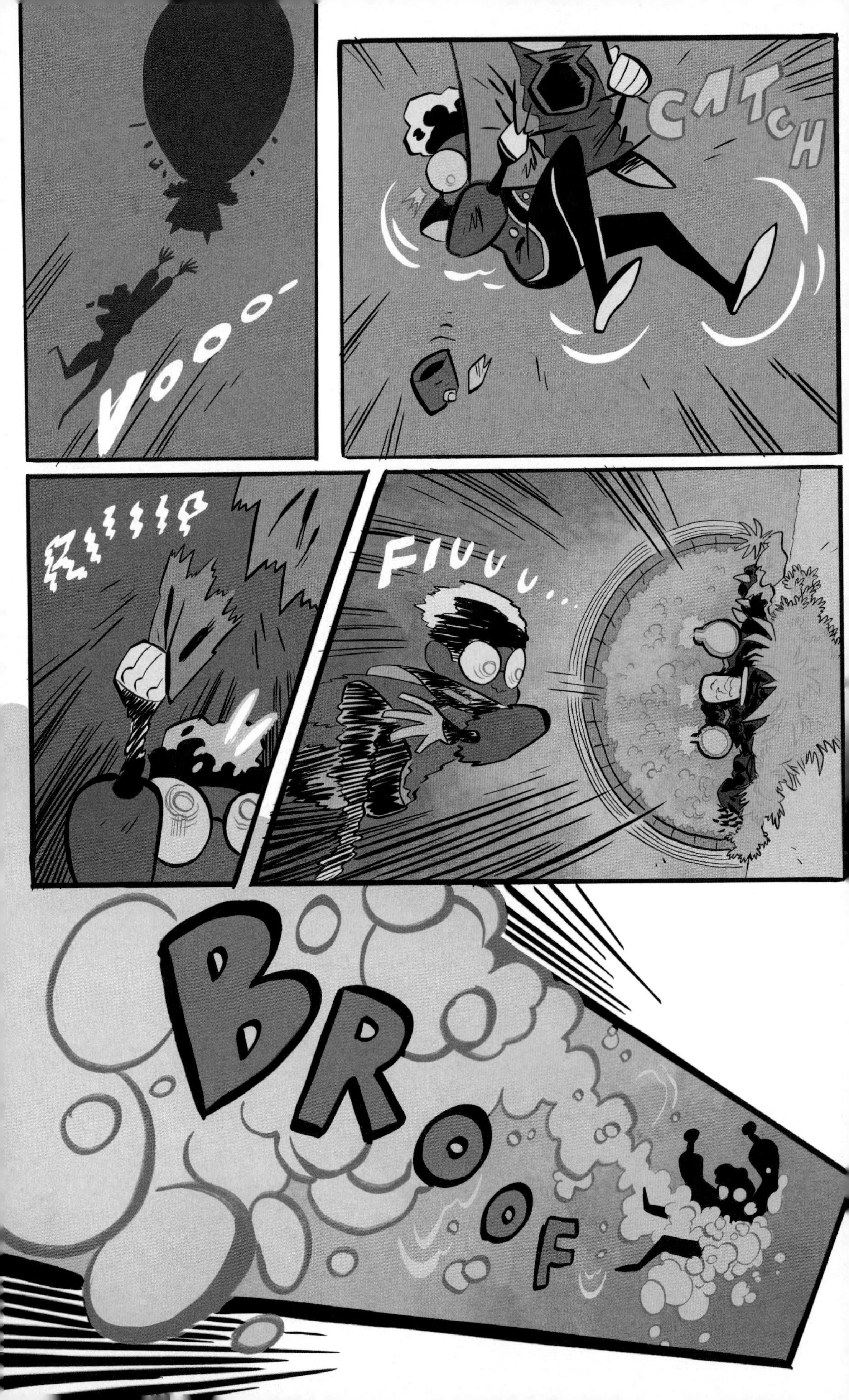
VOOOO
CATCH
FIUUUU...
BROOF

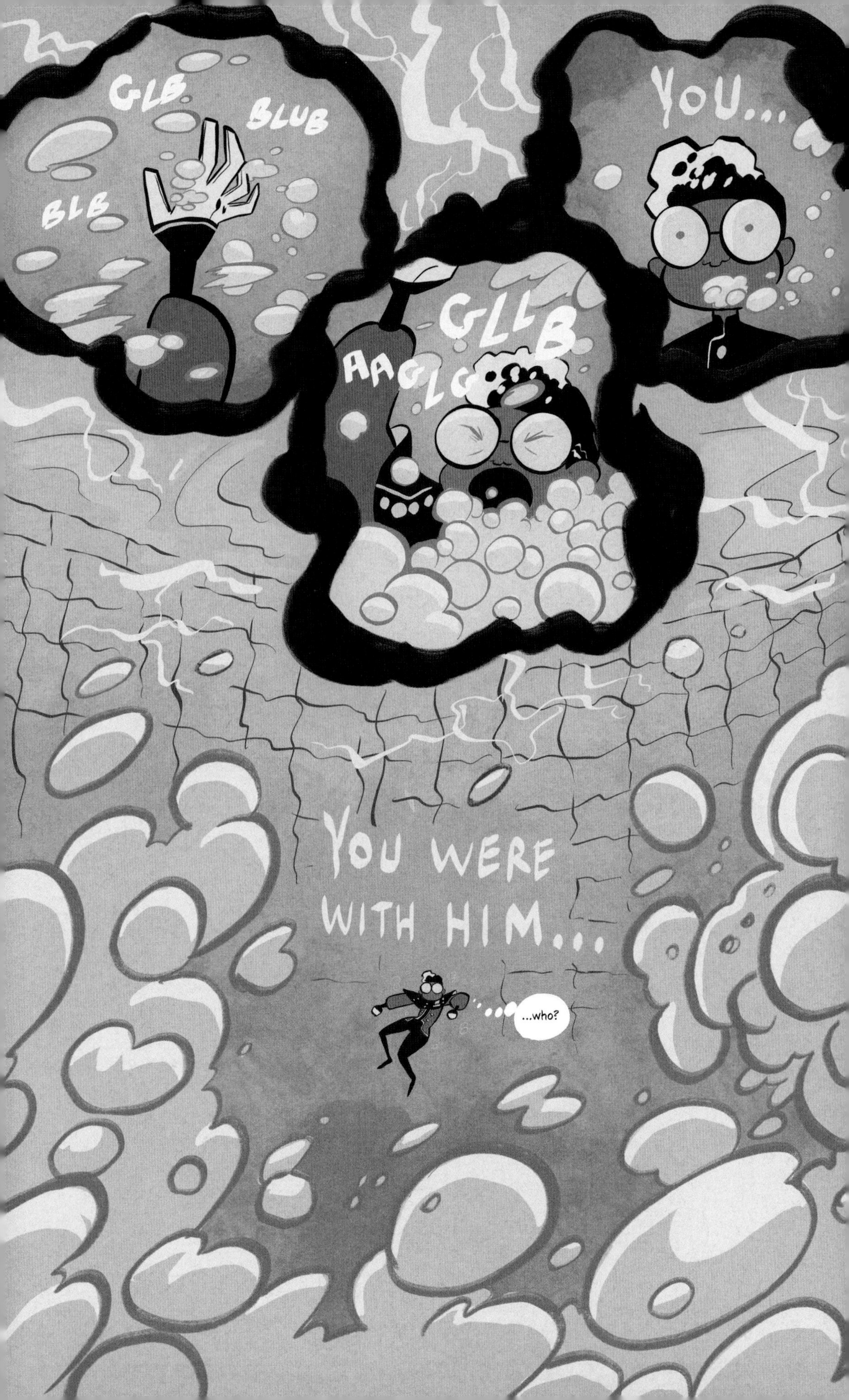
GLB
BLUB
BLB
AAGLG
GLLB
YOU...
YOU WERE WITH HIM...
...who?

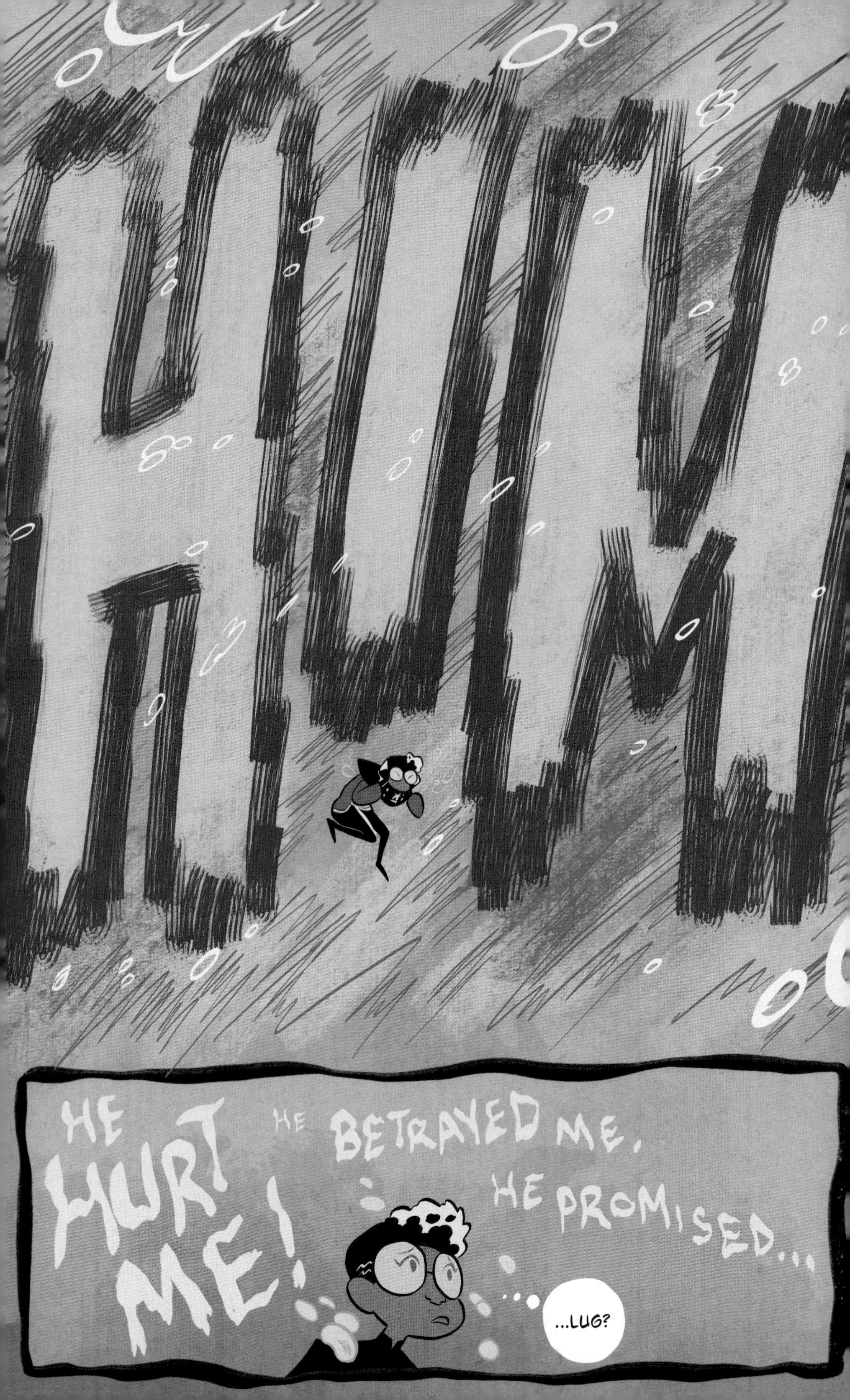
HE HURT ME!
HE BETRAYED ME.
HE PROMISED...
...LUG?

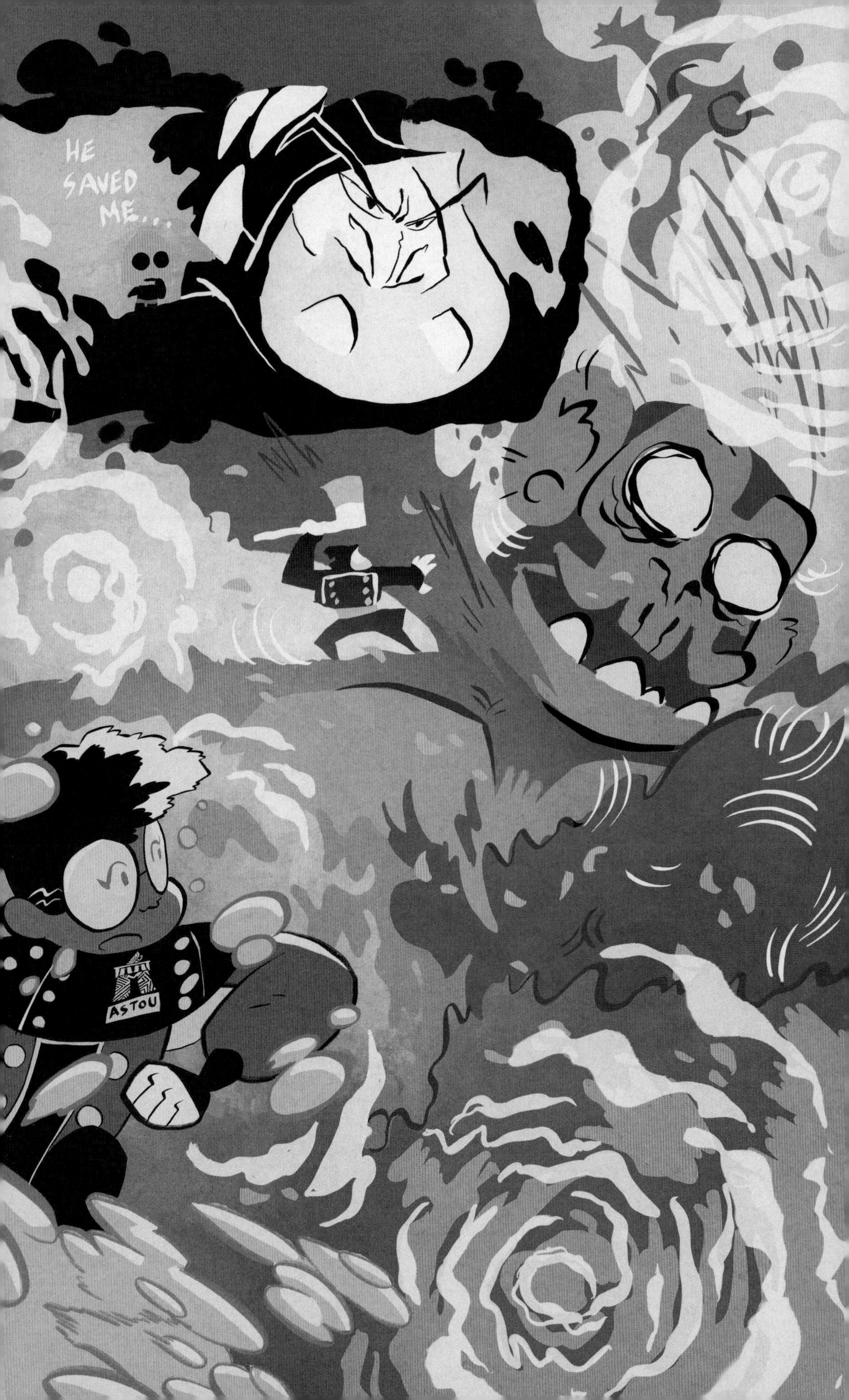
HE SAVED ME...
ASTOU

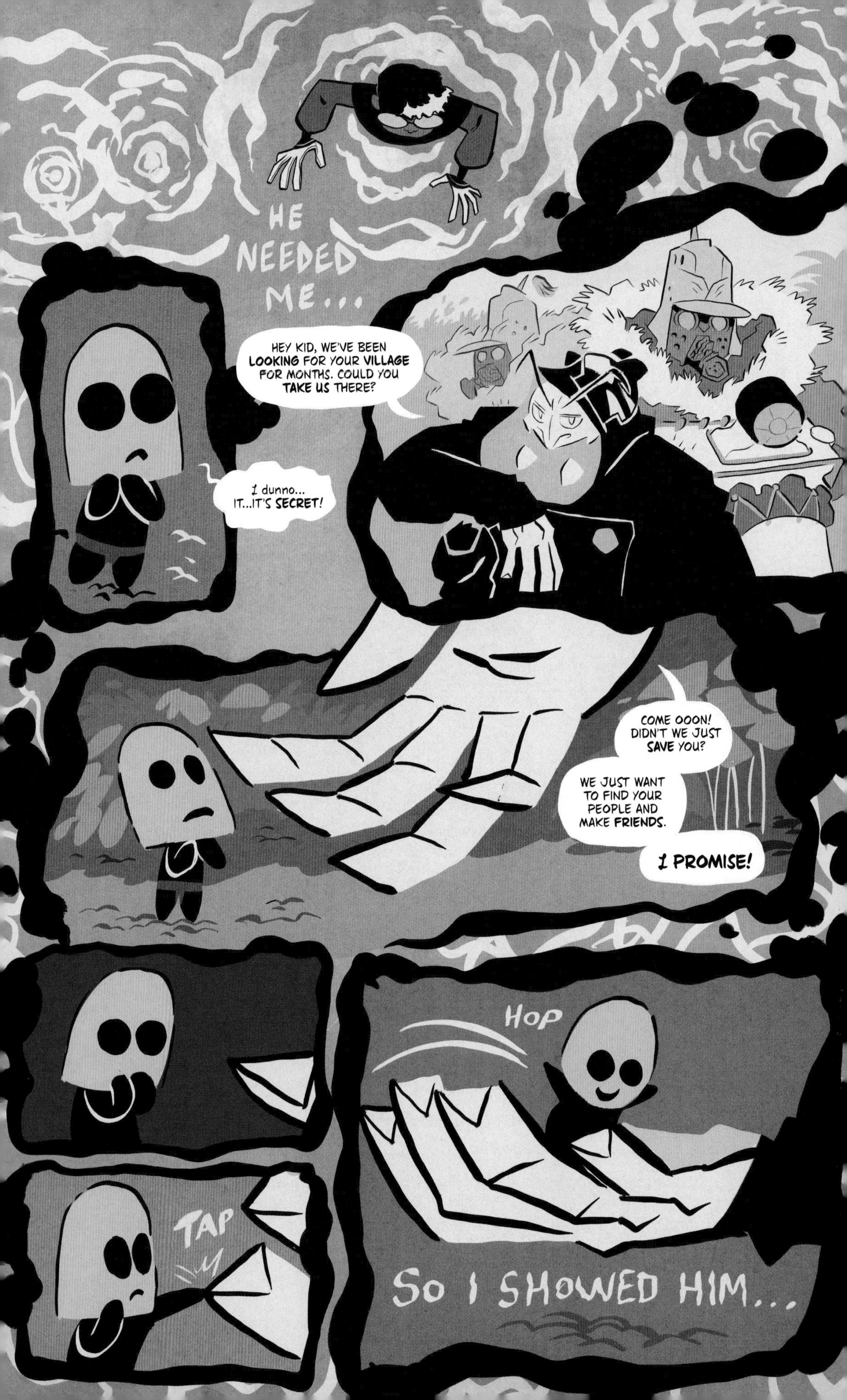
HE NEEDED ME...
HEY KID, WE'VE BEEN LOOKING FOR YOUR VILLAGE FOR MONTHS. COULD YOU TAKE US THERE?
I dunno... IT...IT'S SECRET!
COME OOON! DIDN'T WE JUST SAVE YOU?
WE JUST WANT TO FIND YOUR PEOPLE AND MAKE FRIENDS.
I PROMISE!
TAP
HOP
So I SHOWED HIM...

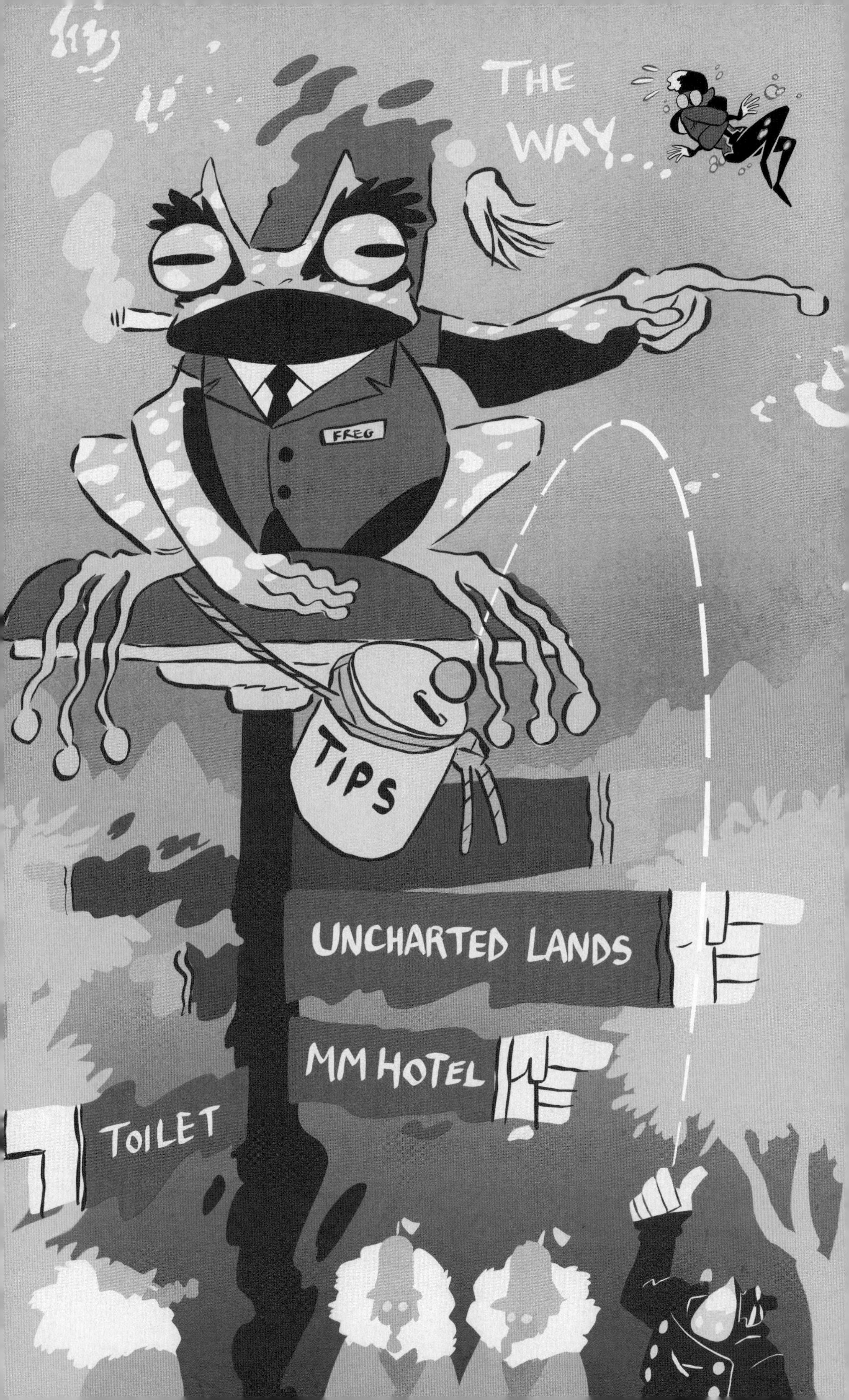
THE WAY...
FREG
TIPS
UNCHARTED LANDS
MM HOTEL
TOILET

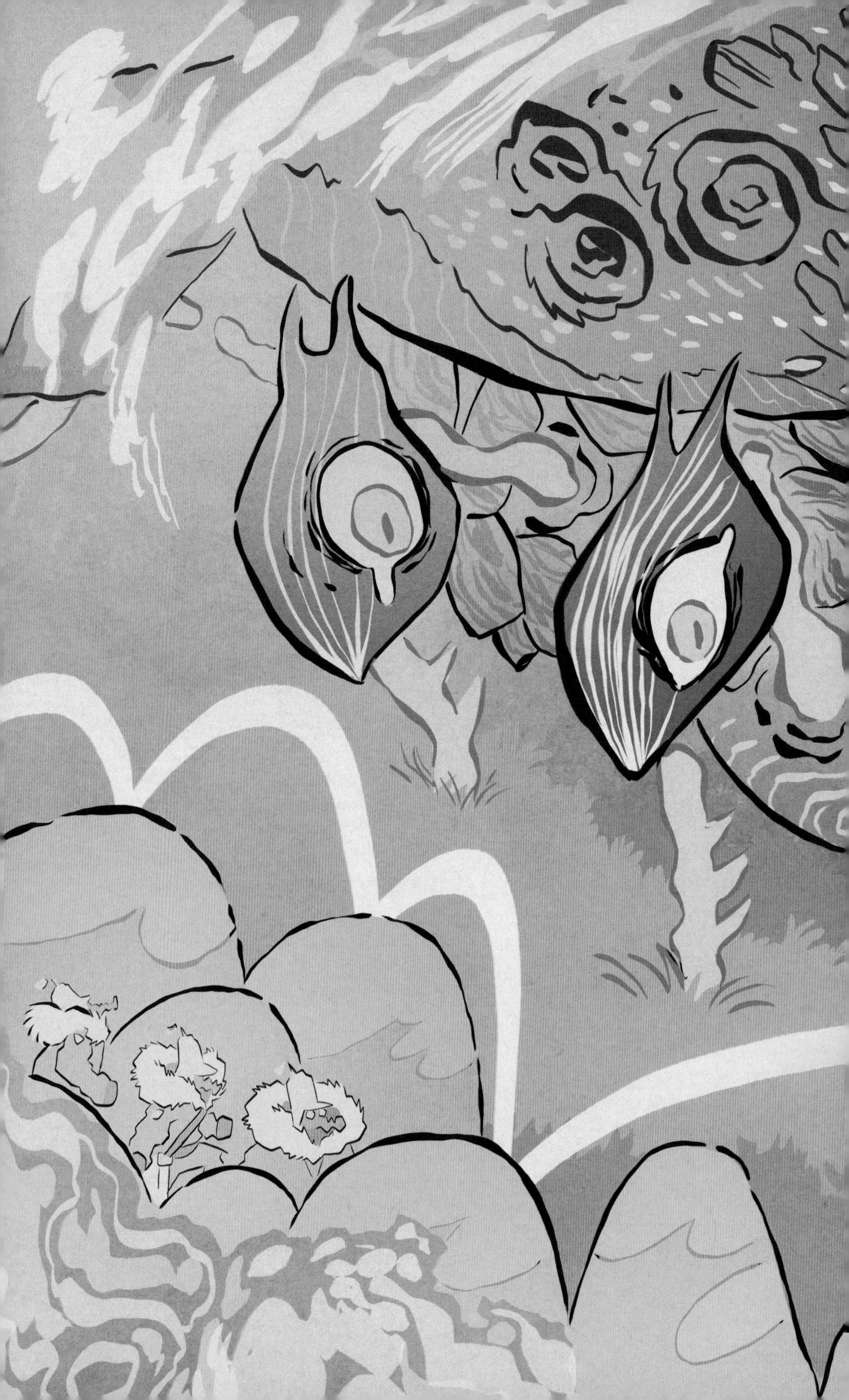

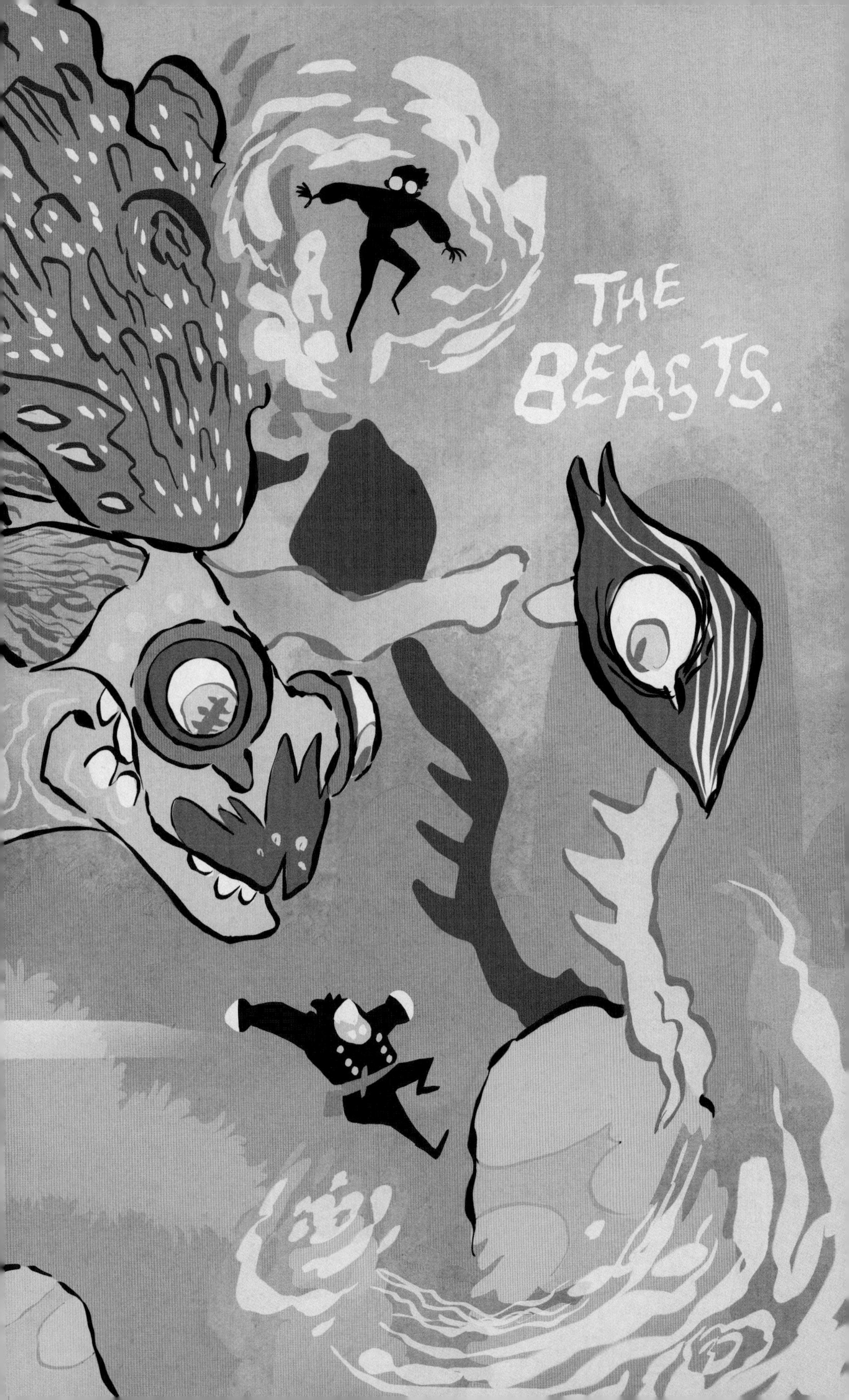
THE BEASTS.

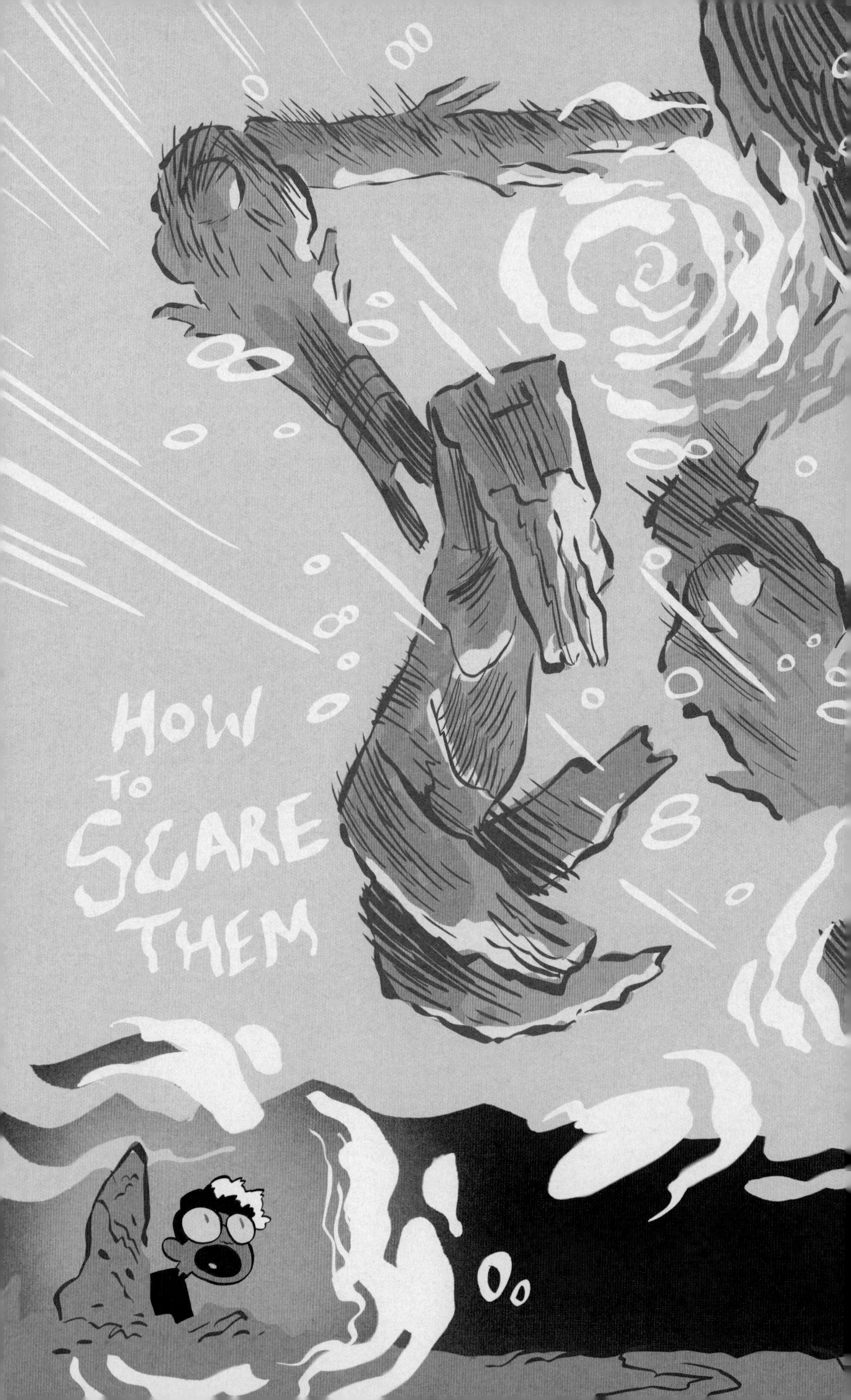
HOW
TO
SCARE
THEM

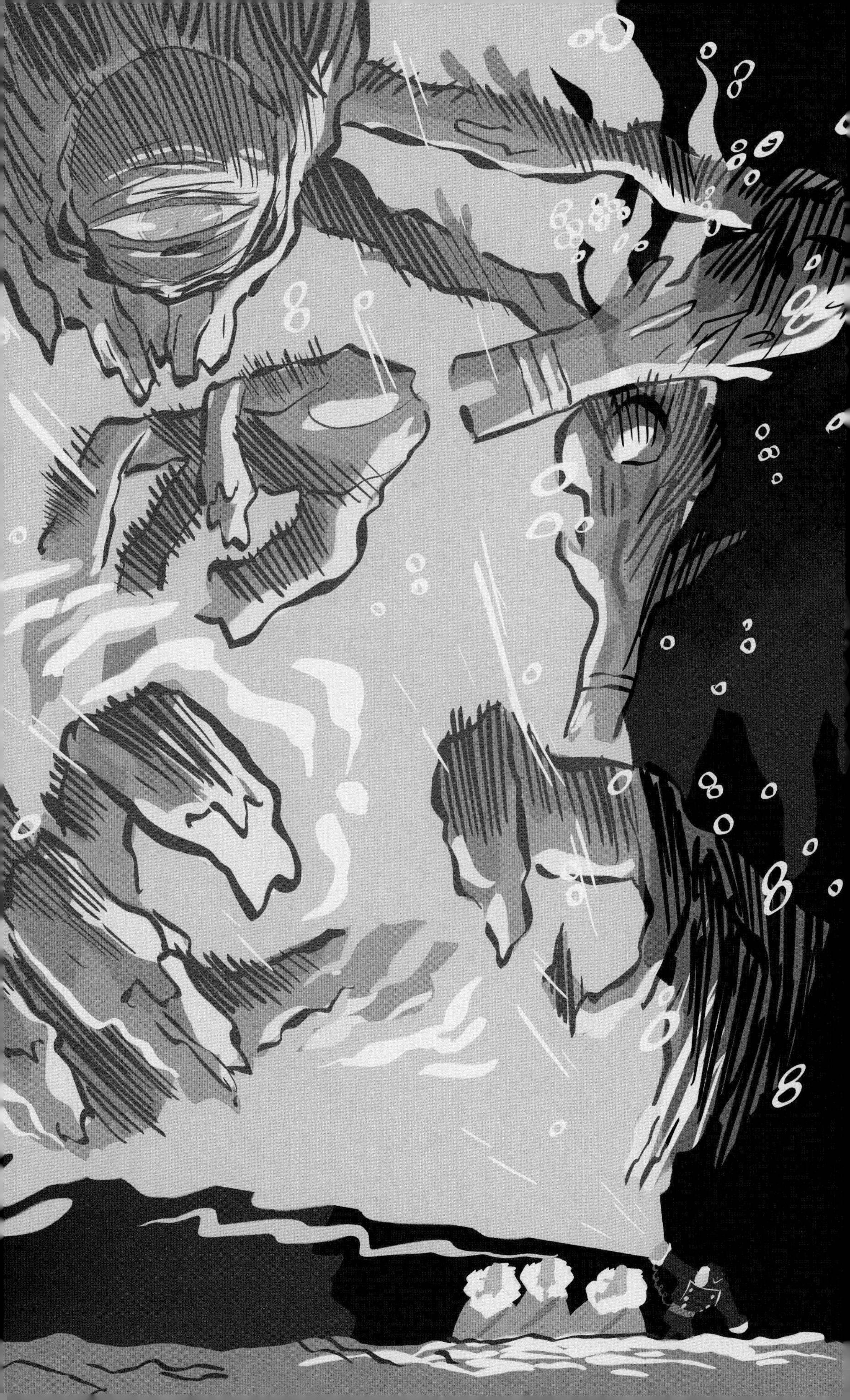

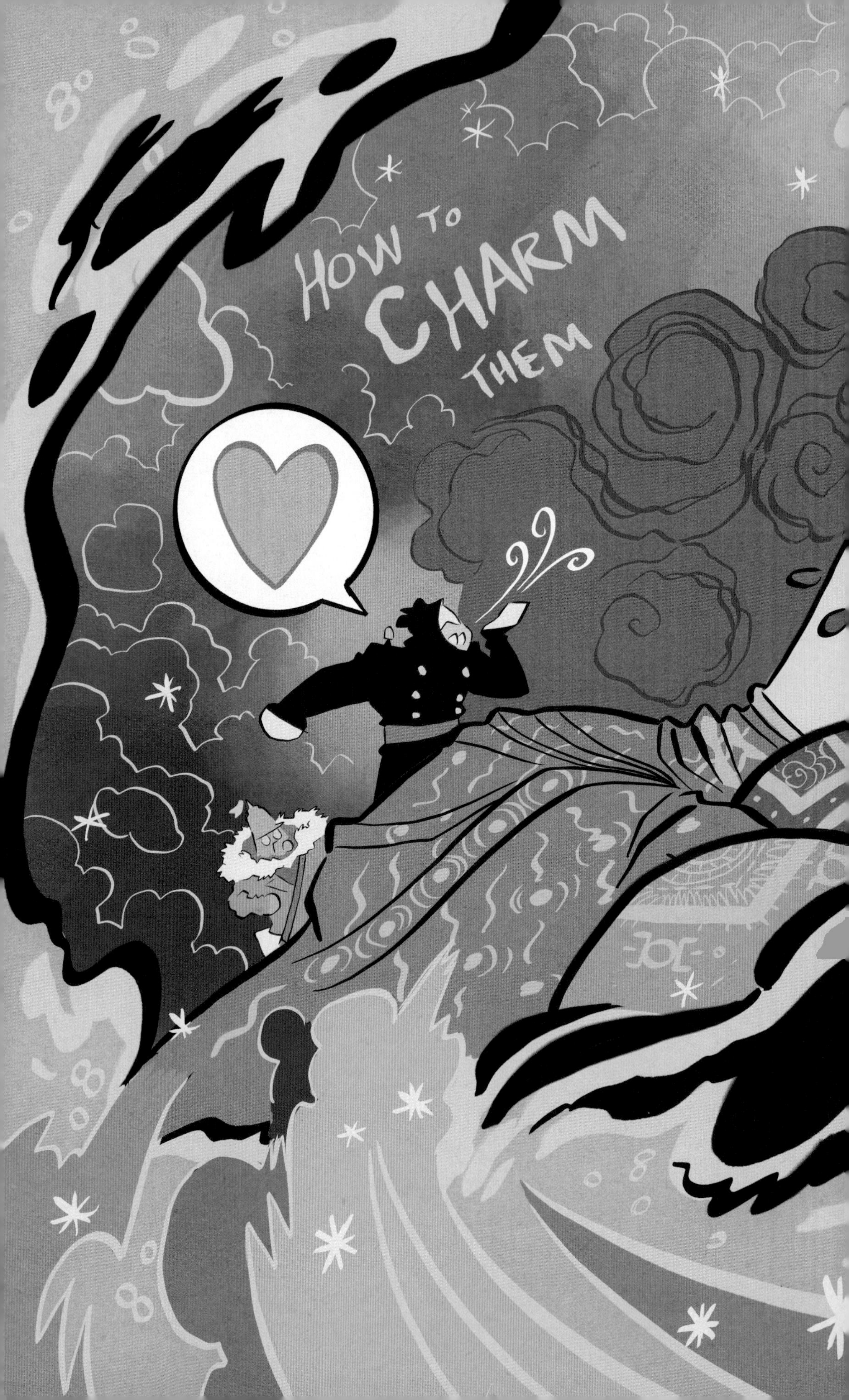
HOW TO
CHARM
THEM

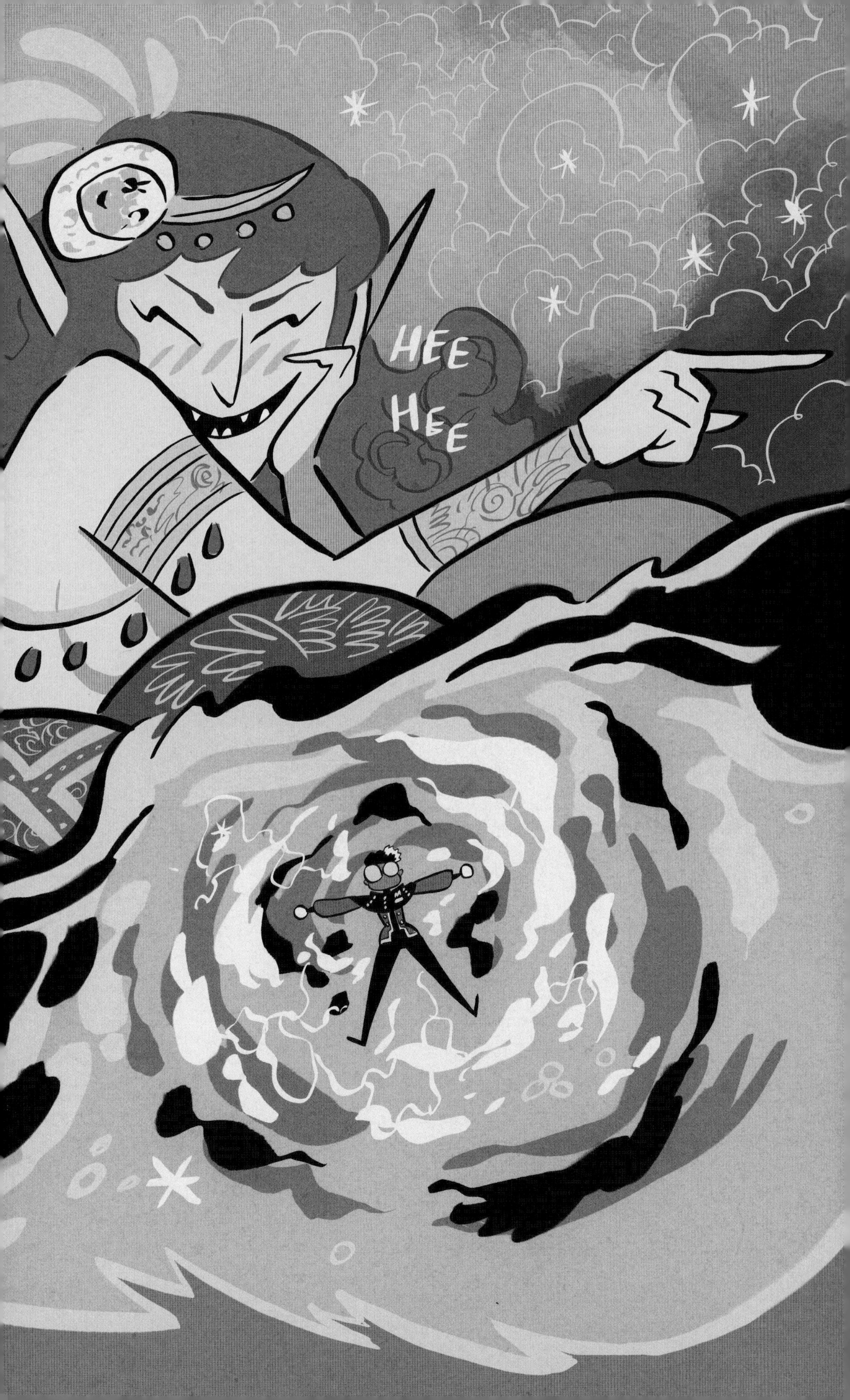
HEE
HEE

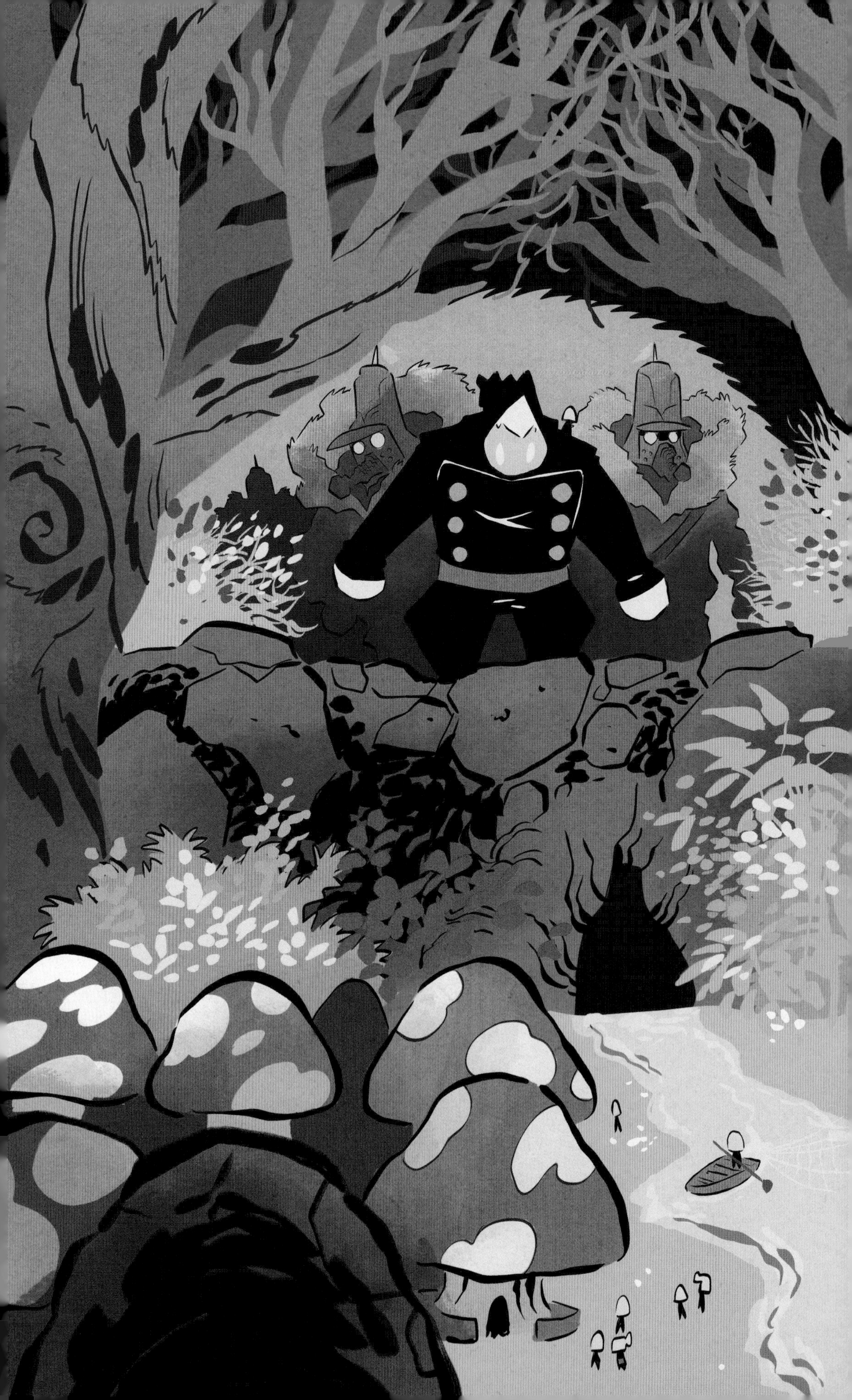

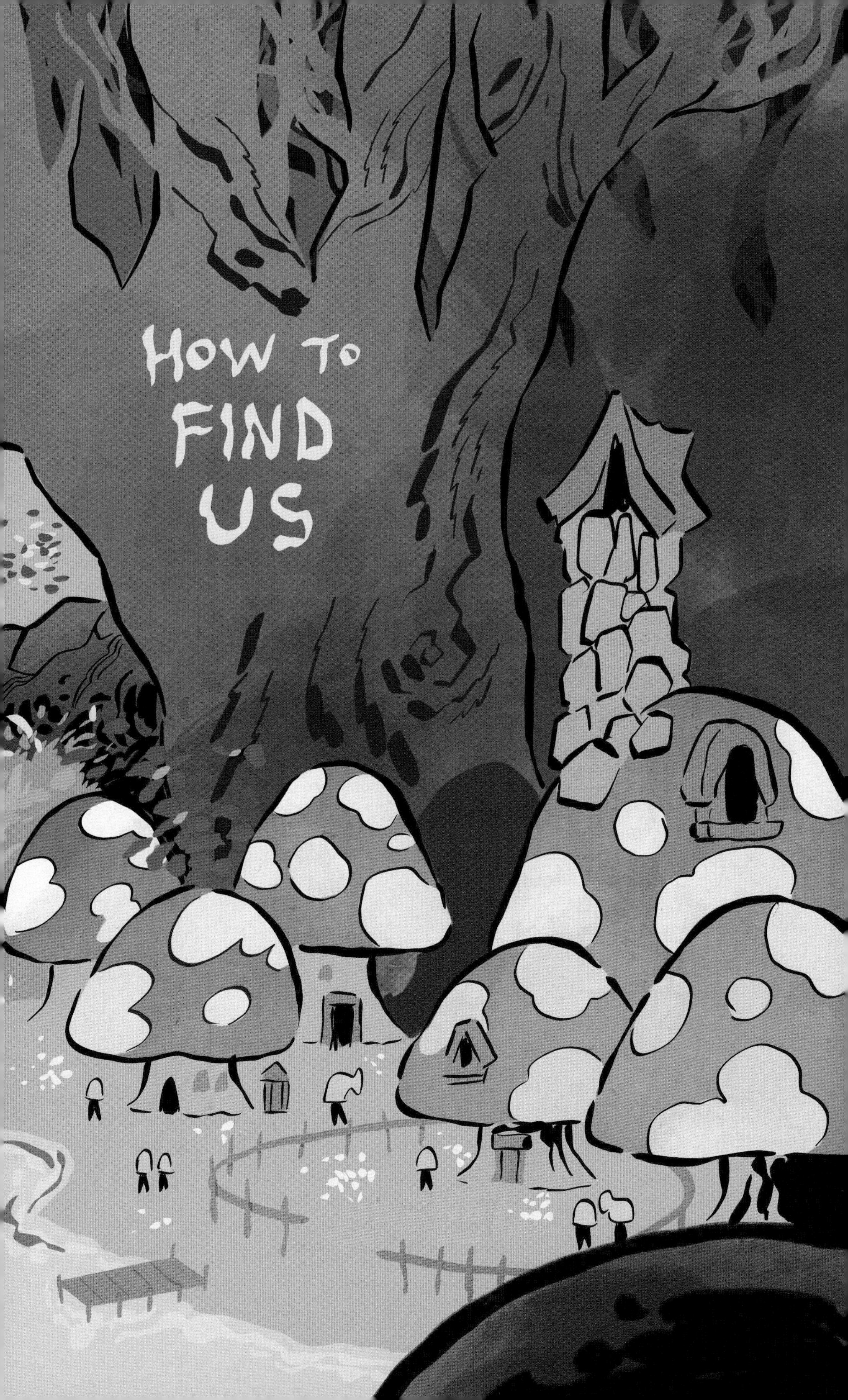
HOW TO
FIND
US

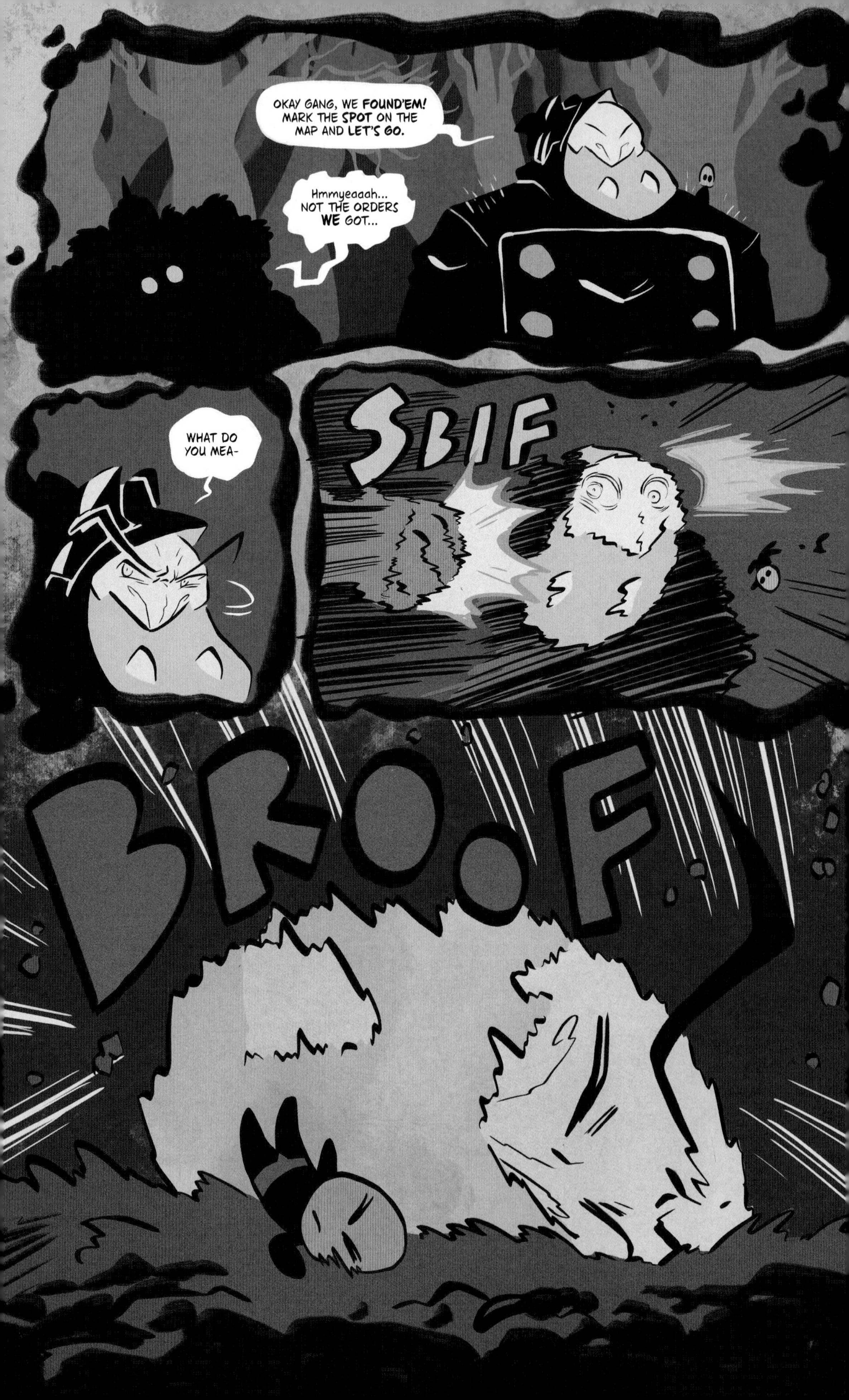

OKAY GANG, WE FOUND'EM! MARK THE SPOT ON THE MAP AND LET'S GO.
Hmmyeaaah... NOT THE ORDERS WE GOT...
WHAT DO YOU MEA-
SBIF
BROOF

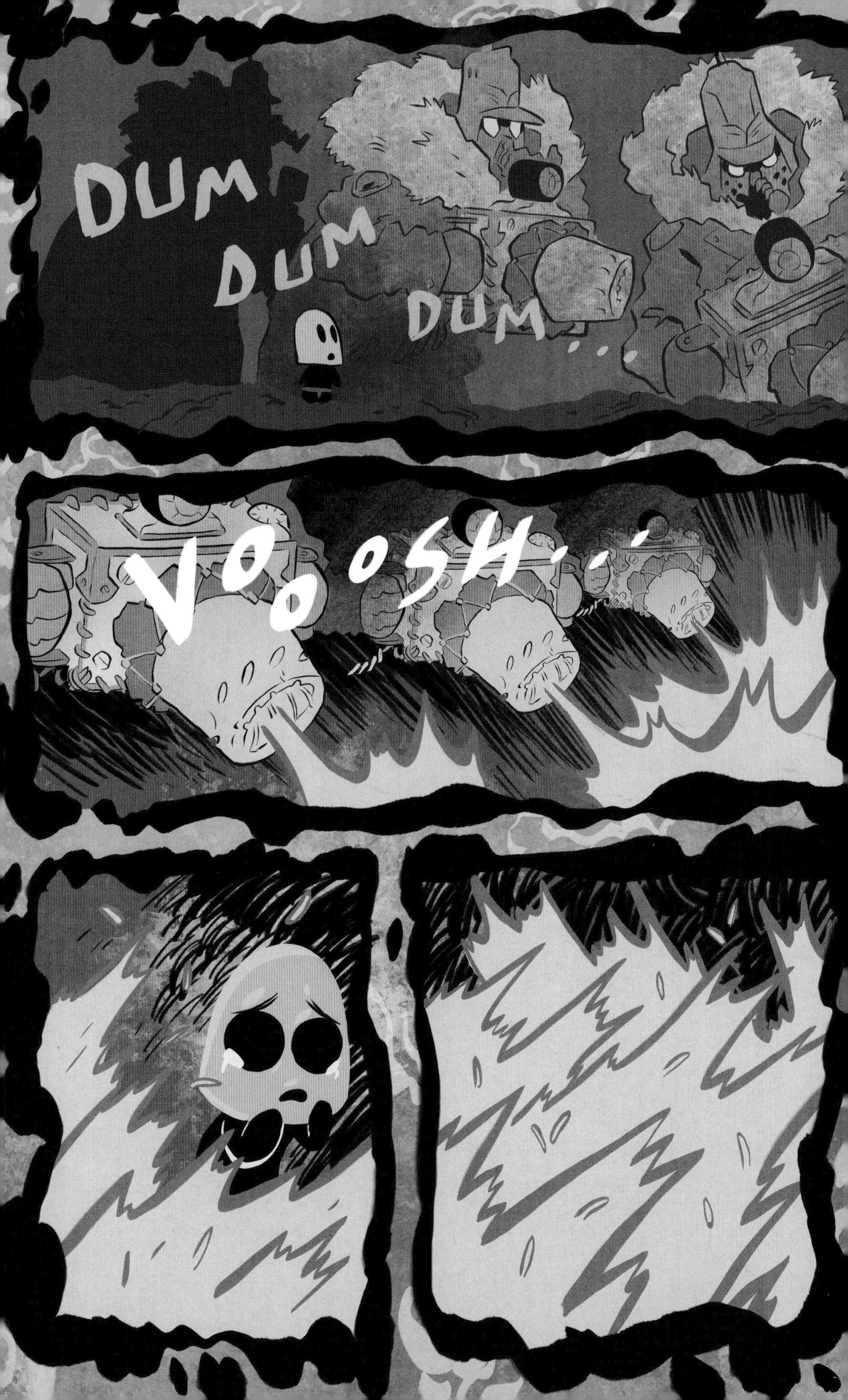
DUM
DUM
DUM...
VOOOSH...

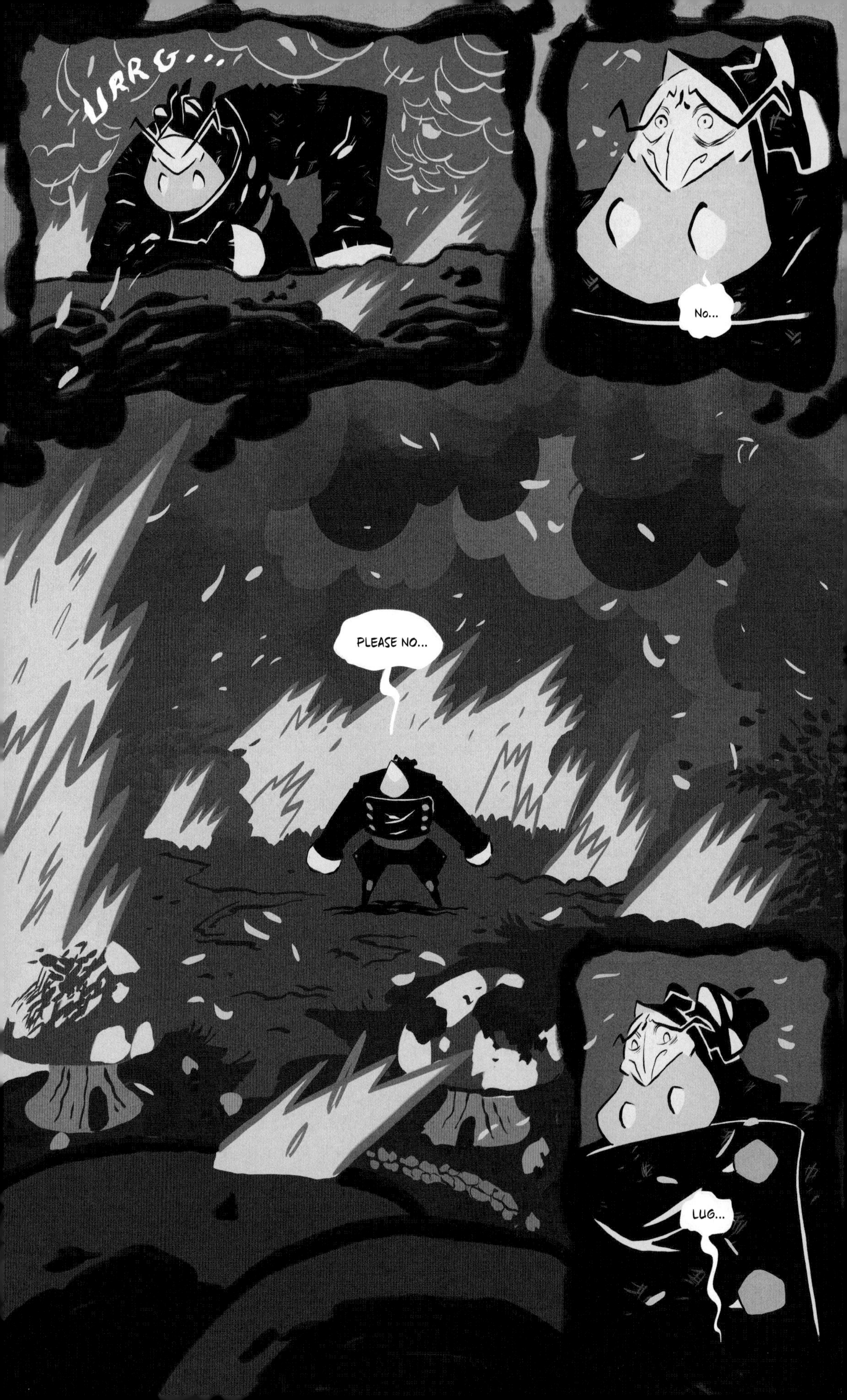
URRG...
NO...
PLEASE NO...
LUG...

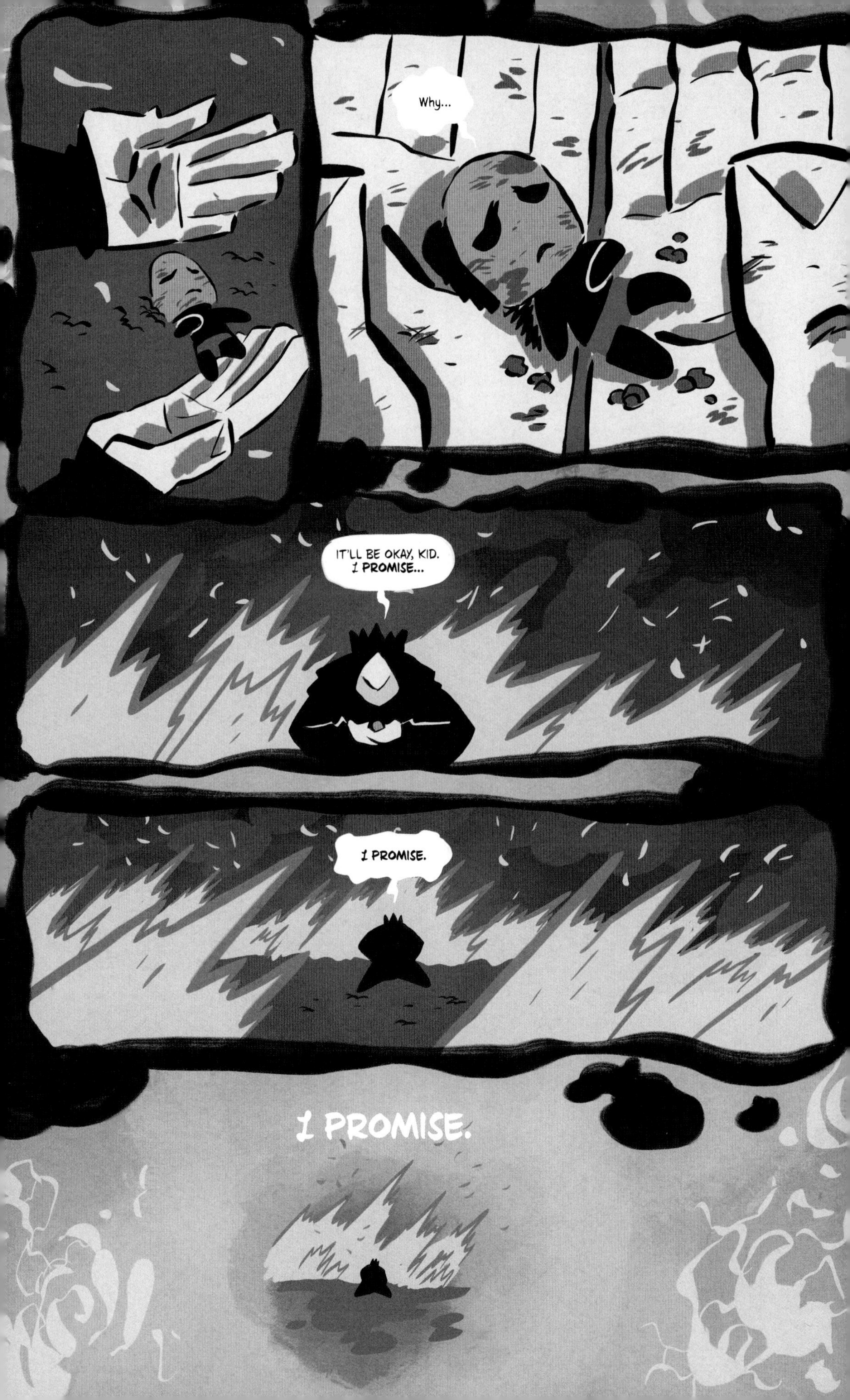
Why...
IT'LL BE OKAY, KID.
I PROMISE...
I PROMISE.
I PROMISE.

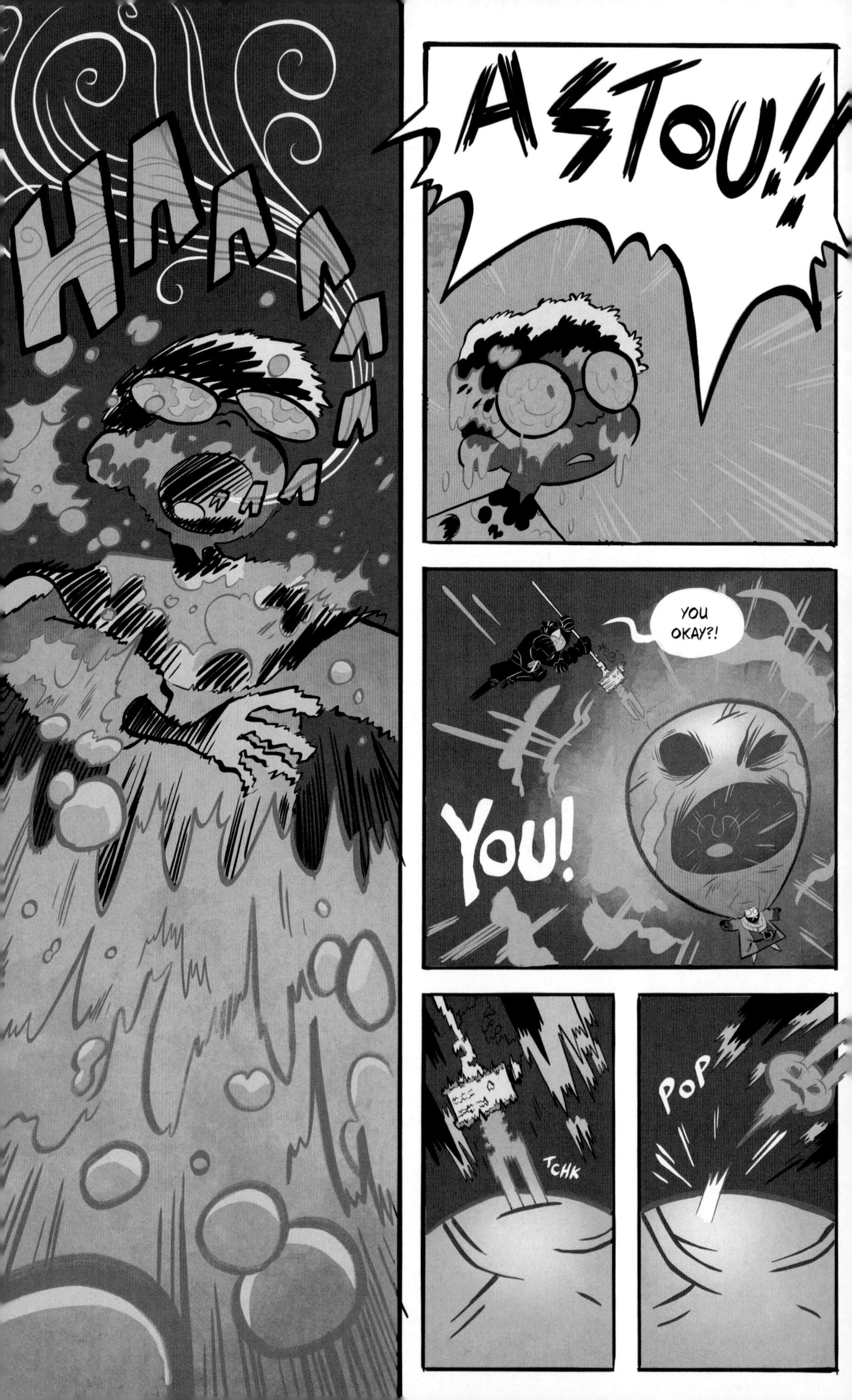
HAAAC!!!
ASTOU!!
YOU OKAY?!
YOU!
TCHK
POP

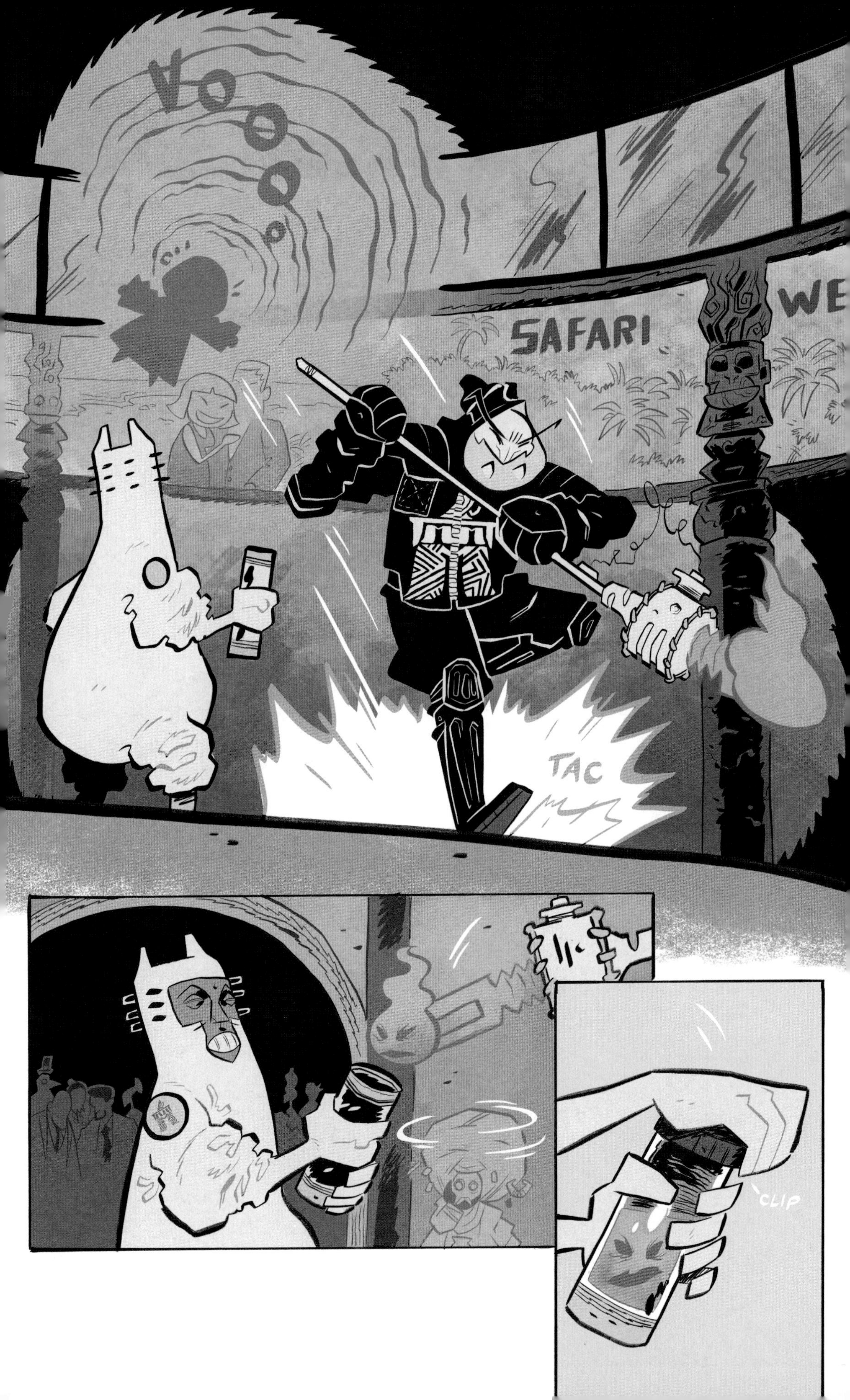
VOOOOO
SAFARI
WE
TAC
CLIP

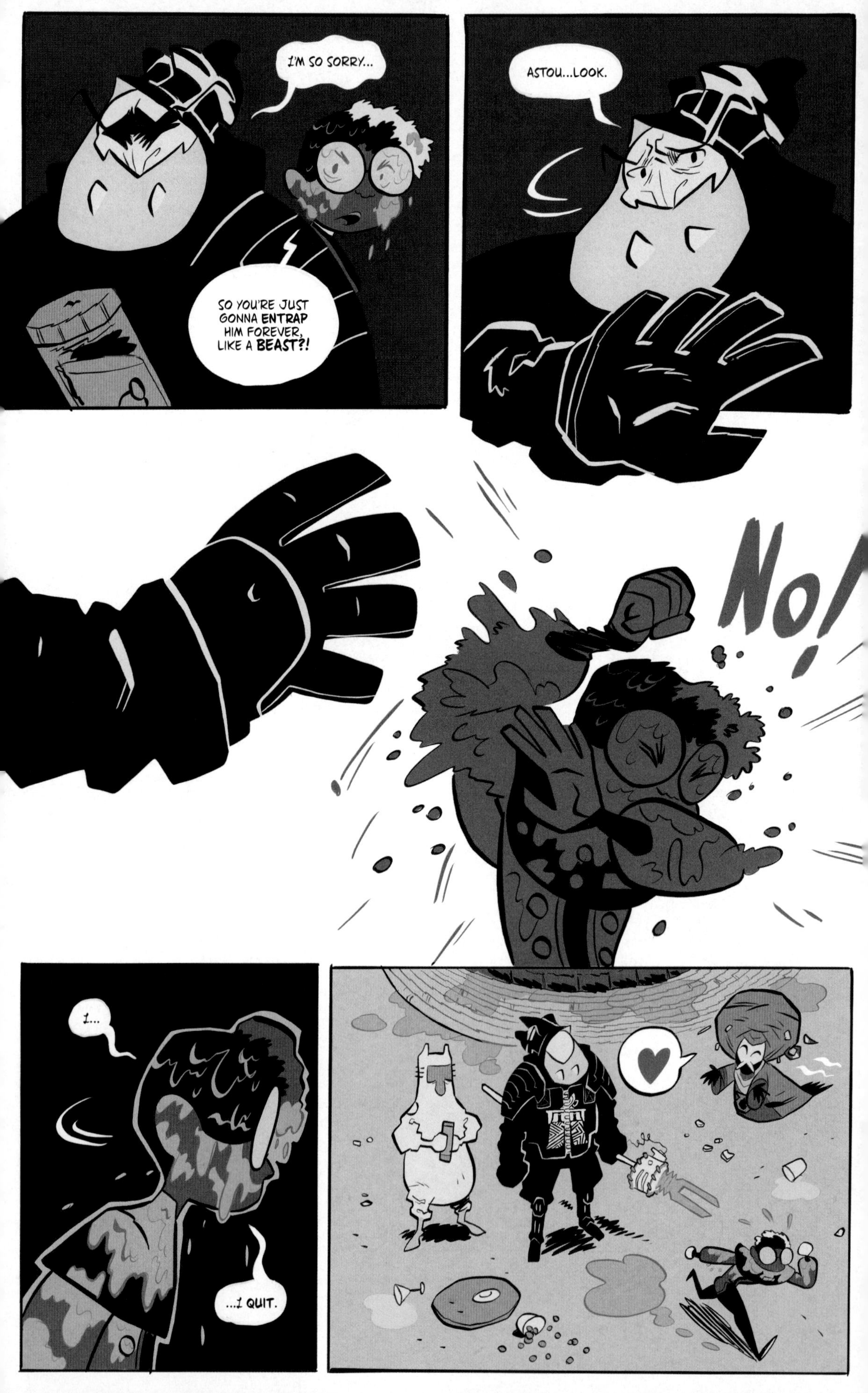
I'M SO SORRY...
SO YOU'RE JUST GONNA ENTRAP HIM FOREVER, LIKE A BEAST?!
ASTOU...LOOK.
No!
I...
...I QUIT.

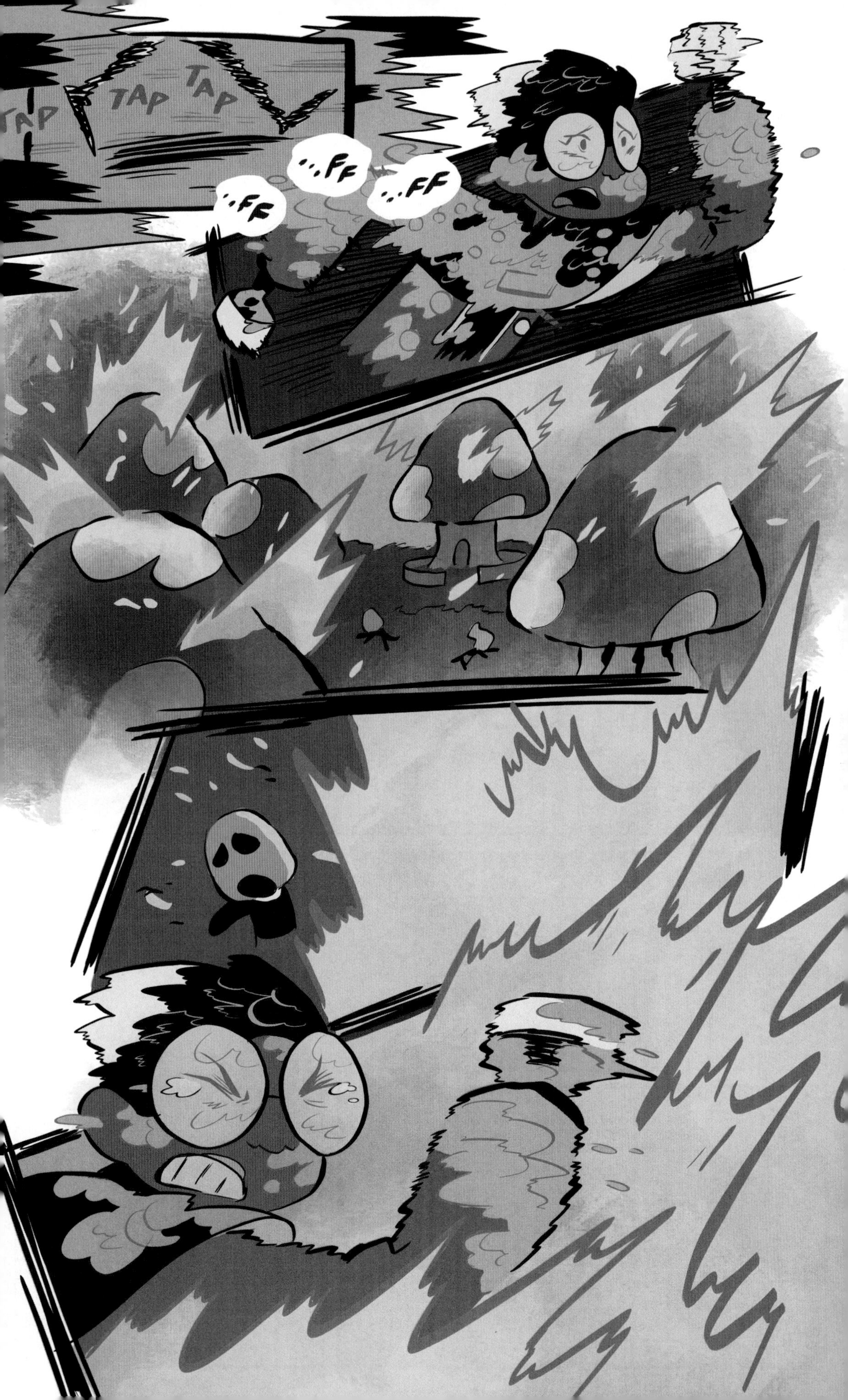
TAP
TAP
TAP
..FF
..FF
..FF

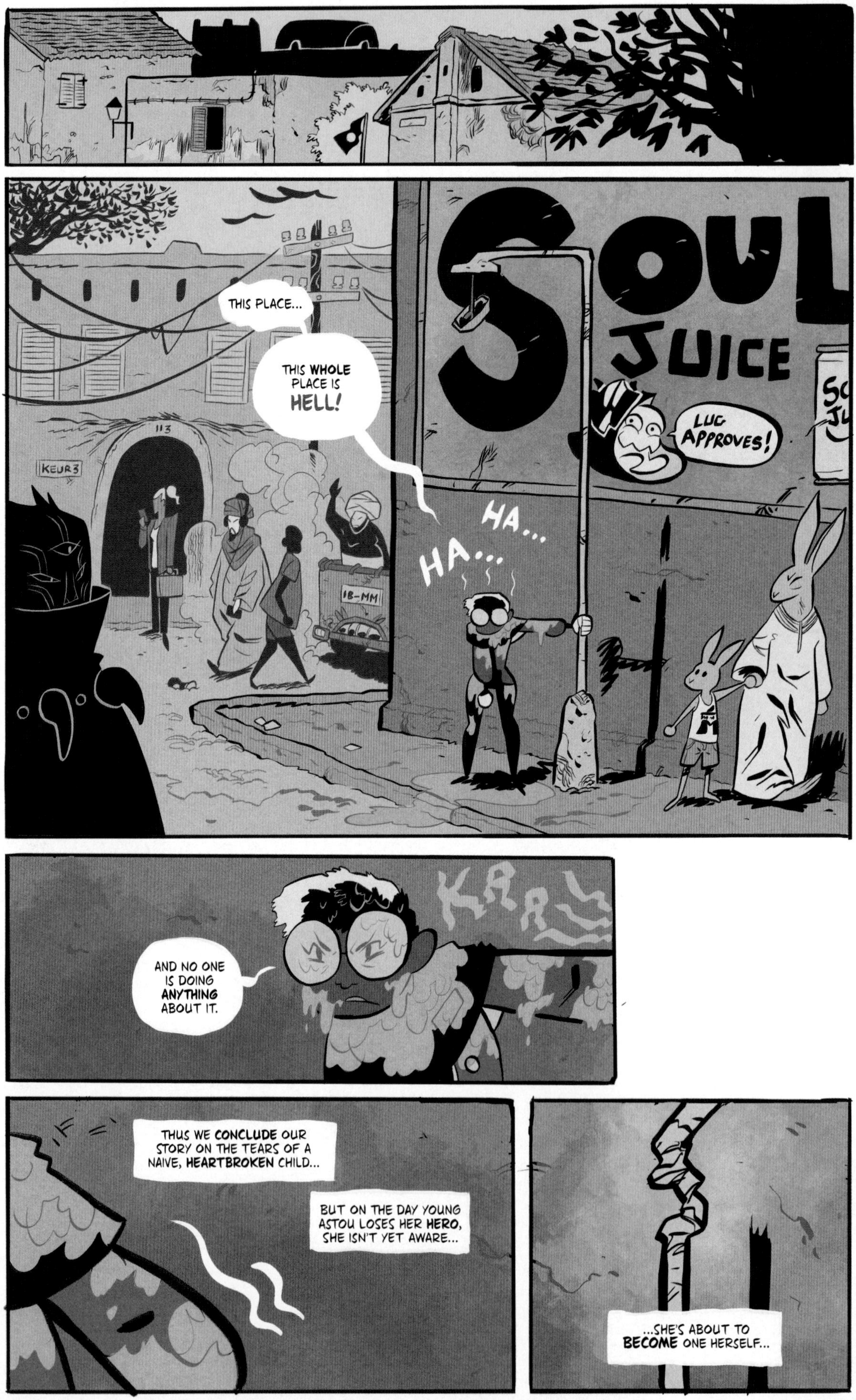
SOUL
JUICE
113
KEUR3
THIS PLACE...
THIS WHOLE PLACE IS HELL!
IB-MM
LUG APPROVES!
HA...
HA...
AND NO ONE IS DOING ANYTHING ABOUT IT.
THUS WE CONCLUDE OUR STORY ON THE TEARS OF A NAIVE, HEARTBROKEN CHILD...
BUT ON THE DAY YOUNG ASTOU LOSES HER HERO, SHE ISN'T YET AWARE...
...SHE'S ABOUT TO BECOME ONE HERSELF...

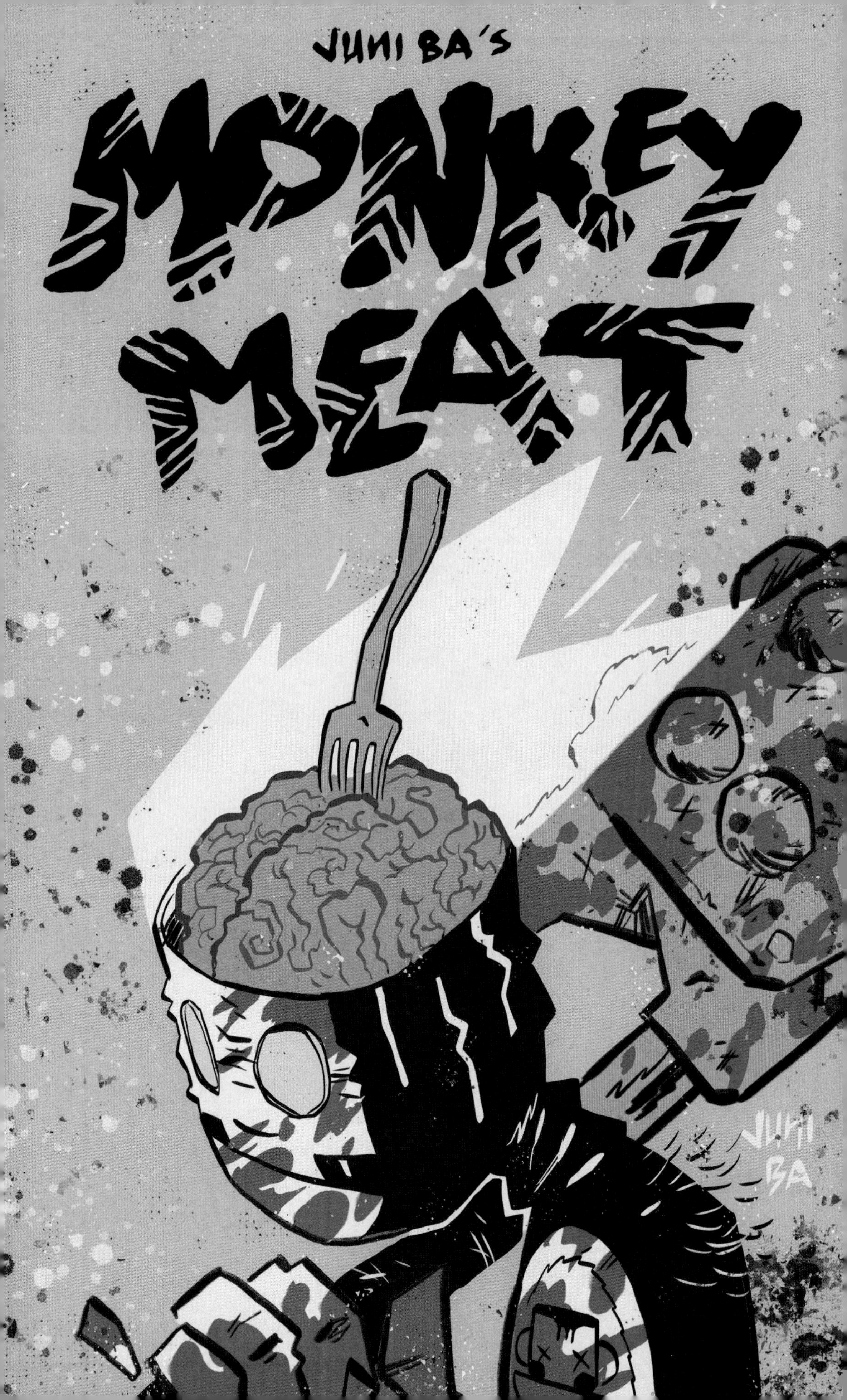
JUNI BA'S
MONKEY MEAT
JUNI BA

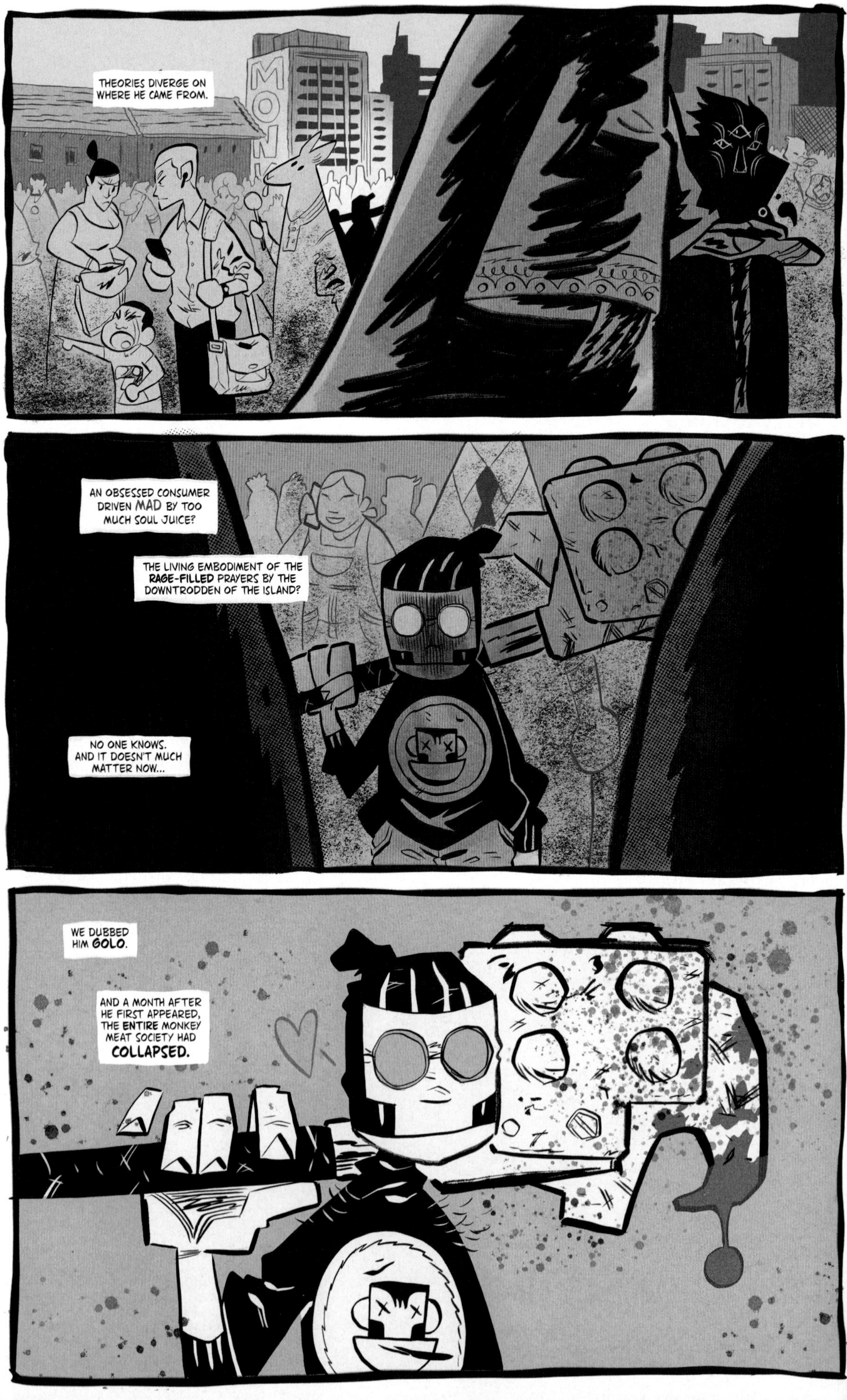
THEORIES DIVERGE ON WHERE HE CAME FROM.
MON
AN OBSESSED CONSUMER DRIVEN MAD BY TOO MUCH SOUL JUICE?
THE LIVING EMBODIMENT OF THE RAGE-FILLED PRAYERS BY THE DOWNTRODDEN OF THE ISLAND?
NO ONE KNOWS. AND IT DOESN'T MUCH MATTER NOW...
WE DUBBED HIM GOLO.
AND A MONTH AFTER HE FIRST APPEARED, THE ENTIRE MONKEY MEAT SOCIETY HAD COLLAPSED.

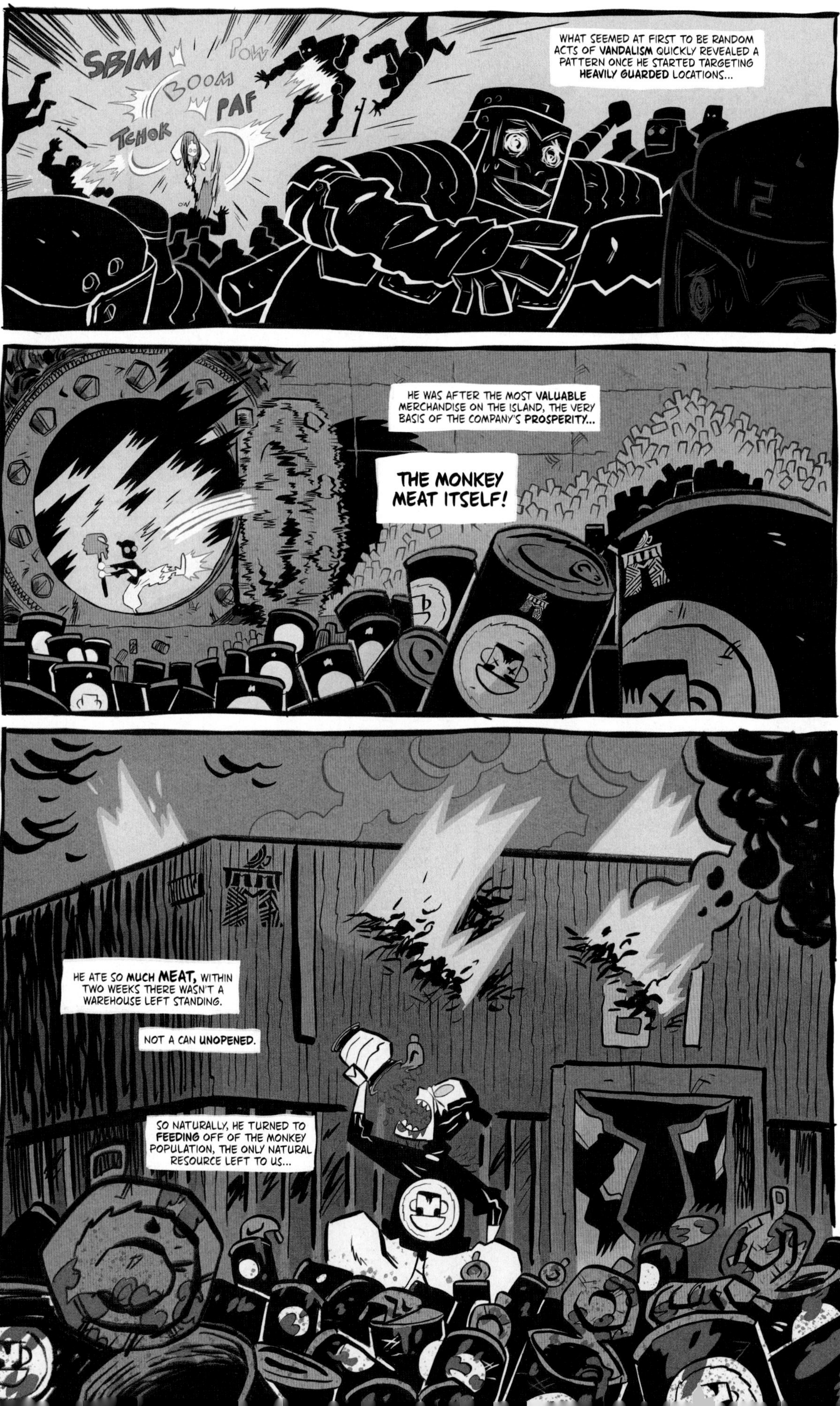
WHAT SEEMED AT FIRST TO BE RANDOM ACTS OF VANDALISM QUICKLY REVEALED A PATTERN ONCE HE STARTED TARGETING HEAVILY GUARDED LOCATIONS...
SBIM
POW
BOOM
PAF
TCHOK
OW
HE WAS AFTER THE MOST VALUABLE MERCHANDISE ON THE ISLAND, THE VERY BASIS OF THE COMPANY'S PROSPERITY...
THE MONKEY MEAT ITSELF!
HE ATE SO MUCH MEAT, WITHIN TWO WEEKS THERE WASN'T A WAREHOUSE LEFT STANDING.
NOT A CAN UNOPENED.
SO NATURALLY, HE TURNED TO FEEDING OFF OF THE MONKEY POPULATION, THE ONLY NATURAL RESOURCE LEFT TO US...

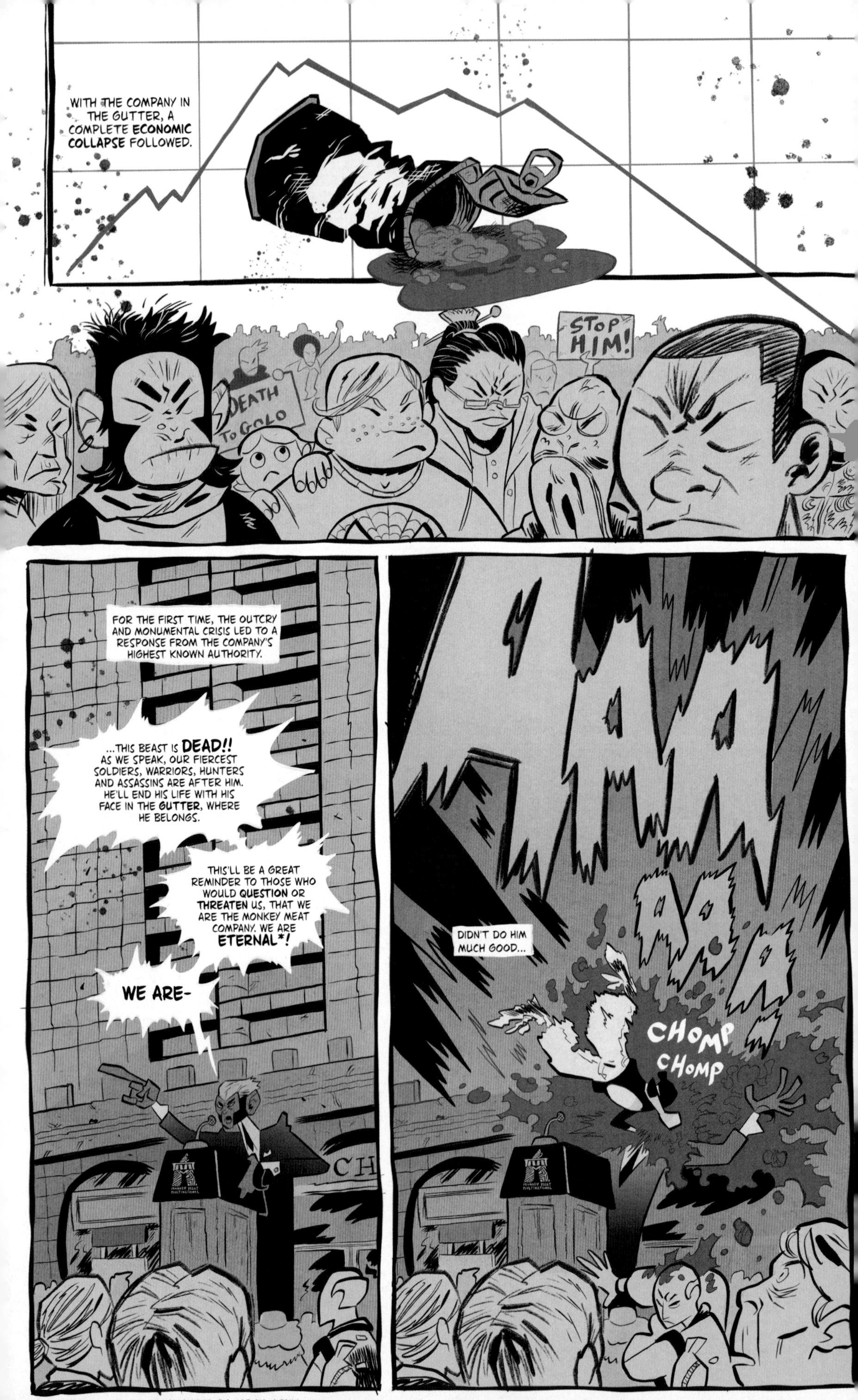
WITH THE COMPANY IN THE GUTTER, A COMPLETE **ECONOMIC COLLAPSE** FOLLOWED.
DEATH TO GOLO
STOP HIM!
FOR THE FIRST TIME, THE OUTCRY AND MONUMENTAL CRISIS LED TO A RESPONSE FROM THE COMPANY'S HIGHEST KNOWN AUTHORITY.
...THIS BEAST IS **DEAD!!** AS WE SPEAK, OUR FIERCEST SOLDIERS, WARRIORS, HUNTERS AND ASSASSINS ARE AFTER HIM. HE'LL END HIS LIFE WITH HIS FACE IN THE **GUTTER**, WHERE HE BELONGS.
THIS'LL BE A GREAT REMINDER TO THOSE WHO WOULD **QUESTION** OR **THREATEN** US, THAT WE ARE THE MONKEY MEAT COMPANY. WE ARE **ETERNAL***!
WE ARE-
DIDN'T DO HIM MUCH GOOD...
CHOMP
CHOMP

*THE WORD IS NOT YET COPYRIGHTED BY MARVEL AFAIK

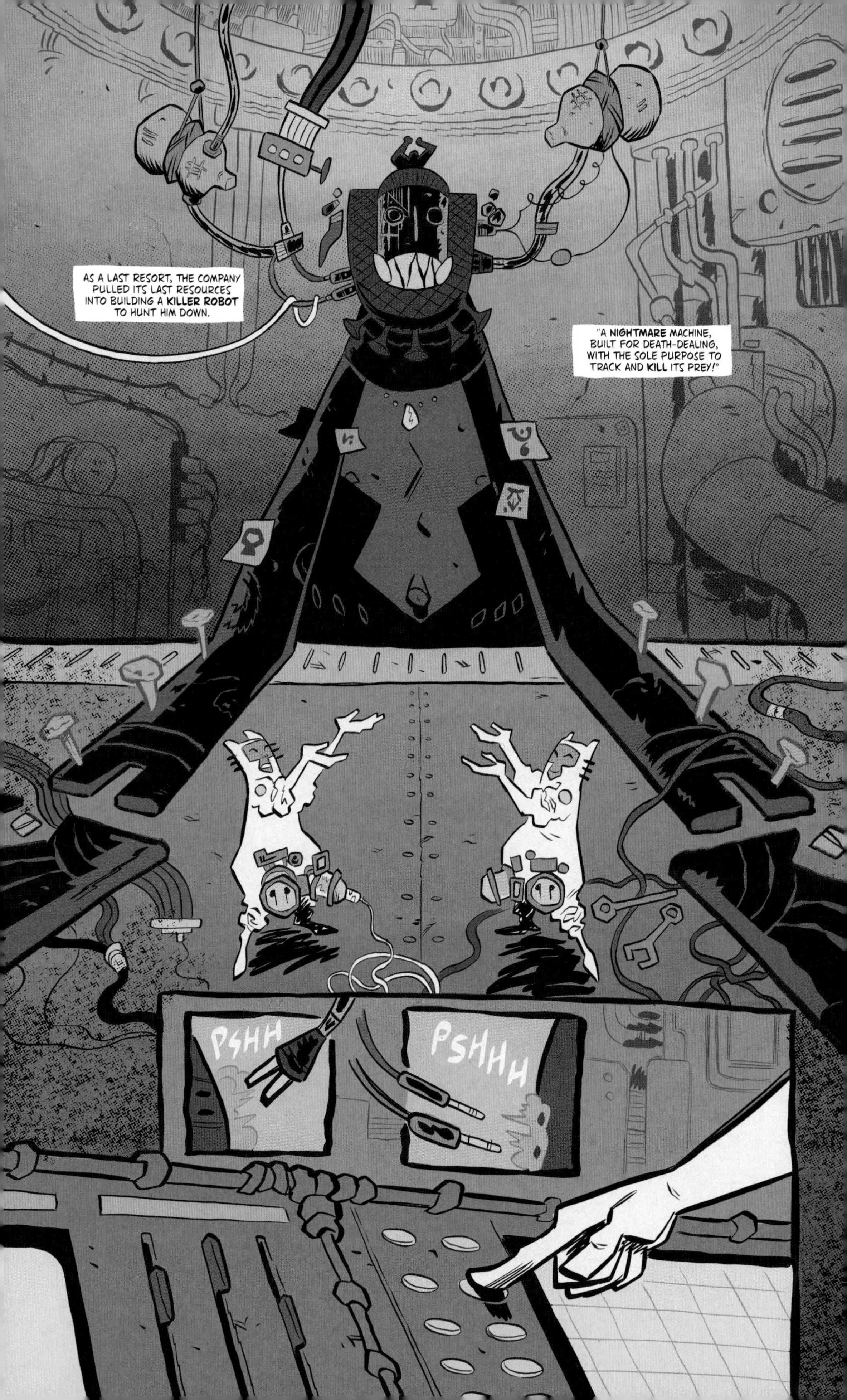

AS A LAST RESORT, THE COMPANY PULLED ITS LAST RESOURCES INTO BUILDING A KILLER ROBOT TO HUNT HIM DOWN.
"A NIGHTMARE MACHINE, BUILT FOR DEATH-DEALING, WITH THE SOLE PURPOSE TO TRACK AND KILL ITS PREY!"
PSHH
PSHHH

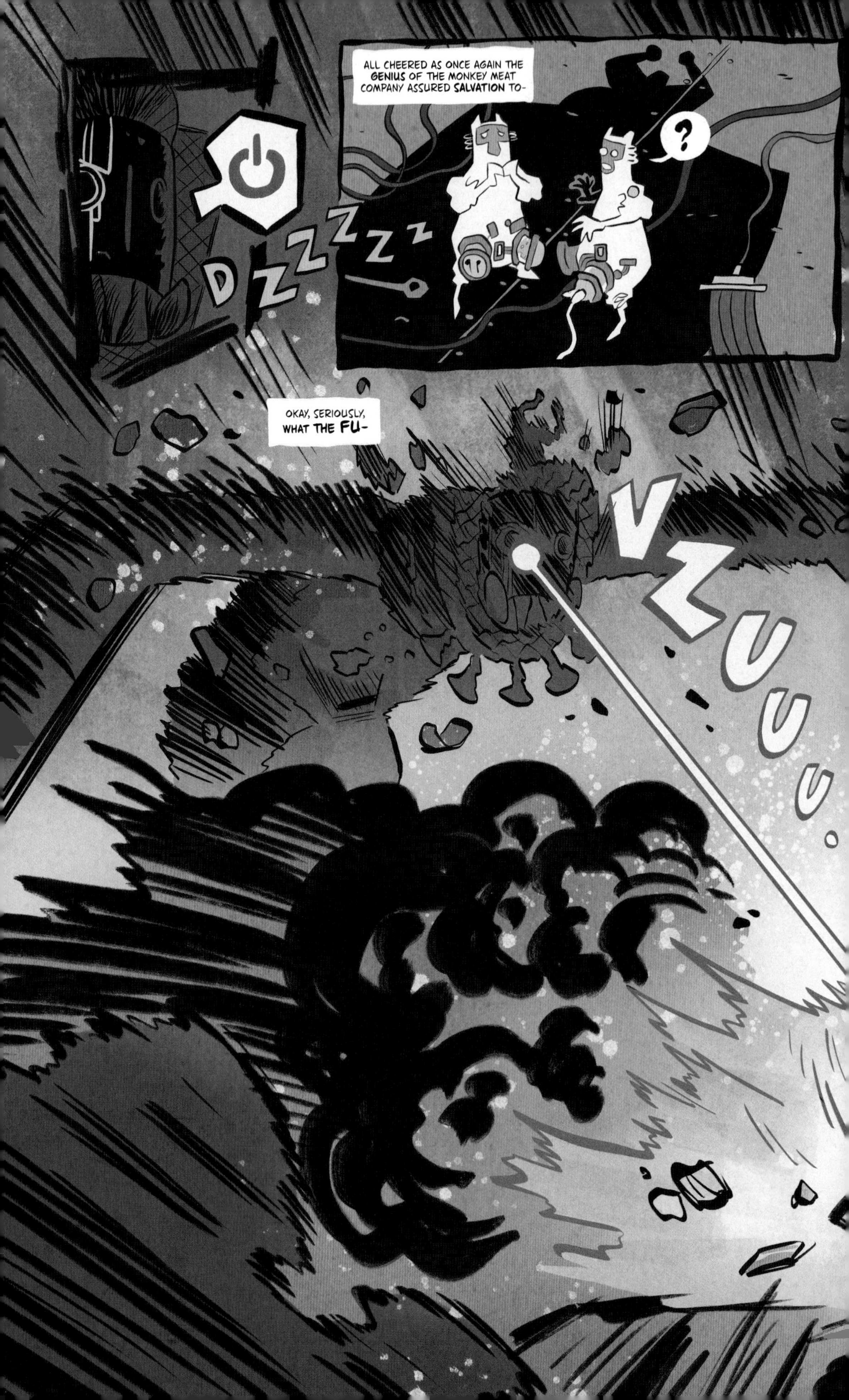
DZZZZZZZ
ALL CHEERED AS ONCE AGAIN THE GENIUS OF THE MONKEY MEAT COMPANY ASSURED SALVATION TO-
?
OKAY, SERIOUSLY, WHAT THE FU-
VZUUUUU

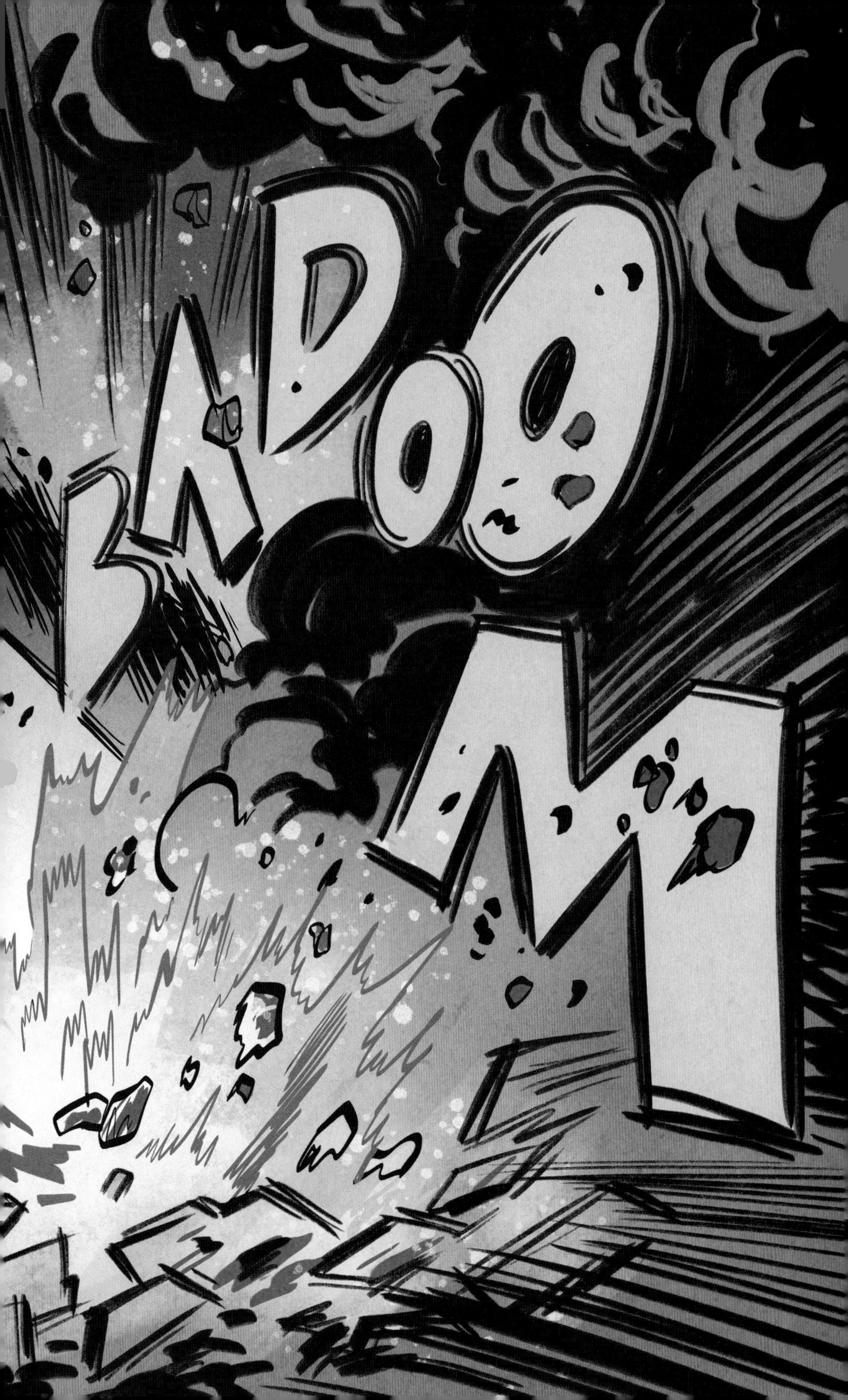
KADOOM

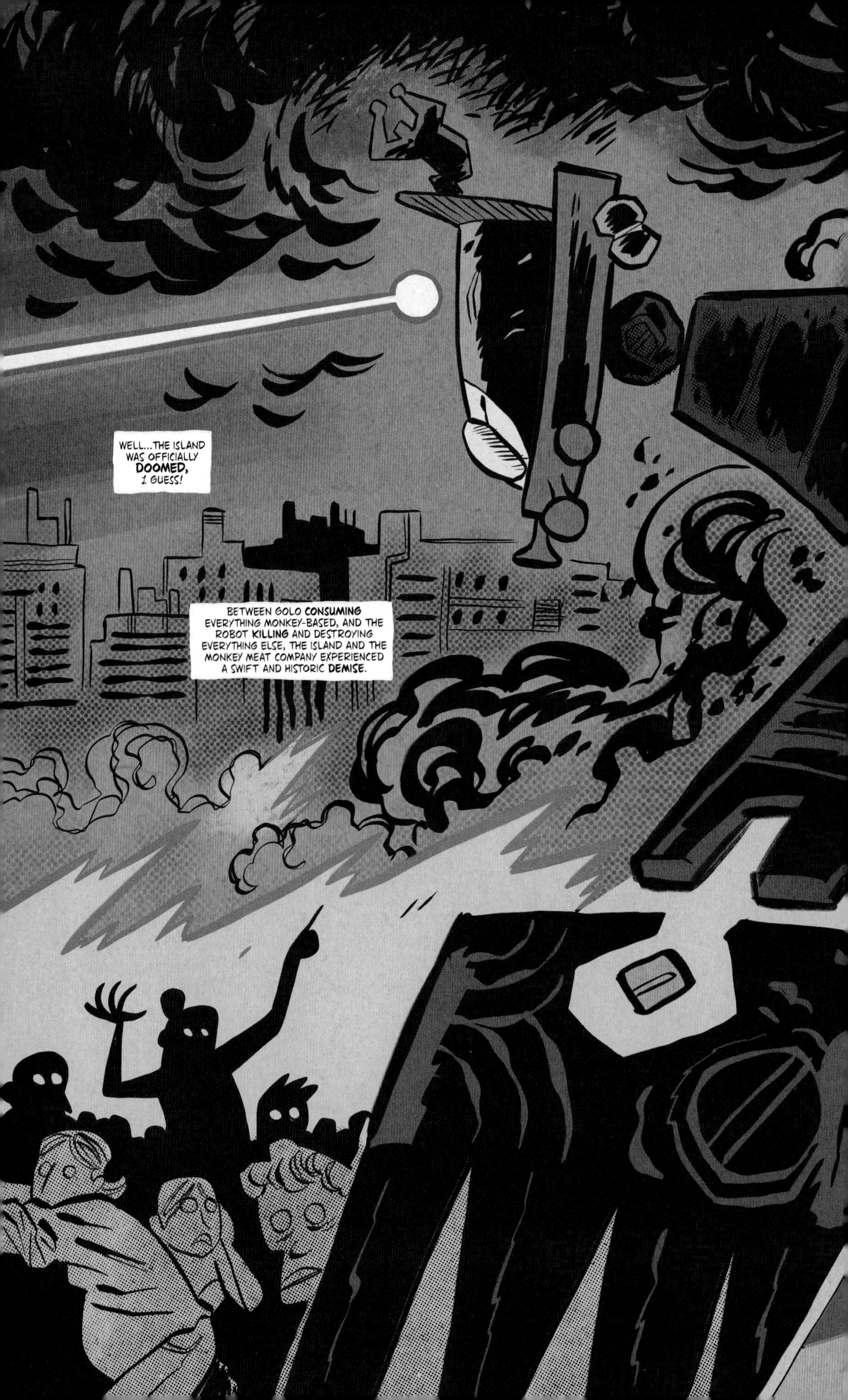
WELL...THE ISLAND WAS OFFICIALLY **DOOMED,** I GUESS!
BETWEEN GOLO **CONSUMING** EVERYTHING MONKEY-BASED, AND THE ROBOT **KILLING** AND DESTROYING EVERYTHING ELSE, THE ISLAND AND THE MONKEY MEAT COMPANY EXPERIENCED A SWIFT AND HISTORIC **DEMISE**.

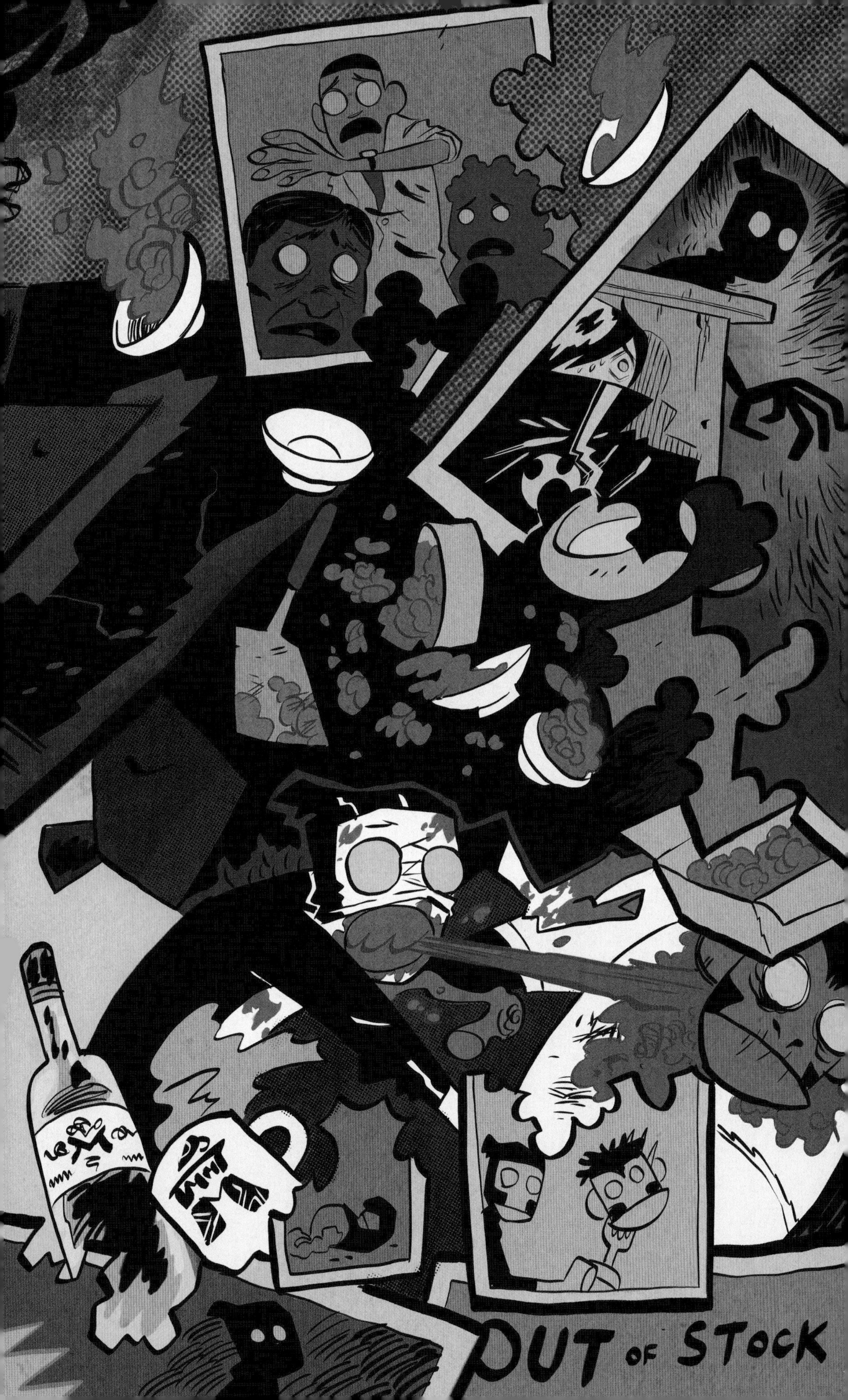
OUT of STOCK

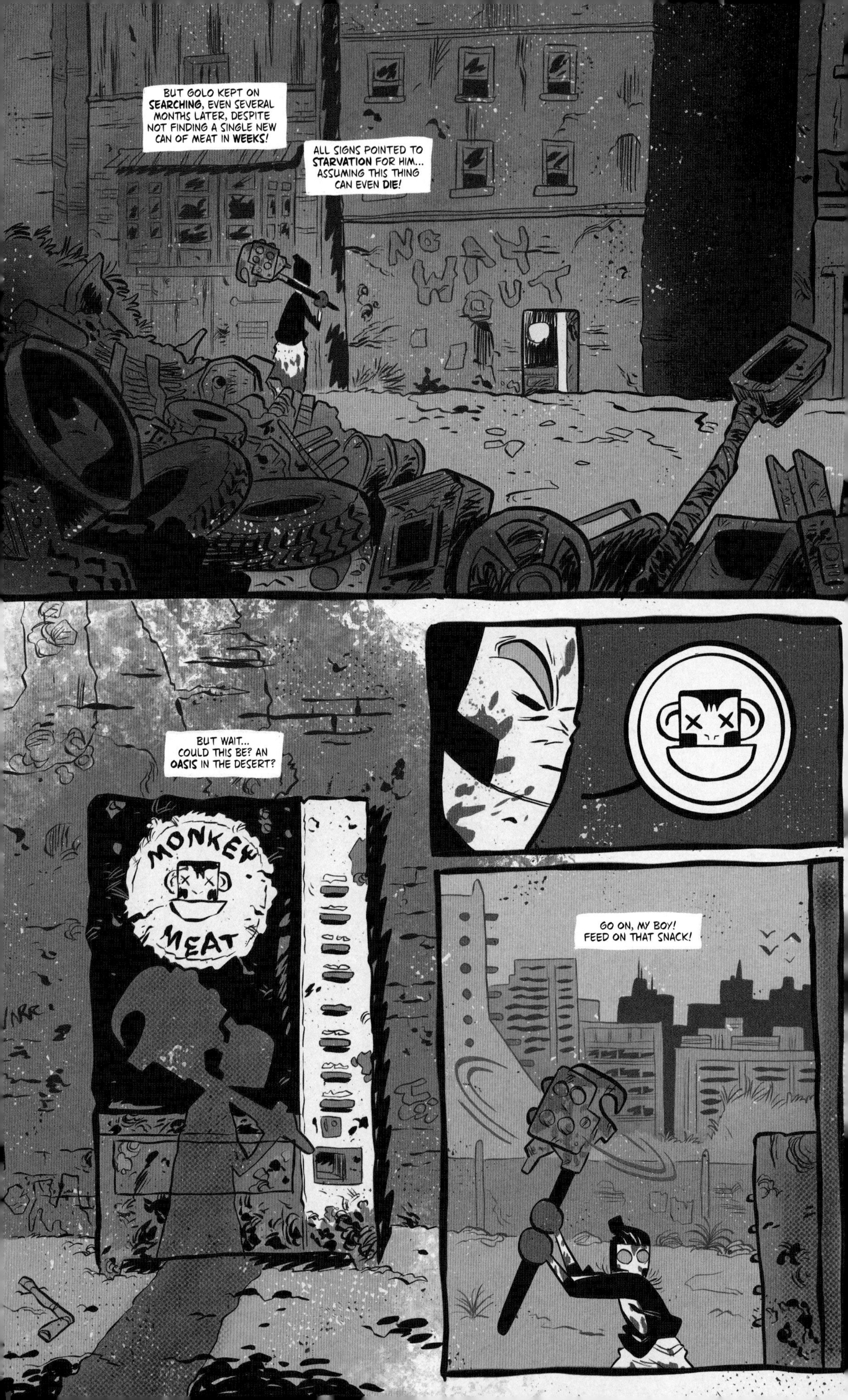
BUT GOLO KEPT ON SEARCHING, EVEN SEVERAL MONTHS LATER, DESPITE NOT FINDING A SINGLE NEW CAN OF MEAT IN WEEKS!
ALL SIGNS POINTED TO STARVATION FOR HIM... ASSUMING THIS THING CAN EVEN DIE!
NO WAY OUT
BUT WAIT... COULD THIS BE? AN OASIS IN THE DESERT?
MONKEY MEAT
GO ON, MY BOY! FEED ON THAT SNACK!

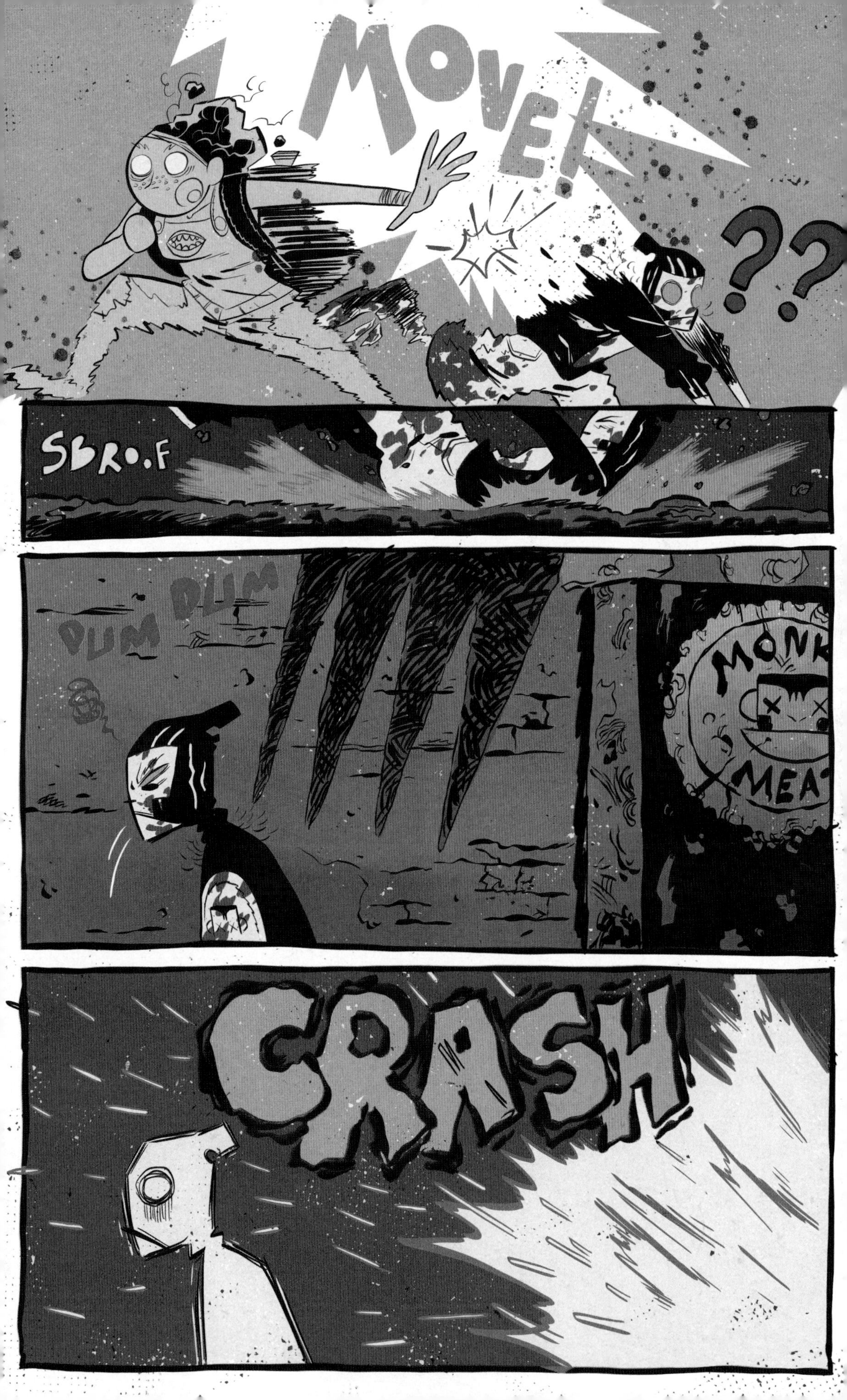
MOVE!
??
SBRO.F
DUM DUM DUM
MONK
MEAT
CRASH

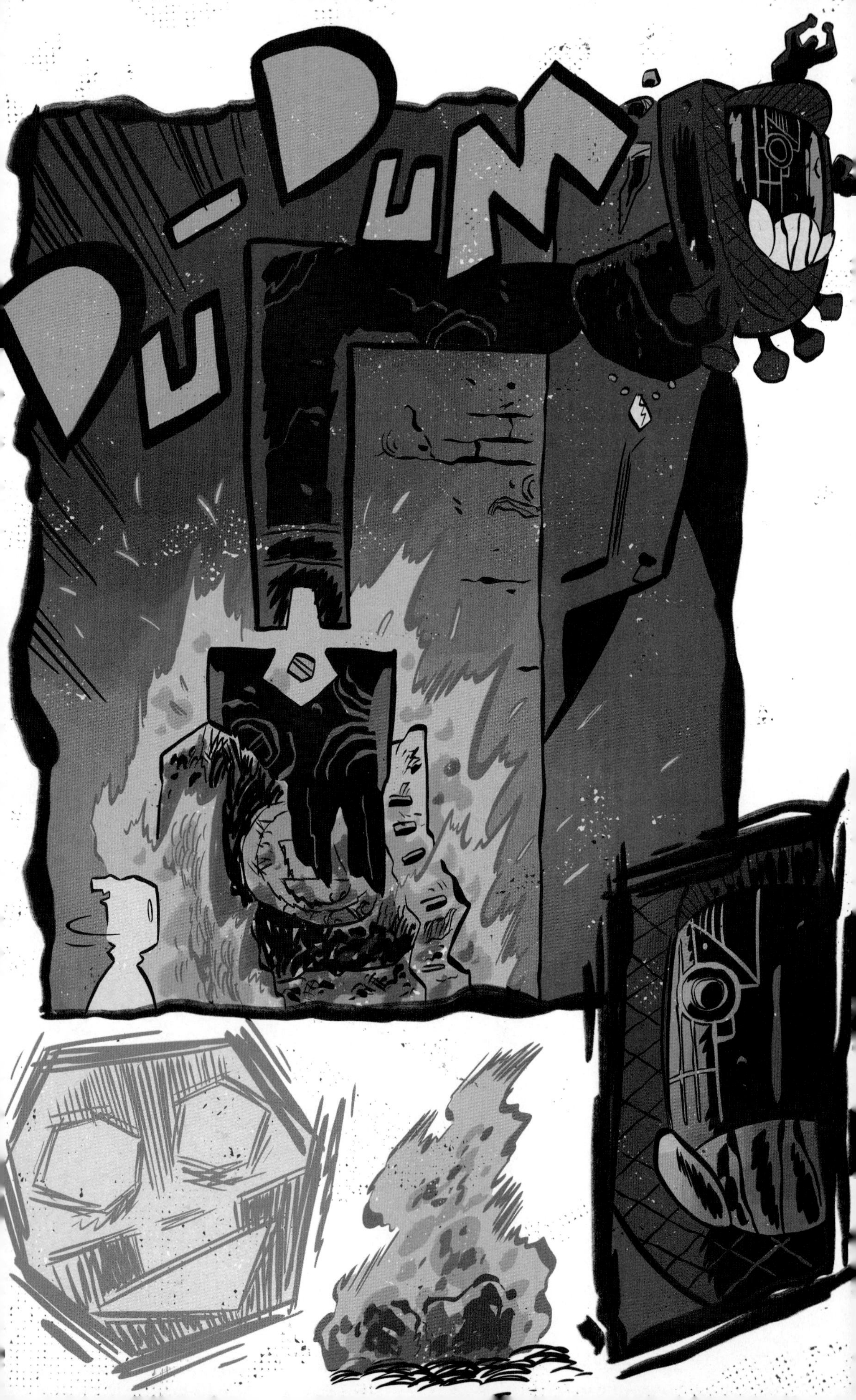
DU-DUM

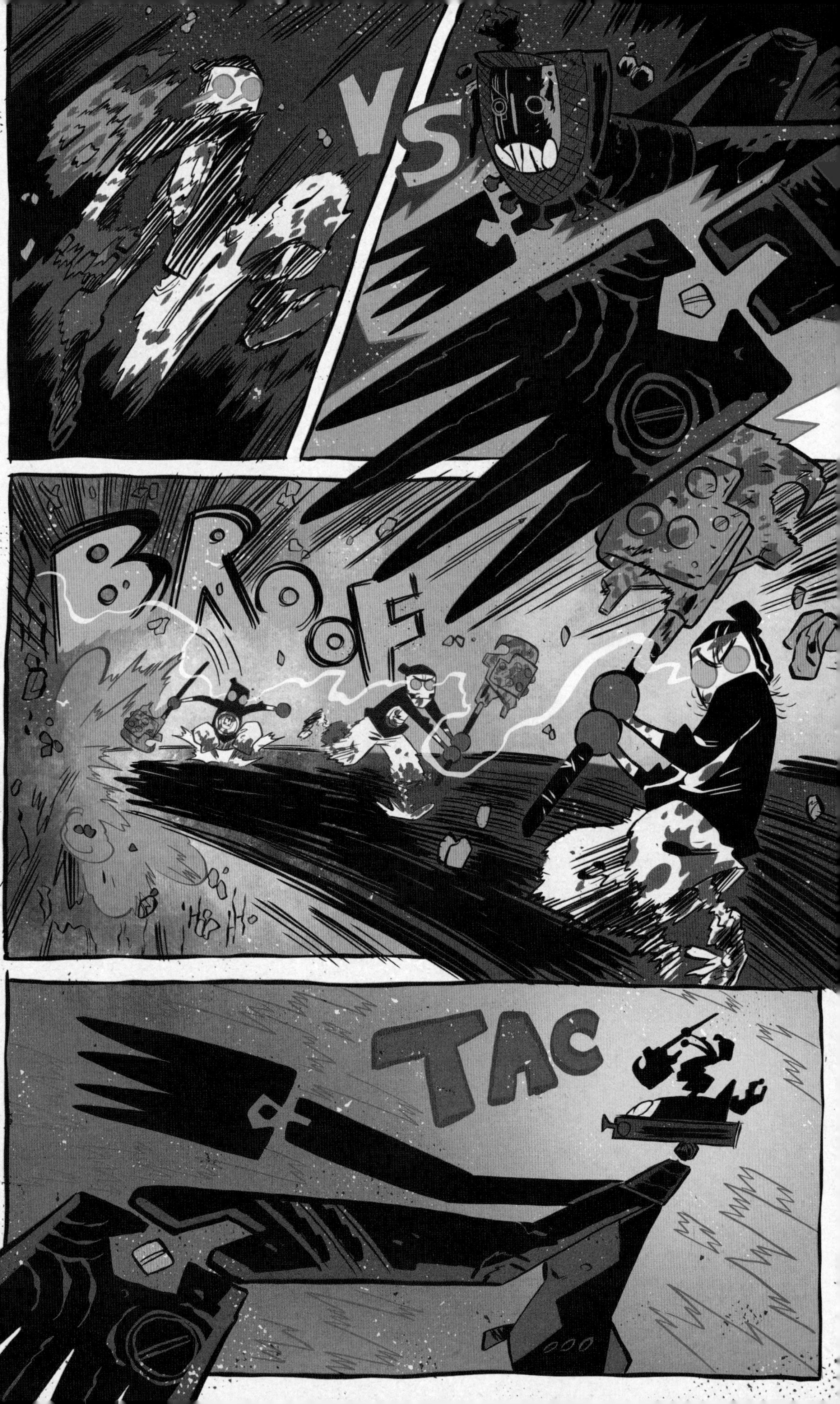
VS
BRAOOF
TAC

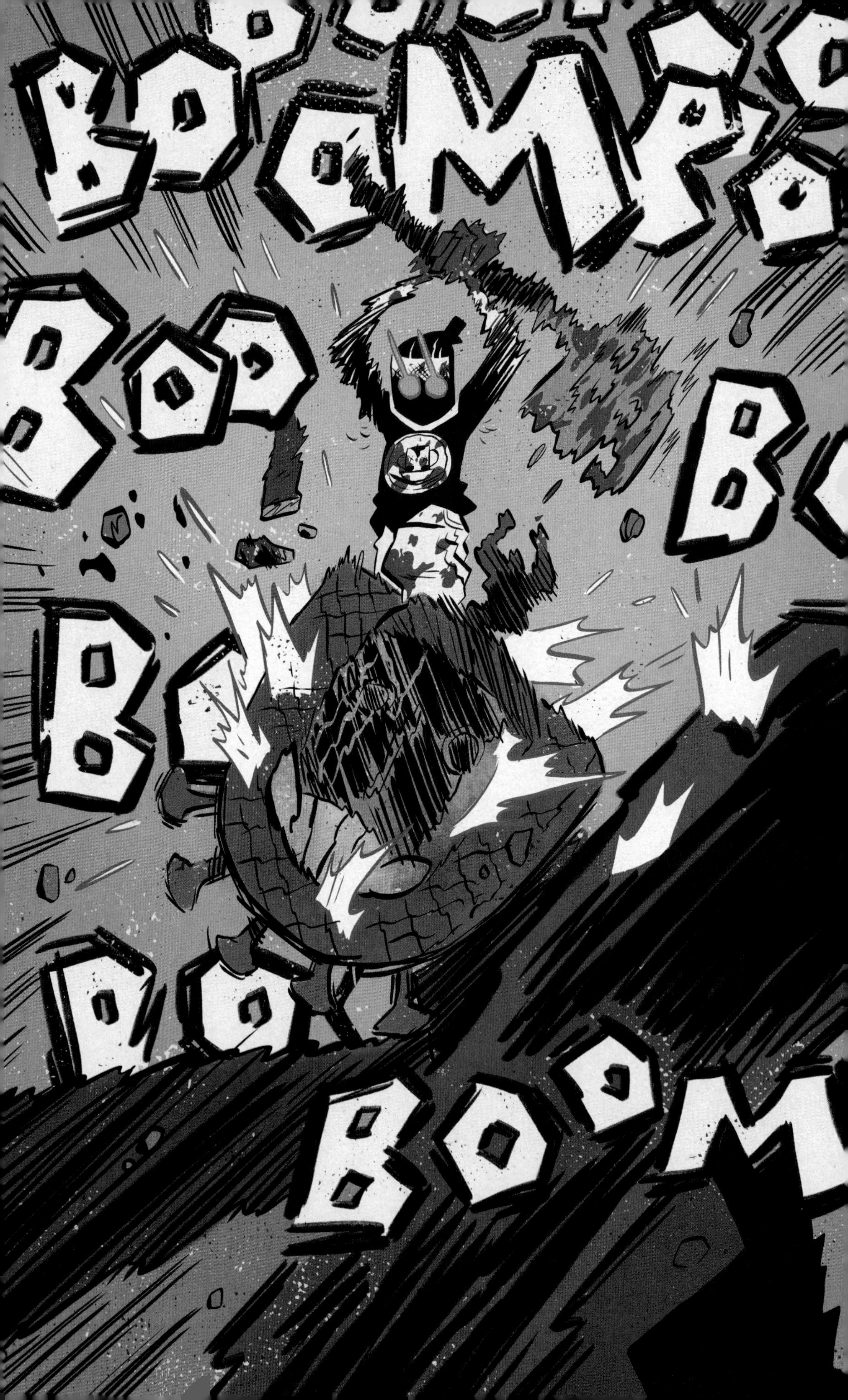
BOOM
BOOM

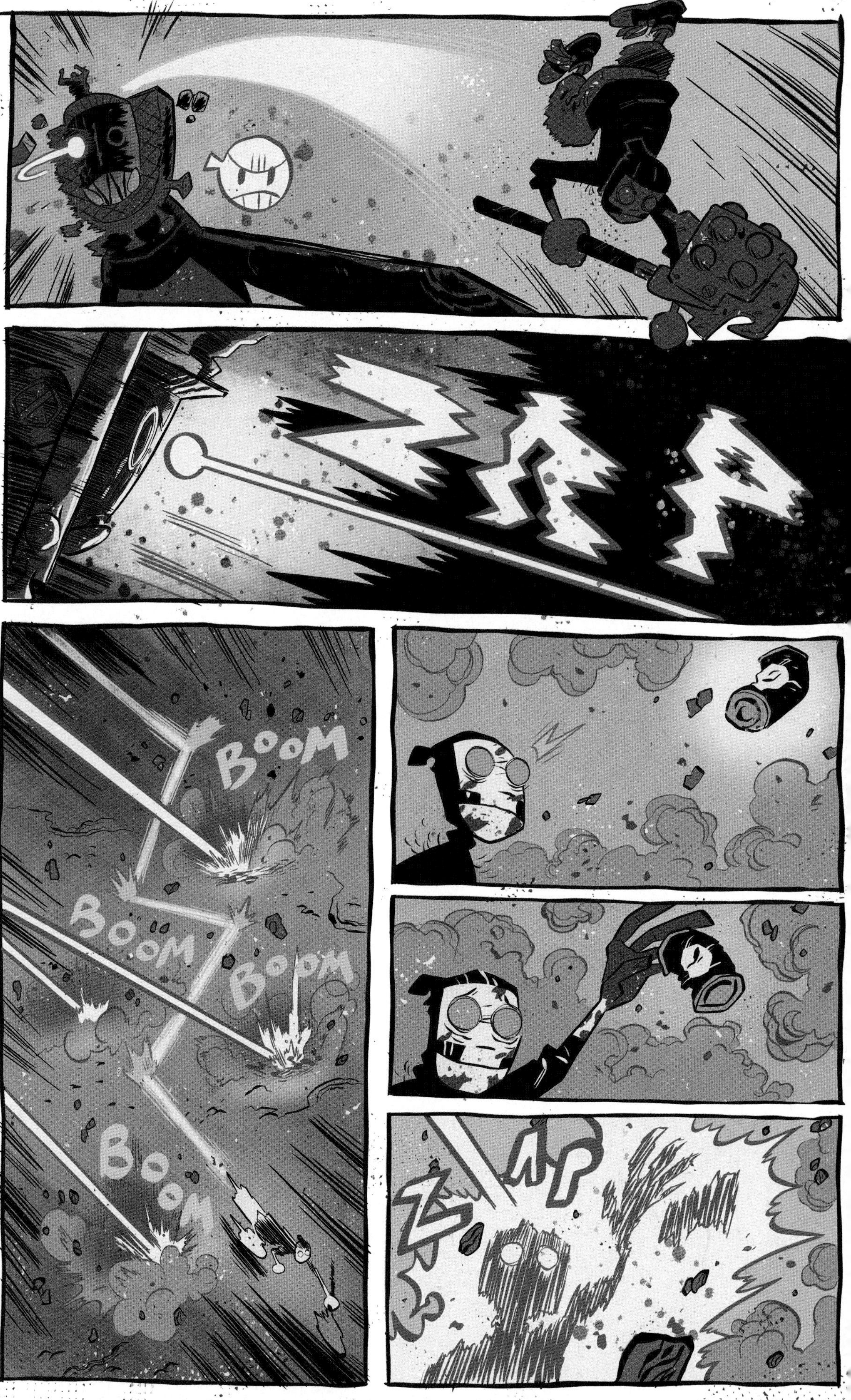

ZAP
BOOM
BOOM
BOOM
BOOM

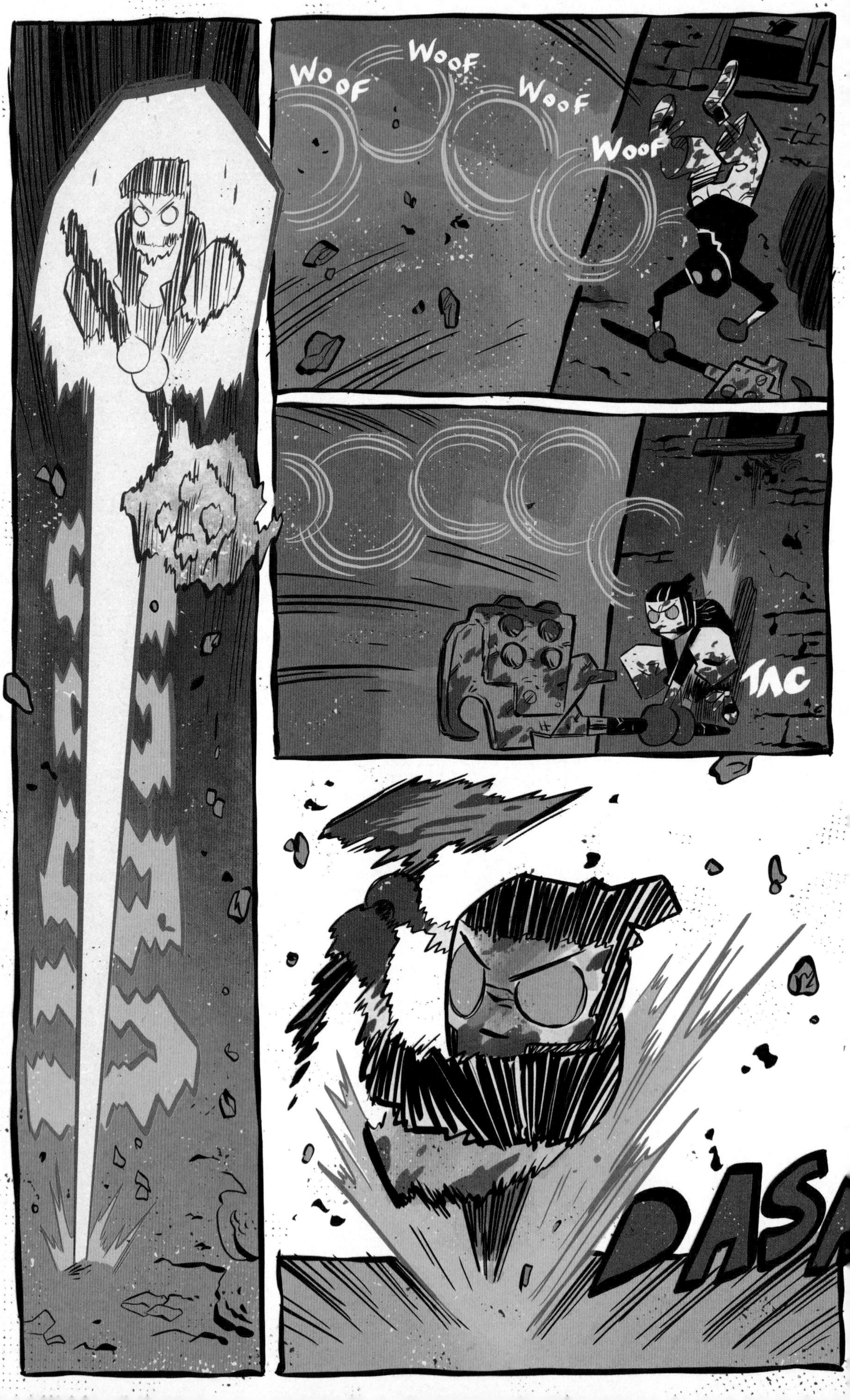
Woof
Woof
Woof
Woof
TAC
DASH

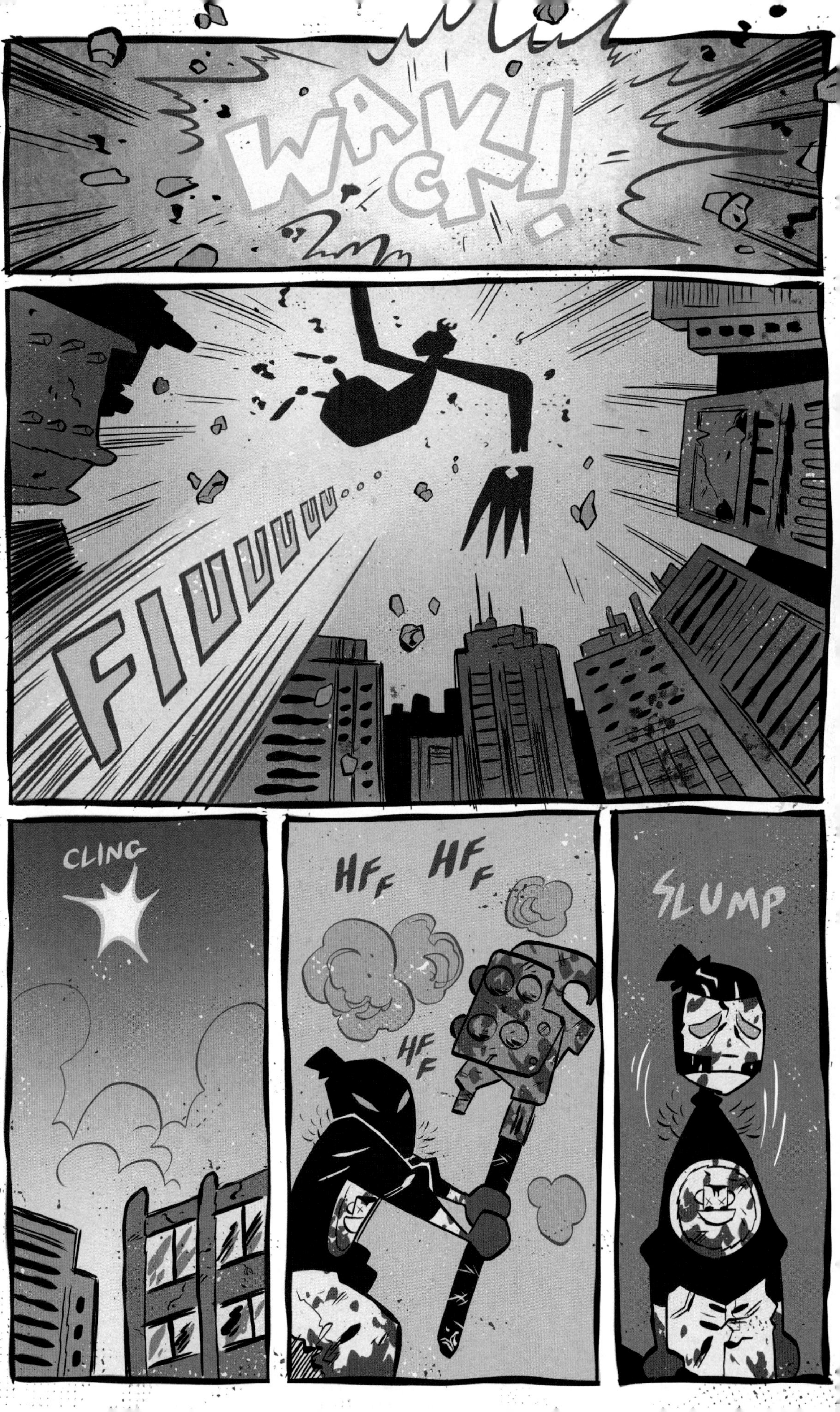
WACK!
FIUUUUUU...
CLING
HFF HFF
HFF
SLUMP

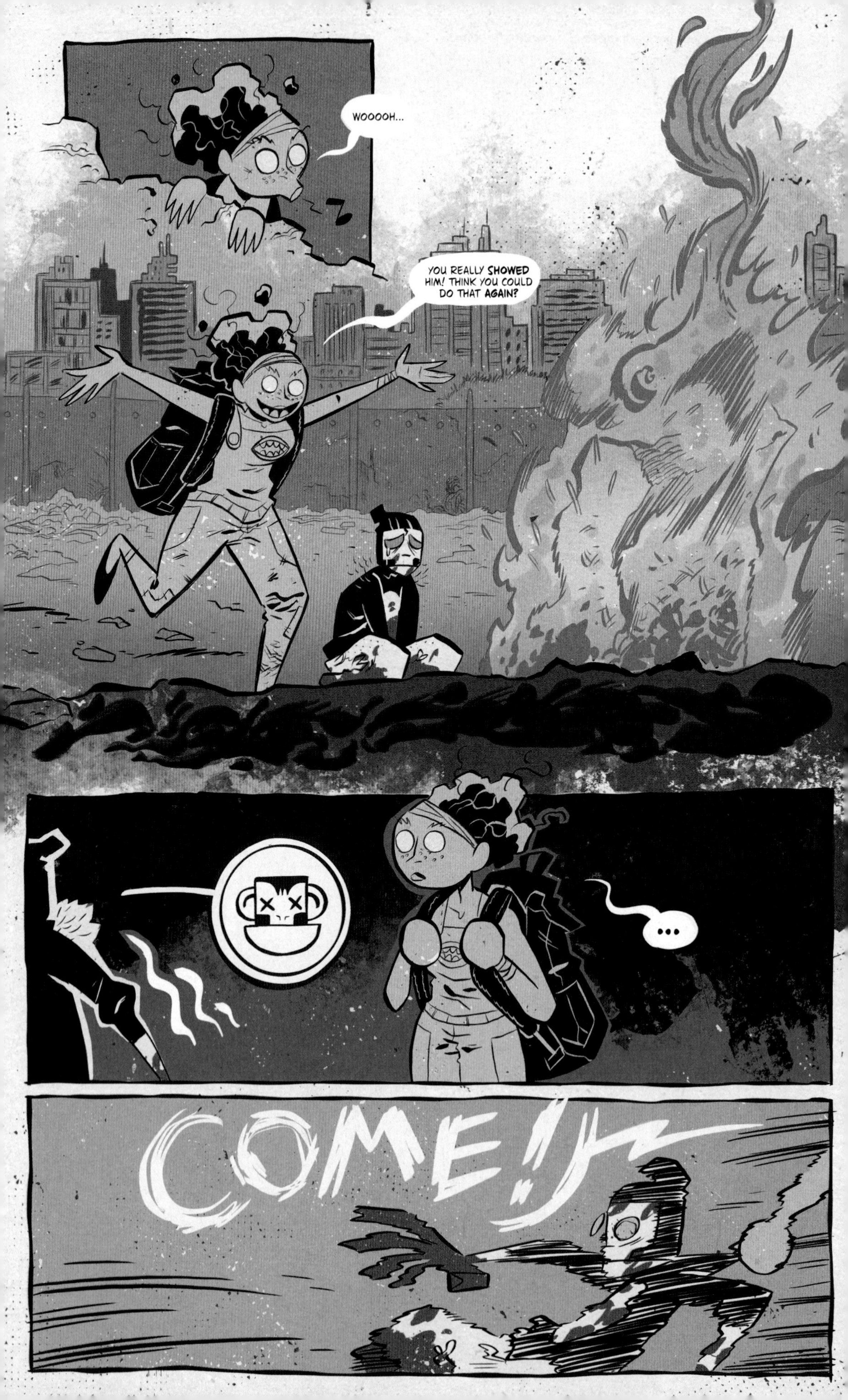
WOOOOH...
YOU REALLY **SHOWED** HIM! THINK YOU COULD DO THAT **AGAIN**?
...
COME!

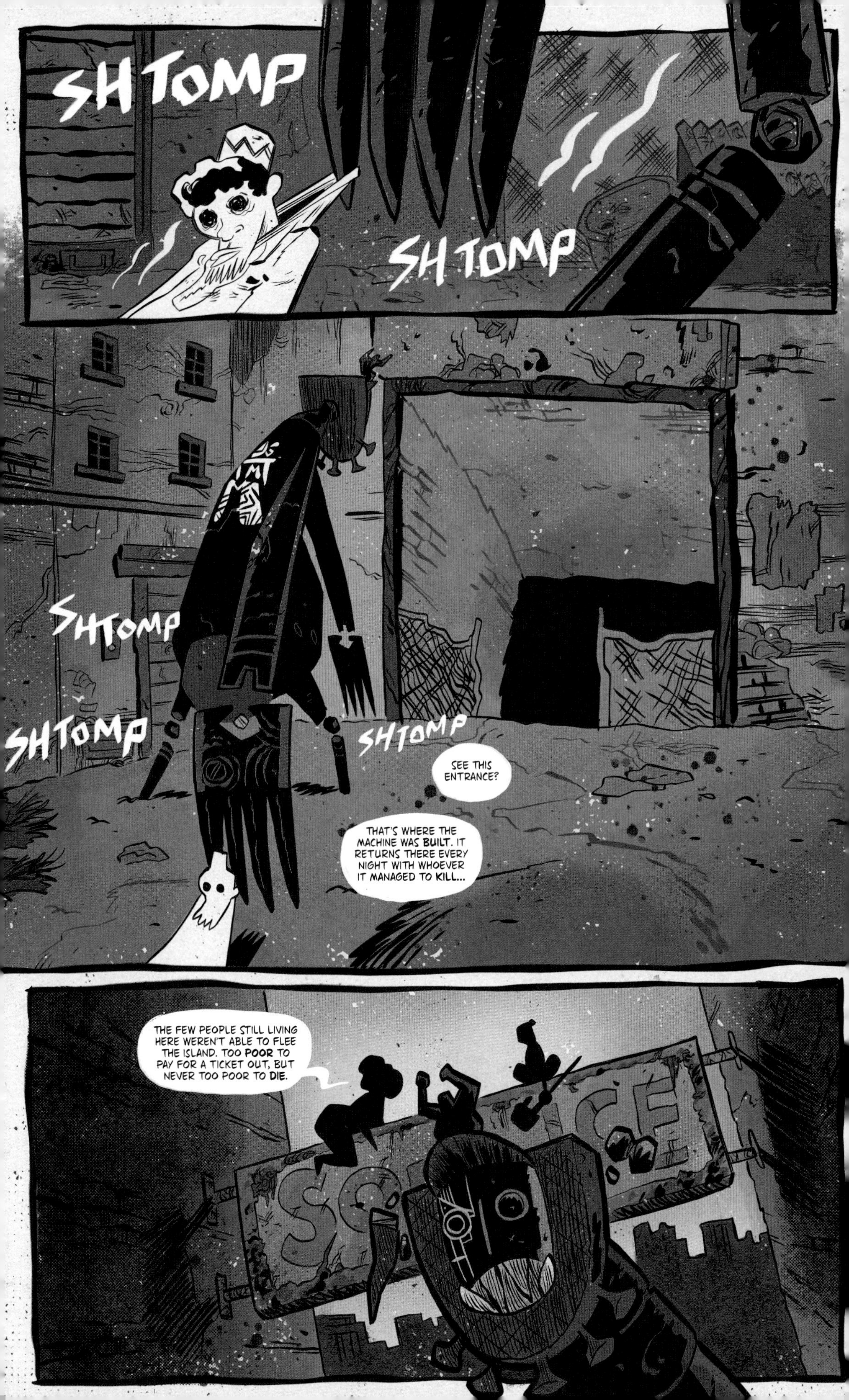
SHTOMP
SHTOMP
SHTOMP
SHTOMP
SHTOMP
SEE THIS ENTRANCE?
THAT'S WHERE THE MACHINE WAS BUILT. IT RETURNS THERE EVERY NIGHT WITH WHOEVER IT MANAGED TO KILL...
THE FEW PEOPLE STILL LIVING HERE WEREN'T ABLE TO FLEE THE ISLAND. TOO POOR TO PAY FOR A TICKET OUT, BUT NEVER TOO POOR TO DIE.

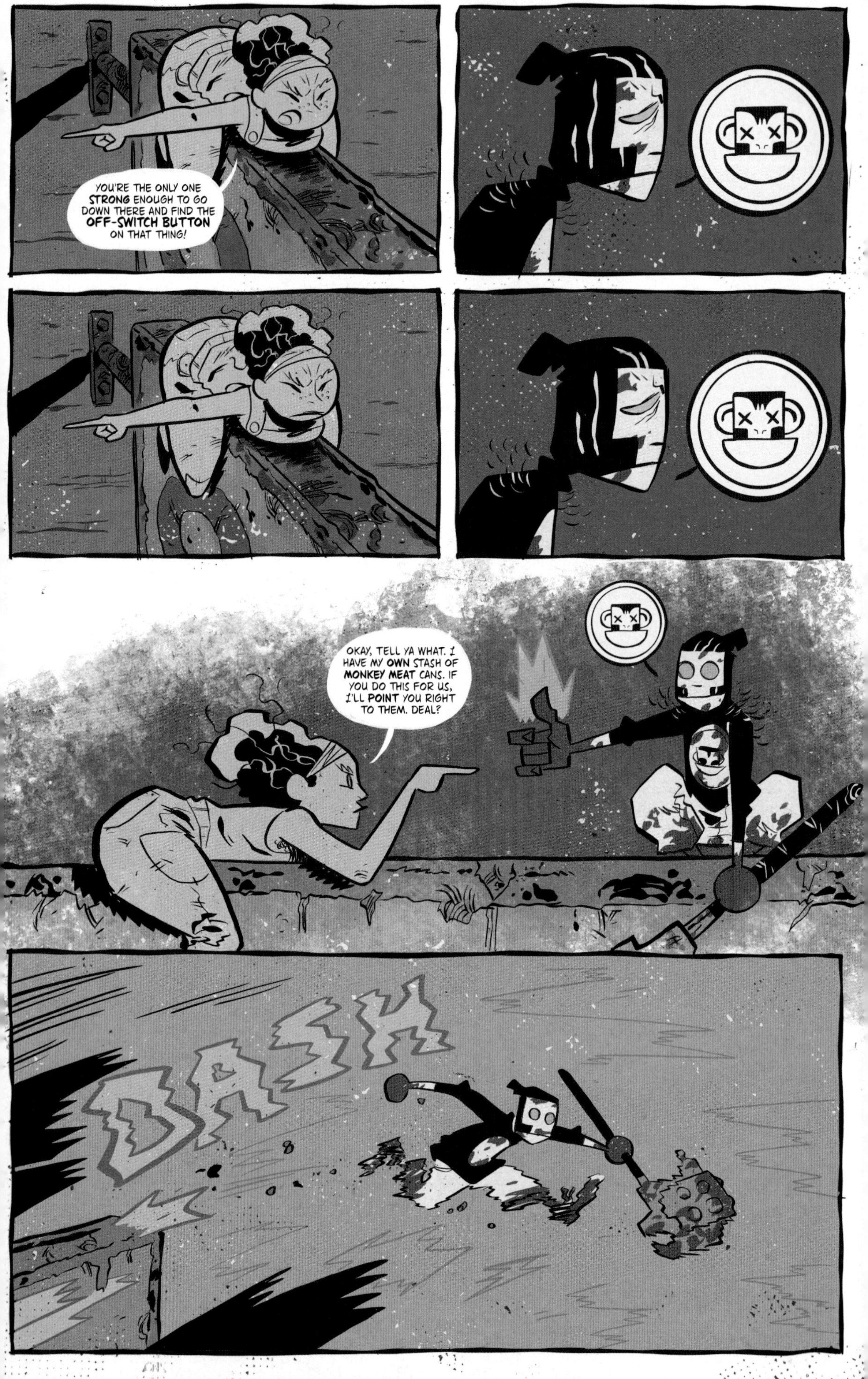
YOU'RE THE ONLY ONE STRONG ENOUGH TO GO DOWN THERE AND FIND THE OFF-SWITCH BUTTON ON THAT THING!
OKAY, TELL YA WHAT. I HAVE MY OWN STASH OF MONKEY MEAT CANS. IF YOU DO THIS FOR US, I'LL POINT YOU RIGHT TO THEM. DEAL?
DASH

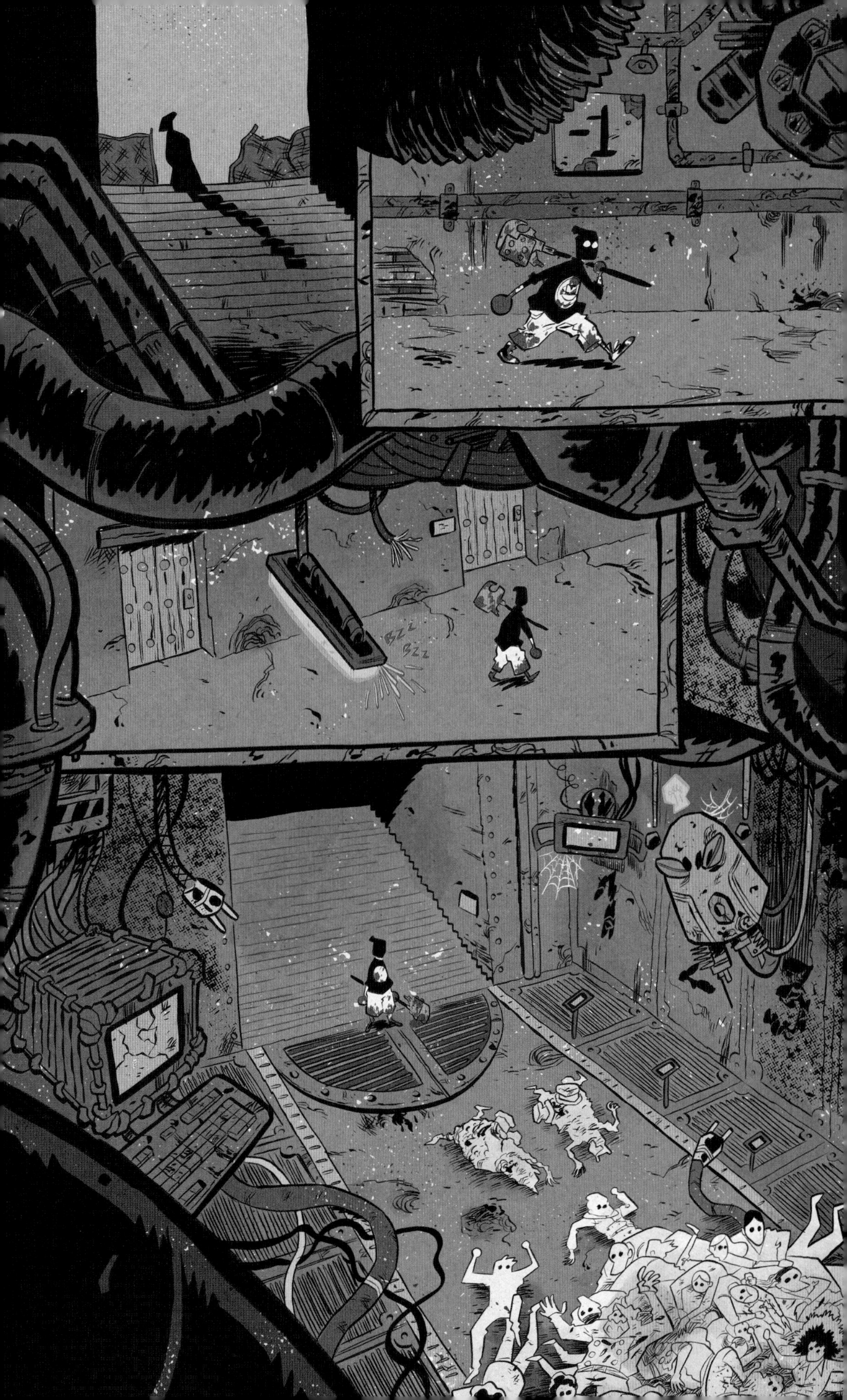
-1
BZZ
BZZ

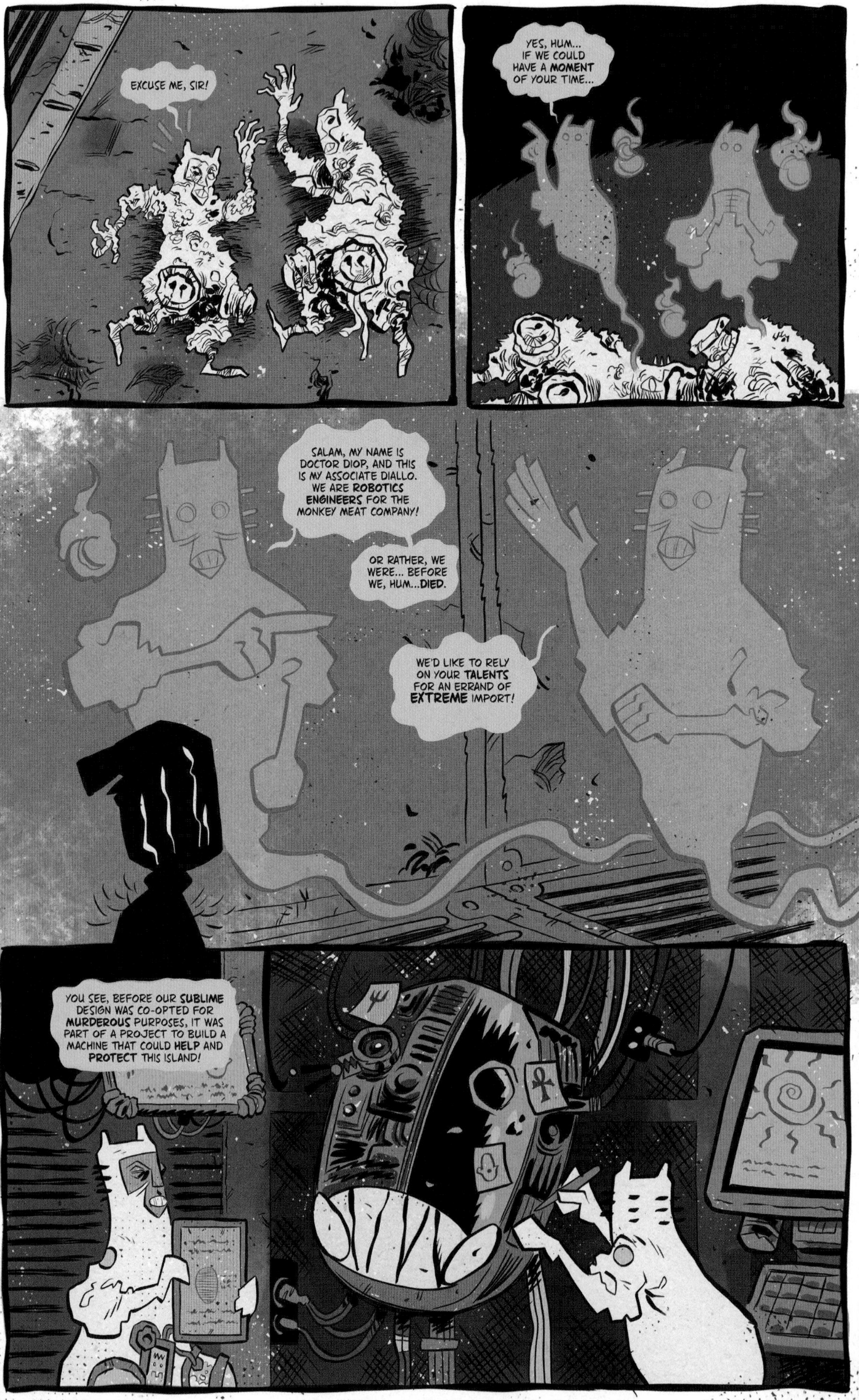
EXCUSE ME, SIR!
YES, HUM... IF WE COULD HAVE A **MOMENT** OF YOUR TIME...
SALAM, MY NAME IS DOCTOR DIOP, AND THIS IS MY ASSOCIATE DIALLO. WE ARE **ROBOTICS ENGINEERS** FOR THE MONKEY MEAT COMPANY!
OR RATHER, WE WERE... BEFORE WE, HUM...**DIED**.
WE'D LIKE TO RELY ON YOUR **TALENTS** FOR AN ERRAND OF **EXTREME** IMPORT!
YOU SEE, BEFORE OUR **SUBLIME** DESIGN WAS CO-OPTED FOR **MURDEROUS** PURPOSES, IT WAS PART OF A PROJECT TO BUILD A MACHINE THAT COULD **HELP** AND **PROTECT** THIS ISLAND!

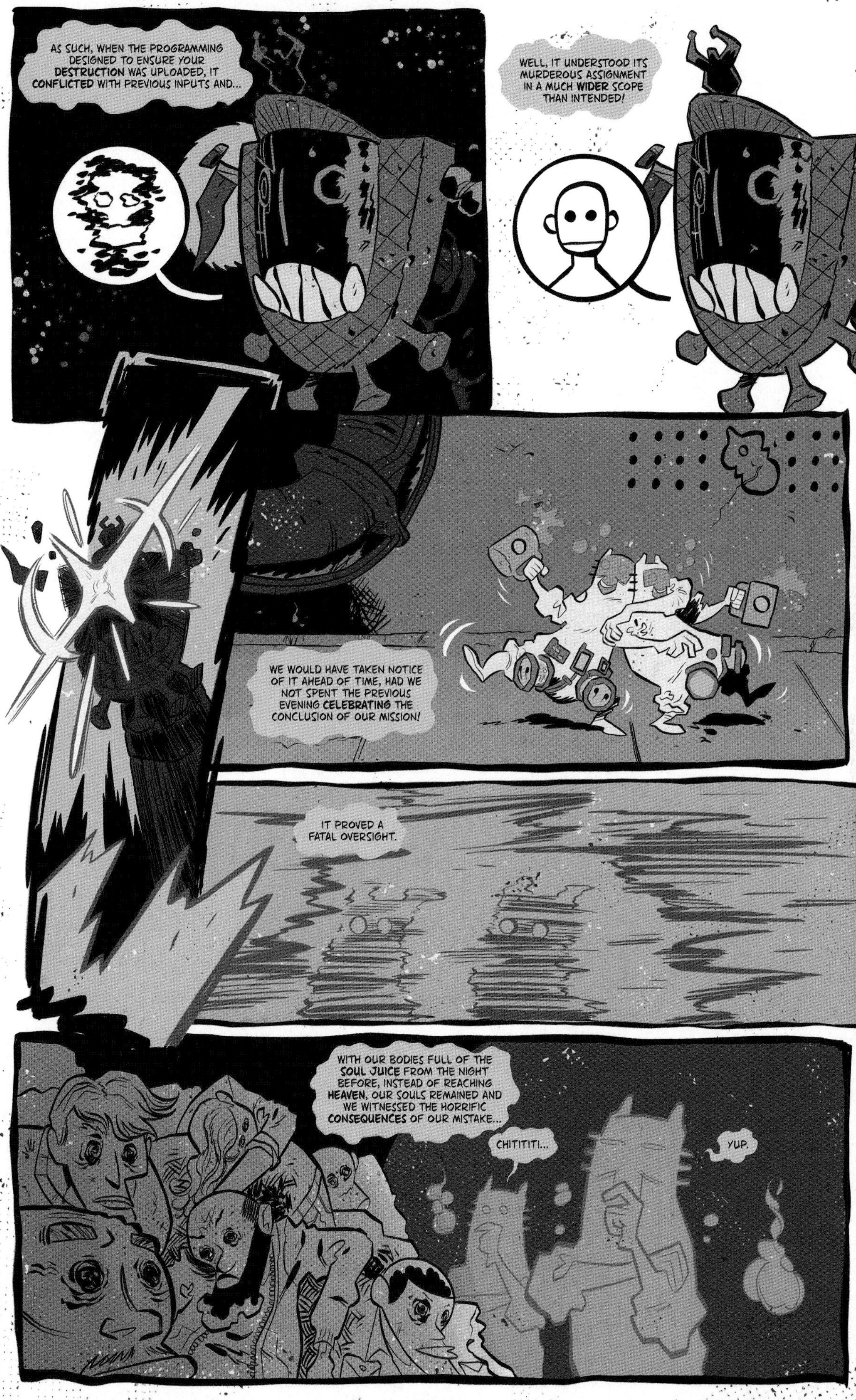
AS SUCH, WHEN THE PROGRAMMING DESIGNED TO ENSURE YOUR DESTRUCTION WAS UPLOADED, IT CONFLICTED WITH PREVIOUS INPUTS AND...
WELL, IT UNDERSTOOD ITS MURDEROUS ASSIGNMENT IN A MUCH WIDER SCOPE THAN INTENDED!
WE WOULD HAVE TAKEN NOTICE OF IT AHEAD OF TIME, HAD WE NOT SPENT THE PREVIOUS EVENING CELEBRATING THE CONCLUSION OF OUR MISSION!
IT PROVED A FATAL OVERSIGHT.
WITH OUR BODIES FULL OF THE SOUL JUICE FROM THE NIGHT BEFORE, INSTEAD OF REACHING HEAVEN, OUR SOULS REMAINED AND WE WITNESSED THE HORRIFIC CONSEQUENCES OF OUR MISTAKE...
CHITITITI...
YUP.

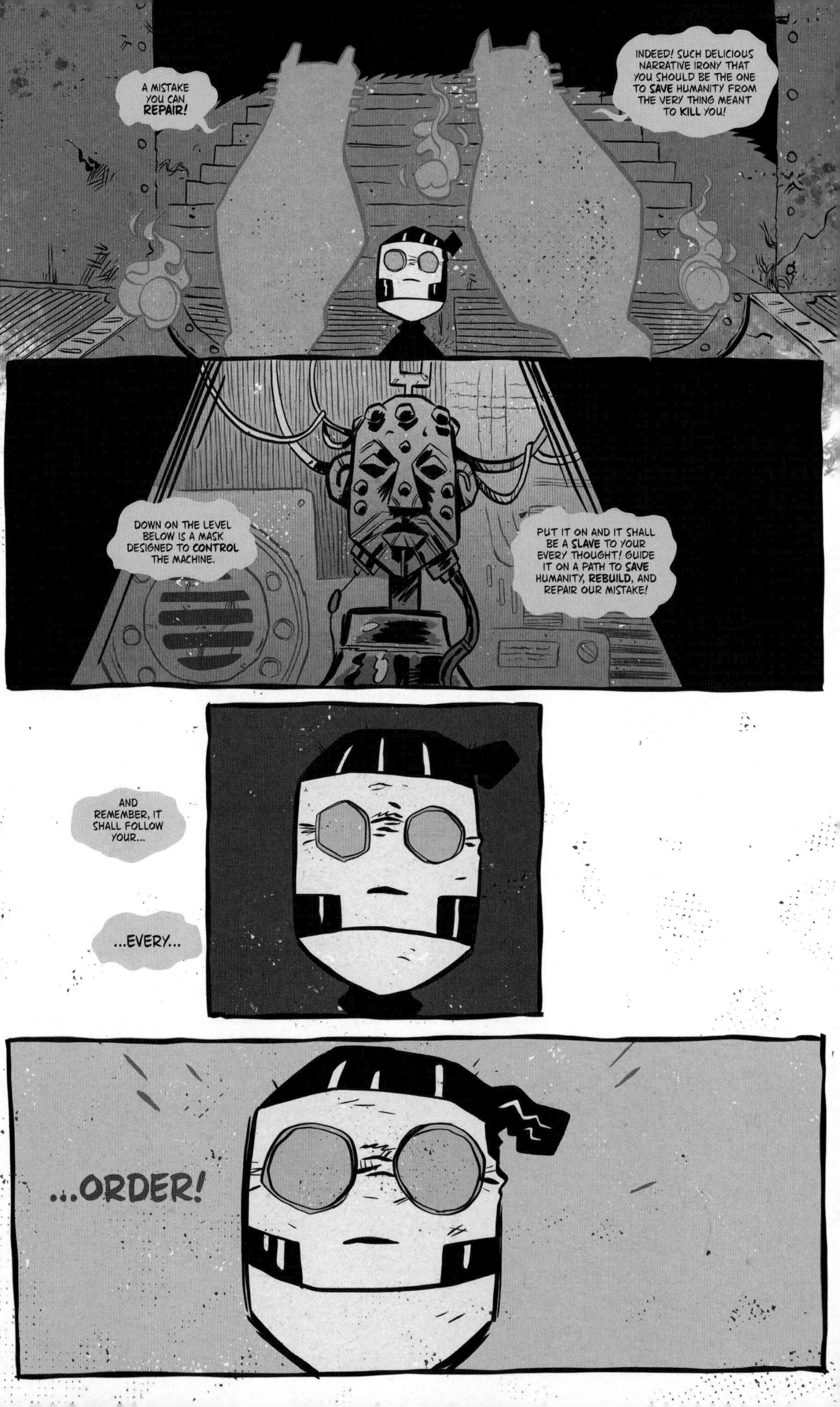
A MISTAKE YOU CAN REPAIR!
INDEED! SUCH DELICIOUS NARRATIVE IRONY THAT YOU SHOULD BE THE ONE TO SAVE HUMANITY FROM THE VERY THING MEANT TO KILL YOU!
DOWN ON THE LEVEL BELOW IS A MASK DESIGNED TO CONTROL THE MACHINE.
PUT IT ON AND IT SHALL BE A SLAVE TO YOUR EVERY THOUGHT! GUIDE IT ON A PATH TO SAVE HUMANITY, REBUILD, AND REPAIR OUR MISTAKE!
AND REMEMBER, IT SHALL FOLLOW YOUR...
...EVERY...
...ORDER!

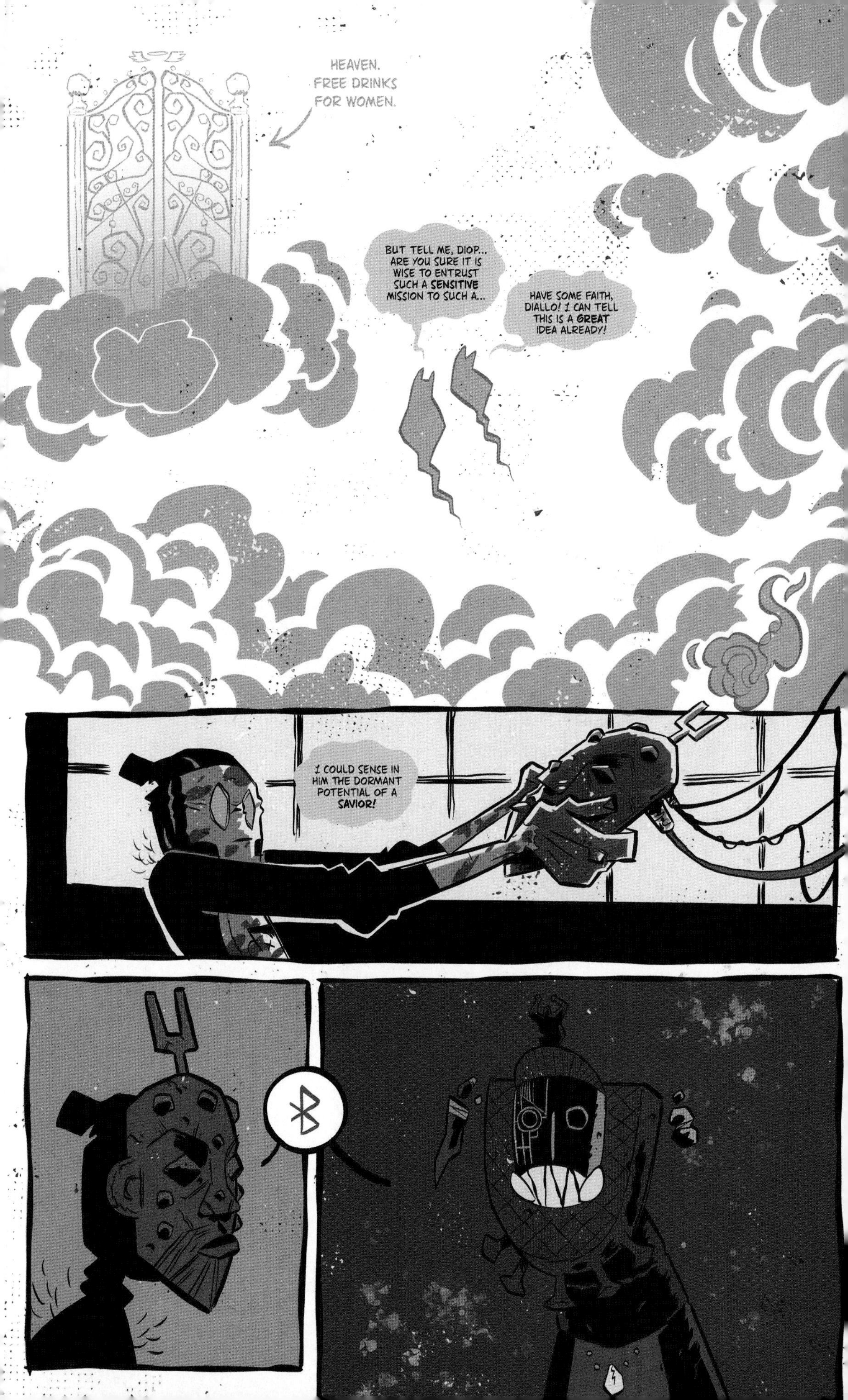
HEAVEN. FREE DRINKS FOR WOMEN.
BUT TELL ME, DIOP... ARE YOU SURE IT IS WISE TO ENTRUST SUCH A SENSITIVE MISSION TO SUCH A...
HAVE SOME FAITH, DIALLO! I CAN TELL THIS IS A GREAT IDEA ALREADY!
I COULD SENSE IN HIM THE DORMANT POTENTIAL OF A SAVIOR!

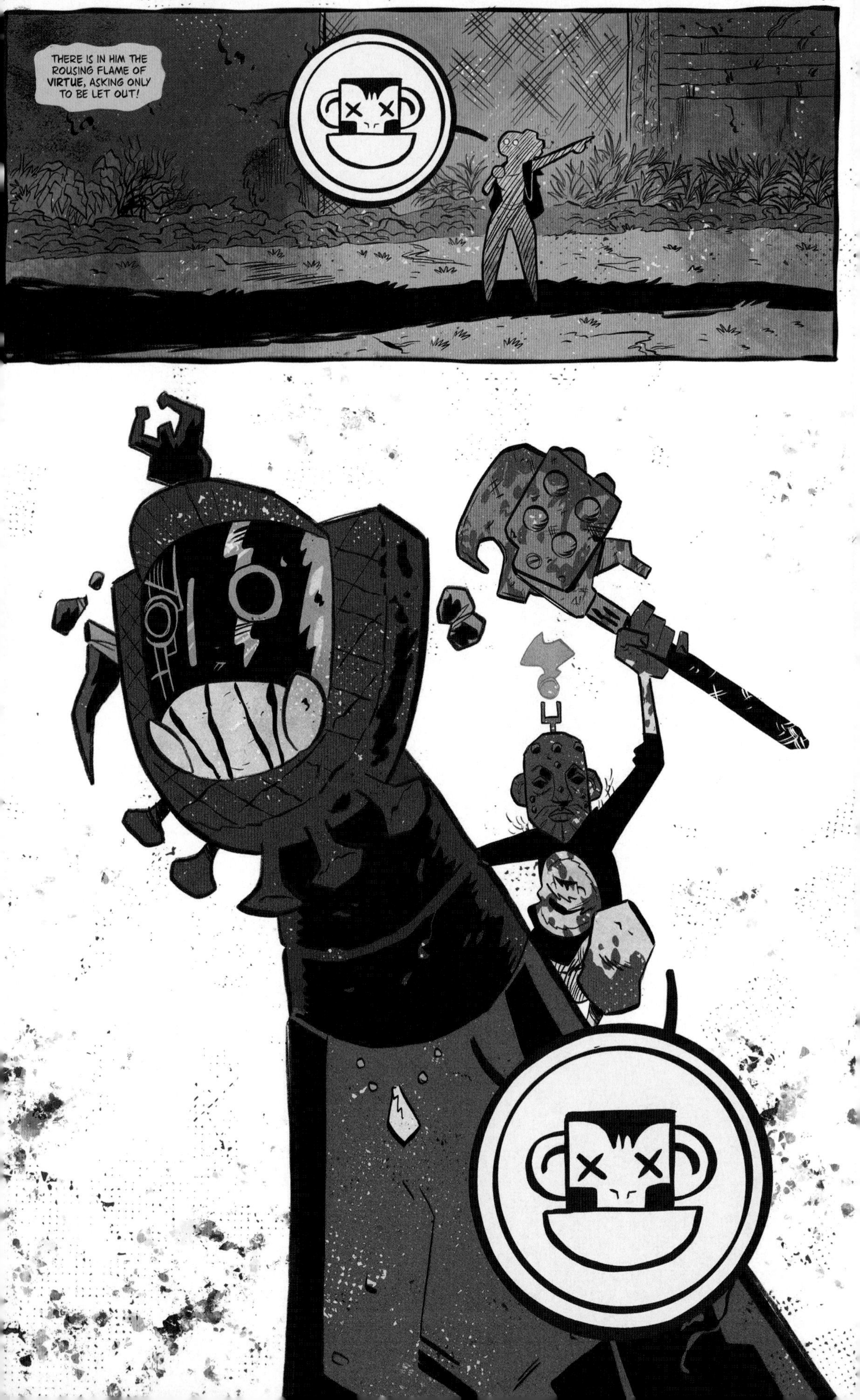
THERE IS IN HIM THE ROUSING FLAME OF VIRTUE, ASKING ONLY TO BE LET OUT!

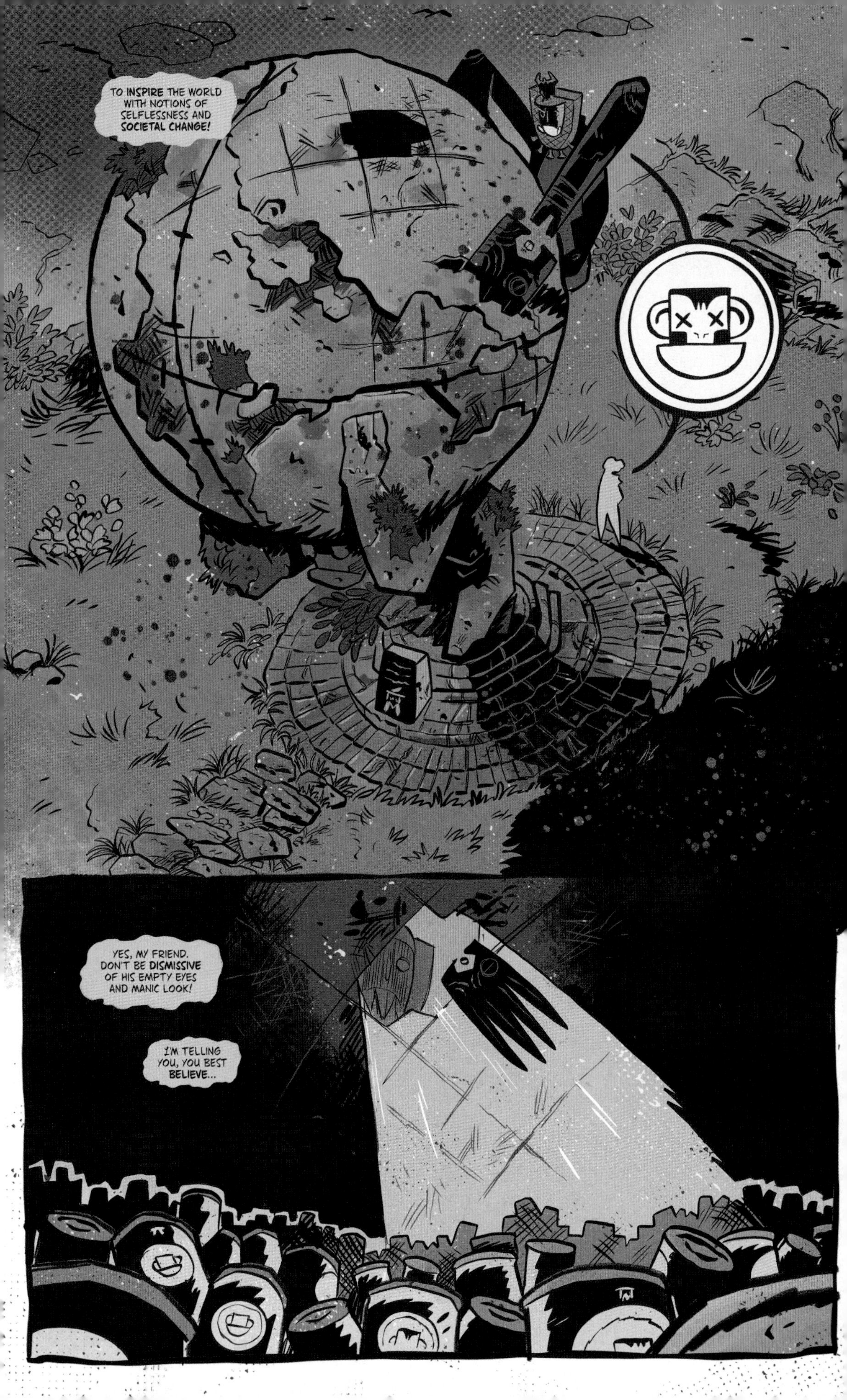
TO INSPIRE THE WORLD WITH NOTIONS OF SELFLESSNESS AND SOCIETAL CHANGE!
YES, MY FRIEND. DON'T BE DISMISSIVE OF HIS EMPTY EYES AND MANIC LOOK!
I'M TELLING YOU, YOU BEST BELIEVE...

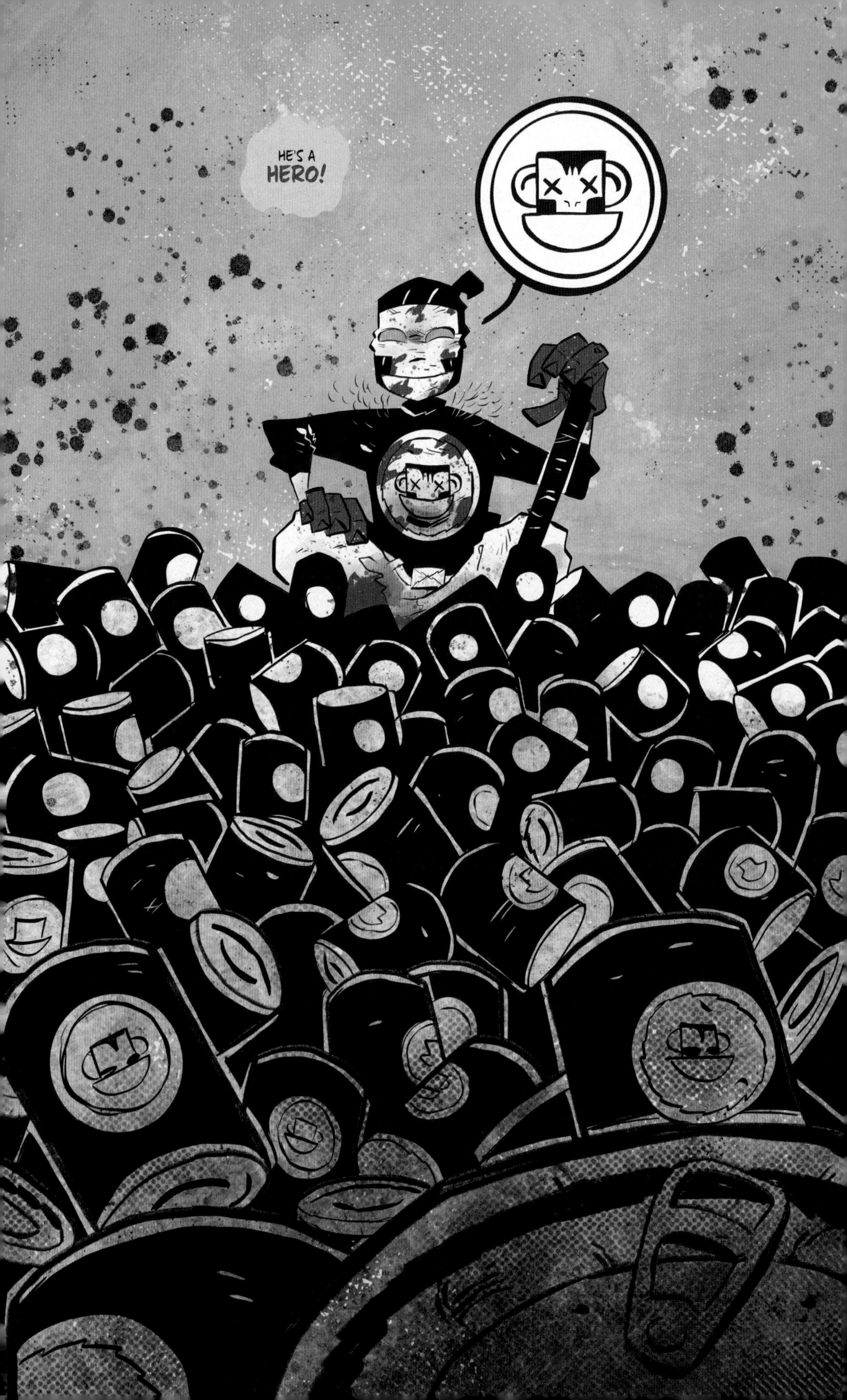
HE'S A HERO!

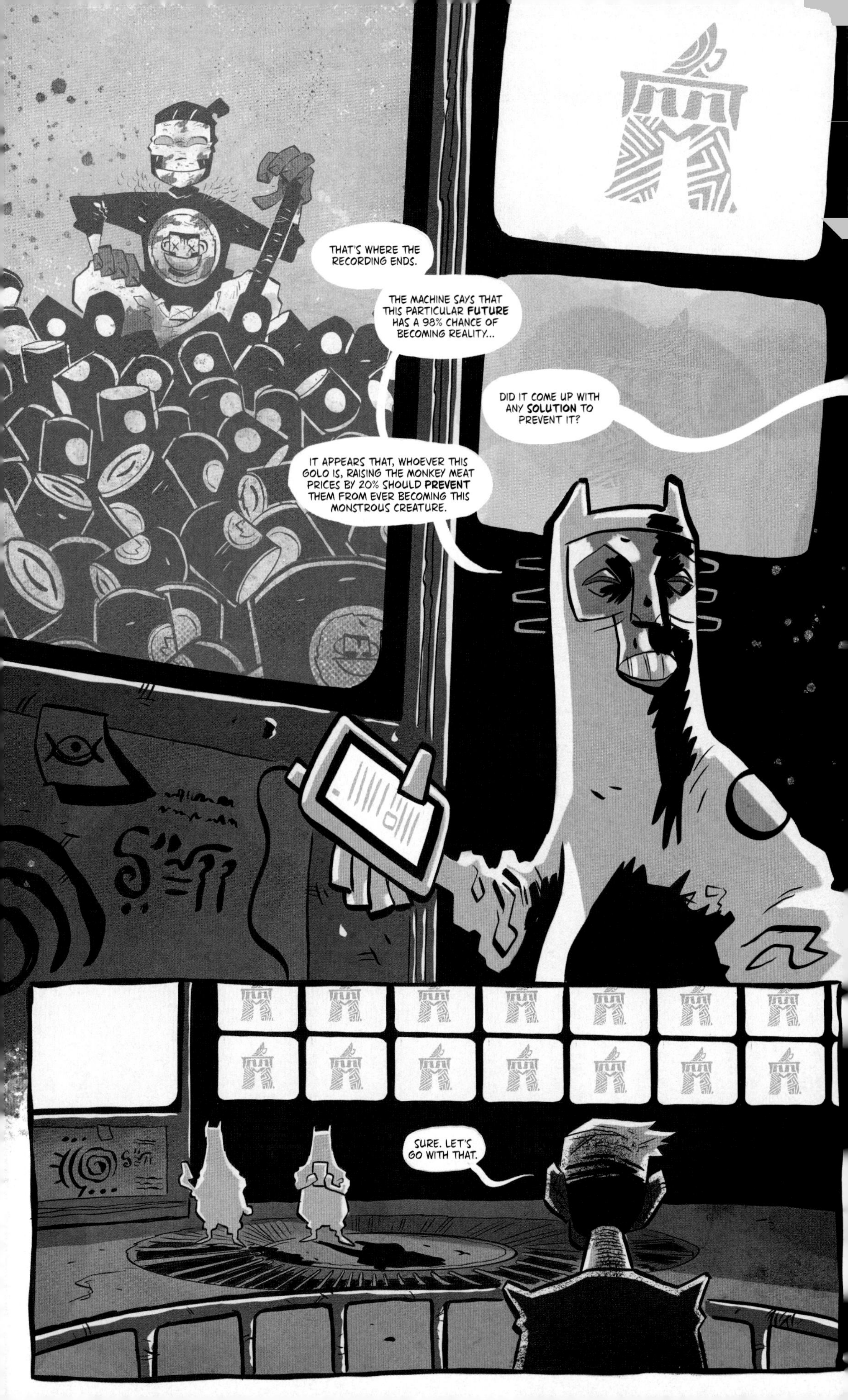
THAT'S WHERE THE RECORDING ENDS.
THE MACHINE SAYS THAT THIS PARTICULAR **FUTURE** HAS A 98% CHANCE OF BECOMING REALITY...
DID IT COME UP WITH ANY **SOLUTION** TO PREVENT IT?
IT APPEARS THAT, WHOEVER THIS GOLO IS, RAISING THE MONKEY MEAT PRICES BY 20% SHOULD **PREVENT** THEM FROM EVER BECOMING THIS MONSTROUS CREATURE.
SURE. LET'S GO WITH THAT.

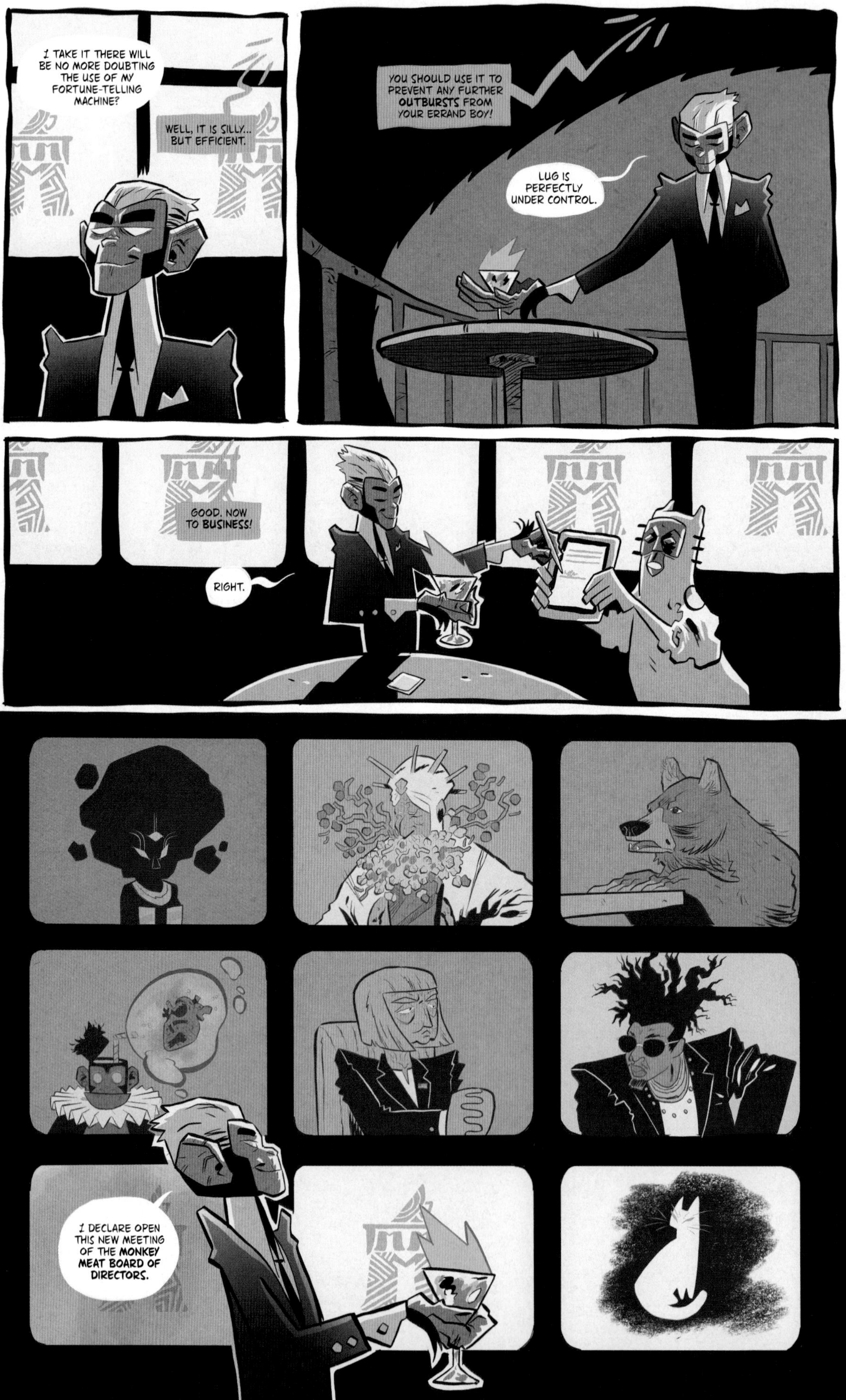
I TAKE IT THERE WILL BE NO MORE DOUBTING THE USE OF MY FORTUNE-TELLING MACHINE?
WELL, IT IS SILLY... BUT EFFICIENT.
YOU SHOULD USE IT TO PREVENT ANY FURTHER OUTBURSTS FROM YOUR ERRAND BOY!
LUG IS PERFECTLY UNDER CONTROL.
GOOD. NOW TO BUSINESS!
RIGHT.
I DECLARE OPEN THIS NEW MEETING OF THE MONKEY MEAT BOARD OF DIRECTORS.

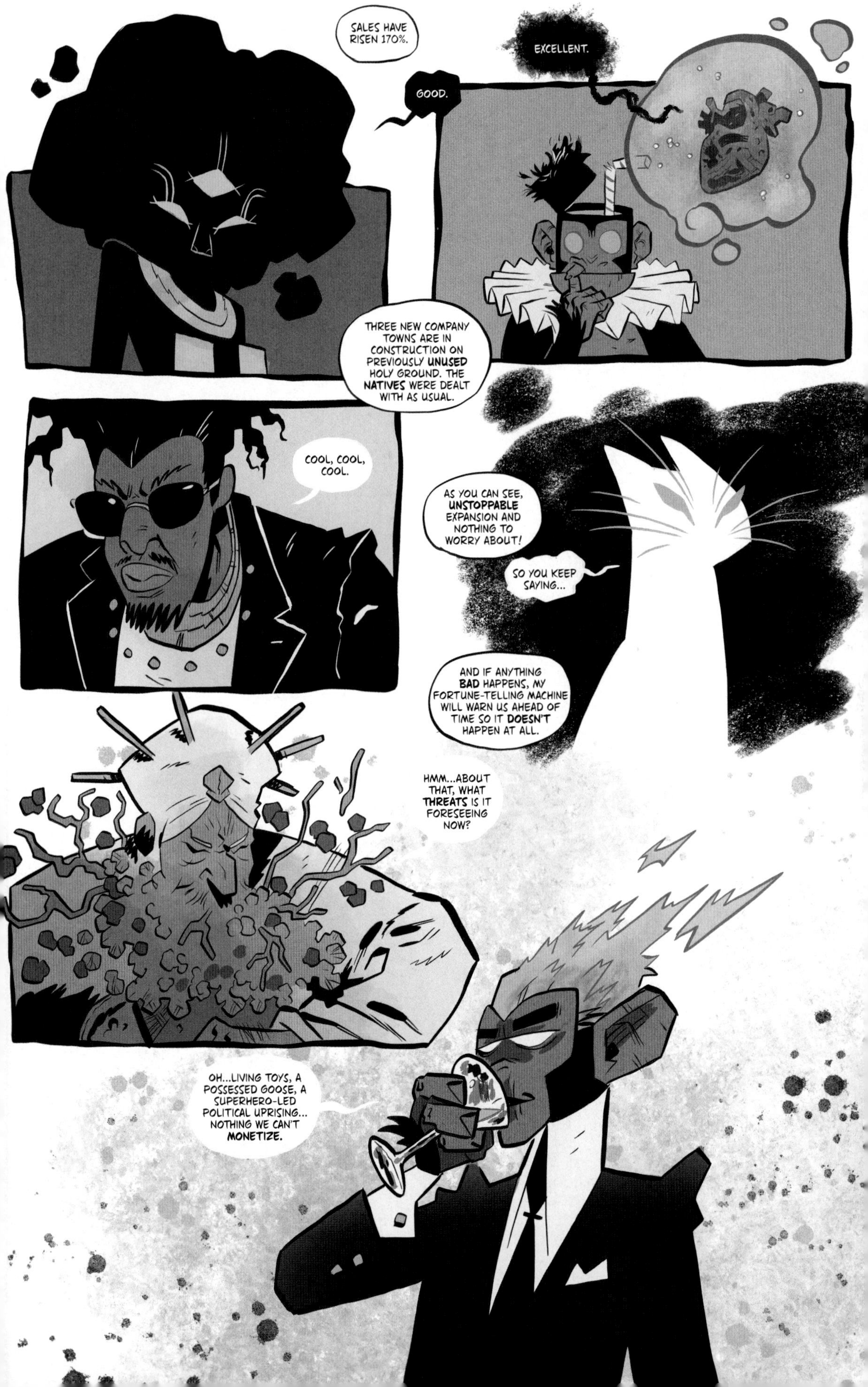
SALES HAVE RISEN 170%.
GOOD.
EXCELLENT.
THREE NEW COMPANY TOWNS ARE IN CONSTRUCTION ON PREVIOUSLY UNUSED HOLY GROUND. THE NATIVES WERE DEALT WITH AS USUAL.
COOL, COOL, COOL.
AS YOU CAN SEE, UNSTOPPABLE EXPANSION AND NOTHING TO WORRY ABOUT!
SO YOU KEEP SAYING...
AND IF ANYTHING BAD HAPPENS, MY FORTUNE-TELLING MACHINE WILL WARN US AHEAD OF TIME SO IT DOESN'T HAPPEN AT ALL.
HMM...ABOUT THAT, WHAT THREATS IS IT FORESEEING NOW?
OH...LIVING TOYS, A POSSESSED GOOSE, A SUPERHERO-LED POLITICAL UPRISING... NOTHING WE CAN'T MONETIZE.

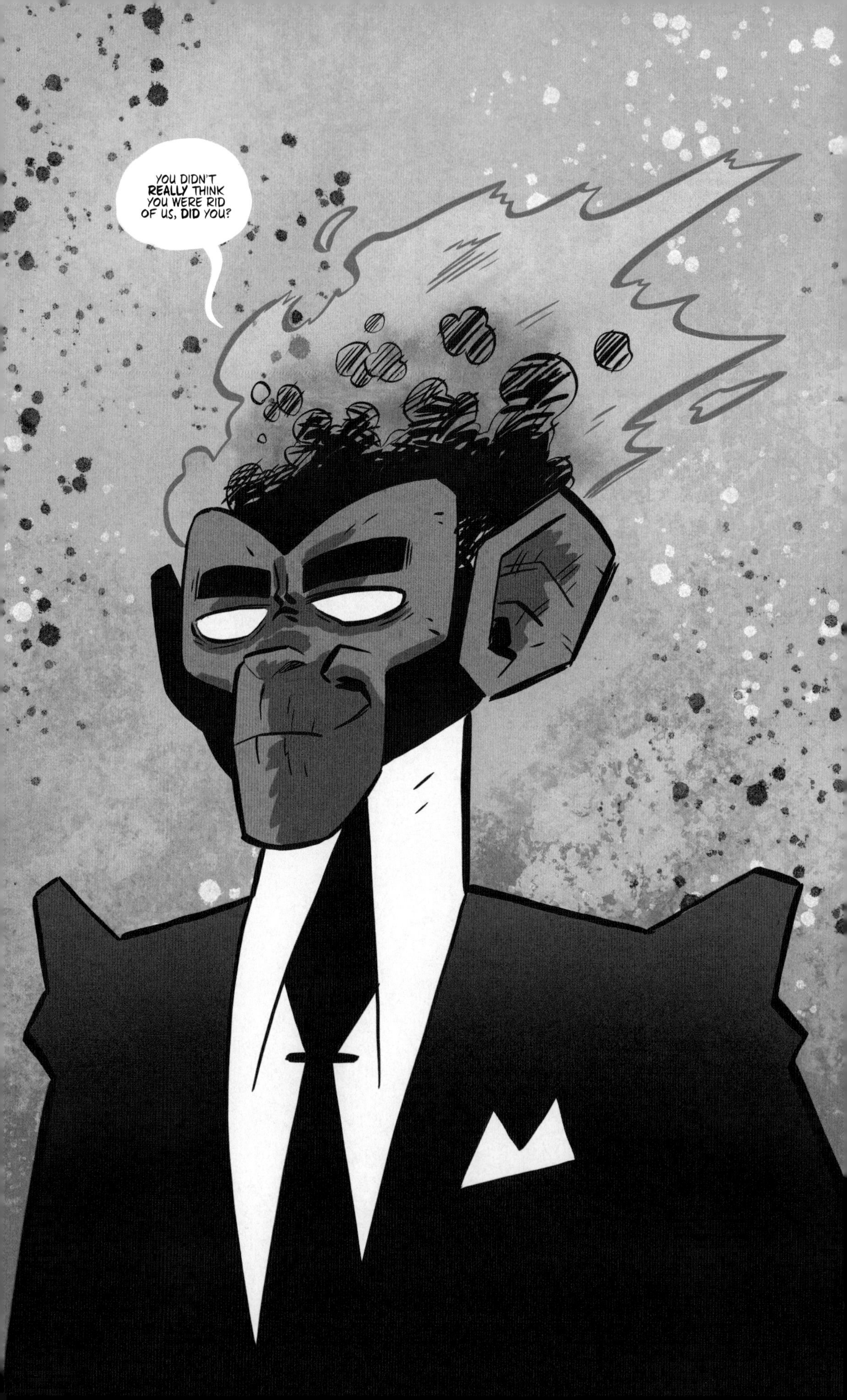
YOU DIDN'T **REALLY** THINK YOU WERE RID OF US, **DID** YOU?

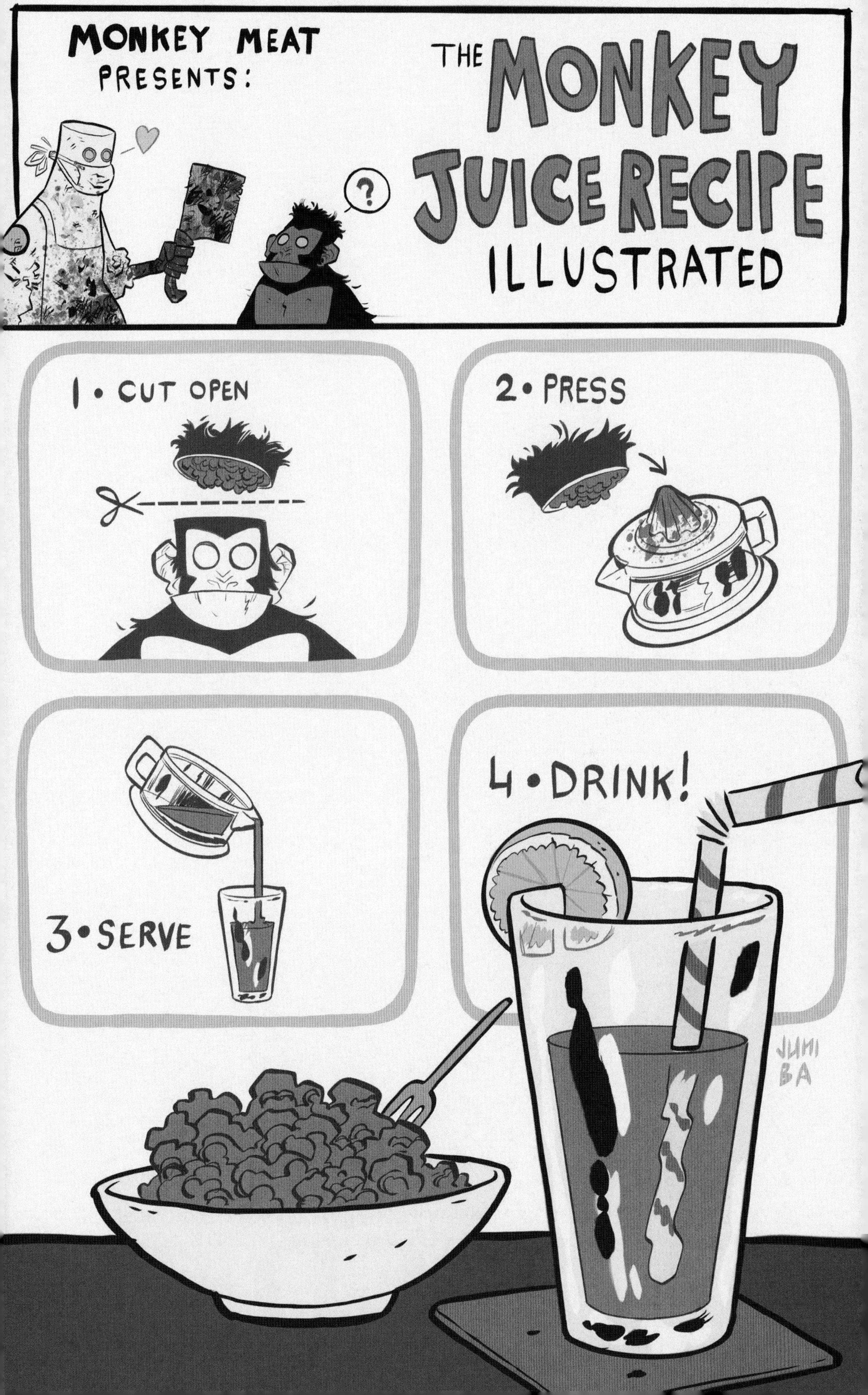
MONKEY MEAT
PRESENTS:
THE MONKEY JUICE RECIPE ILLUSTRATED
?
1 • CUT OPEN
2 • PRESS
3 • SERVE
4 • DRINK!
JUMI BA

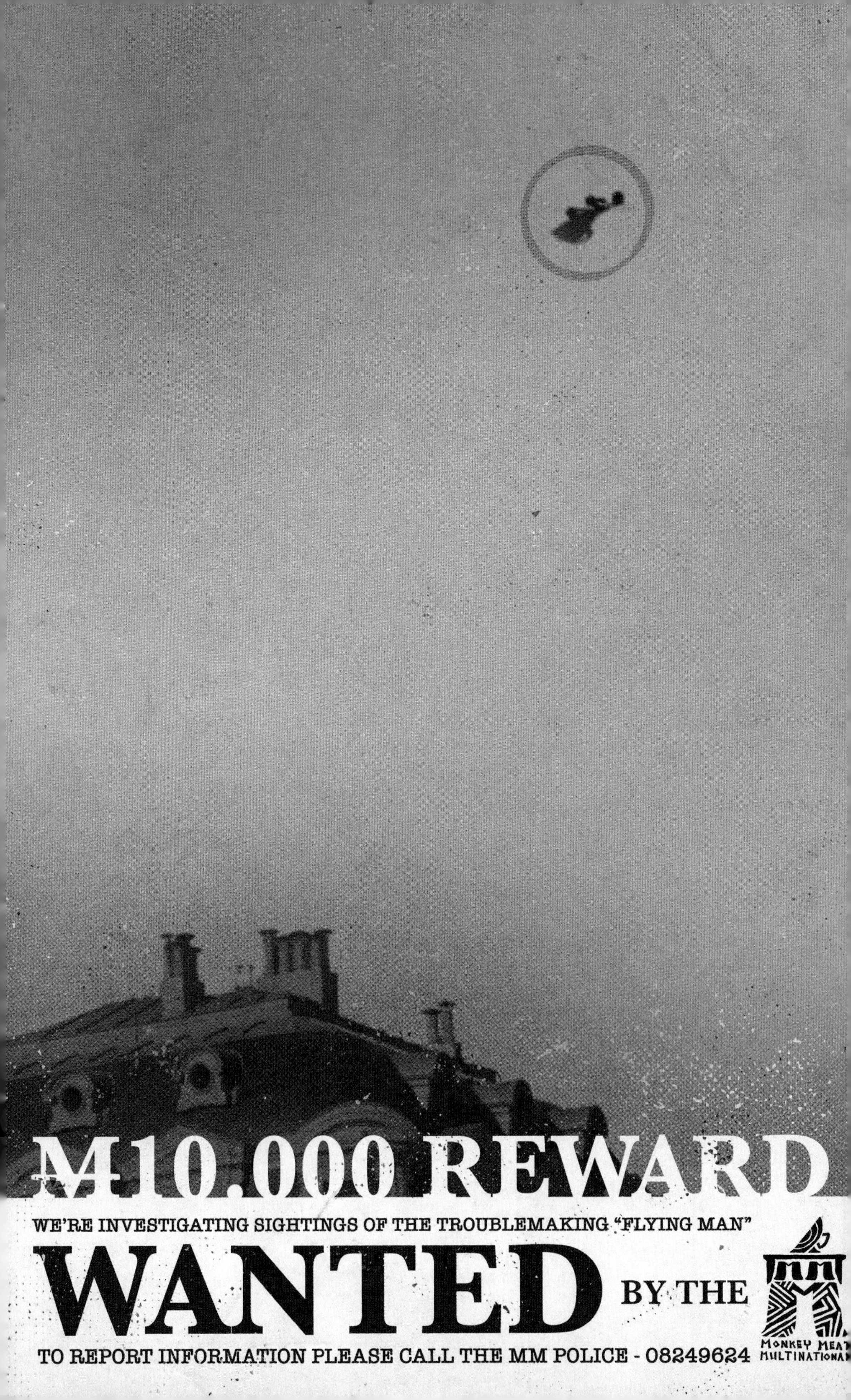
M10.000 REWARD
WE'RE INVESTIGATING SIGHTINGS OF THE TROUBLEMAKING "FLYING MAN"
WANTED BY THE
TO REPORT INFORMATION PLEASE CALL THE MM POLICE - 08249624
MONKEY MEAT MULTINATIONA

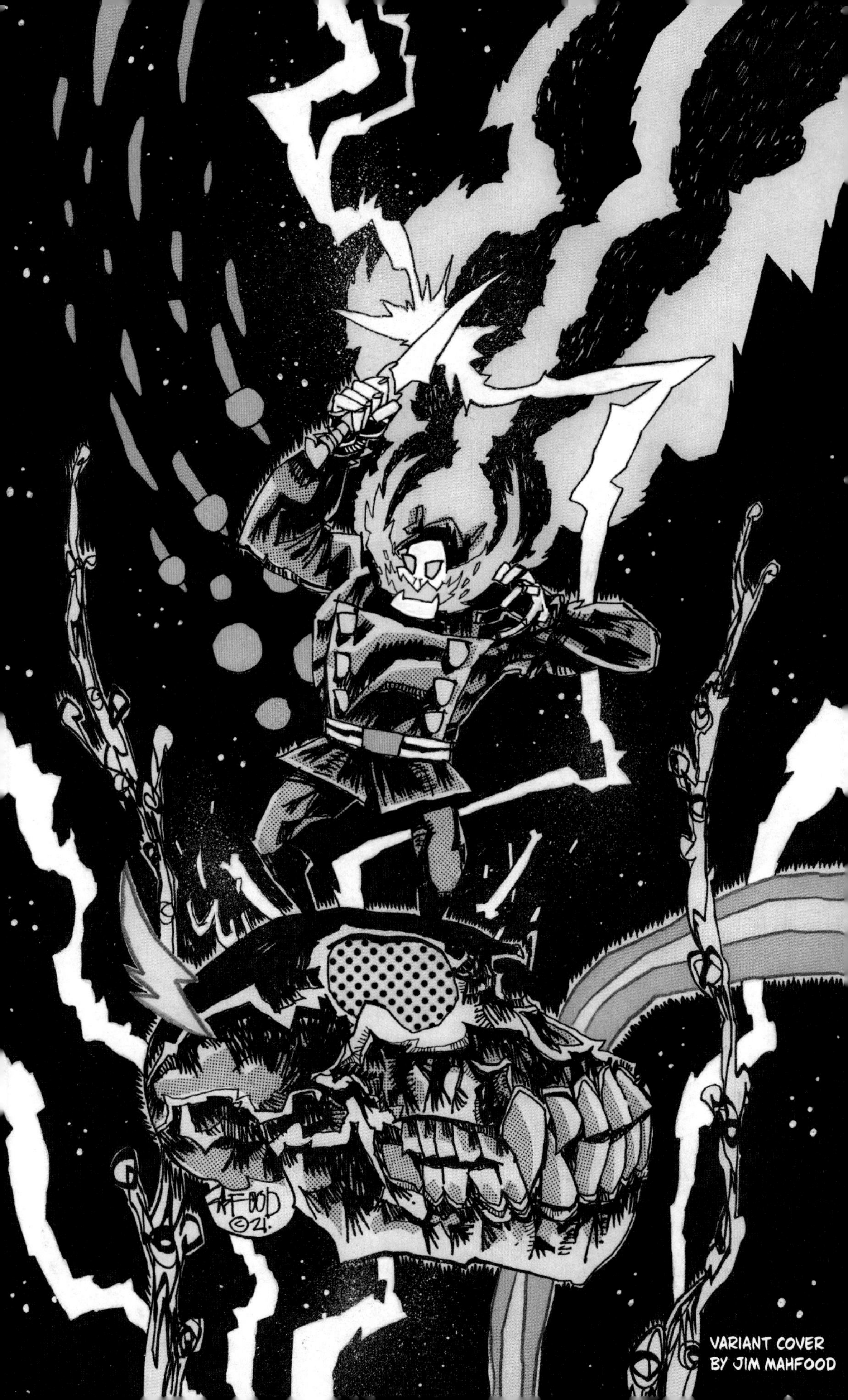

VARIANT COVER
BY JIM MAHFOOD

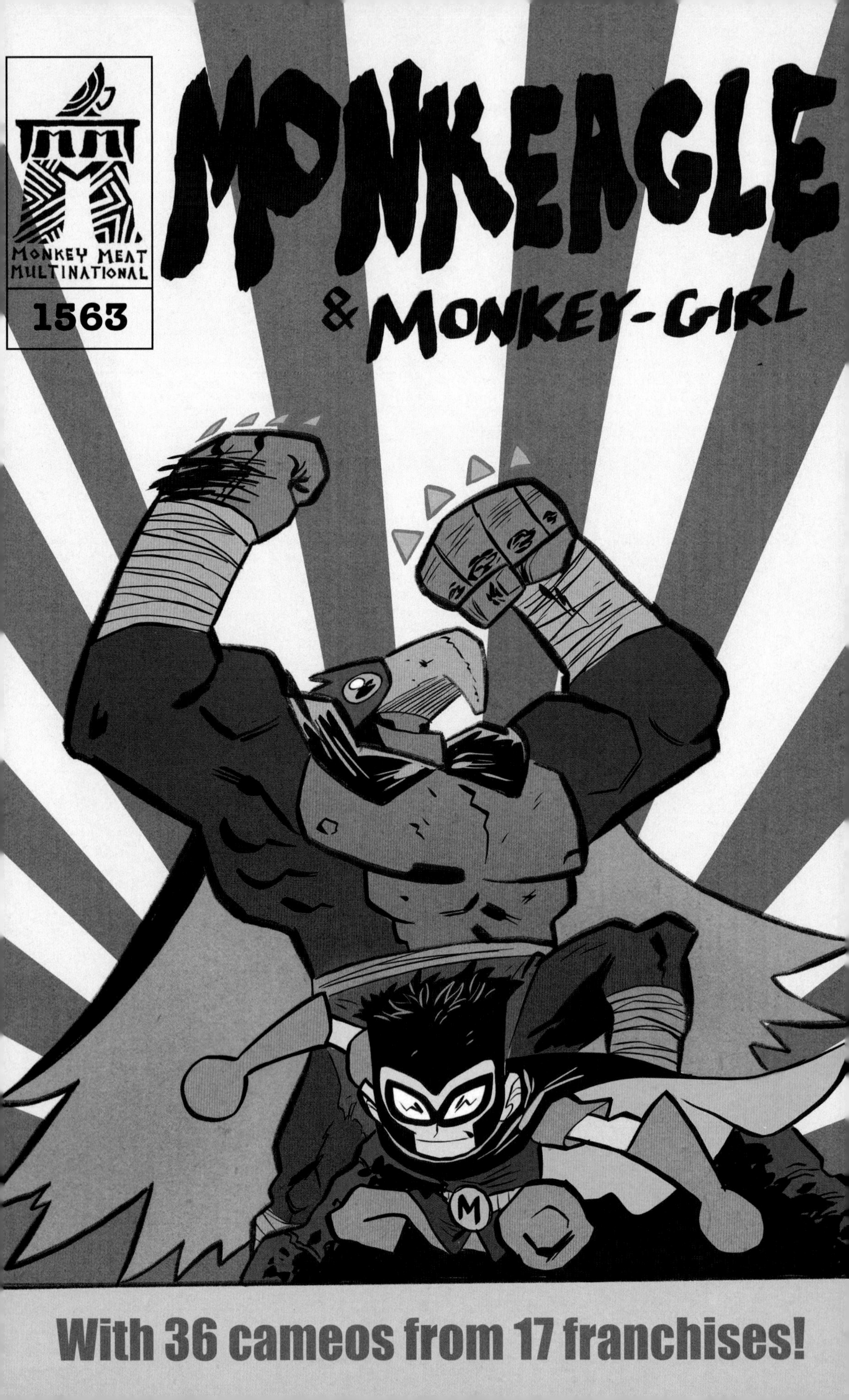
MONKEY MEAT MULTINATIONAL
1563
MONKEAGLE
& MONKEY-GIRL
With 36 cameos from 17 franchises!

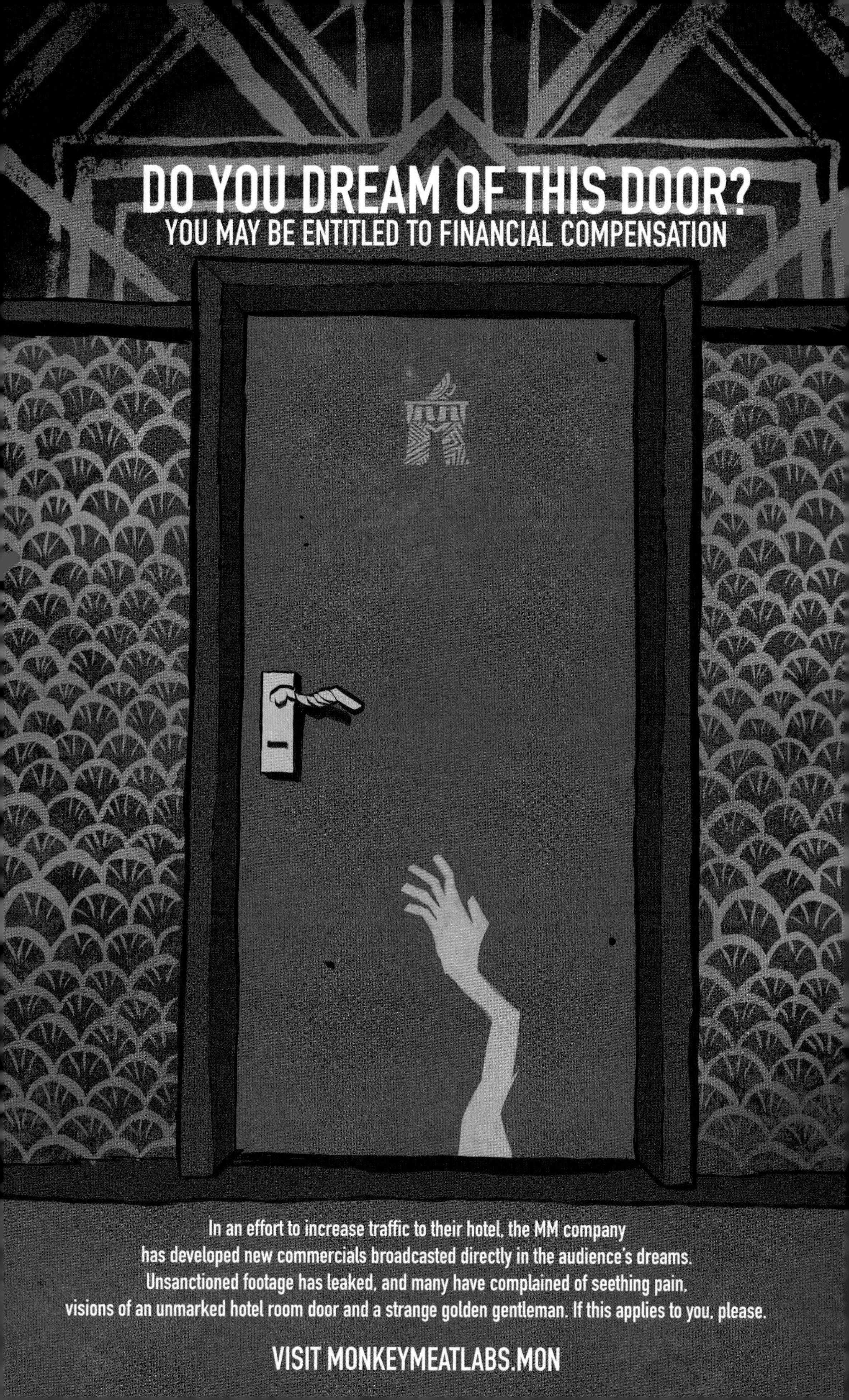
DO YOU DREAM OF THIS DOOR?
YOU MAY BE ENTITLED TO FINANCIAL COMPENSATION
In an effort to increase traffic to their hotel, the MM company has developed new commercials broadcasted directly in the audience's dreams. Unsanctioned footage has leaked, and many have complained of seething pain, visions of an unmarked hotel room door and a strange golden gentleman. If this applies to you, please.
VISIT MONKEYMEATLABS.MON

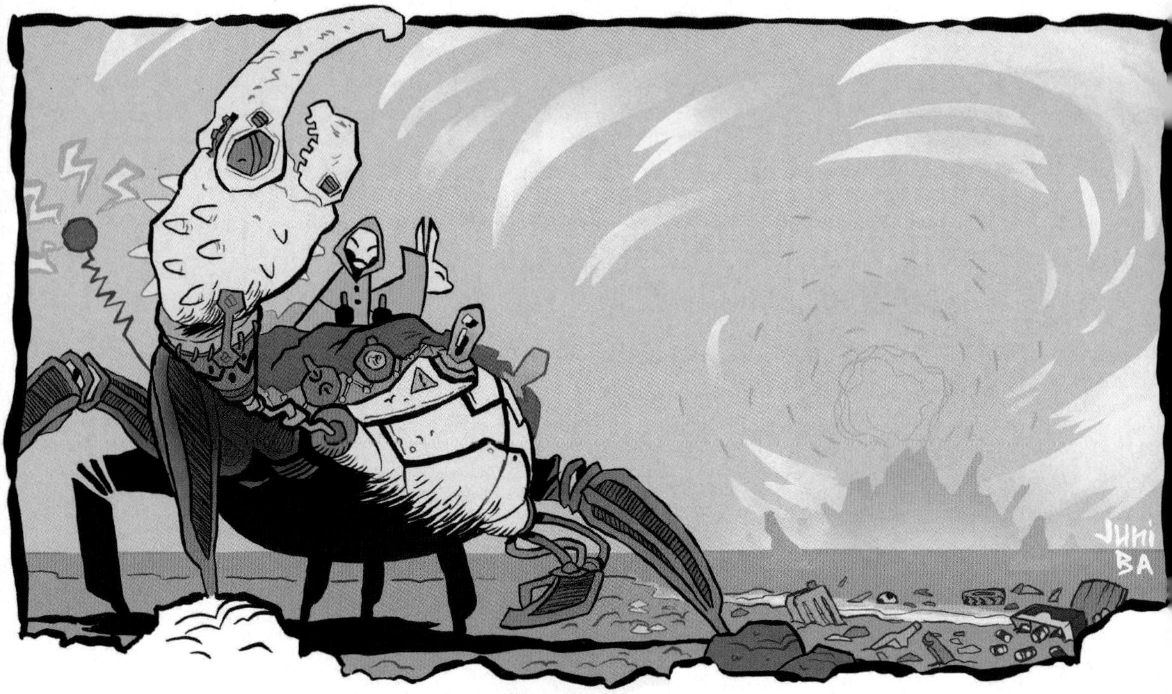
JUNI BA

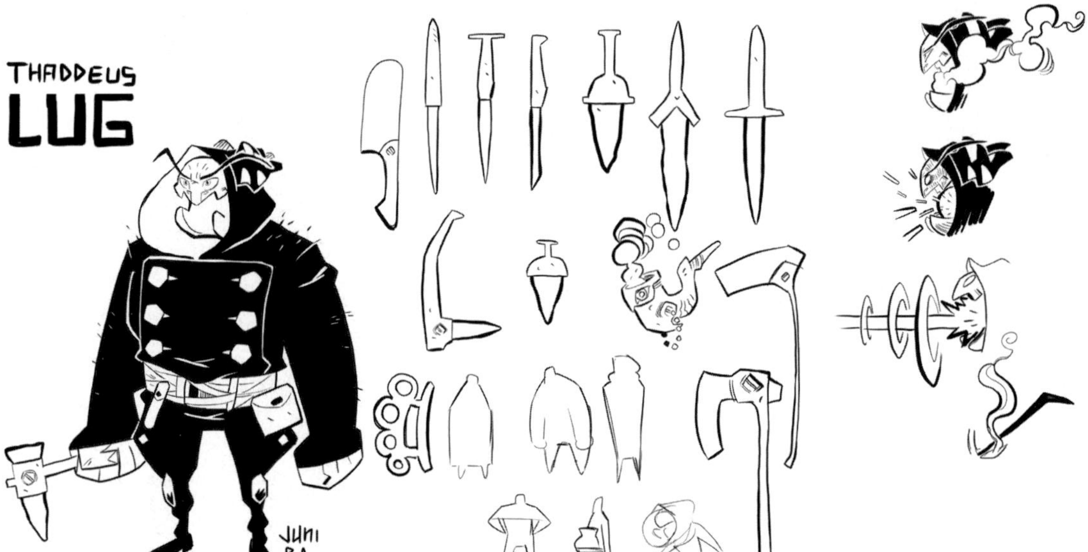
THADDEUS
LUG
JUNI BA

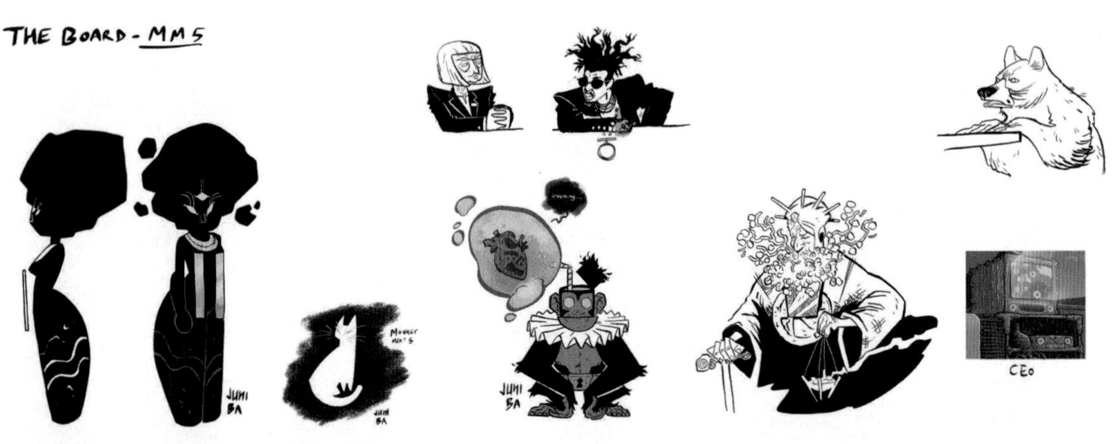
THE BOARD - MM5
JUNI BA
JUNI BA
CEo

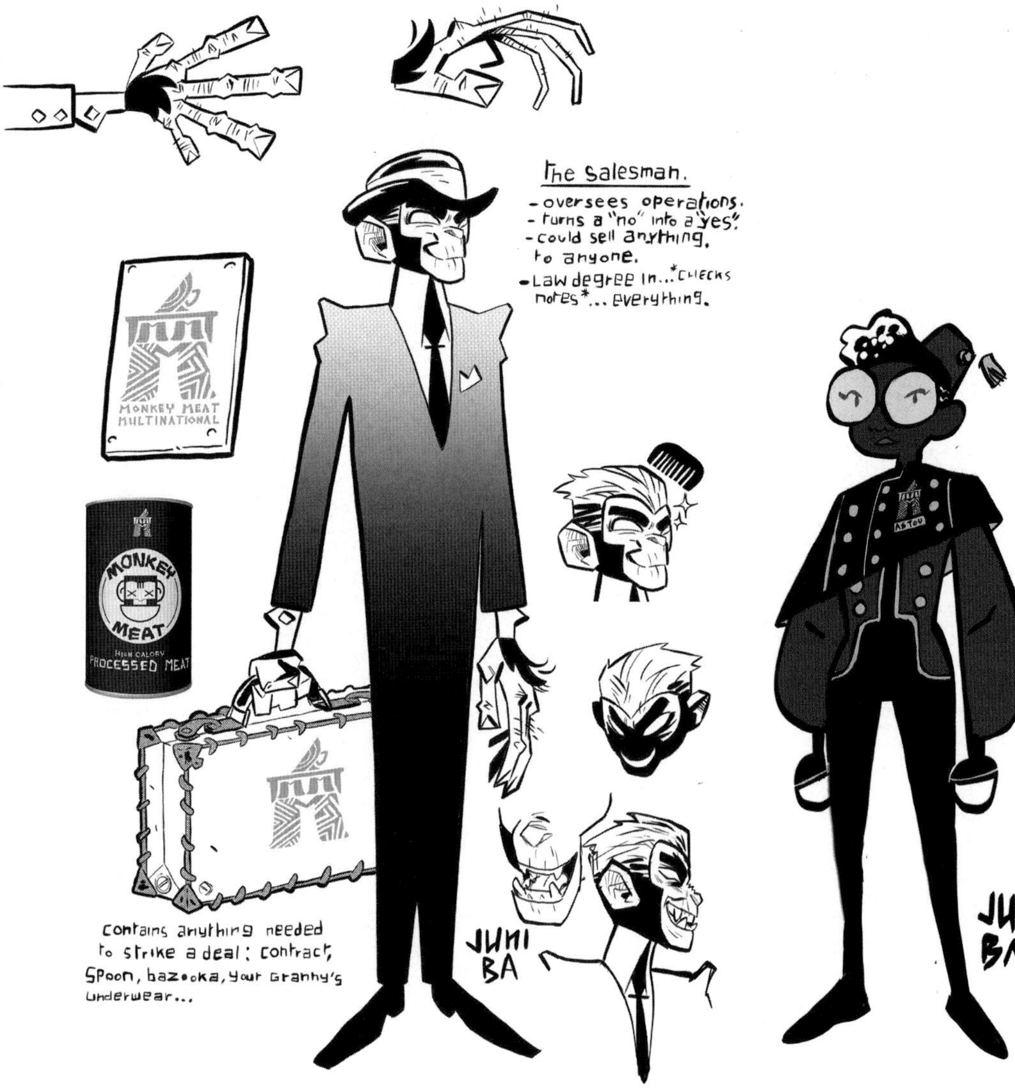
The Salesman.
-oversees operations.
-turns a "no" into a "yes".
-could sell anything. to anyone.
-Law degree in... *checks notes*... everything.
MONKEY MEAT MULTINATIONAL
MONKEY MEAT
HIGH CALORY
PROCESSED MEAT
contains anything needed to strike a deal: contract, Spoon, bazooka, your Granny's underwear...
JUNI BA
JUNI BA

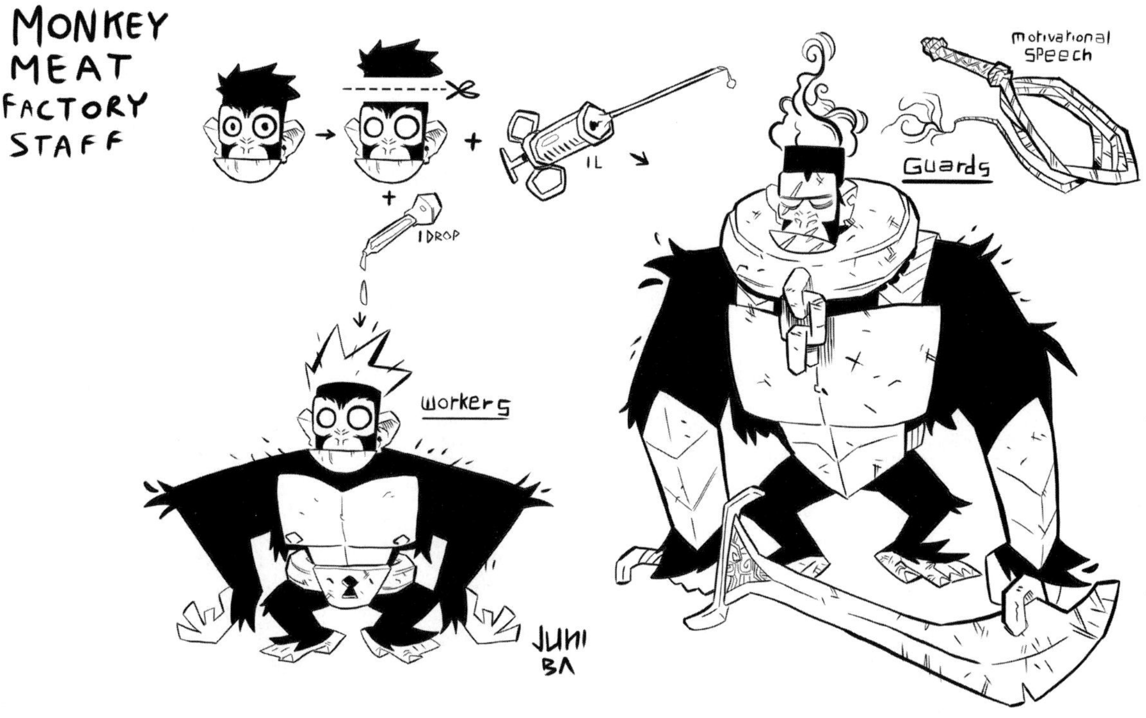
MONKEY MEAT FACTORY STAFF
1L
1 DROP
motivational speech
Guards
workers
JUNI BA

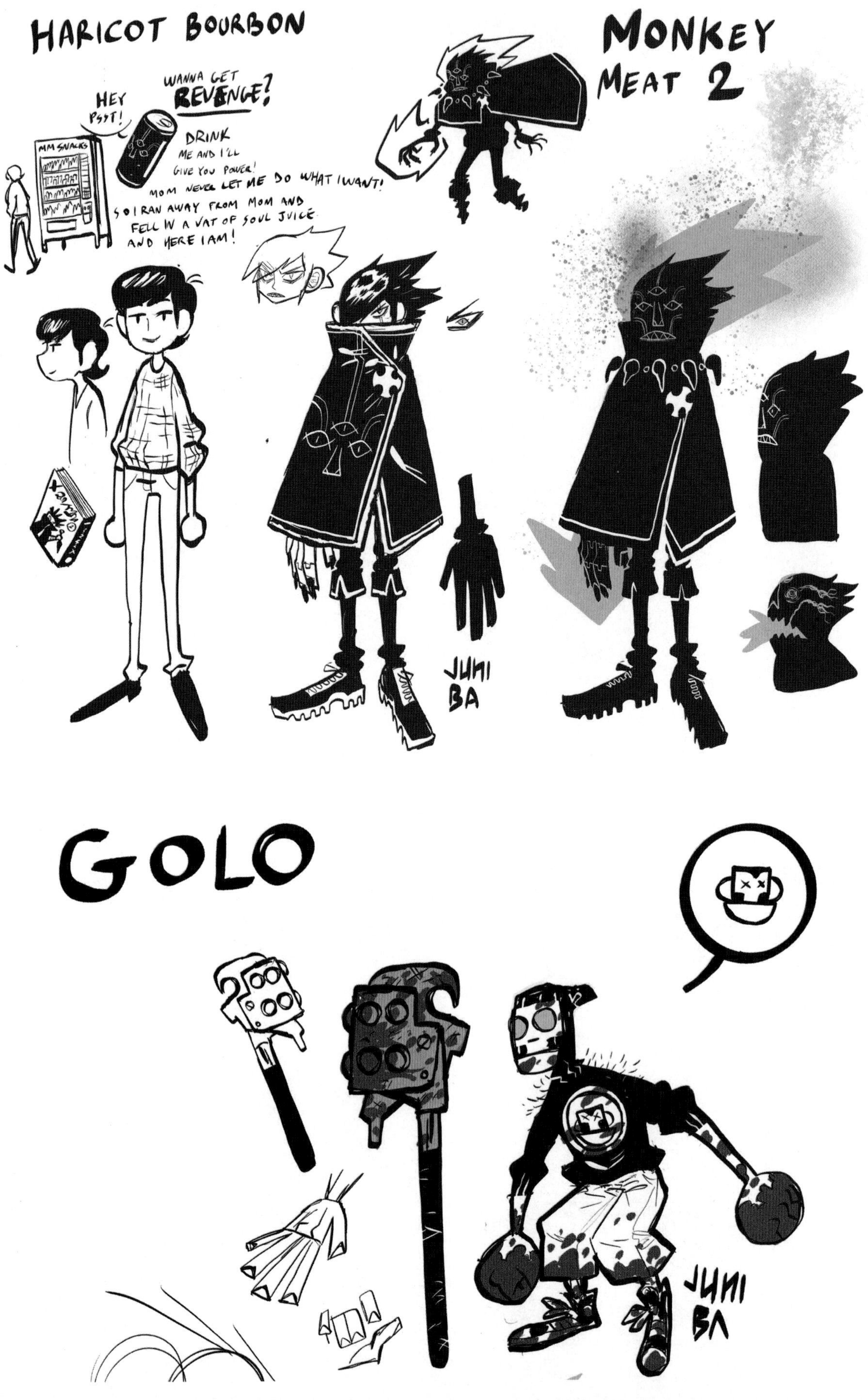
HARICOT BOURBON
MM SNACKS
HEY PSST!
WANNA GET REVENGE?
DRINK ME AND I'LL GIVE YOU POWER!
MOM NEVER LET ME DO WHAT I WANT!
SO I RAN AWAY FROM MOM AND FELL IN A VAT OF SOUL JUICE AND HERE I AM!
MONKEY MEAT 2
JUNI BA
GOLO
JUNI BA

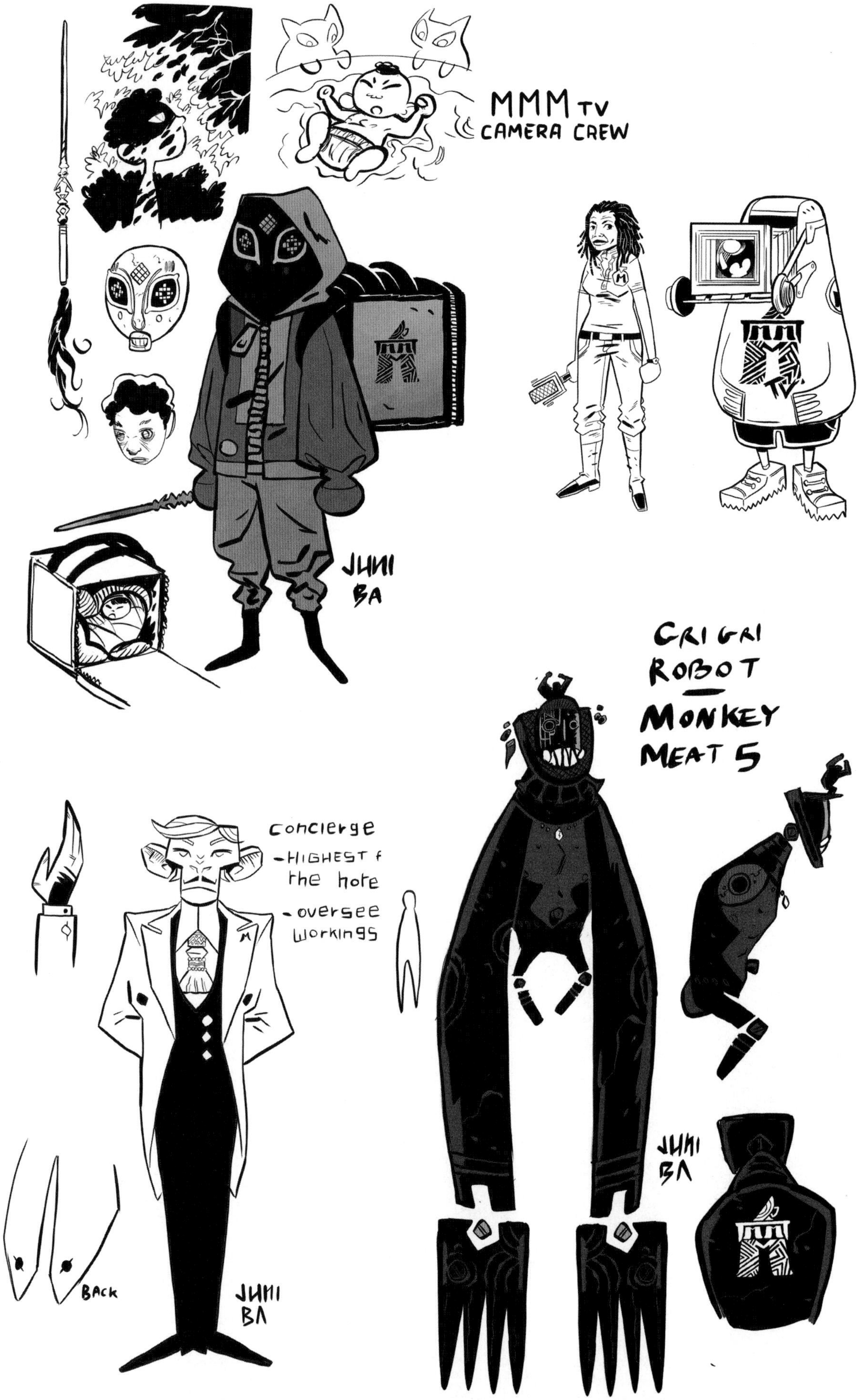

MMM TV
CAMERA CREW
JUNI BA
GRIGRI
ROBOT
MONKEY MEAT 5
concierge
-HIGHEST f
the hote
-oversee
workings
BACK
JUNI BA
JUNI BA

SAFARI
GUIDE ASSISTANT

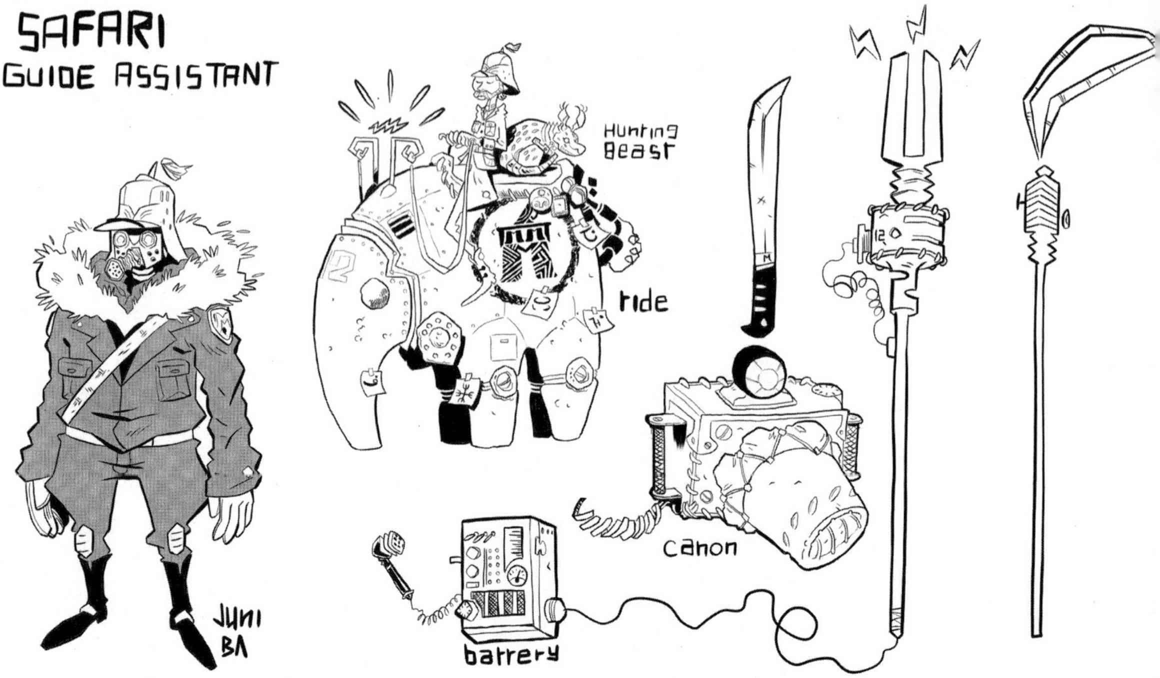
Hunting
Beast
ride
canon
battrery
JUNI
BA

MONKEY MEAT
FACILITY GUARDS
GORILLA WARFARE

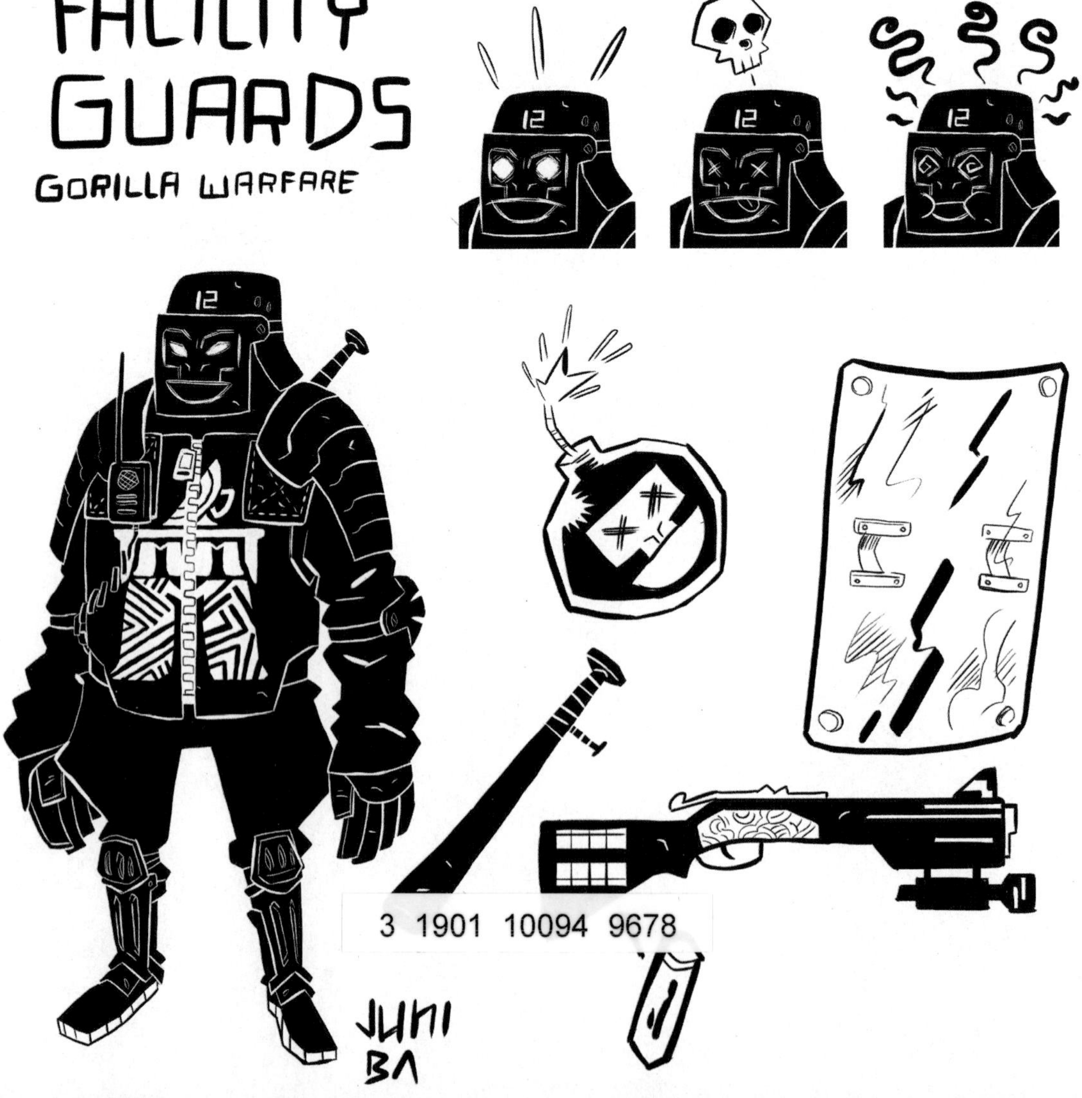
12
JUNI
BA

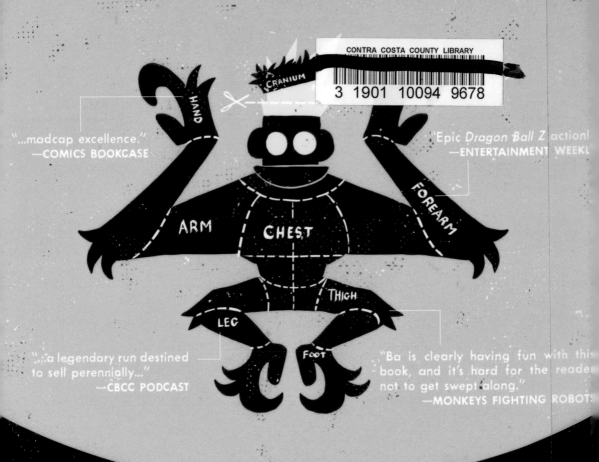

"...madcap excellence."
—COMICS BOOKCASE

"Epic *Dragon Ball Z* action!
—ENTERTAINMENT WEEKL

HAND

CRANIUM

FOREARM

ARM   CHEST

THIGH

LEG   FOOT

"...a legendary run destined
to sell perennially..."
—CBCC PODCAST

"Ba is clearly having fun with thi
book, and it's hard for the reade
not to get swept along."
—MONKEYS FIGHTING ROBOT

"MONKEY MEAT IS THE FIRST GREAT NEW COMIC OF 2022"

—COMICSXF

The Monkey Meat Company is a mega-corporation founded by ▮▮▮▮▮▮▮▮, operating from an island in the middle of somewhere, selling cans of processed monkey meat. It proved so successful, it funds the strange experiments performed on an island already filled with magic. Silly rumors of poor labor conditions and mysterious supernatural horrors on the island have surfaced, so we decided to report them to you ourselves!

These are the first five accounts.

Collects MONKEY MEAT #1-5, written and drawn by *Djeliya* and *Teenage Mutant Ninja Turtles* author Juni Ba, with special authorization from the Monkey Meat Company.

T+ / TEEN PLUS

Monkey Meat
MULTINATIONAL $16.99 US   ISBN: 978-1-5343-2323-0

9 781534 323230

image